Censoring Culture

Censoring Culture

Contemporary Threats to Free Expression

EDITED BY ROBERT ATKINS AND SVETLANA MINTCHEVA

Published in Conjunction with the
National Coalition Against Censorship

THE NEW PRESS

NEW YORK
LONDON

Published in the United States by The New Press, New York, 2006
Distributed by W. W. Norton & Company, Inc., New York

ISBN-13 978-1-59558-097-9 (hc) 978-1-59558-050-4 (pbk)
ISBN-10 1-59558-097-2 (hc) 1-59558-050-6 (pbk)
CIP data available

The New Press was established in 1990 as a not-for-profit alternative to the large, commercial publishing houses currently dominating the book publishing industry. The New Press operates in the public interest rather than for private gain, and is committed to publishing, in innovative ways, works of educational, cultural, and community value that are often deemed insufficiently profitable.

www.thenewpress.com

Composition by dix!

Printed in Canada

2 4 6 8 10 9 7 5 3 1

I dedicate this book to the memory of my loving (and outspoken) parents, Sylvia Bram Atkins and Leonard Thomas Atkins.

—Robert Atkins

To my mother, Daria Velitchkova, who always insists one should balance freedom of expression with respect and consideration for others, and my father, Peter Mintchev, who accepts no limits.

—Svetlana Mintcheva

Contents

PART V: SELF-CENSORSHIP

Acknowledgments

We gratefully wish to acknowledge the role of two individuals who were instrumental to the conceptualization, inception, and realization of this book: Antoni Muntadas, an inspiring artist and friend, with whom we worked on the *Censorship in Camouflage* series of panel discussions at the New School University's Vera List Center for Art and Politics; and Sondra Farganis, the always-supportive former director of the Vera List Center for Art and Politics, who "exec-produced" these panel discussions and arranged for us to meet Diane Wachtell, executive director of The New Press, who was immediately receptive to the idea of publishing this book. For its co-sponsorship of the panels, its support for this book, as well as thirty years' of fighting the good fight for First Amendment freedoms, we thank the National Coalition Against Censorship and its executive director, Joan Bertin. In addition, we are extremely grateful to The New Press staff for its professionalism in guiding us through the complex task of anthologizing so much material.

Five artists graciously contributed artworks for the section-opening pages of the book and we wish to publicly acknowledge those contributors—Kim Dingle, Hans Haacke, Glenn Ligon, Antoni Muntadas, and Carolee Schneemann—as well as that of Jane Hammond, who allowed us to use her intriguing painting for the cover. Writing is always a time-consuming task and we especially appreciate the labors of Jacqueline Livingston, Marian Rubin, Betsy Schneider, and Marilyn Zimmerman, who shared their painful experiences, as we do the efforts of Leeza Ahmadi, Guillermo Gómez-Peña, John Leanos, Glenn Ligon, Barbara Pollack, and Carolee Schneemann. Dee Dee Halleck, Ruby Lerner, and Janice Lieberman artfully adapted their New School panel discussion presentations to the different needs of the book, and we are grateful to them. We would also like thank two additional artists, Hans Haacke and Antoni Muntadas; two museum directors, Tom Finkelpearl and Thomas Sokolowski; and two curators, Norman Kleeblatt and Joanna

Lindenbaum, for allowing us to relentlessly grill them for the interviews published here. Finally, our thanks to Stephanie Elizondo Griest, the kids of Harlem Live (Stephen Opong, Damali Slowe, Ife Collymore, Christopher Davis), Kehinde Togun, and Tynesha McHarris, who participated in a specially convened discussion and shared canny insights with us.

Obviously a work like this depends on the efforts of so many scholars and activists who preceded us. Many of them are anthologized here, and probably, given the cross-disciplinary nature of this volume, are sharing a table of contents for the first time. We thank you all for your willingness to have your essays (re)printed and we are pleased to be able to provide what we hope is a lucid, engaging and original context for them. Equally important, we thank you for your years of advocacy and activism on behalf of unfettered expression. *Censoring Culture* is only the beginning of a project and a discussion, one that we hope every reader will help complete.

Permissions

Grateful acknowledgment is made for permission to print or reprint the following copyrighted material:

Excerpt from "Private Censorship, Corporate Power" by Lawrence Soley. Copyright 2002 by MRPress.

"American Music Challenges the Copyright Tradition" by Siva Vaidhyanathan. From *Copyrights and Copywrongs* by Siva Vaidhyanathan. Reprinted by permission of New York University Press.

"On Edge: Alternative Spaces Today" by Robert Atkins. Originally published in *Art in America,* November 1998, Brant Publications, Inc.

"Market Censorship" from *The Business of Books* by André Schiffrin. Copyright © 2000 by André Schiffrin. Reprinted by permission of Verso.

"Creativity in Real Space" by Lawrence Lessig. Copyright © 2002 by Lawrence Lessig. Reprinted by permission of the author.

"Hacking Culture" from *Hacker Culture* by Douglas Thomas. Copyright © 2002 by Douglas Thomas. Reprinted by permission of University of Minnesota Press.

"How the IP Guerillas Won: ®™ark, Adbusters, Negativland, and the 'Bullying Back' of Creative Freedom and Social Commentary" by Giselle Fahimian. [cc] by Giselle Fahimian.

Excerpts revised for publication from "Media Effects" from *Not in Front of the Children* by Marjorie Heins. Copyright © 2001 by Marjorie

Heins. Reprinted by permission of Hill and Wang, a division of Farrar, Straus and Giroux, LLC.

"Violent Video Game Players Mysteriously Avoid Killing Selves, Others" by Seth Killian. Originally published in *Censorship News* #92 (Winter 2003–2004). Reprinted by permission of the author.

"Censorship: The Sexual Media and the Ambivalence of Knowing" adapted from *Harmful to Minors: The Perils of Protecting Children from Sex* by Judith Levine. Copyright © 2002 by Judith Levine. Printed by permission of the author.

"Pitfalls in Fighting 'Nigger': Perils of Deception, Censoriousness, and Excessive Anger" from *Nigger* by Randall Kennedy, copyright © 2002 by Randall Kennedy. Used by permission of Pantheon Books, a division of Random House, Inc.

"The Past is Prologue, but Is Parody and Pastiche Progress?" Copyright © 1997 by Lowery Sims and Michael Harris. Reprinted by permission of the authors.

"The New Meaning of Bias" from *The Language Police: How Pressure Groups Restrict What Students Learn* by Diane Ravitch. Copyright © 2003 by Diane Ravitch. Reprinted by permission of Knopf.

"Taking Offense" from *Giving Offense: Essays on Censorship* by J.M. Coetzee, copyright © 1996 by The University of Chicago. Reprinted by permission of The University of Chicago Press.

Excerpt from "Censorship: a Personal View" from *Places I Never Meant to Be* by Judy Blume. Copyright © 1999 by Judy Blume. Reprinted by permission of the author.

"Censoring Myself" from *The New Gatekeepers: Emerging Challenges to Free Expression in the Arts* by Betty Shamieh. Copyright © 2003 by National Arts Journalism Program.

Introduction: Censorship in Camouflage

Svetlana Mintcheva and Robert Atkins

Censorship has always been a dirty word. (It derives from the Latin for "census taker" or "tax collector," designating one of the most reviled citizens of the Roman Empire.) In the legal sense, censorship is the governmental suppression of speech. In a broader sense, it refers to private institutions or individuals doing the same thing, suppressing content they find undesirable. The difference is that the former is prohibited by the First Amendment and the latter is not. Regardless of its legality, however, censorship is unpopular. The classic image of the censor depicts a narrow-minded and prudish bureaucrat blind to the transcendent flights of the imagination we call art, burnishing his red pen or his stamp and inkpad with perverse pleasure. This portrayal renders the censor as the very opposite of the creative artist. But censorship often operates more subtly than that, sometimes disguised as a moral imperative, at other times presented as an inevitable result of the impartial logic of the free market. No matter how it may be camouflaged, however, the result is the same: the range of what we can say, see, hear, think, and even imagine is narrowed.

Of the many debates about censorship in recent memory, not one has opened with a public official saying, "Let's censor this." On the contrary, the standard initial talking point is "This is not censorship, we do not censor," followed by: "We need to be sensitive to community standards"; "We need to protect children who might see this"; "We can't spend taxpayers' money to support work that might offend"; or "We don't consider this censorship at all, because you are free to exhibit your work elsewhere." The censor's current disguises of choice are the moral imperatives of "protecting children" and of exercising "respect for religious and cultural beliefs and sensitivities"—both, in themselves, laudable objectives, and for this reason, perfect disguises for other, less savory motives.

A discussion of censorship that only takes into account attempts to repress existing works, however, misses all those works that never came to life: perhaps, because this novel didn't seem sufficiently commercial, there was no chance of it being published or, perhaps, because that play might have offended somebody, the playwright censored himself at the outset and decided not to write it at all.

Censoring Culture expands the notion of censorship beyond the acts of removing a photograph from an exhibition or canceling a performance to include a much larger field of social conditions and practices that prevent artists' works of all kinds from reaching audiences or even from being produced. The narrow collecting purview of a museum, for instance, might be irremediably problematic for contemporary painters if no museum in their country collected work by living artists. Or, consider the modestly successful, mid-career writer: although her books have earned back her publisher's investments, at certain houses, she may be ignored, given the all-consuming editorial quest for the Big Book. Finally, the temporal extension of intellectual property rights practically prohibits American artists from working with images from the cultural vernacular of their day, such as Barbie or Batman and Robin. In few of these cases did somebody make a conscious decision *in order* to frustrate or limit artists' opportunities for expression. Nonetheless, within these situations, we see constraints on creativity and access to needed cultural materials. Such limitations both impoverish our culture and undermine our shared ideal of freedom.

The central goal of *Censoring Culture* is the expansion of the very notion of censorship. The specific disguises, mechanisms, and systemic factors that are discussed within the book—with the exception of the Internet—all predate the culture wars of the 1980s and 1990s. We make no claim to identifying entirely new phenomena. The fact that a phenomenon has been recognized, however, does not mean that it is sufficiently, or well, explored.

The dire effects on free expression of corporate consolidation, especially in the media for example, have been noted. The self-defeating extremes of political correctness have been subject to harsh criticism. (They are often dismissed as the whining of political "others.") The subtle but powerful force of self-censorship, on the other hand, remains little discussed or understood—although its ubiquity in totalitarian societies and familiarity to artists and writers in every society is hardly a secret.

Censoring Culture broadens the debate about culture and free expression by assembling existing contributions into a larger, overarching composition, and by exposing the mechanisms that limit free speech today as part of a complex system of economic, political, cultural, and/or social arrangements. Although the effects of corporate consolidation are most visible in the communications and publishing industries, they are also present in every other aspect of cultural production. Political correctness, though often ridiculed by the right, is similarly invoked by the right and the left to silence unorthodox speech rather than to engage with it.

We have brought together material in a variety of formats ranging from interviews to round-table discussions, and from diary entries to analytical essays. When existing analysis was insufficient, as with self-censorship, we have commissioned essays or conducted interviews with key authorities in the relevant fields. When the views of involved groups or stakeholders were underrepresented, we invited them to speak: a roundtable with teens, for instance, offers an essential reality check for adults who would ban a book from a school library before reading it, much less consider the concerns of the young people they are trying to "protect." Each of the collected pieces touches on one (or more) of a range of sometimes seemingly unrelated issues that affect, directly or indirectly, cultural production and distribution. A number of the writings in this collection do not directly refer to censorship. Nevertheless, within this context they reveal the multiple pressures—social, economic, legal and/or personal—that lead to the shuttering of an exhibition or the decision not to publish potentially controversial material about a particular subject.

Our approach is based on the simple assumption that, to paraphrase the old saw about quacking ducks, if something results in limiting the range of what can be produced, exhibited, printed, imagined, or thought, we are entirely willing to entertain the idea that this condition or phenomenon is censorship. This includes censorship as we know it—a public official making sure that what goes on public exhibition isn't likely to arouse anybody's concerns about "appropriateness" or other subjective criteria for viewing—and censorship outside of our traditional understanding of the concept.

In general, responses to censorship—whether activist or analytical—have come after the fact. By contrast, *Censoring Culture* examines systemic factors, which are poised to bear upon free speech now or at a future moment; that is, it identifies the conditions that present the potential for censorship. This is especially true of new technologies: just as the Internet promised the unfettered exchange of ideas, copyright laws quickly threatened the Net's potential for the uncensored dissemination of ideas. The ability to identify and address systemic factors prior to overt incidents of censorship suggests the possibility of a proactive approach based on dealing directly with the structural conditions that ensure future censorship.

Censorship has generated considerable attention in recent years, primarily because of interest in the issues raised by the recent, arts-oriented phase of the American "culture wars." Writings about the controversies surrounding Robert Mapplethorpe's *Perfect Moment* retrospective or Andres Serrano's photograph "Piss Christ" often focused on the divisive question that fueled the culture wars: "Why should so-called average taxpayers fund art that offends them?" *Censoring Culture* is an effort to get beyond not only this public-funding tug of war, but also beyond the very notion of a culture war. The problem with the media-driven concept of a culture war is that, rather than simply describing a state of affairs, it helps perpetuate an image of a nation in combat, one divided by radically opposed views. And not insignificantly, it diverts the political conversation from class and race to values, moral codes, and lifestyles.

The concept of a culture war creates the illusion of millions of cultural warriors at the ready, muskets—or at least PCs—in hand. This illusion helps magnify the thousands-strong campaigns organized by special interest groups into actions that seemingly represent the views of millions. Although the issues might change, the strategy of creating controversy in order to mobilize a constituency is standard operating procedure for many activist groups: once the National Endowment for the Arts (NEA), a focal point of emotion in the 1990s, stopped funding individual artists or controversial projects, right-wing groups returned to the perennially popular call to arms, "decency on the airwaves." As ever, pundits and politicians can be counted on to exploit—and exaggerate—such cultural fissures. To reenter the realm of reality, the vast majority of Americans do not, in fact, subscribe to the mediagenic, imaginary extremes of the so-called culture wars; they hold judiciously moderate positions. As the texts collected in *Censoring Culture* demonstrate, censorship today is a result of multiple factors, none of them directly related to a cultural rift at the heart of America.

Censoring Culture is divided into five parts that progress from background to foreground, from the systemic and institutional to the personal. The first two parts offer portraits of our era of triumphant capitalism as seen through its effects on contemporary expression within the new, global economic order and the brave new world of digital media. The component writings in the next two sections interrogate, analyze, and deconstruct the disguises from behind which today's censors often operate: the moral imperative of protecting children from "inappropriate" material, exploitation, or molestation; and the imperative of demonstrating respect and sensitivity toward the beliefs of a diverse population. Together the four parts comprise a multifaceted portrait of the conditions and institutions, attitudes and behaviors that limit expression in the varied precincts of cultural life. *Censoring Culture* concludes with material devoted to what is likely the most important and least understood topic under consideration—self-censorship. This is the point where public and private, economics and psychology, social sensitivities and political repression, intersect. It is also the point where censorship becomes invisible.

Contrary to what opponents of public funding in the arts claim, the salvation of free speech is not likely to be found in the marketplace. In fact, possibly the largest threat to free expression comes from the widening influence of corporations. Fewer, larger corporations now wield multinational influence, sharply contrasting with the national reach of previous generations of big business. During the past decade and a half we have seen an unprecedented amount of consolidation within all branches of cultural production. This process of consolidation has frequently resulted in de-facto monopolistic control. Although more books are published than ever, more films are released, and more cable channels seem to go online weekly, quantity should not be confused with diversity, much less quality. Although this anthology focuses on consolidation within the book publishing industry, similar developments affect—and afflict—virtually every other medium.

The pressure corporations exert on expression is also felt in recent, aggressive moves by entertainment and media companies to impose their ownership on material that, by all rights, is part of our shared cultural heritage. Congress has supported this power grab by repeatedly extending the duration of the period of copyright, invariably at the behest of entertainment industry giants such as the Walt Disney Company. But what is a gift to copyright owners is an impediment to the public-at-large, some segment of which is undoubtedly eager to see Mickey Mouse enter the public domain.

In recent years corporations have sued, or threatened to sue, numerous artists for violating copyright or ignoring trademarks. To cite one typical example, Mattel sued a book publisher, a record company, and a photographer for using images of its Barbie doll without permission. Mattel ultimately lost all three cases, but the mere threat of extraordinarily expensive litigation with an unpredictable outcome (Chanel, unlike Mattel, has tended to win suits against artists for trademark violation) is likely to discourage anyone from continuing to use such material in their work or asserting their rights under copyright law's fair use provisions. Ironically, this trend toward stricter control of copyright material flies directly in the face of contemporary artistic methods. Postmodern approaches such as "sampling" in music or "appropriation" in art both rely on the strategic use of already existing material to comment about contemporary matters.

For a while it appeared that the Internet was the answer to corporate domination of cultural production. It made low-cost publishing available to anyone with a computer and an online connection; it revolutionized access to international news, independently-produced music, activist networks, and nonmainstream art works. Best of all, the rhizomatic structure of the Internet made top-down control impossible. However, and somewhat predictably, the Internet's expansion has been paralleled by expanded legal efforts to regulate content.

Those efforts are provoked by both economic and moral motives. Economic concerns have arisen from the ease of disseminating copyrighted material online. Endless rounds of litigation over music file-sharing for noncommercial purposes eventually reached the Supreme Court and essentially put home-grown companies like Napster and Grokster out of business. The morality-derived category of issues ostensibly aims to "protect" children from age-inappropriate material or from pornographers lurking in chat rooms. Instead, these laws have been effective in restricting access by viewers of all ages—especially low-income adults—to constitutionally-protected entertainment and sex sites, as well as sites featuring educational and health information.

Government regulation is not the only problem facing the new medium. The Internet's potentially universal accessibility inevitably clashes with local laws and customs. If a French court could effectively prevent an American Internet Service Provider (Yahoo!) from hosting sites containing hate speech, a Chinese court might well try to suppress information about the Tiananmen Square massacre. It is possible that new and relaxed international regulations will come into play soon, but it is crucial to be aware of the nature of the Internet as contested turf: the conflicts may variously center on the regulation of speech, the ownership of this virtual "real estate," or the possibility of near-monopoly control of bandwidth by large corporations.

Protecting children, one of the rationales for government regulation of the Internet, is also the most convenient disguise under which the impulse to control speech operates in general. Children—a king-size blanket term covering the range from toddlers barely able to walk to seventeen-year-olds on the verge of enlisting in the military—are rarely allowed to speak for themselves or, when they are, hardly ever regarded as credible witnesses. Transformed instead into blank slates for the projection of adult fears and prejudices, children provide an effective pretext for banning the display of nudes, installing filters on computers in public libraries, or censoring TV broadcasts. The evocation of an innocent child is so politically potent that the lack of credible evidence to back up the claims that sexually-oriented material harms children is almost beside the point.

The moral panic accumulating around childhood sexuality has created collateral damage—perhaps most unjustly affecting those mothers who have innocently taken pictures of their naked kids, only to find themselves criminal suspects. Public officials, including police officers, prosecutors, and judges, are mandated to examine photographs of children with a focus on whether these images might appeal to a pedophile, and whether they might constitute evidence of child abuse. Because federal child pornography law makes no exception for writers, scholars, physicians, or journalists researching the traffic in sexually explicit images of children, those undertaking such investigations are themselves subject to prosecution. As a result, the only way to gauge the extent of sexual abuse of children in the production of child pornography is to examine court records, which show little evidence of a rampant problem. This conclusion is seconded by sociologists, who have found that most incidents of child abuse are not sexual. Needless to say, the problems most affecting children—poverty, the state of public education, a lack of health care and, in too many cases, parental neglect—have nothing to do with pedophiles. Hunting for them among middle-class mothers, banning drawn or photographed nudes in public exhibition spaces, or bleeping four-letter words from TV broadcasts is unlikely to solve any of these problems.

Of the disguises worn by censors to mask their generally frowned-upon activites, respect for religious and cultural sensitivities is nearly as popular as the need to protect children. Taking its cue from the left-leaning, cultural diversity movement active in the 1970s and 1980s, the religious right, a decade later, began vociferously to demand sensitivity and respect for its values. The controversies about Martin Scorsese's film, *The Last Temptation of Christ,* Terrence McNally's play, *Corpus Christi,* and Chris Ofili's painting, *The Holy Virgin Mary,* among many examples focused less on the allegedly blasphemous nature of the works than on the offended feelings of Catholics, who saw in them the "desecration" of their symbols.

Aggrieved sensitivities are not the exclusive property of the right or left; they span the entire political spectrum. Ethnic and sexual minorities, empowered by a growing respect for sensitivity toward cultural difference, also grew more public in their complaints about bias in this museum program or that educational curriculum. African American parents called for the removal of *Huckleberry Finn* from schools because of its (historically accurate) use of the term "nigger," while concentration camp survivors called for the cancellation of an exhibition at The Jewish Museum that contained work by an Israeli artist/peacenik/serviceman who approached the Holocaust in unorthodox, critical fashion.

Whose voice matters more? Who is allowed to speak about the painful history of an ethnic, racial, or sexual minority? Does anybody own identity and history? Some questions are so complex they resist resolution. We acknowledge the complexity of such matters, and—in good faith—insist that not every question is answerable. We also assert that the practice of civility and the cultivation of patient listening can transform shouting matches into discussions, enabling everyone involved to actually hear opposing points of view.

The most difficult sort of censorship to analyze—and even recognize—is self-censorship. Self-censorship is the interiorization (conscious or subconscious) of every mechanism and rationale for censorship: it is present when an artist hesitates about creating a work that might disturb viewers or might infringe on copyrighted material; it is operating when a fiction writer decides to purge sexual explicitness from the language of her characters; and it is apparent when museum curators refuse even to consider exhibiting work by artists with politically contentious points of view, fearing that showing such work might lead to losses of support from audiences, public officials, and funders. Typically self-censorship remains unrecognized—even by the person or institution guilty of it.

To be sure, it is often very difficult to draw the line between editing—the discriminations and judgments that are at the heart of the creative process—and the realm of self-censorship. To complicate matters further, there are many motives for self-censorship and some are undeniably legitimate. They range from fear of political retribution or financial fallout, to consideration for one's family or community. Self-censorship is so shaming an activity, though, that those who opt to do it in light of one of the "good" rationales mentioned above—that is, choosing to self-censor rather than to disgrace the family or to avoid facing some unpleasant financial music—tend to deny the nature of their actions. In an informal poll we took, we found that *nobody* wants to admit s/he ever self-censors. Perhaps the single thing we can all agree on about self-censorship is that a more detailed exploration of this uncharted terrain is necessary.

Censoring Culture is an unfinished project, an exercise in connecting the dots. We hope that readers will help continue our work by applying some of the methodological signposts we've outlined to their own lives, to the sometimes-difficult-to-detect habits of the culture at large, and publicly disseminating their findings for the benefit of the rest of us. We hope that *Censoring Culture* might serve as an antidote, however small, to the appalling and disingenuous lip service frequently paid to championing freedom of speech, and the gargantuan volume of hot air expended by those among the powers-that-be who, at the same time, seem neither interested in free expression nor in broadening its reach through promotion or policy.

Happily, the conditions described in this book are not immutable. On the contrary, the mechanisms of censorship also provide openings, possibilities for action, innovation, and change. The censor's disguises are not impenetrable, either. *Censoring Culture* may help, we hope, to identify some of those openings and possibilities, and to provide encouragement for exposing censorship in all its guises. It is time to state the obvious: it is necessary to restore the value, in public life, of reasonableness and respect for others, of truth-telling and plain speaking, and of the freedoms that have previously been broadened and deepened by each generation in succession.

If we are to actually confront the social problems at hand, we must face up to some unpleasant realities as part of the process. If we are to ameliorate the condition of children, we must initiate a truth-telling campaign that encompasses the sometimes disingenuous meaning of "protecting" children and the unscrupulous manner in which politicians have used children to impose their views of what is "appropriate." If the Internet is to fulfill its potential as a site for community building and a space for genuinely open, noncommercial communication, we must be alert to initiatives to privatize its infrastructure or to control its content. We should also reassess the balance between stimulating creativity (through copyright protections) and stifling creativity (through copyright overprotections). And finally, if we wish for a better world for those victimized by historical injustice, we must do more than purge our vocabularies of a dozen unacceptable epithets and deepen—or initiate—efforts to actually improve our fellow citizens' lives.

In an age when representative governments are on the rise worldwide, societies that seem to understand the nature and operation of censorship are surprisingly rare. Tragically, their understanding is all too often a by-product of their experiences with dictatorships. Despite the ignominy of these pasts, their cultivation of present-day liberties reminds us that the very exercise of freedom of expression is both salutary and life-affirming. Free expression resembles nothing so much as art, especially through its provision of pleasure. This makes us hopeful about its future.

Censoring Culture

PART I

Economics

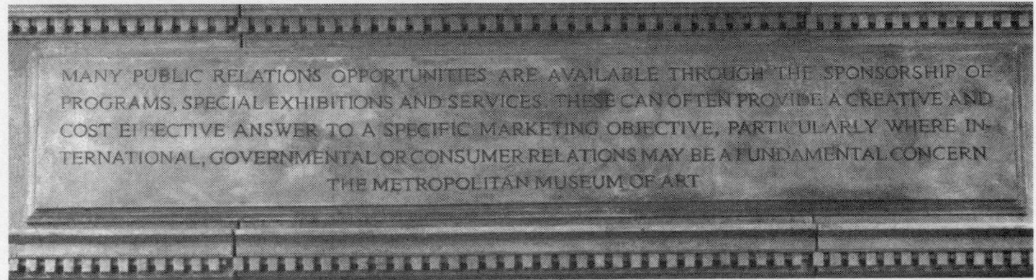

Hans Haacke, *MetroMobiltan* (1985) and detail © 2006 Artists Rights Society (ARS), New York/VG Bild-Kunst, Bonn. Courtesy of the artist.

1

MONEY TALKS: THE ECONOMIC FOUNDATIONS OF CENSORSHIP

Robert Atkins

The battle over federal funding of the arts in the United States—so prominent in the late 1980s and early 1990s—seems to have long ago disappeared from public consciousness. After slashing the National Endowment for the Arts (NEA) budget to $97.6 million in 2000, Congress has annually voted incremental raises for the agency. The 2005 budget stands at $121.3 million (nowhere near the agency's fiscal high-water mark of nearly $176 million in 1992 and again reestablishing the United States among the least generous per capita arts funders of the industrialized nations). Funding for the contentious program of grants to individual artists was eliminated more than a decade ago. To determine now whether the cure for the disregard of the American citizenry that supposedly ailed the agency was better or worse than the malady itself seems pointless, especially in light of vast changes in the nature of arts funding. Today's most vexing issue is not whether strings will be attached to new sources of funding—all funding comes with them—but the nature of the strings.

The early 1990s saw more than merely the downsizing of the U.S. federal government's support of the arts; it was the epochal moment when the so-called global "triumph of capitalism" could be discerned: a new economic order had emerged in China; the realignment of socialist Eastern- and Central-European states after the fall of the Soviet Union was nearly complete; and the rightward drift of Western European labor parties showed no signs of abating. This "triumph" also signaled the expanded power and influence of corporations, evident in the accelerating pace and unprecedented scale of corporate consolidation, and the spread of privatization to previously unaffected properties and locales. Both phenomena would profoundly influence artists' (and non-artists') ability to freely express themselves.

Artists and arts organizations now turn first to foundations and private individuals for support; they contribute the lion's share of U.S. arts funding—$3.1 billion from foundations and $4.7 billion from individuals in 2001. Unlike the NEA of the 1980s, however, these donors tend to direct their resources primarily to capital projects and programs, rather than to living artists and the development of new work, as Creative Capital Fund President and Executive Director Ruby Lerner notes in her essay, "Private Philanthropy and the Arts: Does Anybody Want an Artist in the House?" Although the lack of support for projects by living artists is not surprising given the American track record, the scale of unmet need is. Lerner's plea for a national initiative to "put artists back into the arts" assumes the form of a proposal to designate 10 percent of arts funding from public and private sources to support contemporary creation. Like the new artworks that would result from such a fund, Lerner's plan must reach her intended audience of givers as a first step toward realization.

As I wrote in "On Edge: Alternative Spaces Today," the demise or near-death experiences during the late 1990s of many alternative (or artists') spaces—organizations founded by and dedicated to programmatic support of artists—upset the balance of the art world ecosystem. This decline not only limits the number and diversity of artistic visions presented to audiences through exhibitions, but will impair the vitality of future artists unable to develop their crafts in these laboratory-like milieus.

When it comes to funding alternative spaces, or any other research and development initiative in the arts, corporations tend to show little interest. (Their support for the arts in the United States in 2001 was about equal to the combined expenditures of federal, state, and municipal arts agencies—and about half of the amount given annually by foundations, according to Lerner.) They choose instead to fund high-profile programs such as blockbuster exhibitions. These surrogate, tax-deductible forms of advertising—no different than the corporate sponsorship of mid-twentieth-century radio and TV shows such as *The Camel News Caravan* or *General Electric Theatre*—have been of special interest to artist-social critic Hans Haacke. He tartly sums up corporate motives for supporting the arts in his assertion that the corporation's "fundamental interest in the arts is self-interest," from the interview in this section, "Revisiting *Free Exchange:* The Art World After the Culture Wars."

Like Haacke, many observers and arts professionals worry that arts organizations' and institutions' increasing dependence on corporations for financial support invariably yields pressures for noncontroversial, crowd-pleasing programming. A major downside of the corporate-instigated attention to attendance and demographics is its potential for distracting the staff from its primary mission, which is educational, and from which the institution derives its nonprofit, tax exempt status.

Corporations, on the other hand, are legally mandated to do just one thing: make money—which makes them the particularly strange bedfellows of arts institutions. More than two decades ago, Philippe de Montebello, the venerable director of New York's Metropolitan Museum of Art, famously characterized corporate sponsorship of exhibitions as "an inherent, insidious, hidden form of censorship." Today the institution he continues to direct is deeply beholden to corporations. The museum's marquee-name, 2005 summer show, *Chanel*—almost totally funded by the House of Chanel—was a shameless celebration of Coco Chanel and her most recent successor, Karl Lagerfeld, that omitted any mention of the former's use of Nazi-era laws to consolidate her business interests in Vichy France. Given the museum's educational mission, the term *conflict of interest* seems to apply.

Funding of the arts by corporations is probably less important in the larger scheme of things than the systemic factors or socio-economic conditions—such as corporate consolidation—which have the effect of censorship, despite no censorious intentions on anybody's part, creating the condition of censorship without a censor. Consolidation is the merging of corporations into ever-larger companies or "multinationals." This phenomenon results in less expression of diverse viewpoints and increased (global) distribution of uniform products and services. The areas where consolidation most forcefully brushes up against the arts are the mass media and book industries. Legal limits on the consolidation of mass media companies have been rolled back so far in the United States and Australia that near monopolistic ownership of the traditional communications industries—broadcast, radio, publishing, and entertainment of all kinds—was virtually inevitable. The second phase of consolidation comprises the incorporation of media, arts, and entertainment holdings into noncommunications-based, corporate empires. Their generous campaign contributions and newly acquired power to control media content bring with them close connections to government officials, both politicians and members of regulatory commissions. Dee Dee Halleck, Professor Emerita at the University of California, San Diego, and co-founder of Paper Tiger Television and Deep Dish Satellite Network, describes the close and synergistic connections between communications corporations and government in her essay "The Military-Industrial Complex Is Dead! Long Live the Military-Media-Industrial Complex!" To expect uncensored information about crucial issues of war and peace from a company enmeshed in the military-media-industrial complex is foolish, she suggests, indeed as naïve as believing the assertions of cable television and Internet companies (and consolidation supporters) that five-hundred available cable channels ensures a diversity of editorial viewpoints, rather than simply those of their media mogul owners.

Virtually all large publishing companies are now parts of corporate communication empires. The supposed rationalization of the idiosyncratically tradition-bound book publishing industry has resulted in consideration of books as but one product among many that the company manufactures. Not surprisingly, those books that are unlikely to generate immediate sales are unlikely to be energetically promoted. André Schiffrin, founding director of The New Press, and author of "Market Censorship," notes that one outcome of all the dislocations wrought by the conglomerates' takeover of publishing are smaller profits than before. This may be, he wryly suggests, a product of the blockbuster advances for a relatively small number of already famous authors and the hefty executive salaries that have come to characterize the industry since consolidation.

Book publishing and distribution run along a parallel track. The ranks of diverse, independent bookstores are now drastically depleted vis-à-vis the chain stores, due in part to the deep discounts the mega-retailers receive from publishers. The demise of the nonchain bookstore can also have unsettlingly weighty effects on individuals and even communities. The late, independent bookseller Charles Kuralt sued Borders and Barnes & Noble in 1998 over their monopolistic pricing practices. In "Unfair Trade Practices in Bookselling," a statement announcing the initiation of his suit, he argues that the chain stores' demands for lower-than-wholesale prices from publishers are brutally anticompetitive and antisocial. They benefit only the chains themselves, Kuralt suggests, "[n]ot the authors, agents, publishers, sales reps, independent shops or the economy in general." And because the chain bookstores and general discount stores *are* responsible for selling a majority of the books purchased in the United States, their power to limit expression is vast—and disturbing. Walmart's decisions *not* to distribute a book because of its supposed embrace of homosexuality, or a CD because of its alleged denigration of Christianity, is likely to decide its market success or failure.

One of the most abrasive points of friction between economics and free speech in the United States today is copyright. Copyright legislation grows increasingly restrictive with remarkable regularity. Congress recently extended the copyrighted reach of works by individuals to 70 years beyond the author's death, and to 95 years since creation for those owned by corporations. Recent judicial rulings have also restricted public access to protected works by limiting, in practice at least, the scope of "fair use," that is, the right to make use of a copyrighted work for purposes of commentary or parody.

Unfortunately this limitation of material in the public domain and narrowing of fair use flies directly in the face of contemporary art practice. Although artists have always built on the artistic achievements of the past, during the 1980s a radically new approach that put existing works literally at the center of production developed. The decline of the modernist pursuit of originality during the third quarter of the twentieth century allowed for the emergence of postmodern *modus operandi* based on borrowings and transpositions of existing compositions. Known as "appropriation" in the visual arts and "sampling" in music, these practices are now standard operating procedure for artists in all art forms. Because copyright regulation has grown increasingly restrictive and because their working methods are often incompletely understood by judges, many appropriation artists and sampling musicians have spent more than their fair share of time in court.

Popular music is the art form most afflicted by issues of copyright. Cultural historian Siva Vaidhyanathan argues in "American Music Challenges the Copyright Tradition" that one-size-fits-all copyright law never suited music, which "more than any other vehicle of culture, collapses the gap that separates idea from expression." Musical copyright is traditionally regarded as comprising separate rights—not just of composition, but rights of performance and reproduction, as well. Rap music, with its melodic basis in sampling, conflates the notions of compositional and mechanical (or reproduction) rights. *En masse,* the numerous cases against samplers comprise what may be the largest body of suits by copyright holders against a single group of artists in history. Despite the quantity of cases, no precedent-setting ruling has established definitive boundaries for this practice.

Enforcing its trademark and copyright holdings is often a full-time job for multiple members of a corporate or foundation legal staff. Hundreds of copyright holders—running the gamut from the Walt Disney Company to Barbie-doll-manufacturer Mattel, from the House of Chanel to the estate of novelist Vladimir Nabokov, along with virtually every music publisher—have either threatened or entered into litigation against artists for copyright violation. Artists have been accused of infringing on images of such icons as Mickey Mouse, Barbie, and the Chanel logo, on musical compositions such as the Chiffons' *He's So Fine* (the culprit was George Harrison), and on *Lolita,* the classic novel by Nabokov.

During the 1990s, Barbie doll manufacturer Mattel lost three separate suits against a photographer, a book publisher, and a record company for copyright infringement. Should we regard these incidents as exemplars of the futility of trying to maintain exclusive control over the image of public (toy) figures? Or the heartening triumph of a David against the corporate Goliath? In fact the reverse is probably true: to challenge a major corporation in court is extraordinarily expensive; well beyond anybody's means. (Even multimillionaire, daytime TV diva Oprah Winfrey complained of having insufficient resources to take on in court the Texas cattle industry for her allegedly "disparaging" remarks about Lone Star beef.) The economic power of corporations is so vast today, Lawrence Soley argues in "Private Censorship, Corporate Power," that even the threat of being used acts as a potent deterrent to engaging with corporations in litigation over copyright matters. He concludes that "Because such [coercive] tactics are widely used to restrict speech, businesses and corporations now pose a greater threat to free speech than does government."

Whether government or big business should be crowned the premier threat to contemporary free expression may not be a matter of great concern; surely both are bad and getting worse. A more subtle—and dangerous—hindrance to expression in our era of triumphant capitalism and the new, neo-liberal economic order may be the infiltration of our speech and thought by the *economic:* that is, by economically-determined values and judgments about worth and appropriateness. Symptoms of the dehumanizing, ethics-averse economic include: political candidates who think of themselves as products to be packaged, advertised, and sold to the electorate; international organizations that regard newly emerging states as nascent markets and their citizenry as consumers; and bureaucrats designing plans for the distribution of vital emergency or medical care who place budgetary priorities ahead of human need.

Such thoughts may seem light years removed from debates about the size of the NEA budget or whether, in fact, the agency should exist at all. But it is the increasing hegemony of the economic outlook and its subsuming of the once separate realms of the political and the ethical that probably poses the single greatest threat not only to free expression, but to liberal society today. The arts, on the other hand, through their more experiential and less deterministic modus operandi, offer an antidote. We ignore the necessity of such alternatives at our own peril.

2

PRIVATE PHILANTHROPY AND THE ARTS: DOES ANYBODY WANT AN ARTIST IN THE HOUSE?[1]

Ruby Lerner

When it comes to censorship, attention invariably focuses on the public sector's attempts (usually successful) to withhold funding for what it regards as controversial art. It is much more difficult to assess the subtler role that private sector philanthropy plays in determining what kinds of art and ideas get produced and disseminated.

When discussing support for "the arts," it often seems that what is meant is everything *but* support for living, breathing artists. In 1981, composer Lester Trimble lamented the state of support for contemporary composers. "Year after year we starve the horse while applying layers of gilt to the cart," he wrote in *The New York Times,* "but for all our grand expenditure of money on concert halls and theaters, we are not enriching our culture by one jot." Writer James Baldwin expressed himself more tartly when he observed that, "Everybody wants an artist on the wall or on the library shelf, but nobody wants one in the house."

Just what is the current economic climate for living artists? What are some of the realities of private sector philanthropy that may, intentionally or unintentionally, discourage the fullest expression of contemporary creativity? How much private philanthropy goes to further the original work of contemporary artists? How well do the organizations established to support individual artists fare? Is this an era of cultural necrophilia in which funding practices reward dead artists at the expense of the living? And if so, with what consequences?

Private Dollars: Where They Come from and Where They Go

Private philanthropy consists of support from individuals, foundations, and corporations, in that order of magnitude. It is critical to dissect the path of these private philanthropic dollars because, in 2000, private philanthropy provided an estimated $9.4 billion to nearly 24,000 arts and culture organizations, more than *three times* the amount of government support that year.

The following statistics, from the Foundation Center's most recent report on arts funding, *Arts Funding IV: An Update on Foundation Trends*[2], reveal that the $9.4 billion donated by private philanthropic sources in 2000, breaks down as follows: $4.7 billion from individual giving, $3.1 billion from foundations, and $1.6 billion from corporations. Although it would be fascinating to know more about the characteristics of both the donors and recipients of the $4.7 billion in individual support, the focus of this article is on foundation support and what portion of it funds the creation of new work.

According to *Arts Funding IV,* foundation support in 2001 rose to $4.2 billion. While the Foundation Center does not report on direct giving to individual artists, it looked at the 1,007 foundations sampled and deduced that, in 2001, approximately $53 million was allocated to individual artists. *Alas, $53 million represents just 1.3 percent of $4.2 billion.* And even that $53 million is artificially inflated as it includes a one-time commitment of $10 million to the Creative Capital Foundation by the Andy Warhol Foundation for the Visual Arts. Of the remaining $43 million, a little more than $22 million was allocated by foundations for the creation of new work, with an additional $4.5 million for awards and prizes. Finally, if the one-time Warhol grant to Creative Capital is removed, about $15 million was designated for artists' services. The most troubling news about artist-support is found in the professional development category, which includes fellowships, residencies, internships, scholarships, awards, prizes, and competitions and significantly affects individual artists. This category lost ground between 1998 and 2001, with giving for the subcategory of artist fellowships and residencies suffering a precipitous decline of nearly 50 percent from $42.5 million in 1998 to $22.2 million in 2001.

Of the total $4.2 billion given by foundations in 2001, the three largest allocations were for capital support: general construction support for building expansion or the creation or augmentation of an endowment fund (36%); program or project-specific support (31.6%); and general operating support (18.2%).

What might these numbers tell us? First, that more than one-third of the funding went toward capital expenses. Based on my experience, it is fair to assume that most of this money has gone to larger, probably more traditional or better-known arts organizations that may employ large numbers of interpretive artists but whose support for the development of new work is a tiny part of their mission.

Second, that a much smaller amount went toward the ongoing general operating needs of organizations. This category would include money for small and mid-sized organizations that directly support individual artists and innovators. Often smaller arts organizations are forced to invent new programs to continue attracting project support—a category with greater resources. For a small organization, this endless quest for project-specific dollars eats up far too much time and energy.

How that $4.2 billion of foundation support breaks down by discipline is also revealing: museum activities received 34.4 percent of the pie; performing arts received 29.6 percent, media and communications, which includes public television and radio, received 8.4 percent; multidisciplinary arts, including multipurpose arts centers, arts councils, and arts education programs got 8.3 percent; 6.7 percent went to visual arts; and the remaining 12.6 percent went to arts-related humanities, historical activities, and other activities, such as policy/education. Unquestionably, within each of those broad categories, some support reached artists creating new work as well as the organizations that support them. For example, within the category of performing arts funding, nearly $14 million went to support choreography, playwriting, and musical composition; however, even that represents only 2.4 percent of all performing arts support. Clearly, relative to total arts giving, the amount that actually reaches the hands of artists allowing them to undertake new projects is very small.

A Culture of Creative Voices

The exhibition, presentation, and dissemination of contemporary art is certainly important. In fact, it is possible to judge the health of a community or society by how well it supports and sustains those contemporary creative voices in all arenas: education, science and technology, business, humanities, and, yes, in the arts. However, artists can be relevant to our contemporary culture only if their work is available to the public. Supporting the creation, as well as the distribution of that work must not be undervalued. There are those who believe that an artist's work should not be supported until it has "stood the test of time" (usually after the artist is long dead!). But what if this principle were applied to support for scientific research? There wouldn't be any!

In the past, important pilot programs were created to address the health of the infrastructure that supports artists' work. However, many of these demonstrably valuable programs lasted only for their three-to-five year trial periods, only to be financially abandoned after that. This style of short-term commitment ensures that vital field-wide initiatives never come to full maturity, and the art community is often forced to start again, at point zero. The field is littered with the corpses not only of its failures, but of its successes. The Advancement and Regional Re-grant programs of the National Endowment for the Arts are just two of the many important public sector initiatives that have been lost.

A much-needed strategy for building support for artists would entail the cultural community's development of a better understanding of how well *all* institutions, including large traditional institutions, support original artists. Who asks of any organization: What percentage of your annual operating budget supports original work? When endowment funds are being raised, who asks: What percentage will be allocated to sustain programs that support new artists' projects? If we care about our cultural future, and not just about our cultural heritage, boards and funders must guarantee that appropriate resources go to the creation of new work. Without such a commitment, perhaps we need to define this neglect as a subcategory of censorship: Cultural deprivation due to the withholding of financial life-support.

To achieve a healthier cultural ecology, there needs to be a "Percent for Artists" initiative, representing a national commitment to putting artists back into "the arts." Or, to employ Baldwin's memorable phrase, bringing artists "into the house." Perhaps we could think of it as tithing for the future. What an amazing difference just 10 percent of that $9.4 billion of private support—$940 million—would make for the diverse contemporary artists living and working throughout this country and for the organizations that help to sustain them.

Is that too much to ask? Even if much of the remaining 90 percent must go to the dead, how about just 10 percent for the living?

Additional research for this article was provided by Celia O'Donnell.

Notes

1. This article was adapted from Part One of the series of panel discussions, "Censhorship in Camouflage," held at the New School University, in New York, in June 2002.
2. *Arts Funding IV: An Update on Foundation Trends* (2003, developed in cooperation with Grantmakers in the Arts) is available from The Foundation Center (www.foundation center.org, 1-800-424-9836).

3

PRIVATE CENSORSHIP, CORPORATE POWER

Lawrence Soley

The tobacco companies have repeatedly squawked about their First Amendment right to advertise cigarettes. In 1998, as Congress considered a bill that would ban outdoor and sports advertising reaching adolescents and children, the tobacco companies denounced the proposed legislation for trampling on their free speech rights. "We intend to assert our First Amendment, due process, and other constitutional rights to overturn [this legislation] in courts," threatened tobacco industry attorney J. Phil Carlton, as the companies withdrew from negotiations on the bill until it offered them more protection from liability suits. The tobacco company representatives asserted that they would not surrender their First Amendment rights to promote cigarettes unless Congress capped the industry's annual liability claims.[1] In other words, the tobacco companies were willing to give up their cherished First Amendment rights for the right price.

In an effort to derail a proposed federal ban on cigarette advertising a decade earlier, the Philip Morris Corporation sponsored an essay-writing contest about the First Amendment rights of cigarette advertising. The contest was a continuation of an earlier Philip Morris promotional campaign, inaugurated during the American Bicentennial, heralding the Bill of Rights and the freedoms it enshrines.

Advertisements for the contest appeared in large circulation magazines and newspapers, including *The New Yorker* and the *New York Times,* asking entrants to write about why a ban on cigarette advertising infringed on free speech. The purpose of the heavily advertised contest was to suggest that the proposed ban threatened the average citizen's First Amendment rights.[2]

The campaign represented the height of corporate hypocrisy, suggesting that billion-dollar, multinational conglomerates such as Philip

Morris are just "average citizens" being pushed around by big government. Philip Morris is not, after all, an average citizen; it is a multibillion-dollar, multinational conglomerate, whose annual sales exceed the gross domestic product of Iraq, Chile, and many other nations, and whose Kraft Food and Miller Brewing divisions produce more food and drink annually than most countries consume.[3]

The contest also erroneously implied that commercial advertising has the same First Amendment protection as political and social speech, which is untrue. While commercial speech enjoys First Amendment protection, that protection is less than that afforded political and social speech.

Ironically, at the same time they were clamoring about free speech rights, the tobacco companies were using their profits and power to suppress information about the health hazards of cigarette smoking. This corporate-sponsored censorship had been ongoing for decades.

When the tobacco companies sponsored television programs in the 1940s and 1950s, they prohibited shows from mentioning the health risks of cigarette smoking, using words that might suggest smoking was unhealthy, or inadvertently referring to marketplace competitors. For example, Jack Benny refused to mention a cancer treatment center on his show, admitting that "I am sponsored by a cigarette maker, [and] we are not permitted at any time to mention the word cancer."[4] In the 1950s, R. J. Reynolds, the sponsor of NBC's *Camel News Caravan,* even banned the filming of news events where "No Smoking" signs were observable and prohibited dramatic shows from naming characters "Lucky," the brand name of its chief competitor.[5]

When magazines ran articles about the hazards of smoking, the tobacco companies quickly withdrew their advertising to financially punish the magazines. *Mother Jones, Reader's Digest,* and other magazines had their tobacco advertising accounts cancelled after publishing articles about the health hazards of smoking.[6] Having learned that the tobacco companies will not allow magazines in which they advertise to publish stories about the hazards of smoking, magazines carrying cigarette advertising have studiously avoided the subject.[7]

> Even advertising agencies have felt the wrath of the tobacco conglomerates. When Saatchi and Saatchi developed an advertisement for Northwest Airlines promoting the airline's nonsmoking flights, R. J. Reynolds

> had its parent company, R.J.R. Nabisco, pull its advertising business from the agency. Because Saatchi did not handle any of the tobacco company's cigarette advertising, R.J.R. Nabisco pulled its accounts for biscuits and sweets, part of its Nabisco division.[8]

The problems of tobacco company censorship are far graver than suggested by these neanderthal attempts to directly pressure the media. Magazines that carry cigarette advertising frequently act as tobacco company toadies, refusing to carry antismoking advertisements. Of thirty-six magazines carrying such advertisements, twenty-two refused outright to run ads for antismoking clinics, an investigation of magazine advertising practices found. In rejecting antismoking advertisements, *Cosmopolitan* explained that it would not "jeopardize $5 or $10 million worth of business" from the tobacco companies. An executive with *Psychology Today,* a self-help magazine that claims to be devoted to readers' well-being, said the magazine would not accept the antismoking ads because "we have a lot of money that comes in from tobacco companies, and frankly, we don't want to offend our tobacco advertisers."[9]

Not content with merely stopping magazines from publishing antismoking articles, the tobacco companies have recently moved into the publishing business, producing their own magazines with tobacco-friendly content. Brown & Williamson produces *Simple Living* and *Flair* with Hearst Publications and *Real Edge* with EMAP Peterson Publishing. The three are written by employees of Hearst and EMAP Peterson so they appear to be bona fide consumer magazines. However, the contents are carefully controlled by Brown & Williamson, which determines what can be written about, forbids references to cancer or other tobacco-induced diseases, and even prohibits mentions of cigarette smoking in stories. Smoking is promoted through advertising and other visuals, rather than hard-sell stories.[10] Philip Morris and R. J. Reynolds produce similar magazines. Philip Morris produces *Unlimited* with Hachette Filipacchi Publishing and R. J. Reynolds produces *CML* with Time, Inc.

Tobacco companies employ many other methods to suppress information about the hazards of smoking, one of which is to have tobacco company employees sign confidentiality agreements that prohibit them from speaking about the company and its products during and after their employment. When Dr. Victor DeNoble, a scientist working for

Philip Morris, discovered that nicotine was not just addictive, but altered smokers' brain chemistry, he was fired. To ensure DeNoble's silence, Philip Morris reminded him that a secrecy clause in his employment contract prohibited him from speaking publicly about his research, warning him that if he violated his contract, Philip Morris would sue.[11]

The same fate befell Jeffrey Wigand, a Brown & Williamson employee, who became aware of the company's research demonstrating the addictive nature of nicotine and its manipulation of cigarette nicotine levels. When Brown & Williamson discharged Wigand, he was warned to remain silent about the company and repeatedly threatened with legal action if he violated the secrecy clause in his employment contract. Eventually, Wigand told his story to *60 Minutes.*

Brown & Williamson then threatened to sue CBS if *60 Minutes* broadcast Wigand's interview, claiming that *60 Minutes* had intentionally interfered with a civil contract by encouraging Wigand to violate his confidentiality agreement with the company.[12] The threat of legal action came as CBS's owners were negotiating the sale of the network. Fearing that the lawsuit would lower CBS's value, CBS suppressed the interview, an act of self-censorship criticized by many newspapers. For example, the *New York Times* called the suppression "a chilling message to journalists investigating industry practices everywhere."[13] The *Wall Street Journal* also scooped CBS, publishing a story based on interviews with Wigand. After being denounced and scooped, CBS allowed *60 Minutes* to air the Wigand interview, hoping to salvage its by then tarnished reputation as a muckraker.

A movie, *The Insider,* was subsequently made about the Wigand–*60 Minutes* debacle. Although *The Insider* was based on widely known events, Brown & Williamson threatened to sue the film's distributor for libel, alleging that scenes suggesting that the tobacco company physically threatened Wigand were untrue.[14] Significantly, the tobacco company didn't challenge the main premise of the movie, which was that Brown & Williamson sought to silence former employees and even reporters who sought to expose its potentially criminal practices.

Several years earlier, Brown & Williamson publicly discussed suing cartoonist Gary Trudeau for defamation after his *Doonesbury* comic strip showed Thomas Sandefur, the company's CEO, being indicted for perjury because of his testimony before Congress. Sandefur testified that nicotine wasn't addictive, even though company documents show that he was well aware of nicotine's addictive power.[15]

Such tactics have not been unique to Brown & Williamson. R. J. Reynolds threatened to sue Dr. Paul M. Fischer, who published research showing that children were well acquainted with Joe Camel, the cartoon character used to promote Camel cigarettes. As a result of the threats, Fischer gave up studying tobacco advertising.[16]

Philip Morris and Reynolds filed libel suits against ABC after the network's Day One program featured a segment alleging that the tobacco companies "spiked" the nicotine in cigarettes. During those suits, the tobacco companies sought and obtained a court order limiting the number of ABC executives who were allowed to see subpoenaed tobacco company documents. Each Philip Morris document delivered to ABC carried legal warnings stamped on it that "this document and its content shall not be used, shown, or distributed as provided in the court's order."[17]

An out-of-court settlement was reached on the eve of ABC's sale to Disney Corporation, in which ABC agreed to publicly apologize for the segment and pay the tobacco companies' legal costs. The carefully worded apology stated that ABC could not prove that the companies "spiked" or increased nicotine levels, even though ABC had evidence clearly showing they manipulated and controlled the levels. Critics charged that ABC settled the suit to allow the sale of the network to proceed without impediments.

The settlement prohibited ABC and Philip Morris executives from commenting on the case and required the sealing of the briefs filed by Philip Morris and ABC.[18] *USA Today* nevertheless obtained a copy of the secret ABC brief, discovering that accompanying Philip Morris documents showed that the tobacco company did indeed add nicotine to cigarettes. The newspaper concluded that the "evidence appears at odds with both the tobacco company's public statements and the network's apology," suggesting that ABC might have settled in order to make the network's sale easier.[19]

Lawsuits such as these, which are filed to stifle criticism rather than remedy injustice, are called Strategic Lawsuits Against Public Participation, or SLAPPs. These suits tie up critics in court for years, forcing them to incur massive legal expenses. Burdened by such suits, critics often gag themselves. Shortly after Philip Morris filed its $10 billion libel suit against ABC over the spiking segment on *Day One,* the network cancelled a one-hour documentary on *Turning Point* about tobacco companies, suggesting that SLAPPs are an effective form of censorship.[20]

When sued or being sued, the tobacco companies also seek and obtain protective orders to suppress information about tobacco industry practices. As Marc Z. Edell, an attorney who sued the tobacco companies, explained, the companies "have protective orders [gag orders] entered in every case, you can't share information among plaintiff's lawyers, and they try to paper you to death and outspend you, which they are quite capable of doing."[21] These tactics have been used repeatedly in civil and class-action suits filed against the tobacco companies, making it very hard for injured parties to finance their suits against the tobacco companies because each suit begins at square one.

The tactics used by the tobacco companies to suppress information—advertising pressures, secrecy agreements, defamation suits, and protective orders—are not unique to the tobacco industry. A survey of television news reporters and editors found that more than two-thirds of television stations had been threatened by advertisers, who tried to intimidate the stations with threats to withdraw advertising because of the content of news stories. Forty-four percent of the television journalists reported that advertisers had "actually withdrawn advertising because of the content of a news report."[22]

Corporations even withdraw funding to punish nonprofit institutions and community groups, just as they withdraw advertising to punish media. For example, Nike Chairman Philip Knight cancelled a promised $30 million contribution to the University of Oregon for renovating the athletic stadium when the university joined the Workers' Rights Consortium, which had criticized the use of foreign sweatshops by U.S. manufacturers.[23] Holland America Cruise Line cut off contributions to several charitable groups in Juneau, Alaska, after Juneau voters approved a tax on cruise ship passengers who arrive annually in that city. When the cruise line withdrew support for the arts council, Civil Air Patrol, and other nonprofit organizations, it said it was reassessing its relationship with the city as a result of the vote.[24]

General Growth Properties, Inc., which operates 130 malls nationwide, banned Salvation Army bell ringers from its Wisconsin properties during the 1999 holiday season. The corporation wasn't punishing the

Salvation Army because of anything it did or said. Rather, as Bernie Freibaum, the chief financial officer of General Growth, explained, the company's motivation for acting like Scrooge was that "if you let one group in, then all of a sudden you have to let the rest in and the next thing you know you're in court arguing the First Amendment."[25] In Wisconsin, like most other states, mall owners can prohibit all free expression on their property. General Growth feared that the presence of the Salvation Army might set a precedent for other nonprofit groups, which might then demand to distribute handbills or engage in other forms of free expression.

Corporations also commonly seek protective orders sealing evidence or impose confidentiality agreements in the settlement of civil cases, as Philip Morris did in its lawsuit against ABC. "This practice has exploded in the last twenty years," reports Arthur Bryant of the nonprofit Trial Lawyers for Public Justice. "Corporations have realized how they can be successful, and it's cheaper to hide the truth from the public."[26] Secret settlements are often reached by the manufacturers of pharmaceuticals, medical devices, and hazardous products such as lead paint, but are also used by retailers such as Home Depot, Inc., and Wal-Mart, which successfully keep secret information about injuries sustained by shoppers in their stores, who are struck by merchandise falling from shelves or tripped by goods lying on the floor.

Bridgestone, Inc., the manufacturer of the dangerous ATX tires that came on Ford sports utility vehicles and delaminated in hot weather, quietly settled many cases arising from crashes and injuries caused by the tires over an eight-year period. The settlements usually included secrecy agreements, barring parties in the suits from discussing the case. The court files and evidence were also sealed, keeping information about the dangers posed by the tires from reaching the public.[27]

Secrecy clauses such as those used by Philip Morris and Brown & Williamson to silence Victor DeNoble and Jeffrey Wigand are not just used by the tobacco companies or in employment contracts. They have increasingly been inserted into a variety of other contracts, including university-corporate research contracts, which often contain clauses restricting when researchers can publish their findings. For example, a study published in the *New England Journal of Medicine* reported that a majority of companies entering into biomedical research agreements with universities require that the findings be "kept confidential to protect [their] proprietary value beyond the time required to file a patent."[28]

According to the National Cancer Institute's Steven Rothenberg, these restrictions on publishing impede scientific research because uninhibited "discussion among scientists, even about preliminary results of ongoing experiments . . . can play an important part in advancing research."[29]

Some university-corporate contracts restrict more than when research findings can be published. They contain paragraphs giving the corporate sponsor the right to determine whether the results can ever be released. A British pharmaceutical corporation, the Boots Company, gave $250,000 to the University of California San Francisco for research comparing its hypothyroid drug, Synthroid, with lower-cost alternatives. Instead of demonstrating Synthroid's superiority, as Boots had hoped, the study found the drugs were bioequivalents. Professor Betty Dong, who conducted the study, submitted her findings to the *Journal of the American Medical Association,* which, after subjecting the study to rigorous blind review, agreed to publish it. The information could have saved consumers $356 million if they had switched to cheaper alternatives, but would have undermined Synthroid's domination of the $600 million synthetic hormone market.

When Boots found out about the scheduled article, it stopped publication, citing provisions in the research contract that results "were not to be published or otherwise released without [Boots'] written consent." After Boots blocked publication of the article, it announced that Dong's research was badly flawed, and that Sythroid was actually superior to alternatives. Dong was unable to counter the claim because she could not release the study.[30]

Some research contracts have even had speech restrictions imbedded in them. In 1996, the University of Wisconsin signed a multimillion-dollar contract with Reebok, granting the running-shoe manufacturer exclusive rights to make and market athletic apparel bearing the Wisconsin logo. In addition to paying coaches for promotional appearances and giving financial support for the university's athletic program, the contract included this speech-restricting clause: "The university will not issue any official statement that disparages Reebok . . . [and] will promptly take all reasonable steps to address any remark by any university employee, including a coach, that disparages Reebok."

Although university administrators publicly disclosed many other provisions of the contract, they kept the speech-restriction clause secret until the last moment. When news of it did become public, dozens of professors signed a letter of opposition. Embarrassed by the flak and the exposure of their willingness to sell out free speech, university administrators retreated, asking Reebok to cancel the speech-prohibition paragraph. Facing a public relations disaster, Reebok quickly agreed.[31]

Because such tactics are widely used to restrict speech, businesses and corporations now pose a greater threat to free speech than does government.

The Growth of Corporate Power

As railroads in the United States developed and grew in the last half of the nineteenth century, American industry was transformed. The railroad companies became the first large interstate corporations, but they also built the infrastructure that allowed other corporations to become large national operations. The size of U.S. companies is reflected in the number of miles of railway track laid. Between 1840 and 1850, 7,000 miles of track were opened; between 1850 and 1860, 24,000 miles were opened; between 1860 and 1870, another 24,000; and between 1870 and 1880, 51,000 miles of track were laid and opened.[32]

During these decades of railway expansion, businesses intrinsically tied to the railway industry, such as telegraph, steel, and oil, evolved into large corporations. Other corporations became national once the railways allowed goods to be easily distributed nationally.

During the same era that corporations grew from local to national enterprises, labor unions developed. The Knights of Labor, which was forced to organize underground beginning in 1869, emerged publicly in 1881. In 1886, thirteen unions merged to form the American Federation of Labor. These unions protected workers from exploitative companies, which used numerous tactics to keep wages down and unions out. The tactics included dismissal, blacklists, lockouts, brutality, and yellow dog contracts, which employees signed, promising never to join a union.

When unions gained enough power to influence legislation, such as state laws passed during the 1890s that prohibited blacklisting, companies used a variety of methods to circumvent the laws or to challenge them in court. An important method for countering legislation protecting workers came in 1886 when the Supreme Court ruled in *Santa Clara County* v. *Southern Pacific Railroad* that corporations were legally "persons" and entitled to protection under the equal protection clause of the Fourteenth Amendment to the Constitution.[33] The Fourteenth Amendment, written to redress the legal inequality between whites and blacks in former slave states, prohibits states from "depriv[ing] any person of life, liberty, or property without due process." Rather than protecting blacks, the Fourteenth Amendment after 1886 was primarily used to challenge child labor, health, and safety laws imposed by states, and to protect corporations from any state actions that limited corporate activities. "Of the Fourteenth Amendment cases brought before the Supreme Court between 1890 and 1910, nineteen dealt with the Negro, 288 dealt with corporations," reports historian Howard Zinn.[34]

Using the Fourteenth Amendment as the basis for their claims, corporations filed suits claiming that state laws creating the eight-hour day, prohibiting employers from discharging pro-union employees, and banning yellow dog contracts were unconstitutional abridgements of employers' rights. The employers frequently won. In 1895, the Supreme Court struck down an Illinois law establishing the eight-hour day, ruling that the law "substitutes the judgement of the legislature for the judgement of the employer and employee in a matter which they are competent to agree with each other. But the police power of the state can only be permitted to limit or abridge such a fundamental right as the right to make contracts, when the exercise of such power is necessary to promote the health, comfort, welfare, or safety of society to the public; and it is questionable whether it can be exercised to prevent injury to the individual engaged in a particular calling."[35] The Supreme Court's thinking in this case—that state laws designed to protect workers rather than society as a whole violated due process—was repeated in many cases until 1937. Between 1897 and 1937, the Supreme Court frequently invalidated state and federal legislation that the court perceived to regulate economic activity.[36]

Corporations also used the Sherman Antitrust Act of 1890, passed to curb the monopolistic practices of large corporations, to sue unions, claiming that unions were "combinations" that restrained trade. This practice continued until the passage of the Norris-LaGuardia Act of

1932, the later interpretation of which exempted labor unions from prosecution under the antitrust laws.[37]

The legacy of *Santa Clara County* v. *Southern Pacific Railroad* is that corporations have extended their powers far beyond those of individuals. As author Robert Sherrill observed, "The inequality between black and white that the 14th Amendment was supposed to overcome has instead been transformed into perhaps an even greater inequality between the corporate person and the natural person."[38] With their greater financial clout and power, corporations have successfully used the courts and Fourteenth Amendment protections to curb attempts to police their abuses.

Santa Clara County v. *Southern Pacific Railroad* isn't the only court decision or government action that has contributed to the growth of corporate power during the past century. One of the most important has been the U.S. government's perception that big businesses are needed to compete globally. This perception has permitted mergers, such as the 1999 merger between Exxon and Mobil, the nation's two largest oil companies, that would have been banned under antitrust laws in another era.[39] It has produced legislation such as the Telecommunication Act of 1995 that allowed large corporations like General Electric to grow even larger.

Part of the reason why legislation like the Telecommunication Act has been passed by Congress and state legislatures is that several Supreme Court decisions, particularly *Buckley* v. *Valeo,* have allowed corporations to become active in the political process, lobbying extensively and contributing money to candidates running for public office. The *Valeo* decision allowed corporations, through their political action committees (PACs), to donate money directly to political candidates and indirectly through unlimited "soft money" contributions to political parties. In federal elections, the largest contributions now come from corporate PACs. Corporate PACs contributed $48 million to Republican House candidates in 1998 and $23 million to Democratic candidates, more than any other group.[40] Corporate PACs also contributed the most money to political party organizations. For example, nearly half of the money flowing into the National Republican Congressional Committee during the 1998 elections came from corporations.[41]

Political parties and elected officials dependent on these contributions lobby federal agencies on behalf of, or vote for legislation benefitting their contributors. An example of this is provided by Arizona senator John McCain, who campaigned in the 2000 Republican presidential primary against the corrupting influence of political contributions. Despite his campaign message, McCain lobbied extensively on behalf of his contributors. McCain wrote regulators on behalf of America West Airlines, Ameritech, BellSouth, Paxson Communications, and other financial backers. He asked the Federal Communications Commission to give "serious consideration" to BellSouth's proposal to offer long-distance telephone service, asked the FCC to approve Paxson Communication's request to buy a television station, and castigated the FCC in a letter for being unfair toward Ameritech's proposed merger with another regional telephone company.[42]

Not only have laws and regulations been adopted that have allowed corporations to expand their size and power, but U.S. tax policies during the last half-century have benefitted corporations at the expense of citizens. The federal tax burden has been shifted from corporations to individuals since the 1950s, giving corporations more money to use for acquisitions and to influence legislation. In 1952, corporate income taxes accounted for 32.1 percent of federal revenues. By 1970, federal revenues coming from corporate taxes dropped to 17 percent, and, by 1980, they had fallen to 6.6 percent.[43] Relieved of their tax responsibilities, corporate coffers have swelled, allowing them to evolve from multidivisional organizations to national conglomerates to multinational entities rivaling the size and power of many nation states.[44] Because they have more assets available to them than most governments and because they lack public accountability, corporations now wield immense power, which they often use to restrict speech or silence critics.

Notes

1. Henry Weinstein, "Tobacco Firms Threaten Assault on Cigarette Bill," *Los Angeles Times,* April 4, 1998.
2. For a discussion of the contest, see Bruce Horowitz, "Essay Contest Touches Off Ethics Contest," *Los Angeles Times,* December 23, 1986.
3. According to Philip Morris (see www.philipmorris.com/corporate/ir/investor/sec_filings.htm), the corporation's operating revenues for 1998 were $74.4 billion and its net earnings were $7.8 billion. By comparison, the gross domestic product of Iraq,

the United States' bête noire, was $41.1 billion, according to *The World Almanac 1998* (Mahwah, NJ: World Almanac Books, 1997), 775.

4. Robert Laurence, "Sponsors' Ties to Content Could Bind TV," *San Diego Union-Tribune,* August 17, 1999.
5. Louis Banks, "Memo to the Press: They Hate You Out There," *The Atlantic,* April 1978, 38.
6. Ben Bagdikian, *The Media Monopoly,* 5th ed. (Boston: Beacon Press, 1997), 156, 171.
7. K. E. Warner, L. M. Goldenhar, and C. G. McLaughlin, "Cigarette Advertising and Magazine Coverage of the Health Hazards of Smoking—A Statistical Analysis," *New England Journal of Medicine,* January 30, 1992, 305–11.
8. "Saatchi Plays Down RJR's Move," *Financial Times,* April 7, 1988, 26.
9. Quoted in Kenneth Warner, "Cigarette Advertising and Media Coverage of Smoking and Health," *New England Journal of Medicine,* February 7, 1985, 387.
10. Alex Kuczynski, "Big Tobacco's Newest Billboards Are on the Pages of Its Magazines," *New York Times,* December 12, 1999, 1.
11. Amanda Locy, "Tobacco Industry Secret Project Goes Up in Smoke," (Wauwatosa, WI) *Express News,* October 25, 1999.
12. Howard Kurtz, " '60 Minutes' Kills Piece on Tobacco Industry," *Washington Post,* November 10, 1995.
13. "Self-Censorship at CBS," *New York Times,* November 12, 1995.
14. Judith Michaelson, "Morning Report," *Los Angeles Times,* November 9, 1999.
15. For examples of the evidence, see discussions in Henry Weinstein, "Key Tobacco Witness Gets Immunity, Sources Say," *Los Angeles Times,* July 13, 1997; "Tobacco Firm Chief Lied in Testimony Before Congress, Ex-Employee Says," *Chicago Tribune,* January 28, 1996; "UC to Release Tobacco Firm's Papers in Wake of Ruling," *Los Angeles Times,* July 1, 1995.
16. Barry Meier, "Cigarette Makers' Strategy of '94 Is Echoed Today," *New York Times,* May 2, 1998; Philip J. Hilts, "A Law Opening Research Data Sets Off Debate," *New York Times,* July 31, 1999.
17. John Schwartz, "ABC Issues Apology for Tobacco Report," *Washington Post,* August 22, 1995.
18. Benjamin Weiser, "ABC and Tobacco: The Anatomy of a Network News Mistake," *Washington Post,* January 7, 1996; Steve Weinberg, "Smoking Guns," *Columbia Journalism Review,* November 1995, 29.
19. Doug Levy, "ABC Brief Backs Nicotine Claim," *USA Today,* January 16, 1996.
20. Robert P. Laurence, "ABC's Snuffing of Tobacco Film Leaves Foul Odor," *San Diego Union Tribune,* April 22, 1996.
21. Quoted in Larry C. White, *Merchants of Death* (New York: Beech Tree Books, 1988).
22. Lawrence Soley, "The Power of the Press Has a Price," *Extra!,* July/August 1997, 11–13.
23. "University Won't Get Donation," *Milwaukee Journal Sentinel,* April 25, 2000.
24. Douglas Frantz, "Alaskans Choose Sides in Battle Over Cruise Ships," *New York Times,* November 29, 1999.

25. "Company Policy Bans Solicitation of Money at Malls," *Milwaukee Journal Sentinel,* November 14, 2000.
26. Quoted in Davan Maharaj, "Firestone Recall Puts Spotlight on Secret Liability Agreements," *New York Times,* September 10, 2000.
27. Ibid.
28. David Blumenthal, et. al., "Relationships Between Academic Institutions and Industry in the Life Science—An Industry Survey," *New England Journal of Medicine,* February 8, 1996, 371.
29. Steven A. Rothenberg, "Secrecy in Medical Research," *New England Journal of Medicine,* February 8, 1996, 392.
30. Ralph T. King, "How a Drug Firm Paid for University Study, Then Undermined It," *Wall Street Journal,* April 25, 1996.
31. "Campus Fight Leads Reebok to Modify Shoe Contract," *New York Times,* June 28, 1996.
32. Statistics from E. J. Hobsbawm, *Industry and Empire* (New York: Penguin Books, 1977), 115. For a discussion of the importance of railways in corporate evolution, see Oliver E. Williamson, "The Modern Corporation: Origins, Evolution, Attributes," *Journal of Economic Literature,* December 1981, 1537–68.
33. *Santa Clara County* v. *Southern Pacific Railroad,* 118 U.S. 394 (1886).
34. Howard Zinn, *A People's History of the United States* (New York: Harcourt Brace Jovanovich, 1980), 255.
35. Quoted in Frank Tracy Carlton, *The History and Problems of Organized Labor* (New York: D.C. Heath & Co., 1911), 273.
36. Laurence H. Tribe, op. cit., 567–74.
37. *U.S.* v. *Hutcheson,* 312 U.S. 219 (1941).
38. Robert Sherrill, "Big Business Takes the First," *Harper's,* January 1988, 22.
39. Mark Curriden, "Exxon-Mobil Merger Assured, Lawyers Say," *Dallas Morning News,* November 27, 1999.
40. Associated Press, "Big Business Reroutes PAC Money," *Chicago Tribune,* September 16, 1999.
41. Juliet Eilperin, "House Whip Wields Fund-Raising Clout," *Washington Post,* October 18, 1999.
42. Robert R. Rankin and Josh Goldstein, "Ethics Flap Seen as Threat to McCain's Image," *Milwaukee Journal Sentinel,* January 8, 2000.
43. Herbert I. Schiller, *Culture, Inc.* (New York: Oxford University Press, 1989), 28–29.
44. For a discussion of this evolution, see Alfred D. Chandler, Jr., "The Structure of American Industry in the Twentieth Century: A Historical Overview," *Business History Review,* Autumn 1969, 473–503. Chandler's approach was criticized by Richard B. Du Boff and Edward S. Herman, "Alfred Chandler's New Business History: A Review," *Politics and Society* 10 (1), 87–110.

4
AMERICAN MUSIC CHALLENGES THE COPYRIGHT TRADITION

Siva Vaidhyanathan

Music, more than any other vehicle of culture, collapses the gap that separates idea from expression. Is the string of six notes that initiates "Happy Birthday to You" an idea, an expression, or both? If it is an idea, there must be another way to express the same idea. Would playing the same notes at a different tempo constitute a new expression of the same idea? Would playing it in a different key be an exercise in novel expression? Is there an idea behind a particular arrangement of musical notes? Is there an idea behind a tone, texture, timbre, or "feel" of a song? Are these features of a song ideas in themselves?

If copyright law is charged with protecting a particular arrangement of notes, should it protect the melody, the harmony, the rhythm, or all of the above? How long must that string of notes be to constitute a protectable segment of expression? Should music copyright law be most concerned with the "total concept and feel" of a protected work, or particular elements such as solos, riffs, or choruses? The twelve-bar I-IV-V chord pattern runs through most songs within the blues tradition, so that pattern is generally considered unprotectable. It is considered "common property," drawn from the "deep well" of American blues. However, an identifiable one-measure guitar riff—such as the opening to the Rolling Stones song (and Microsoft Windows advertisement) "Start Me Up"—could be protectable. At what point between general chord patterns and specific strings of notes does repetition constitute an infringement of a protectable expression? None of the answers to these questions is clear. Creative infringement cases have been interpreted on an almost ad hoc basis. Maintaining a healthy measure of freedom for "second takers" to build upon an expressive tradition demands other strategies, because the traditional safeguard of the idea-expression dichotomy does not operate the same way in music as in other fields.

Because these questions yield unsatisfying answers, many disputes among artists get expressed in moral or ethical terms. Led Zeppelin, like many rock groups, did not have an unsullied reputation for granting credit to blues artists. The group had covered and properly credited two other Dixon compositions, "You Shook Me" and "I Can't Quit You Baby," on its first album in 1968, *Led Zeppelin I.* During the early 1970s, the group had befriended the Dixon family on its visits to Chicago and had publicly paid homage to American blues pioneers. The group had failed to credit two other songs from *Led Zeppelin II,* "Bring It on Home" and "The Lemon Song," which resembled other Dixon compositions. Unbeknownst to Dixon, his publishing company, Arc Music, had negotiated a settlement with Led Zeppelin over those uncredited songs, but had neglected to inform Dixon or pay him the recovered royalties until long after the settlement. By the late 1980s, Led Zeppelin would not eagerly grant either writing credit or royalties to Dixon over "Whole Lotta Love."[1] The proceeds of that settlement helped Dixon start the Blues Heaven Foundation, dedicated to helping aging composers and performers recoup some of the rewards for their work in years before they had a chance to develop sophisticated business and legal acumen. When Dixon passed away in 1992, his legend had grown from brilliant composer and performer to brave business pioneer. Dixon was among the first blues artists to wrest control of rights and royalties from exploitative record and publishing companies.[2]

The relationship between blues composers and rock artists is complex. There are rarely obvious good guys and bad guys in the stories of disputes over credit, influence, and royalties. In 1956, Elvis Presley revolutionized popular music by introducing stripped-down, high-power southern rhythm and blues to mainstream white audiences around the world. He did so by recording some songs that African American artists had distributed to lesser acclaim just a few years before, such as Big Mama Thornton's "Hound Dog." While Thornton's version gained legendary status among blues fans in the 1950s, it barely scratched the white pop market. Presley's version, on the other hand, sold two million copies in 1956 and simultaneously topped the pop, country, and rhythm and blues charts. Presley's appeal transcended racial and regional lines and opened up several generations of young people from around the globe to the power of African American music.[3] Yet Presley remains a controversial figure to many critics, who consider his work "inauthentic" because he reaped far greater rewards than previous or contemporary black artists whose work was just as exciting. Music journalist Nelson George has called Presley "a damned lazy student" of black culture and a "mediocre interpretive artist." Chuck D, the leader and lyricist of the rap group Public Enemy, sings "Elvis was a hero to most, but he didn't mean shit to me." Whether in good faith or bad, white performers almost always reaped larger rewards than their black influences and songwriters. As Tricia Rose has argued, whiteness matters in the story of the commodification of black cultural expression. By virtue of their whiteness, many artists participated in styles and subcultures that emerged from the rhythm and blues tradition and "crossed over" what was until only recently a gaping social and economic chasm between black music and white consumers. White rockers went where black artists could not. Even when blacks could cross over, white artists have had better opportunities to capitalize on the publicity and distribution systems. For instance, many "alternative" or "rock" radio stations will occasionally play rap music, but only if it is by white artists such as the Beastie Boys, Limp Bizkit, or Kid Rock.[4]

But the politics and economics of cultural exchange and translation are not simple and unidirectional. Like Elvis, many later blues-rock stars such as Eric Clapton, the Rolling Stones, and Bonnie Raitt helped publicize the work of almost forgotten blues artists. Others, such as Led Zeppelin and the Beach Boys, have granted credit to composers such as Dixon and Chuck Berry under legal duress. There is very little difference in the passion or sincerity behind the work of Muddy Waters and that of Eric Clapton. However, there is an indisputable chasm between the reception of Waters's work in the 1950s and that of Clapton's hits of the 1970s: Because he is white, Clapton was in a better position to exploit vastly better business conditions and broader consumer markets than Waters was. Clapton emerged at a very different time. Nonetheless, many music fans now know and appreciate the work of Willie Dixon, Muddy Waters, and Robert Johnson because of Elvis Presley, Eric Clapton, Jimmy Page, and others.

The simplistic story of the relationship is that younger white performers "stole" material from aging "authentic" composers such as Willie Dixon, Sonny Boy Williamson, or Son House. But tracing influence through something as organic and dynamic as American music is never simple. Blues-based music is often the product of common and standard chord structures and patterns. Relying on or referring to a particular influence can be as important as any "original" contribution to a work. A composer might employ a familiar riff within a new composition as a signal that the new song is part of one specific tradition within the vast multifaceted canon of American music. Influence is inspiration, and songs talk to each other through generations. As Willie Dixon wrote: "When you're a writer, you don't have time to listen to everybody else's thing. You get their things mixed up with your ideas and the next thing you know, you're doing something that sounds like somebody else." Because repetition and revision are such central tropes in American music, rewarding and encouraging originality is a troublesome project in the music industry.[5]

In 1948, Muddy Waters released a song for the Chess brothers' Aristocrat label called "Feel Like Goin' Home." It was Waters's first national rhythm and blues hit. "Feel Like Goin' Home" was a revised version of a song Waters had recorded on his front porch in Mississippi for the folklorist Alan Lomax in 1941. After singing that song, which he told Lomax was entitled "Country Blues," Waters told Lomax a story of how he came to write it. "I made that blue up in thirty-eight," Waters said. "I made it on about the eighth of October, thirty-eight. . . . I was fixin' a puncture on a car. I had been mistreated by a girl, it was just running in my mind to sing that song. . . . Well, I just felt blue, and the song fell into my mind and it come to me just like that and I started singing." Then Lomax, who knew of the Robert Johnson recording of a similar tune called "Walking Blues," asked Waters if there were any other blues songs that used the same tune. "There's been some blues played like that," Waters replied. "This song comes from the cotton field and a boy once put a record out—Robert Johnson. He put it out as named 'Walking Blues.' . . . I heard the tune before I heard it on the record. I learned it from Son House. That's a boy who could pick a guitar."[6]

In this brief passage, Waters offers five accounts of the origin of "Country Blues." At first, Waters asserts his own active authorship, saying he "made it" on a specific date under specific conditions. Then Waters expresses the "passive" explanation of authorship as received knowledge—not unlike Harriet Beecher Stowe's authorship of *Uncle Tom's Cabin*—that "it come to me just like that." After Lomax raises the question of Johnson's influence, Waters, without shame, misgivings, or trepidation, says that he heard a version of that song by Johnson, but that his mentor Son House taught it to him. Most significantly, Waters declares in the middle of that complex genealogy that "this song comes from the cotton field."

Poisoning the Well

Just before the Beatles broke up, lead guitarist George Harrison was busy composing songs for his first solo album, *All Things Must Pass.* Harrison and his new band, which included keyboard player Billy Preston, were playing a concert in Copenhagen, Denmark, in 1970. During a backstage press conference, Harrison slipped away, grabbed an acoustic guitar, and started playing around with simple chord structures. He eased into a pattern of alternating a minor II chord with a major V chord. Then he chanted the words "Hallelujah" and "Hare Krishna" over the chords. Soon other members of his band and entourage gathered around him, joining in on the song in four-part harmony. Between choruses of "Hallelujah" and "Hare Krishna" Harrison improvised some verses that included lyrics such as "My Sweet Lord," "Dear, dear Lord," and "I really want to see you; I really want to be with you." Over the next few weeks, Harrison and Preston returned to that jam, composing and recording the entire text of what became Harrison's first solo hit, "My Sweet Lord."[7]

After the song gained wide acclaim and broad distribution, a band called the Belmonts recorded a tongue-in-cheek version of "My Sweet Lord" that appended the chorus lyrics from the 1962 Chiffons tune "He's So Fine," composed by Ronald Mack and produced by Phil Spector, to the Harrison hit. The similarities between "My Sweet Lord" and "He's So Fine" were not lost on Bright Tunes Music Corporation either. Bright Tunes was the publishing company that controlled the rights to "He's So Fine." Bright Tunes filed suit against Harrison, and the case went to trial in 1976. In his decision, the district judge closely examined the building blocks of both songs. "He's So Fine" consists of two "motifs," Judge Richard Owen concluded. The first motif (A) is the array of notes "sol-me-re." The second motif (B) is the phrase "sol-la-do-la-do." Owen granted that standing alone neither of these motifs is novel enough to qualify for protection.

However, what matters is not the building blocks themselves, but their arrangement and order within the greater structure. "He's So Fine" contains the pattern A-A-A-A-B-B-B-B. The pattern of four repetitions of A followed by four repetitions of B is "a highly unique pattern," Owen ruled. Then, examining "My Sweet Lord," Owen stated that the Harrison song used the same motif A four times, and then motif B three times. In place of the fourth repetition of B, Harrison employed a transitional passage (T) of the same length as B. "My Sweet Lord" goes A-A-A-A-B-B-B-T. In both songs, the composers used a slippery "grace note" in the fourth refrain of B (or in the substituted transitional phrase T, in the case of "My Sweet Lord"). In addition, Owen wrote, "the harmonies of both songs are identical." Harrison's expert witnesses asserted that the differences between the songs mattered more than the similarities. They argued that the lyrics, the syllabic patterns, and syncopations distinguished each song. For instance, the highly meaningful terms "Hallelujah" and "Hare Krishna" in "My Sweet Lord" replace the nonsense word and rhythmic placeholder "dulang" from "He's So Fine."[8]

Federal courts ask two questions to determine whether a song infringes on the copyright for an earlier song: The plaintiff must show that the second composer had access to the first song and that the second song shows "substantial similarity" to the first. Similarity without access, the result of a random coincidence, would not infringe. There are only eight notes in a major scale, after all. Accidents do happen. The need to establish access necessarily protects hits better than obscure songs. On the other hand, hits are more likely to stick in people's minds, more likely to flow through musical communities as influences and inspirations, and more likely to add elements to the musical "well."[9]

George Harrison went to the well once too often. He was raised in the blues tradition, as embodied by the English working class in the 1950s and 1960s. He and his pals spent their youth memorizing riffs from Chuck Berry, Muddy Waters, and Buddy Holly records. American rhythm and blues were irresistible sources of powerful stories and emotions, and influenced everything Harrison and his peers did. Both Harrison and Preston testified vehemently that neither one of them considered "He's So Fine" an inspiration for "My Sweet Lord." The Chiffons song never entered their minds, they said. But "He's So Fine" topped the pop music chart in the United States for five weeks in the summer of 1963. It reached the number 12 spot in England during that same time—a summer when the top song on the British pop charts belonged to the Beatles. Both Preston in the United States and Harrison in England had ample access to the Chiffons' recording. They both knew of the song, but neither consciously appealed to it as a source for "My Sweet Lord." Judge Owen agreed: "Seeking the wellsprings of musical composition—why a composer chooses the succession of notes and the harmonies he does—whether it be George Harrison or Richard Wagner is a fascinating inquiry. It is apparent from the extensive colloquy between the Court and Harrison covering forty pages in the transcript that neither Harrison nor Preston were conscious of the fact that they were utilizing the 'He's So Fine' theme. However, they in fact were, for it is perfectly obvious to the listener that in musical terms, the two songs are virtually identical except for one phrase." Then, precipitously employing the passive voice, Owen leapt to a conclusion that poisoned the well for subsequent artists:

> What happened? I concluded that the composer, in seeking musical materials to clothe his thoughts, was working with various possibilities. As he tried this possibility and that, there came to the surface of his mind a particular combination that pleased him as being one he felt would be appealing to a prospective listener; in other words, that this combination of sounds would work, Why? Because his subconscious knew it already had worked in a song his conscious mind did not remember. Having arrived at this pleasing combination of sounds, the recording was made, the lead sheet prepared for copyright and the song became an enormous success. Did Harrison deliberately use the music of "He's So Fine"? I do not believe he did so deliberately. Nevertheless, it is clear that "My Sweet Lord" is the very same song as "He's So Fine" with different words, and Harrison had access to "He's So Fine." This is, under the law, infringement of copyright, and is no less so even though subconsciously accomplished.[10]

Under this standard, which makes "subconscious" influence illicit, something an artist must struggle to avoid, Muddy Waters would have had great difficulty keeping up with who had recorded and marketed particular arrangements that were considered common property in the Mississippi Delta, music that came "from the cotton field," or from the well of tradition. The standard used in the Harrison case puts a heavy burden on those who snatch a groove out of the air and insert it as one part of a complex creative process.

Over the next twelve years, emboldened by the Harrison suit, composers and publishing companies that retained rights to classic American songs considered pursuing legal action against more recent songwriters. In 1981, the company that owned the rights to the 1928 Gus Kahn and Walter Donaldson standard "Makin' Whoopee" filed suit against Yoko Ono, collaborator and spouse of former Beatle John Lennon, for her song "I'm Your Angel" on the 1981 album *Double Fantasy.* Jazz pianist Keith Jarrett pursued action against Steely Dan songwriters Donald Fagen and Walter Becker for jazz-tinged cuts from their album *Gaucho.* Actions such as these did nothing to promote originality and new music. In fact, the publicity about such suits probably retarded creativity by generating an aura of fear and trepidation.[11]

Then, in 1988, another artist who "went to the well" of the American rhythm and blues tradition won a major case that was strikingly similar to the Harrison ordeal. Only this time, the songwriter in question, John Fogerty, had written both the original song and the later one. Fogerty was accused of copying from himself. Fogerty had been the leader, driving force behind, and chief songwriter of the successful 1960s country-blues-rock band Creedence Clearwater Revival. Like many young and naive songwriters, including Willie Dixon, Fogerty had signed a contract earlier in his career that granted all rights to his songs to a publishing company, Jondora, which was owned by Fantasy Records. After Fogerty split with his band and Fantasy in the early 1970s, he refused to play hits from his old catalogue because he resented the performance royalties flowing to Fantasy and its president, Saul Zaentz. Those years of bitterness pushed Fogerty out of the rock spotlight. His refusal to play his old songs disconnected Fogerty from his fans. Then, in 1985, Fogerty released his "comeback" album, *Centerfield.* The album yielded a number of hits that generated airplay and sales, including "Rock and Roll Girls," which shares a chord pattern and beat with classics such as Ritchie Valens's "La Bamba" and the Isley Brothers' "Twist and Shout," and the title cut "Centerfield," which quotes a line from Chuck Berry's song "Brown-Eyed Handsome Man," signifying that the album was just the latest link in the rhythm and blues chain. However, two of the songs on the album seemed to be direct attacks on Fogerty's nemesis, Fantasy president Zaentz. "Mr. Greed, why you gotta own everything that you see? Mr. Greed, why you put a chain on everybody livin' free?" Fogerty sang on the song "Mr. Greed." And the final song on the album was called "Zanz Kan't Danz." The refrain includes the line "but he'll steal your money."[12]

Zaentz filed suit. But he had found a stronger claim than defamation or libel on which to attack Fogerty. Zaentz argued that the opening song on *Centerfield,* "The Old Man down the Road," contains a bass line, rhythm, and guitar bridge that are similar to those of the 1970 Creedence Clearwater Revival hit "Run through the Jungle." While Fogerty had written "Run through the Jungle," Zaentz still owned the rights to it. During the jury trial in San Francisco, both sides called a series of musicologists to discuss influence and originality in music. Then Fogerty took the stand with his guitar in hand. Over a day and a half, Fogerty played for the jury such songs as "Proud Mary," "Down on the Corner," and "Fortunate Son" to explain his creative process. Most importantly, Fogerty played tapes of old Howlin' Wolf and Bo Diddley songs, then picked up his guitar and played a Bo Diddley song called "Bring It to Jerome," which contains riffs and rhythms similar to both "Run through the Jungle" and "The Old Man down the Road." The jury found for Fogerty after two hours of deliberation.[13]

The Harrison and Fogerty cases show that the case law concerning the reuse of tropes and elements from older songs makes little or no space for performance-based models of originality—contributions of style or delivery. Judges such as Owen in the Harrison case have tried to employ the structuralist reading method that Judge Learned Hand developed (although Owen's opinion seems to owe something to Freud as well). But these cases have not yielded anything close to a simple or clear standard for determining whether one song in the blues tradition infringes on another. The ruling in the Harrison case seemed to bend in favor of older composers, putting the burden of clearing influences on newer songwriters. Yet the judgment in the Fogerty case seemed to grant "creedence" to the notion that songwriters should be allowed to draw from the blues tradition well.

The Harrison and Fogerty cases are concerned with how songwriters might trample on the composition rights—that is, the actual notes and structure—of an older song. But there are two other major rights in the "bundle" of rights that make up musical copyright: performance rights and mechanical rights. Performance rights concern public concerts, radio play, jukebox play, and other media exhibitions. Performance rights are usually licensed—and royalties collected—through consortiums such as the American Society of Composers, Authors, and Publishers (ASCAP) and Broadcast Music, Inc. (BMI). Mechanical rights are the rights to reproduce particular recordings of the song or album. Before the 1980s, infringement suits that dealt with mechanical rights generally concerned large-scale pirating of records and tapes. Suits over composition rights dealt with the re-use of melody, harmony, or lyrics.[14]

However, digital technology and the rise of urban hip-hop culture complicated that dichotomy. Rap does not use melody and harmony in the same ways that other forms of music do. In fact, rap artists often "sample" bits of others' melody and harmony, and use those "samples" as part of a rhythm track, completely transforming and recycling those pieces of music. Rap is revolutionary because it did not emerge directly from the American blues tradition. It is an example of and expression of "Afrodiasporic" black culture, derived in form and function from Caribbean music more than from American rhythm and blues.[15] However, in the United States, rap artists used whatever building blocks they found in their environment to construct an American rap tradition. So instead of playing similar riffs or melodies from other artists on their own instruments, early rap composers weaved samples from familiar songs into a new montage of sound. By the early 1990s copyright cases concerning mechanical rights intersected with the unstable principles of composition rights.

Fear of a Sampling Planet: How Rap Bum-rushed Copyright Law

Over the raunchy, driving Jimmy Page guitar chords of the Led Zeppelin song "Kashmir," Philadelphia rapper Schoolly D bellows the words "Way way down in the jungle deep"—signature of the African American folk poem "Signifying Monkey." In the traditional poem, the trickster monkey uses his wits and his command of diction to outsmart a more powerful adversary. The "Signifying Monkey" has appeared in various forms in blues recordings, folktale ethnographies, the poetry of Larry Neal, and the blacksploitation film *Dolomite.* Only this time, the trickster tale turns up as the lyrics to the song "Signifying Rapper" on Schoolly D's 1988 album *Smoke Some Kill.* Jimmy Page did not join D in the recording studio. Nor did Page or Led Zeppelin garner any credit on the label of *Smoke Some Kill.* But the contribution—and the message—is unmistakable. Schoolly D is "signifying" on Led Zeppelin, a more powerful cultural force than he is. Among the raw materials available to creative black youth in the deindustrialized Reagan-era cities were piles of warped vinyl, scraps of sounds. Pretentions to "authenticity" seemed silly. "Credit," in all its various meanings, was not forthcoming to black youth or black culture. Why should they give it when they weren't receiving it? Led Zeppelin did not "credit" the blues masters as often as they could have, so why should Schoolly D do anything but reciprocate? Yet by rapping an updated and unexpurgated version of an African American folktale, Schoolly D was proclaiming his connection to something that was once "real," by constructing a musical work that felt nothing like "real" music. Repeating and reusing the guitar riff from "Kashmir" was a transgressive and disrespectful act—a "dis" of Led Zeppelin and the culture that produced, rewarded, and honored Led Zeppelin.[16]

Schoolly D released "Signifying Rapper" a decade after rap first attracted the attention of young people and music executives around the world. The first rap record to attract radio play and widespread sales, the Sugarhill Gang's "Rapper's Delight" (1979), rode the thumping instrumental track from Chic's "Good Times," a disco hit that also served as the backing track for many free-form rap songs of the 1970s. From the late 1970s through the early 1990s, most rap songs adhered to and improved on the formula popularized by "Rapper's Delight," spoken rhymes punctuating a background montage constructed from unauthorized pieces of previously recorded music. The expansion of the market for rap music was phenomenal. In 1987, rap records represented 11.6 percent of all the music sales in the United States. By 1990, rap was 18.3 percent of the music business.[17]

Rap's rise from an urban hobby to a major industry rocked the status quo of not only the music industry, but the legal world as well. Since the late 1970s, rap artists have pushed the boundaries of free expression with sexually explicit lyrics and descriptions of violence by and against law enforcers. They have raised questions about society's power structures from the ghettos to the Gallerias. In many cases, legal and societal traditions had no way to deal with these fresh and strong sentiments that drove through America in an open jeep, powered by a heavy beat.

That's what happened when an entrenched and exciting hip-hop tradition, sampling, energized by digital technology, encroached upon one of the most ambiguous areas of the American legal tradition: American copyright law. Complicating the clash, the concept of copyright has been deeply entrenched in western literary tradition for centuries, but does not play the same role in African, Caribbean, or African American oral traditions. It's far too simple and inaccurate to declare that copyrighting has been a white thing; sampling, borrowing, or quoting has been a black thing. The turmoil that rap has created in copyright law is more complex than just a clash of stereotypically opposed cultures. It's not just a case of mistrust and misunderstanding. Rap—for a moment—revealed gaping flaws in the premises of how copyright law gets applied to music and shown the law to be inadequate for emerging communication technologies, techniques, and aesthetics.

The tension in the law is not between urban lower class and corporate überclass. It's not between black artists and white record executives. It's not always a result of conflicts between white songwriters and the black composers who sample them. It is in fact a struggle between the established entities in the music business and those trying to get established. It is a conflict between old and new.

Sampling, as opposed to simply imitating, became a big issue in American music after digital technology became cheap and easily available and its products became immensely popular.[18] Digital sampling is a process by which sounds are converted into binary units readable by a computer. A digital converter measures the tone and intensity of a sound and assigns it a corresponding voltage. The digital code is then stored in a computer memory bank, or a tape or disc, and can be retrieved and manipulated electronically.[19]

But why do rap artists sample in the first place? What meanings are they imparting? Some songs grab bits and pieces of different pop culture signposts, while others, such as Tone Loc's "Wild Thing" or Hammer's "U Can't Touch This," which lays lyrics upon a backing track made up almost entirely of Rick James's "Super Freak" instrumentals, hardly stand alone as songs, but are truly "versions" of someone else's hits.[20] Sometimes, as with Schoolly D's sampling of Led Zeppelin's "Kashmir" for his song "Signifying Rapper," it can be a political act—a way of crossing the system, challenging expectations, or confronting the status quo. Often, the choice of the sample is an expression of appreciation, debt, or influence. Other times it's just a matter of having some fun or searching for the right ambient sound, tone, or feel. Certainly Rick James's funky hits of the late 1970s and early 1980s influenced not only artists of the 1990s but their audiences. Sampling is a way an artist declares, "Hey, I dug this, too." It helps form a direct connection with listeners, the same way a moviemaker might throw in a Motown hit in a soundtrack. By the early 1990s, at least 180 recordings by more than 120 artists contained samples by some of funk godfather George Clinton's P-Funk school, which included 1970s bands Funkadelic, Parliament, and various other bands headed by Clinton or his bassist, Bootsy Collins.[21] It's tough to say whether a new song that relies almost completely on some older hit riffs can achieve financial success on its own merits. Two of the best-selling rap hits are entirely dependent on massively danceable older songs and are, sadly, lyrically limited. They are Hammer's "U Can't Touch This" and Vanilla Ice's 1990 single "Ice Ice Baby," which was a stiff and meaningless rap over the backing track to the 1982 David Bowie–Queen hit "Under Pressure."[22] *Village Voice* music critic Greg Tate explained the aesthetic value of sampling: "Music belongs to the people, and sampling isn't a copy-cat act but a form of reanimation. Sampling in hip-hop is the digitized version of hip-hop DJing, an archival project and an art form unto itself. Hip-hop is ancestor worship."[23]

Sampling helps forge a "discursive community" among music fans. Rap music first made that connection to white audiences—and thus expanded the discursive community exponentially—in 1986, when Run DMC released its version of the 1977 Aerosmith song, "Walk This Way."[24] Within the African American discursive community, rap songs serve, in historian George Lipsitz's words, as "repositories of social memory."[25] Lipsitz particularly credits the matrix of cultural signs highlighted by sampling and realistic lyrics that document the struggles of inner-city life. Sampling can be transgressive or appreciative, humorous or serious. It gives a song another level of meaning, another plane of communication among the artist, previous artists, and the audience.

Digital sampling also had a powerful democratizing effect on American popular music. All a young composer needed was a thick stack of vinyl albums, a $2,000 sampler, a microphone, and a tape deck, and she could make fresh and powerful music. She could make people dance, laugh, and sing along. She might, under the right conditions, be able to make money from the practice. As critic John Leland wrote in *Spin:* "The digital sampling device has changed not only the sound of pop music, but also the mythology. It has done what punk rock threatened to do: made everybody into a potential musician, bridged the gap between performer and audience."[26]

Clearly, sampling as an American expression was raised in the Bronx, but was probably born in the Caribbean. Its aesthetic appeal is deeply embedded in African American and Afro-Caribbean culture, if not for most of this half century, then certainly over the last twenty-five years. More significantly, for a while in the late 1980s, it looked as if transgressive sampling was not going to go away. It made too much money and was too important to the meaning and message of rap. During the first decade of rap, the legal questions surrounding sampling grew more troublesome for both artists and labels as rap became more popular and the economic stakes rose. Sampling seemed to undermine the very definitions of "work," "author," and "original"—terms on which copyright law rests.

The Illin' Effect: How Copyright Bum-rushed Rap

All was not well for the creative process before courts weighed in on sampling issues. Anarchy was not paradise. Artists also suffered because of the confusion the practice caused in the record business. Record companies were understandably risk averse. Because sampling raised so many questions, labels pushed their more successful acts to get permission for samples before releasing a record. The problem was that no one knew what to charge for a three-second sample. As a 1992 note in the *Harvard Law Review* stated: "Consequently, the music industry has responded with an ad-hoc, negotiated licensing approach to valuing music samples."[27] As industry leaders and lawyers, and older songwriters, grew more aware of the prevalence of sampling and of the potential monetary gain from challenging it, artists became more concerned with the potential costs of sampling. This certainly retarded the creative process. Artists chose to sample less-well-known works, works published or produced by their own companies and labels, or works with a lower licensing price. When the Beastie Boys wanted to sample the Beatles song "I'm Down," Michael Jackson informed them that he owned the rights to the song and denied them permission to use it. The Beastie Boys eventually opted against using that song.[28]

Until 1991, no one in the rap or licensing businesses knew what the guidelines for digital sampling were. This means that on any given day, an artist may have been ripped off by an overpriced licensing fee, or a publishing company may have gotten burned by charging too little for a sample that helped produce a top hit.[29] That's why several legal scholars in the late 1980s and early 1990s tried to formulate licensing systems based on the use, length, and type of sample. Still, the industry was waiting for a court to weigh in so there could be some predictability and stability in the system.[30]

Several sampling cases were settled out of court before December of 1991, postponing the inevitable guidance a judicial decision would bring. Nonetheless, the publicity surrounding these cases made older artists hungry to cash in on the potential sampling licensing market. A song that had ceased bringing in royalties decades ago could suddenly yield a big check. In 1991 Mark Volman and Howard Kaylan of the 1960s pop group the Turtles sued the rap trio De La Soul for using a twelve-second piece of the Turtles' song "You Showed Me" in the 1989 rap track "Transmitting Live from Mars." Volman and Kaylan sued for $2.5 million, but reached an out-of-court settlement for $1.7 million. De La Soul paid $141,666.67 per second to the Turtles for a sliver of a long-forgotten song.[31]

Then in December 1991 a federal judge issued a terse sixteen-hundred-word ruling that all but shut down the practice of unauthorized sampling in rap music. In August of 1991, Warner Brothers Records distributed an album released by a small record label called Cold Chillin' Records. The artist was a young New Jersey rapper named Biz Markie. The album was called *I Need a Haircut*. There was nothing particular, unique, or special about the album. It was pretty substandard fare for rap albums from the late 1980s and early 1990s. The rhymes were simple. The subject matter was juvenile. The production was pedestrian. The choice of samples was neither funny nor insightful. *I Need a Haircut* might have been a trivial footnote in rap history but for the second-to-last cut on the album: "Alone Again." For that song, Biz Markie took the first eight bars of the number one single of 1972, Gilbert O'Sullivan's "Alone Again (Naturally)." Markie used only about twenty seconds of piano chords from the original song, which he looped continually to construct the musical background of the song. O'Sullivan's song was a sappy ballad about family loss. Markie's song was about how the rapper received no respect as a performer back when he played in combos with old friends, but since he had become a solo performer his career had been satisfying. Markie's use of O'Sullivan's sample did not directly parody it, but it was essential to setting the minor-chord mood of Markie's tale of determination and self-sufficiency.[32]

Markie's lawyers did not claim that sampling in this context was fair use. They could have argued that only a small section of O'Sullivan's song contributed to a vastly different composition that did not compete with the original song in the marketplace. This fair use defense probably would not have swayed the judge either. But they didn't even attempt to mount one.[33]

U.S. district judge Kevin Thomas Duffy's ruling did not articulate any nuanced standard by which a song could be sampled, manipulated, or revised without permission. It left no "wiggle room" for fair use. It did not consider whether the new use affected the market of the original song in any way. It did not try to clarify how long a sample must be to qualify as an infringement. The fact that the sample in question was a mere twenty seconds did not bode well for fair use. Duffy's brevity clarified these issues by ignoring them: "how much?" and "for what purpose?" need not even be asked after Duffy's ruling. It was safe to assume that any sample of any duration used for any purpose must be cleared.

There could be room for unauthorized sampling within American copyright law. It could and should be considered fair use. Digital samples are more often than not small portions of songs. These portions are being used in completely different ways in the new songs. Because they are not working in the same way as in the original song, they are inherently different from their sources. But most importantly, samples add value. They are pieces of language that generate new meanings in their new contexts. The new meanings are clear and distinct from their original meanings. A new song that samples an old song does not replace the old song in the marketplace. Often, it does the opposite. Despite all the panic digital sampling generated among legal experts in the late 1980s, sampling does not threaten the foundation of the law. In fact, if copyright law is to conform to its constitutional charge, to "promote the progress of science and useful arts," it should allow transgressive and satirical sampling without having to clear permission from original copyright owners. A looser system—and a broader definition of fair use—would encourage creativity. A tightly regulated system does nothing but squeeze new coins out of old music and intimidate emerging artists.

As Funny as They Wanna Be

There is social value in allowing transformative uses of copyrighted music without permission. The U.S. Supreme Court in 1994 articulated this principle in a landmark case that involved rap music. But it was not a case about sampling per se. It was the case that made America safe for parody.

Despite its brief tenure on the music charts, no group in the history of rap has been as controversial as the 2 Live Crew. A Broward County sheriff prosecuted a record store owner for selling the group's 1990 album *As Nasty As They Want to Be,* which relied on sexist and explicit lyrics and a complex montage of digital samples. Scholars and musicologists lined up both for and against the group and its leader, Luther Campbell. Within a year, Campbell had recast himself from nasty rapper and talented producer to a hero for the First Amendment. But it was 2 Live Crew's "nice" version of the album, *As Clean As They Want to Be* that brought the group to the U.S. Supreme Court. It contained a cut entitled "Pretty Woman" that relied heavily on the melody and guitar riff of Roy Orbison's 1964 hit "Oh, Pretty Woman." Orbison's publishing company, Acuff-Rose Music, Inc., had denied 2 Live Crew permission to parody the song. Campbell decided to do it anyway, and relied on a fair use defense when the lawsuit came. The U.S. district court granted a summary judgment in favor of 2 Live Crew, ruling that the new song was a parody of the original and that it was fair use of the material. But the Sixth Circuit Court of Appeals reversed that decision, arguing that 2 Live Crew took too much from the original and that it did so for blatantly commercial purposes. The U.S. Supreme Court ruled unanimously that the appeals court had not balanced all the factors that play into fair use. The Supreme Court reversed the appeals court and ruled in favor of Campbell and 2 Live Crew.[34]

Justice David Souter also concluded that a parody is unlikely to directly compete in the market with an original work because it serves a different function—criticism. Souter wrote,

> Suffice it to say now that parody has an obvious claim to transformative value, as Acuff-Rose itself does not deny. Like less ostensibly humorous forms of criticism, it can provide social benefit, by shedding light on an earlier work, and, in the process, creating a new one. Parody needs to mimic an original to make its point, and so has some claim to use the creation of its victim's (or collective victims') imagination, whereas satire can stand on its own two feet and so requires justification for the very act of borrowing.

Souter concluded that 2 Live Crew did target Orbison's song, not just society at large. But Souter also warned that this case should not be read as an open license to revise others' works for merely satirical purposes, and that each case should be considered individually. "The fact that parody can claim legitimacy for some appropriation does not, of course, tell either parodist or judge much about where to draw the line. Accordingly, parody, like any other use, has to work its way through the relevant factors, and be judged case by case, in light of the ends of the copyright law."[35]

While Souter was careful not to send too strong a message to potential parodists, his ruling set down some pretty firm principles upon which future cases might be decided. Significantly, Souter declared from the highest perch that parody has social value, and that courts must take such fair use claims seriously. But the U.S. Supreme Court has not considered a case in which transgressive or parodic sampling in rap music was defended as fair use. Based on the principles Souter outlined, it's not likely that the court would smile upon unauthorized digital sampling that indirectly commented on the culture at large—that is—most sampling. But sampling that directly comments upon its source, positively or negatively, might have a chance for consideration. Fundamentally, courts, Congress, and the public should consider how creativity happens in America. Ethnocentric notions of creativity and a maldistribution of political power in favor of established artists and media companies have already served to stifle expression—the exact opposite of the declared purpose of copyright law.[36]

Notes

1. Led Zeppelin, "Whole Lotta Love," on *Led Zeppelin II* (New York: Atlantic Records, 1969). In the 1994 digitally remastered release of *Led Zeppelin II,* Willie Dixon receives co-songwriting credit for "Whole Lotta Love" after Jimmy Page, Robert Plant, John Paul Jones, and John Bonham.
2. Willie Dixon and Don Snowden, *I Am the Blues: The Willie Dixon Story* (New York: Da Capo Press, 1989), p. 223. Information on the Blues Heaven Foundation can be found on the World Wide Web at http://www.island.net/-blues/heaven.html. The troubling relationship between blues composers and their record and publishing companies is much clearer. More often than not, it was blatantly exploitative. For an account of the relationship between Chicago rhythm and blues labels and their exploited artists, see Mike Rowe, *Chicago Breakdown* (New York: Da Capo Press, 1979). Also see Robert Pruter, *Chicago Soul* (Urbana: University of Illinois Press, 1991). For a study of the cultural and social meaning of blues in Chicago, see Charles Keil, *Urban Blues* (Chicago: University of Chicago Press, 1966). For the most penetrating study of the blues aesthetic in American culture, see Albert Murray, *Stomping the Blues* (New York: McGraw Hill, 1976).
3. David Halberstam, *The Fifties* (New York: Villard Books, 1993), p. 478.
4. Nelson George, *The Death of Rhythm and Blues* (New York: Pantheon, 1988), pp. 62–64. Public Enemy, "Fight the Power," from *Fear of a Black Planet* (New York: Def Jam Records, 1990). Tricia Rose, *Black Noise: Rap Music and Black Culture in Contemporary America* (Hanover, N.H.: Wesleyan University Press, 1994), pp. 4–8. The observation about "alternative" playlists is my own, drawn from hundreds of hours of frustrating radio listening.
5. Dixon and Snowden, p. 224. The essential books about Delta blues include Robert Palmer, *Deep Blues* (New York: Penguin Books, 1982), and William Ferris, *Blues from the Delta* (New York: Da Capo, 1978).
6. Muddy Waters, interview with Alan Lomax in Stovall, Mississippi, August 1941, on *Muddy Waters: The Complete Plantation Recordings* (Universal City, Calif.: MCA Records, 1993). Thanks to Gena Dagel Caponi for insisting that I listen to this interview.
7. George Harrison, "My Sweet Lord," from *All Things Must Pass* (London: Apple Records, 1970). The account of Harrison's composition process is from *Bright Tunes Music Corp. v. Harrisongs Music, Ltd.,* 420 F. Supp. 177, U.S. District Court Southern District of New York, Aug. 31, 1976.
8. *Bright Tunes Music Corp. v. Harrisongs Music, Ltd.*
9. Sidney Shemel and M. William Krasilovsky, *This Business of Music,* 5th ed. (New York: Billboard Publications, 1985), pp. 265–66.
10. *Bright Tunes Music Corp. v. Harrisongs Music, Ltd.*
11. Robert Palmer, "Today's Songs, Really Yesterday's," *New York Times,* July 8, 1981, p. C21.
12. John Fogerty, *Centerfield* (Burbank: Warner Brothers Records, 1985). See George Varga,

"A Good Moon Rising: Legal Troubles behind Him, Fogerty Takes Back His Own," *San Diego Union-Tribune,* August 13, 1998, p. E4. Also see Hank Bordowitz, *Bad Moon Rising: The Unauthorized History of Creedence Clearwater Revival* (New York: Shirmer Books, 1998), pp. 202–6.

13. *Fantasy, Inc. v. Fogerty,* 664 F. Supp. 1345, Northern District of California, 1987. Also see *Fantasy Inc. v. Fogerty,* 984 F. 2d 1524, U.S. Ninth Circuit Court of Appeals, 1993. Also see Katherine Bishop, "A Victory for the Creative Process," *New York Times,* November 11, 1988, p. B5.
14. See Shemel and Krasilovsky. For the history of the development of this "bundle" of rights, especially the rise of ASCAP and BMI, see Russell Sanjek (updated by David Sanjek), *Pennies from Heaven: The American Popular Music Business in the Twentieth Century* (New York: Da Capo Press, 1996).
15. Rose, pp. 21–26.
16. Schoolly D, "Signifying Rapper," from *Smoke Some Kill* (Philadelphia: Zomba Recording Corp., 1988). For an example of the "Signifying Monkey" tale, see Langston Hughes and Arna Bontemps, eds., *Book of Negro Folklore* (New York: Dodd, Mead, 1958), pp. 365–6. Also see Roger Abrahams, ed., *Afro-American Folktales: Stories from Black Traditions in the New World* (New York: Pantheon, 1985), pp. 101–5. For the transgressive and political potential of "signifying" during African American slavery, see Abrahams, *Singing the Master: The Emergence of African American Culture in the Plantation South* (New York: Pantheon, 1992). For an account of the urban twentieth-century uses of both the practice of "signifying" and the "Signifying Monkey" tale, see Abrahams, *Deep Down in the Jungle: Negro Narrative Folklore from the Streets of Philadelphia* (Chicago: Aldine Publishing, 1970). Also see John W. Roberts, *From Trickster to Badman: The Black Folk Hero in Slavery and Freedom* (Philadelphia: University of Pennsylvania Press, 1989). For a theory of the transgressive and unifying functions of tricksters, signifying, and the "Signifying Monkey" in forging an African American literary tradition published the same year as Schoolly D's "Signifying Rapper," see Henry Louis Gates, *The Signifying Monkey: A Theory of African American Literary Criticism* (New York: Oxford University Press, 1988). For an introduction to the Afro-Caribbean roots of the Signifying Monkey, see Thompson.
17. Theresa Moore and Torri Minton, "Music of Rage," *San Francisco Chronicle,* May 18, 1992, p. 1.
18. Roland and Yamaha began marketing digital samplers in the United States in 1983, at a cost of up to $20,000. These days, they cost as little as $2,000. See David Sanjek, " 'Don't Have to DJ No More': Sampling and the 'Autonomous' Creator," *Arts and Entertainment Law Journal* 10, no. 2 (1992): 612.
19. Allen, p. 181.
20. Hammer freely admits his dependence on other artists for his danceable beats. He is paid for his dancing and rapping, one of which is impressive. Hammer was quoted in *People* magazine saying, "Right after I did the song, I said, 'Hey, I gotta pay Rick for this.' I didn't need a lawyer to tell me that." See Peter Castro, "Chatter," *People,* July 30, 1990,

p. 86. Hammer frequently bases his most catchy jams on popular hits, and some of them are not old enough to be called classic. His hit "Pray" was laid down over riffs from Prince's 1984 hit "When Doves Cry," from the album *Purple Rain*.

21. Whitney C. Broussard, "Current and Suggested Business Practices for the Licensing of Digital Samples," *Loyola Entertainment Law Journal* 2 (1991): 479.
22. "Ice Ice Baby" was certified platinum on Oct. 9, 1990, when its sales exceeded one million. After the success was certified, the original artists, record company, and publisher all sought compensation for the use of the sample. The matter was settled out of court for an undisclosed amount. See *Harvard Law Review* 105 (1992): 728.
23. Greg Tate, "Diary of a Bug," *Village Voice,* Nov. 22, 1988, p. 73.
24. Run DMC, "Walk This Way," from *Raising Hell* (New York: Profile Records, 1986). This was the first rap hit to get extensive play on MTV and more "mainstream" rock radio. It had a profound effect on those of us who grew up during the 1980s in suburban America. When we heard that three Adidas-clad men from Hollis, Queens, were down with mid-seventies rock like Aerosmith, it showed us that rap might just have something to say to us, or at least some fun to offer us. For an explanation of how "discursive communities" create meaning, see Stanley Fish, *Is There a Text in This Class?* (Cambridge: Harvard University Press, 1980).
25. George Lipsitz, "The Hip Hop Hearings: Censorship, Social Memory, and Intergenerational Tensions among African Americans," in Joe Austin and Michael Nevin Willard, eds., *Generations of Youth: Youth Cultures and History in Twentieth-Century America* (New York: New York University Press, 1998), p. 405.
26. John Leland, "Singles," *Spin,* August 1988, p. 80. Urban hip-hop is not the only subculture assaulting the foundations of creative ownership. Cyberpunk theory frequently pushes the notion of the end of proprietary information. Cybermusician Lisa Sirois of the Boston band DDT says: "We're no longer playing instruments, we're programming. We sequence music on a computer, store it on a hard disc, and then record it onto digital audio tape. Then, when we perform, we supplement it with live drums and keyboards. We're live and on tape. We play on an electronic stage." See Nathan Cobb, "Terminal Chic: Cyberpunk Subculture Swimming Closer to the Surface," *Boston Globe,* Nov. 24, 1992.
27. Note, "A New Spin on Music Sampling: A Case for Fair Play," *Harvard Law Review* (Jan. 1992): 726.
28. Allen, p. 102.
29. "A New Spin on Music Sampling," p. 729.
30. Broussard, p. 502.
31. Richard Harrington, "The Groove Robbers' Judgement," *Washington Post,* December 25, 1991, p. D1.
32. Biz Markie, "Alone Again," from *I Need a Haircut* (New York: Cold Chillin' Records, 1991). Since the lawsuit, this original version of the album has been very hard to find. Printings after 1991 do not contain "Alone Again." Warner Bros. ordered all record stores to return copies of the album after the settlement. I searched used record stores for

five years to get a copy so I could hear the song in question. Fortunately, in the fall of 1998, I discovered that Wesleyan University student Kabir Sen owned a copy of the original pressing. He lent it to me so I could complete this section.

33. Harrington. Also see Susan Upton Douglass and Craig S. Mende, "Hey, They're Playing My Song! Litigating Music Copyrights," *New York Law Journal* (July 14, 1997): S1.
34. *Campbell v. Acuff-Rose Music, Inc.*, 510 U.S. 569 (1994). See Mel Marquis, "Fair Use and the First Amendment: Parody and Its Protections," *Seton Hall Constitutional Law Journal* (1997).
35. *Campbell v. Acuff-Rose.*
36. Souter's ruling, however, came a couple of years too late for two other parodists who were denied relief by federal courts. For the painful ordeal that the avant-garde music group Negativeland had to endure when Island Records filed suit against the group and its label for a sampled parody of the Irish rock group U2, see Negativeland, *Fair Use: The Story of the Letter U and the Number 2.* (Concord, Calif.: Seeland, 1995). Just as painful, artist Jeff Koons designed a sculpture that parodied a photograph postcard of a rural American couple holding a litter of puppies. Art Rogers, the photographer of the original, sued Koons and won. *Rodgers v. Koons,* 960 F. 2d 301 (2d Cir. 1992). See Vilis Inde, *Art in the Courtroom* (Westport, Conn.: Praeger, 1998). Also see Rosemary Coombe, *The Cultural Life of Intellectual Property: Authorship, Appropriation, and the Law* (Durham: Duke University Press, 1998). The culture industries and their lawyers still seem to resist the idea that parody is fair use. See Alex Kuczynski, "Parody of Talk Magazine Upsets Disney," *New York Times,* July 19, 1999, p. C10.

5

REVISITING *FREE EXCHANGE:* THE ART WORLD AFTER THE CULTURE WARS

Hans Haacke
in conversation with Robert Atkins and Svetlana Mintcheva

Question: We would like to revisit some of the issues you explored in the early nineties in *Free Exchange* as a starting point for thinking about developments in art during last decade. While your friendly back and forth with Pierre Bourdieu for *Free Exchange* was going on, the acrimonious public debate about funding for the arts in the United States was in full swing. It resulted in a focused consideration of government versus private funding and the strings attached to each of them. But since then, the Supreme Court has approved decency considerations in the National Endowment for the Arts grant-awarding process and the NEA, in practice, no longer funds controversial art. In 1995 all direct grants to individual artists were terminated. The burden of supporting the arts is increasingly shifting to private corporations and foundations. But has anything really changed? Did we lose the "culture wars" of the past fifteen to twenty years?—And what are the "culture wars" anyway?

Hans Haacke (HH): In the arts, the "culture wars," as we have come to call the conflict between those who would like to keep this country an open society versus one regimented by self-proclaimed defenders of "values," began in the late 1980s with the Congressional assault on the NEA. Since then, the agency has become a shadow of its former self. Its budget today is well below what it was fifteen years ago. As opposed to the past, it rarely acts as a financial backup for programs that could not attract corporate sponsors.

For the NEA to be "sensitive to general standards of decency and respect the diverse beliefs and values of the American public," as the law demands since 1990, sounds uncannily like the Nazis' invocation of the "gesundes Volksempfinden," when they purged German museums of what they called "degenerate" art. A U.S. District Court ruled that this 1990 law violated the Constitution. This decision was upheld at the Circuit Court level. It is the shame of the Clinton Administration to have appealed both rulings, all the way to the Supreme Court. Overturning the lower courts in an 8 to 1 decision, Justice Sandra Day O'Connor wrote for the majority, that the law posed: ". . . not a realistic danger that . . . it will compromise First Amendment values." Ignoring what had happened during the four years since the law had been enacted, she added that if the NEA were "to leverage its power to award subsidies on the basis of subjective criteria into a penalty for disfavored viewpoints, then we would confront a different case." Without equivocation, Justice David Souter wrote in his lone dissenting opinion: ". . . viewpoint discrimination in the exercise of public authority over expressive activities is unconstitutional."

Fortunately, the Supreme Court's double-speak did not deter federal district judge Nina Gershon from ruling that Rudolph Giuliani had violated the Constitution in 1999, when, as mayor of New York, he tried to shut down the Brooklyn Museum for exhibiting Chris Ofili's "Holy Virgin Mary." The judge didn't mince words: "There is no federal constitutional issue more grave than the effort by government officials to censor works of expression and to threaten the vitality of a major cultural institution as punishment for failing to abide by government demands for orthodoxy."

You would think the New York museums would have closed ranks and rushed to the defense of one of their peers. Their reaction was, in fact, rather tepid. A few years later, the director of the Museum of Modern Art [Glenn Lowry] even honored the censor-mayor with a garden party. His rationale was simple: "Under Mr. Giuliani's leadership, the Museum received $65 million in capital support for our new building . . ." Glenn Lowry had no reason to fear that Ronald Lauder, the Museum's chairman, would oppose honoring his fellow Republican in such an artful way. Like the money Giuliani was withholding from the Brooklyn Museum until he was stopped by the Court, the subsidy for MoMA's new building comes out of the pockets of New York taxpayers. While Ronald Lauder's contributions to the Museum are tax-deductible, contributions to the American Civil Liberties Union, which took up the cause of the Brooklyn Museum, are not.

Lauder (net worth $2 billion) is a prominent member of the Club for Growth, a "club" that promotes the election of candidates favoring tax cuts for the wealthy. After its reopening, in a twisted recognition of the $65 million New York City subsidy, MoMA raised its entrance fee to $20.

Question: Everything—even the events of 9/11—seems to become a new rationale for silencing outspoken artists.

HH: Yes.

Recently the zeal to go after artists who, in the view of the current administration, do not sufficiently conform reached a frightening and bizarre level. In May 2004, the Patriot Act was used to go after Steve Kurtz and the Critical Art Ensemble, artists whose work raises questions about the consequences of bioengineering. The prosecution, seeking to indict Kurtz on bioterrorism charges, called him, as well as other members of CAE, to appear before a federal grand jury. One of the works the FBI singled out and confiscated was scheduled to be part of an exhibition at the Massachusetts Museum of Contemporary Art in North Adams. The bioterrorism case did not hold up. Instead, Steve Kurtz and the Head of the Department of Genetics at the University of Pittsburgh's School of Public Health were indicted for sending $265 worth of harmless bacteria for Kurtz's work through the mail without strictly adhering to regulations.

Question: Since art is always produced within a social context of money and power—whether pressures come from the government or from corporations and private foundations—it is arguably never really free. However, artists like you manage to make important critical interventions in public discourse. What makes work like yours possible? What directions in the development of arts funding do you think would enable more such work and what, on the contrary, might inhibit it?

HH: When the Deutsche Bank established a foundation for culture in the mid-nineties, Hilmar Kopper, who was then the Bank's CEO and is now the chairman of its supervisory board, pithily declared: "He who pays, controls." In private institutions, and in this country most are private, it depends on the degree to which boards are willing to grant the director and the curators independence in their professional decisions and are ready to promote the creation of an open forum for a culture that is worthy of a democratic society. The record is checkered. In too many places, *noblesse oblige* has become a quaint watchword.

It would be naïve though to assume that publicly funded institutions are, by definition, free of coercion and that those who are spending the public's money can fend off attempts to turn their institutions into private or political fiefdoms. Whether such ventures succeed depends a great deal on how alert and courageous the press, the public, and the people in these institutions prove to be.

Question: What are the key distinctions, in practice, between public and private funding? Your reference to the massive amount of public funds that went into the creation of the newly enlarged MoMA is a reminder of how difficult it is, sometimes, to even differentiate the two kinds of institutions.

HH: A fundamental difference between the two types of funding is that public institutions are answerable to the public and, as we have seen in the case of the Brooklyn Museum, must abide by the First Amendment. Even though private institutions are co-financed by the public through their tax-exempt status, the tax-deductibility of the contributions of their donors, and the favorable tax treatment sponsors get for underwriting their programs, the decisions of the boards of trustees are considered to be at their sole discretion.

On the whole, I have fared better with critical works in publicly funded exhibition venues than in private ones. Even though sponsors and collectors have increasingly gained influence in public institutions, there still remains a comparatively greater degree of independence. In most cases, the curators' and the director's job are not at risk.

In liberal societies, a tacit understanding exists that the mission of public institutions is to provide an open forum and not to serve private/corporate interests. It is a long-term project to preserve this consensus and to introduce it where it does not exist. The recent success of those who do not subscribe to the First Amendment and are indifferent, if not hostile, to a generally shared common good is the result of pushing their undemocratic agenda over many decades. I am afraid it will require tenacity, intelligence, and a good deal of cunning to reverse this socially destructive trend. Yes, it is about good old values, about liberty, equality, and communality!

Question: In the book you discussed two developments—the then-new NEA directives, such as the decency clause, and the increasing reliance of the arts on corporate sponsors. You noted that both often lead to self-censorship. How can we gauge the extent of self-censorship today?

HH: Self-censorship occurs behind closed doors. There are practically no whistle-blowers. It would be too risky for survival in one's chosen field. Many have internalized this mode of operation to the extent that they are not even aware of practicing self-censorship. Or they are in denial because it would undermine their self-respect. In private, museum people have told me that self-censorship is indeed the order of the day.

But it is quite rare for an official to speak about it in public. One such instance occurred about twenty years ago. Philippe de Montebello, the director of the Metropolitan Museum, was quoted in *Newsweek* about his experience with corporate sponsors. He called it "an inherent, insidious, hidden form of censorship." For their financial survival, museums are more than ever dependent on the box-office success of expensive blockbuster shows. But blockbusters can be staged only with corporate funding. It's a vicious circle. Corporations, in their view quite legitimately, are looking for a public relations dividend. Critical rather than celebratory presentations risk being counterproductive to that business goal, a goal that is increasingly shared by museums.

Question: Recently corporate and political interests have become more visibly entangled. The oil conglomerates' vested interests in the Middle East are arguably at the base of United States military intervention in the region, while much to the chagrin of free-speech advocates, an increasingly docile and uncritical media results in the near absence of real debate on issues of public concern. Despite this, broadcast media are subject to a veritable governmental campaign to further regulate content. These may be direct prohibitions, as in the ban on showing the coffins of soldiers killed in Iraq returning home, or the Federal Communication Commission's (FCC) decency regulations, or sternly paternalistic rebukes, as with NBC's axing of Bill Maher's *Politically Incorrect*

TV show after White House spokesman Ari Fleischer criticized it and warned Americans to "watch what they say." Given governmental regulation, that is control, of media ownership, content, and FCC licensing, can one imagine a space for free and critical debate at all?

HH: I'm not without hope. The Internet already has an amazing reach and it will become more common as a source of information and uncensored communication in the future. It simply cannot be controlled. I also see that the *New York Times,* after it shamelessly toed the "patriotic" line, before and long after the invasion of Iraq, has regained a relative degree of independence and, in some departments, has become an important critical voice. I hope that attitude spreads within the paper and there will be imitators elsewhere.

Question: Do you see a politicization of artists over the war in Iraq and the presidency of George Bush comparable to the mostly non-art, anti-Vietnam activism by artists of the sixties or the recent AIDS-art movement? Do you see a possibility for an enlivened public dialogue led by artists transcending the all-absorbing logic of the "free market"?

HH: Compared to just a few years ago, there are more artists today who are not totally obsessed by what they think it takes to make a career—often a synonym for market success. The mood seems to be changing. In view of the November elections, for *ARTFORUM* to devote its entire September issue to art manifestations of a social and political nature is perhaps indicative. There are many ways to engage with society through images, performances or text, both inside as well as outside the art world. They all have the potential of affecting how we see ourselves and the world and of shaping the complex set of ideas, aspirations, and goals that a society embraces—whether we are conscious of these dynamics or not.

Question: Your work has dealt critically with economic and cultural processes of globalization. Have you thought about globalization in relation to "values"-based American censorship; i.e., can it be that the increasing international mobility of artists, the expansion of the art festival circuit, the growth of an international art market, et cetera, are perhaps making the defenders of "traditional values" obsolete at the very moment when they are claiming political dominance?

HH: For many decades now, the art fairs in Basel, Paris, Cologne, Berlin, to name only some of the more well known, have been selling works by American artists with little consideration of so-called "traditional values." Art fairs are driven by a competing set of "values": market values. These have their own, sometimes censorious, effect. Depending on the curators and the openness of the regions in which the various biennials, Documenta, and other such international art festivals take place, these events have, in many instances, offered a relatively unfettered forum. Editors permitting, so have art magazines. More recently, the Internet has emerged as an uncontrolled venue. At least for North American and European art, "globalization" has existed for quite some time. Seen from the outside, the bigotry of a minority that's now reigning in America is difficult to understand. The country looks pathetic and has become the world's laughingstock.

But recognizing that there is a life offshore is hardly comforting. The false-value mongers have an influence on the public discourse, on what American institutions present or exclude from their exhibition programs, on what the public is taught to admire and reject, and how the press spins it. Controversy is rarely suitable as a fund-raising tool. With the exception perhaps of artists in major centers like New York, Los Angeles, and a few others (and sometimes even in those places), the institutionalized disrespect for the First Amendment *does* affect what artists produce. But similar to the self-censorship in institutions, most of them are probably not even aware of the adjustments they make.

6

ON EDGE: ALTERNATIVE SPACES TODAY

Robert Atkins

Winter 1998: I received two startling missives from alternative spaces—an invitation to discuss Franklin Furnace's revised mission as a virtual organization on Feb. 4 and a press release announcing the demise of Randolph Street Gallery on Feb. 13. The news about Randolph Street Gallery was personally saddening. I'd worked with the Chicago space on its production of Antonio Muntadas's *File Room* (1994), the pioneering online archive of social and cultural censorship. Franklin Furnace's situation is more ambiguous. The meeting to which I was invited was called to discuss the New York organization's new cyber-orientation—visionary or elitist? Although a healthy debate ensued, I left concerned that this well-intentioned group of arts professionals hadn't a clue about creating opportunities for artists in a radically reconfigured turn-of-the-twenty-first-century art world.

Pondering some recent developments in alternative-space history, my concerns mounted: N.A.M.E. (in Chicago) and WPA (Washington Project for the Arts) went bankrupt in 1996. (The latter was absorbed by the Corcoran Gallery of Art.) San Francisco's Capp Street Project is closing its space, in part because founder Ann Hatch's philanthropic priorities have shifted. (Its residency program is being incorporated into the exhibition program of the California College of Arts and Crafts.) The Alternative Museum in New York hasn't paid employee salaries since last fall, according to its founder, Geno Rodriguez, who termed the past year "our worst time ever." Roberto Bedoya, then head of the National Association of Artists' Organizations (NAAO), the alternative spaces' lobbying organization in Washington, commented that "there's a kind of malnutrition or fading away. Many organizations are doing far less programming than they used to and some like COCA [Seattle's Center on Contemporary Art], LACPS [Los Angeles Center for Photographic Studies], and LACE [Los Angeles Contemporary Exhibitions] are really stressed." Although spaces like Hartford's Real Art Ways and New York's Artists Space are thriving, the alternative art scene, en masse, is in crisis. As Peter Taub, the former executive director of Randolph Street Gallery, put it: "It's desperate out there. The field is currently defined by adversity." Has an era already ended?

The adversity identified by Taub assumes at least three forms: generational change, the Culture Wars and a decade of public disinvestment, and ill-considered foundation mandates. Only the first of the three could have been anticipated nearly three decades ago when alternative spaces emerged as a new phenomenon. The first of these small nonprofit organizations initiated by and for visual artists appeared in New York in 1969 and 1970 with the founding of 98 Greene Street, Apple and 112 Workshop (aka 112 Greene Street and now White Columns). For many of us baby boomers, at least, the term "alternative space" remains synonymous with the network of seemingly institutionalized spaces such as San Francisco's New Langton Arts, Houston's Diverse Works, Buffalo's Hallwalls, Atlanta's Nexus Contemporary Art Center, New York's Kitchen and San Diego's Sushi, to mention only a few.

Some came into being with a little help from friends within the "establishment." New Langton Arts (then 80 Langton St.), for instance, was founded in 1975 and originally funded by the local art dealers' association, and Artists Space opened its doors in 1973 as a project of the New York State Council on the Arts. For artists of the '70s, the new alternative spaces offered virtually the only venues for the development of conceptually oriented, noncommercial forms such as video, installations and actions (the term "performance art" wasn't commonly used until the late 1970s). This conceptualist bent separated alternative spaces from artists' cooperative galleries, usually commercial spaces where artists banded together to exhibit traditional-format work and collectively pay the rent. Nontraditional curatorial practices also characterized the new alternative spaces: most relied on artists to curate shows, rather than professional curators. And, most radical of all, artists received fees for exhibiting.

Not every space fits this general model and sometimes appearances can deceive. The Drawing Center in SoHo, for example, presents an annual historical show, and boasts an elegant loft space and a well-heeled board of directors. It may not look like an alternative space, but, according to departing executive director Ann Philbin, it is. "The majority of our shows are artist-curated and we pay fees." Other organizations, like P.S. 1 and the New Museum of Contemporary Art, have evolved into full-fledged kunsthalles, that is, contemporary art museums which don't build permanent collections. The NAAO roster now lists more than 700 full and associate members that range widely from established institutions (such as Rochester's Visual Studies Workshop) and publications (Atlanta's *Art Papers*) to their far smaller counterparts such as Los Angeles' VIVA! Lesbian and Gay Latino Artists and Art FBI (Artists for a Better Image), Jeff Gates's publication-oriented, artist-advocacy operation. The NAAO only requires that its members be nonprofits devoted to contemporary art and committed to guaranteeing artists both policy-making roles and fees for presenting their work. Today, an artists' organization may be as much a mind-set as anything else, and not necessarily a physical space.

Since the original flowering of alternative spaces in the 1970s, much has changed. During the first half of the 1980s, East Village artists rejected both the nonprofit and conceptualist orientations of the generation that preceded them and founded their own galleries, including Civilian Warfare, Nature Morte, International with Monument, Fun, and Gracie Mansion. (Although this was largely a New York phenomenon based on a then-thriving market for emerging art, it mirrored an international revival of painting and blunted the razor-sharp divide that once separated commercial galleries from alternative spaces.) Other venues began to enter what had been exclusive alternative-space turf. Object-making artists such as Cindy Sherman and Robert Longo first showed their work at Hallwalls and Artists Space, and then moved with Artists Space director Helene Winer to Metro Pictures, the high-profile commercial gallery she opened (with Janelle Reiring) in 1980. Museums also got into the act by establishing project-type programs, which showcase contemporary art in varied mediums not necessarily by renowned artists.

The second generation of alternative spaces—including Newark's Aljira and San Francisco's Artists Television Access, which were both founded in 1983—were more diverse than their predecessors. The former tends to focus on traditional work, the latter on work in nontraditional formats and distribution systems including cable television. The new role of these spaces in the 1980s and '90s came to be assisting artists (working in all forms) by providing exhibition or performance venues. The term artists' organization began to seem more appropriate, if far less precise, than alternative space.

Alas, the salad days of such organizations would prove to be short-lived. The elimination in 1981 of NEA grants for critics (a group alleged by Hilton Kramer and other enemies of the program to be overly politicized) and of the Neighborhood Arts Program (a component of CETA, the Comprehensive Employment Training Act) were harbingers of the Culture Wars to come. That the NAAO was the only organization-plaintiff in the so-called NEA Four legal battle over the congressionally mandated "decency" standards for the awarding of grants to artists is a reminder that the majority of the cultural warriors' organization-targets have been alternative spaces. To put it bluntly, the Radical Right has triumphed in this and virtually every other decisive engagement of the Culture Wars. The NEA long ago gutted its operational support for many alternative spaces; one of the causes of WPA's bankruptcy was the reduction of annual NEA support from $200,000 to $10,000—a 95-percent cut.

The Radical Right's continuing scrutiny of the NEA has been extended to the state and municipal levels. Programming about the flag, multicultural identities (especially queer ones), and sexuality (even plain old nudity) is likely to invite protest. Numerous alternative spaces have been defunded and some funding programs—such as Cobb County, Georgia's—have been eliminated entirely in order to abolish support for venues that feature such work. If stories like these no longer hit front pages with the frequency they used to, it's not because artists have purified their work. The mass media has little attention span for news that no longer seems new, and the administrators of publicly funded exhibition spaces now have a financial interest in avoiding controversy.

Ironically, Randolph Street Gallery's offerings were never a magnet for censors; the School of the Art Institute of Chicago tended to be the arena in which Chicago scandals of the past decade erupted. Nor was Randolph Street Gallery totally abandoned by the NEA. It received a $30,000 programming grant for its final series of exhibitions and performances, the racial-identity-oriented "T-Race," organized by Kerry James Marshall and Jane M. Saks, which ran from October to December 1997. But in most other regards, its demise seems all too typical.

Founded by a small group of artists in 1979, Randolph Street Gallery moved from its Randolph Street storefront to its location on North Milwaukee Avenue in 1982. The capacious loft encompassed an exhibition gallery, black-box performance space for time-based arts, and a project space. (The organization acquired the space in 1993.) More than a thousand artists and performers have presented their work there, including Xu Bing, Robert Blanchon, Leon Golub, Eve Andrée Laramée, Lauren Lesko, James Luna, Rosy Martin, Muntadas, Esther Parada, Carolee Schneemann, Andres Serrano, Spiderwoman Theatre, and Rirkrit Tiravanija. Randolph Street Gallery administered a regranting program for regional artists that distributed close to $200,000 between 1989 and 1996, and also produced 44 issues of *P-Form,* a savvy quarterly journal devoted to performance and interdisciplinary art between 1986 and 1997. Remarkably, all of these activities were coordinated by five volunteer committees of artists. But despite the exemplary efforts of volunteers, staff and operating expenses increased dramatically, from one part-time staffer in 1986 to five full-time staffers a decade later administering a budget of $450,000.

A turning point for the organization came in 1995, when Peter Taub, its longtime executive director (and current director of performance programs at Chicago's Museum of Contemporary Art), resigned. "I didn't have any energy left from trying to keep it [Randolph Street Gallery] afloat. . . . I also believed the organization needed a radical change and that it would work better with a new executive director," he recalled. According to Paul Brenner, Randolph Street Gallery's former program director, the problems didn't surface until after Taub's departure. "There wasn't enough long-term planning. Grants didn't come in and nobody wants to fund operating expenses anymore." By the end of 1995, 10 percent across-the-board programming cuts were made; quickly increasing to 20-and then 30-percent cuts, because much of the budget was committed to operating expenses. At this point the staff included two full-time development directors, a business/office manager, but no executive director. "The lack of an ED [executive director] was a problem," Brenner observed. "Nobody could do it for the $30,000 we offered and not having an ED hurt us with private funders."

In January 1997, Randolph Street Gallery took a nine-month hiatus from public programming to consider its options. Its board and staff organized roundtables with educators, representatives of larger institutions like the School of the Art Institute of Chicago, and peer organizations. Despite few concrete measures of support, RSG decided to give it one more shot. But things did not improve. "T-Race" closed on Dec. 13, 1997, and the gallery shuttered its operations exactly two months later. Randolph Street Gallery's 19-year history embodies the vital roles that many effective alternative spaces have played: serving artists as research-and-development facilities, while serving audiences as facilitators and bellwethers of cultural discourse in the U.S.

In essence, Randolph Street Gallery was bedeviled with two seemingly intractable problems inherent to alternative spaces today: how to attract an executive director with the business and administrative skills necessary to run a large and complex organization for a modest salary, and how to increase earned income when the audience is largely made up of low-income artists and students. With radical reductions in public funding, alternative spaces are now chiefly at the mercy of private funders, rather than the public funding that subsidized their initial growth. According to Brenner, one Randolph Street Gallery board member went to Chicago's richly endowed MacArthur Foundation seeking additional funding to pay an executive director. What it received instead was a handsomely paid consultant who earned $25,000 for a short report asserting that since Randolph Street Gallery was not likely to generate much earned income, it might as well close. "We would have laughed, if we hadn't felt like crying," commented Brenner.

The problem with such foundation-world thinking is that it proceeds from the arguable (and very American) notion that cultural institutions are businesses and need to adopt corporate models in order to survive. Arts-fundraiser Jeff Jones, author of 2,200 successful grant applications for progressive organizations such as the San Francisco Mime Troupe and the Women's Philharmonic Orchestra, is a veritable one-man history of funding developments of the past decades. "Artists with good artistic sense could start organizations but that's no longer enough. Now you have to be a financial expert who understands marketing and personnel issues. The MBA-skills-bar is impossibly high but you need these skills in order to talk the language funders want to hear," he said. "Every one of the five biggest arts funders in the Bay Area—

where I live—encourages administrative-heavy and art-light organizations. The problem is that these corporate models are fine for large museums and big-budget opera companies, but they have no relevance at all for artist-run organizations. They're a consultant's dream."

Robert Crane, president of the Joyce Merz Gilmore Foundation in New York, concurs that financial accountability and market models are de rigueur among private foundations, while providing much-needed operating support is unfashionable. "This [lack of operating support] has hurt small organizations especially. Alternative institutions must feel that they've taken a beating at every level," he said "Because the work they present isn't immediately popular they particularly need support. Most art organizations can't really open a gift shop and increase earned income." The Joyce Merz Gilmore Foundation, whose founder is a dance patron, recently made its last grants in the visual arts, preferring instead to focus its limited resources on dance and theater.

In the past decade, the notion that organizations of all kinds need to locate and develop alternative streams of earned income has gained currency among funders. Most alternative spaces have considered such ideas, and more than a few have implemented them. Real Art Ways (RAW) in Hartford, for instance, opened a screening room for independent and foreign films in 1996. The cinema generated $80,000 in ticket sales its first year, and the next phase of RAW's $1.4-million expansion includes a café, a performing arts theater, and a second screening room. (This will be funded in part by $550,000 in state and city monies.) Aljira opened a graphic design studio in 1996 with a $50,000 grant from the Arts Challenge Fund, a consortium headed by the Geraldine R. Dodge Foundation; it has yet to turn a profit. Holly Block, executive director of Art in General, noted that her organization provides daytime and after-school education programs for K-12 students and at-risk youths. "This would be earned income if we could charge the Board of Ed a fee for each student," she said. "But we would have had to negotiate their bureaucracy 20 years ago. We do these programs because we're not in SoHo and need to reach a wider audience. So they pay for themselves [via grants] and help us meet other goals." Programs like Art in General's and RAW's at least support their organizations' missions of investigating visual culture and serving audiences.

Perhaps the boldest recent experiment in earned-income initiatives was that of Art Matters, the New York–based foundation. Although not an alternative space, Art Matters attempted to generate substantial earnings by developing a mail-order catalogue of artist-designed products in order to increase artist funding after the NEA eliminated grants to individual artists. The first catalogue appeared in fall 1995 and by all the standards of direct-marketing was an unqualified success: two percent of catalogue recipients made purchases and the dollar amount spent per customer exceeded, on average, those of the Metropolitan Museum of Art's catalogue customers. When it came time to up the ante and expand operations, Art Matters asked the same foundations which constantly preach entrepreneurship to arts organizations to invest $2.5 million. Art Matters received not a dime. As Cee Scott Brown, former executive vice-president of Art Matters, told the *Chronicle of Philanthropy,* "that was just lip service, just buzz words. . . . They [program officers] don't have the ability to convince the boards to follow them." In October 1996, Art Matters declared its direct-mail venture dead and is currently considering whether—and how—to continue awarding grants. If a sophisticated foundation can't, in Jeff Jones's words, talk the language funders want to hear, what success is the typical artist-run organization likely to have?

But perhaps there are larger, philosophical issues at play. Should an alternative space want to become a major wholesaler of tchotchkes? Or as Holly Block put it, "We thought of doing a printing business. But I'm not a printing expert and I don't want to be. One full-time job is enough." Happily, Art in General is in no danger of failing, although Block (among anonymous others) cautioned that the number of alternative spaces facing financial problems is even greater than I think, noting that "people are not very open about their finances."

What's at stake if dozens of alternative spaces fail over the next few years? Plenty, if you regard the art world as an ecosystem. Such an outlook implies that the withering away of alternative spaces not only limits diversity—that is, the range of artistic visions presented to audiences—but impairs the prospects of the vast number of future artists who might develop their skills at these art-making laboratories. As Robert Crane observed, "The entire ecology needs to be supported.

The collapse of small organizations will have an effect, but probably not an immediate one. Everyone, funders included, has short visions when we need ten- to twenty-year horizons."

Are there solutions? Might newer alternative spaces spring up to take the places of those that have vanished? A number of the new storefront/garage galleries started by artists throughout the country (like Pierogi 2000 in Brooklyn) utilize many of the curatorial practices pioneered by nonprofit alternative spaces, while operating as commercial venues. Because the founders of these hybrid spaces are not interested in the onerous task of building and running nonprofit institutions, their access to funds is extremely limited.

The biggest problem may be that "the issue of a crisis in the field gets talked about, but mostly within the field," says Anne Pasternak, head of Creative Time. "You never read about it in the *New York Times.*" Jeff Jones believes that the field's first order of business is to challenge the Darwinian proposition that only well-funded organizations deserve to survive. "Values matter, the Right Wing taught us that," Jones commented. "Cultural equity demands that everybody—artists and audiences alike—has access to cultural resources. Nobody expects the opera to turn a profit, [but] the conversation never begins there." Or as Will K. Wilkins, executive director of Real Art Ways, observed upon returning from a NAAO conference in Chicago in May 1998, "The aftermath of the demise of Randolph Street and N.A.M.E. wasn't really talked about in official sessions there. I was puzzled. . . . Aren't the failures as instructive as the successes?"

7
MARKET CENSORSHIP

André Schiffrin

The recent changes in publishing demonstrate the application of market theory to the dissemination of culture. After the pattern of Ronald Reagan's and Margaret Thatcher's probusiness policies, the owners of publishing houses have increasingly "rationalized their activities." The market, it is argued, is a sort of ideal democracy. It is not up to the elite to impose their values on readers, publishers claim, it is up to the public to choose what it wants—and if what it wants is increasingly downmarket and limited in scope, so be it. The higher profits are proof that the market is working as it should.

Traditionally, ideas were exempted from the usual expectations of profit. It was often assumed that books propounding new approaches and different theories would lose money, certainly at the outset. The phrase "the free marketplace of ideas" does not refer to the market value of each idea. On the contrary, what it means is that ideas of all sorts should have a chance to be put to the public, to be expressed and argued fully and not in soundbites.

For much of the twentieth century, trade publishing as a whole was seen as a break-even operation. Profit would come when books reached a broader audience through book clubs or paperback sales. If this was true of nonfiction, it was doubly true of literature. Most first novels were expected to lose money (and many authors have been described as writing a lot of first novels). Nonetheless, there have always been publishers who regard publishing new novelists as an important part of their overall output.

New ideas and new authors take time to catch on. It might be years before a writer finds an audience large enough to justify the costs of publishing her book. Even in the long run the market cannot be an appropriate judge of an idea's value, as is obvious from the hundreds, indeed thousands, of great books that have never made money. Thus, the new approach—deciding to publish only those books that can be counted on for an immediate profit—automatically eliminates a vast number of important works from catalogs.

There is a further complication. While fiction and poetry may well be written by authors working full-time elsewhere, authors of important works of nonfiction require advances or some other form of assistance to enable them to undertake their research. It is in this area of important work that we have seen the sharpest decline. The "mute, inglorious Milton" of Gray's *Elegy Written in a Country Churchyard* has been replaced by the "mute, inglorious Foucault," the thinker who does not have the wherewithal to write the book that will change the way we think, which may happen even if only a small number of people buy it.

Finally, as in every other aspect of the free market, there is the problem that the playing field is far from level. The larger firms, publishing the more commercial books, have vast advertising budgets at their disposal, enormous sales forces, and an extremely efficient network of press contacts, all of which helps ensure that their books get a certain amount of attention. Smaller publishers are unable to compete on an equal footing and have a much harder time finding space for their books, both in stores and in review columns.

The prevalence of market ideology has affected other spheres in society that in turn have changed the nature of book publishing. In both the United States and Britain, for example, public library purchases were once large enough to cover most of the costs of publishing meaningful works of fiction and nonfiction. I remember Gollancz would always order the same number of copies of a book from Pantheon—1,800—whether it was a mystery or a political treatise. Intrigued, I eventually asked him why this number. Simple, he answered. He could count on orders for 1,600 copies from Britain's libraries. When, in recent years, library funding was drastically cut, an infrastructure supporting the publication of many challenging books was leveled.

But this is only one of many forces affecting the demise of "challenging" books. The change in editorial procedures at large firms has also had a broad impact. This process has been skewed by the fact that decisions on what to publish are made not by editors but by so-called publishing boards, where the financial and marketing staff play a pivotal role. If a book does not look as if it will sell a certain number—and that number increases every year (it's about 20,000 in many of the larger houses today)—then the publishing board decides that the company cannot afford to take it on. This is usually the case when a new novel or a work of serious nonfiction is being discussed. What *El País* called "market censorship" is increasingly in force in the decision-making process based on the requirement of a pre-existing audience for any book.[1]

In the past, an editor would be asked to estimate the sales of the titles he or she proposed. But of course these calculations, infused by the editor's commitment to the book's ideas, were often unreliable, so print runs gradually became the province of salespeople. Nowadays, the figure settled upon is usually decided according to what the author's previous book has sold. This has necessarily led to a marked conservatism, both aesthetic and political, in what is chosen: a new idea, by definition, has no track record.

For obvious reasons, editors have been reluctant to talk about the commercial pressures they face. A rare exception, reported by Janice Radway in *A Feeling for Books,* is Marty Asher, now head of Vintage but at the time with the Book-of-the-Month Club. In an interview with him in 1990, Asher said,

> When you get a large corporation taking over they're interested in the bottom line. . . . Some of them are just merciless, you know "if it doesn't make money we don't want it." Of course if you applied that logic you'd probably eliminate half of the most successful books ever published because it takes a while and nobody wants to wait. . . . The house I came from, if you couldn't get out 50,000 copies they didn't want to bother. It just wasn't worth it. In a mass market now you're talking 100,000 copies.

In time, the system became even more "scientific." Just as an editor was required to run a "profit-and-loss statement" on each book before being allowed to sign it up, a similar running "P & L" is now kept on the editor themselves, with each editor expected to bring in a certain amount of money every year. Strict controls are maintained on editorial choices. The big companies impose sales quotas, so that even Oxford University Press demands that a young editor sign up enough books in a year to bring in a million dollars—obviously discouraging the acquisition of smaller, more challenging titles. Young editors often tell me exactly what the return on their investments have been down to the last decimal point. These numbers determine their salary and status. It is now extremely difficult to publish smaller books: editors see that their own careers will be hampered if they are identified with such titles. The more an editor spends, the more promising he or she seems. Young people in particular have realized that the way to make their mark is to give authors as large an advance as possible, as early in their own careers as they can. Many will have moved on to other firms by the time the book is published and has failed to earn out its advance.

Caught up in this financial machinery, editors are perceptibly—and understandably—less willing to take a gamble on a challenging book or a new author. And the system has become internalized. Publishers and editors alike now explain that they "can no longer afford" to take on a certain kind of book. Literary agents complain bitterly about these changes. The fall 1999 issue of the newsletter of the Association of Authors' Representatives quotes one of its members as saying, "These mergers have increased the obsession with the bottom line. I can't tell you how many editors say to me these days, 'We aren't buying mid-list.' They want everything totally assured up front." Even houses as successful as Knopf now reject books in areas in which they had traditionally published, explaining that they "can no longer afford to do these books," though the profits generated by Knopf are a major source of income for the Random House group. I used to joke with my editors that we were being paid in kind, that a good part of our salary consisted of the books that we could do when we wanted to do them. This kind of thinking is now safely eliminated from the major publishing houses in the United States and increasingly in Europe as well. A look at some of the major American houses clearly reveals this transformation.

The paperback industry has not been exempt from these pressures. When I was studying in England, a Penguin book would sell for around 2 shillings and 6 pence, or 35 cents. This was in keeping with the prices being charged in the United States for equivalent paperbacks and clearly did not bring in enormous profits. After Pearson's takeover, the existing backlist titles, whether fiction or nonfiction, were reprinted in a larger trade paperback format and prices increased dramatically. The original trade paperback in America, a format started in the 1950s, had been only a little more expensive than the mass-market paperbacks with which I was working. The first list of trade paperbacks issued by Anchor Books ranged in price from 65 cents to $1.25. For many years the average Vintage book, still in its smaller format, was $1.95. Marginally increasing the size of the books, Vintage ultimately increased its prices to $10 and above. I remember at the time arguing that this would greatly diminish the number of people buying new Vintage books. "You may be right," I was told, "but the dollars will remain the same." This phrase seems to me to mark the transition from the old ideology to the new. The idea that a book ought to be inexpensive in order to reach as broad a public as possible was being replaced by accounting decisions that looked only at cash totals. It was not a question of simply making money or avoiding a loss—the Vintage list, consisting of the best backlist titles from Random House, Knopf, and Pantheon, was already guaranteed a substantial annual profit. The rule now was that profit *per book sold* had to be as high as possible.

Si Newhouse's decision to sell the Random House group in 1998 to the massive German firm Bertelsmann shocked the publishing world. Random was still the leading U.S. publisher even if its reputation had become tarnished. William Styron, one of Random's most important literary authors, was quoted in *The Washington Post* as saying that Random had become so gigantic and bloated that it now no longer mattered to whom it belonged. But in spite of such observations, Random's end came like a thunderbolt out of the murky skies of American publishing. After eight years of Vitale's stewardship, Newhouse decided that the firm would never reach the profitability he had been promised.

There had been no indication that Newhouse was tired of his role as publisher, no hint that Random House was losing money. The figures that came out were surprising even to those who had followed Random House's fortunes closely. In 1997, it was revealed that the company wrote off $80 million of unearnable advances. That is to say, the policy of risking more and more money on books had been an enormous failure. Apart from the write-offs, the house itself had declared a profit of only 0.1 percent, a figure so low that many initially thought the *New York Times* had made a typographical error reporting it. Such profits were far lower than anything Random House had ever recorded in the years before Newhouse took over. Vitale's promises of spectacular increases in profit had clearly been unrealizable. And though Newhouse himself had expressed great interest in his publishing conglomerate, one of his friends was quoted in the *New York Observer* as saying, "He didn't get to be worth billions of dollars by indulging his own intellectual interests." Random House's losses were clearly too much to take.

The sale price was surprising, too. While the value of Random House had risen from the $60 million that Newhouse had paid for it to $800 million or so in the final decade of Bob Bernstein's direction, its growth had slowed markedly during the Vitale years. Random House was sold for a little over a billion dollars, suggesting that in the preceding eight years of profit-obsessed management, the value of the firm had only crept up. Newhouse and Vitale had achieved the remarkable result of lowering the intellectual value of the firm, cheapening its reputation, and losing money, all at the same time.

Around the same time, Murdoch's HarperCollins announced that it had written off $270 million worth of unearned advances. Apparently unheeded internal memos at Harper's urged a return to the more traditional approach to publishing, suggesting that efforts be focused on trying to rebuild the backlist and that wild speculation on possible best-sellers cease. As part of the attempt to increase profits, HarperCollins decided to discontinue and then sell off its distinguished Basic Books imprint, known primarily for its titles on psychoanalysis and the social sciences. As was the case with Pantheon, Basic had never lost money, but the scale of its publishing was geared to a professional rather than a mass-market readership. Consequently, the books could never sell in large enough quantities to meet Harper's expectations of profit and contribution to overhead. After two years, in which the firm's editors desperately tried to find more popular books, the ax finally fell.

A similar decision was made by Simon & Schuster, which had taken over The Free Press, the most devotedly reactionary of American publishers. During the Reagan years, The Free Press had made a fortune publishing books that were fully in keeping with the political zeitgeist. Subsequently, however, the company lost substantial amounts of money on gambles. A biography of Hillary Clinton proved to be insufficiently hostile for its intended conservative audience. Determined that such a mistake not be made again, Simon & Schuster gutted The Free Press, keeping its name but turning it primarily into a publisher of business books. Even the revolutionaries of the right discovered that revolutions will devour their children, whatever their political coloration. With these changes, the major conglomerates had all divested themselves of their more intellectual, Pantheon-like divisions.

One might think that such massive losses by the two leaders in corporate makeovers would have given others pause for thought. But as soon as Bertelsmann had taken over Random House, they issued a press release saying they expected Random House to make a 15 percent profit in the next few years. That meant a change in profit from $1 million to $150 million (on their annual sales of a billion or so). At the same time, Bertelsmann's corporate handouts made clear that its American holdings, which now included Random, Bantam, Doubleday, and Dell, would also be expected to deliver the 10 percent annual growth that was policy throughout the company; that is, another $100 million. How all this was to be accomplished was not outlined. Perhaps the most telling statistic published about Bertelsmann is that four thousand accountants were reported to be working at its headquarters—many times the number of editors in all its holdings worldwide. The new combined corporation would be responsible for one out of every three trade books published in the United States and would account for 40 percent of Bertelsmann's worldwide sales. Yet in spite of its gigantic size, appeals by authors' groups and others to the attorney general to investigate possible antitrust infringements went unheeded. A mammoth new conglomerate was now in charge of a very important part of American publishing. To make matters worse, Bertelsmann proceeded to acquire part of Barnes & Noble's online book-selling operation.

The metamorphosis of publishing is not abating. The French conglomerates regularly announce further purchases abroad, particularly in France and Britain. Hachette recently bought the British Orion group, itself the owners of such distinguished older firms as Weidenfeld and Gollancz. Orion is now reported to be looking for an American firm to buy, perhaps Simon & Schuster. The Anglo-Dutch Reed Elsevier group, which owns *Publishers Weekly,* bought up several of Britain's most distinguished publishing houses including Methuen, Heinemann, and Secker & Warburg, and then resold them to Random House in August 1995, citing inadequate profitability (which was later reported to be 12 percent of sales). A parallel development took place in Sweden when another Dutch firm, Wolter Kluwer, bought Norstedts, the second most important publishing house in the country with an illustrious record stretching back nearly two hundred years. Norstedts's profits were soon deemed insufficient, and Kluwer decided to keep only the parts of the company producing legal and reference texts. The general publishing division, whose books had formed a central part of Swedish culture, was cast adrift in search of a potential buyer. It was finally bought by the country's cooperative movement, which, in Sweden, still wields considerable power in retailing and distribution; they integrated it into their publishing holdings. But a great deal of damage had already been done by these changes, and Norstedts lost many of its key authors and much of its momentum.

Reed's and Kluwer's decision to concentrate on reference books and information retrieval represents a general trend. Publishers are talking more and more about concentrating on the profitable tip of the information pyramid. They want to make information that used to be found only in books available through new media. Whatever the merits of this technology, and it is undoubtedly of great importance, there is some concern in the United States that public libraries and other open institutions will have less free access to information as a result of it.

All these mergers invariably follow the same pattern. The conglomerate issues a glowing statement lauding the value of the firm it has bought and promising to maintain its traditions. Everyone is assured that no major changes will be made and that as few people as possible will be fired. Later it is announced that simple economies are essential for the sake of efficiency and that "back office" functions will be merged. Accounting, shipping, and warehousing soon find themselves under a common roof. Then the sales forces are amalgamated, since there is no need to have different people covering the same territory. After that an unfortunate overlap in editorial output is discovered, and rationalizations are seen to be required there, too. A number of editors and their assistants are fired, since, after all, the total number of books being published must decrease. Gradually it becomes difficult to tell which firm is publishing which books. In Random House UK, for instance, the same people are responsible for several lists that were once issued by individual, distinctive, and independent publishing houses; now these companies are merely names to be affixed to the title pages of new books. Older books, meanwhile, are ruthlessly pulped or put out of print if they do not sell an ever stricter minimum amount of copies, often as few as 2,000 a year. As a result, many classics are no longer available. Finally, new imprints are set up to run groups of lists, paperback reprints of older books, and new categories of publishing that can overcome the former, "inefficient" divisions of labor.

As we have seen, accelerating corporatization has been accompanied by an upsurge in the amount of profit sought by the major publishing houses. In American publishing since the 1920s, throughout periods of prosperity and depression, average profit for all of the houses was around 4 percent after taxes. (This includes companies that were intensely commercial, generating only those books they felt to be moneymakers, as well as the more intellectual houses that sought to balance profitability with responsibility.)

It is instructive to look at recent figures for those few houses that have not yet been corporatized. In a fascinating survey of European publishing that appeared in 1996, *Le Monde* provided specific numbers. In France, for instance, the most prestigious of the established book houses, Gallimard, makes an annual profit of a little over 3 percent, despite a strong backlist and a flourishing children's book program. Éditions du Seuil, perhaps the second most impressive of the French independents, comes up with a profit of just over 1 percent. At present, both houses are still owned by the founding families and their allies, but because of internal disputes, Gallimard has had to sell some of its holdings to outsiders and its future independence is not to be taken for granted.

As one publishing house after another has been taken over by conglomerates, the owners insist that their new book arm bring in the kind of revenue their newspapers, cable television networks, and films do—businesses that have always enjoyed far higher profit margins. New targets have therefore been set in the range of 12–15 percent, three to four times what publishing houses have made in the past.

To meet these new expectations, publishers drastically change the nature of what they publish. In a recent article, the *New York Times* focused on the degree to which large film companies are now putting out books through their publishing subsidiaries, so as to cash in on movie tie-ins. In 1990, The Disney Corporation established its own publishing arm, Hyperion, to exploit Disney releases. The thrust of this effort was described in the *Times* by Robert Gottlieb, a leading agent: "We are not dealing with Farrar, Straus here. Remember this is a very commercial entertainment business."

The changes that have taken place in publishing are increasingly mirrored in the bookselling business as well. One of the first titles I commissioned at Pantheon was a survey of monopoly practices in America. *In a Few Hands* was publicly presented as the work of the late populist senator from Tennessee, Estes Kefauver. In reality, it was written by his very able staff, who ran a series of exemplary hearings over the years on the way monopolies had grown in the American economy. In addition to chapters on the steel industry and pharmaceuticals, the book included an account of a public inquiry into bakeries. C. Wright Mills originally organized the inquiry that showed how national brands such as Tip Top and Wonder had replaced the small bakeries that used to be in every town. The large industrial outfits initially offered bread at prices that greatly undercut local bakeries. They also encouraged local grocery stores to give more shelf space to their bread by hiking up discounts. Price differentials were at first sufficiently attractive to drive the smaller producers into bankruptcy. Having eliminated the competition, the companies raised their prices in predictable monopolistic succession and Americans were left with plastic-wrapped and plastic-tasting bread that was more expensive than the locally produced loaves it replaced. Only many decades later did specialist bakeries begin to flourish again in large cities, selling excellent but very expensive loaves to the small numbers that can afford them.

The fate of the small American baker has stayed in my mind as I have watched the progressive disappearance of independent bookstores from America's main streets. Such independents should not be romanticized. Many were small, illstocked, and as interested in selling greeting cards and stationery as they were in books. But they were numerous and an essential part of American life. The following 1945 survey lists the number of stores that were deemed worthy of a visit by a publisher's sales representative. New York had 333 stores, Chicago had 88, and Los Angeles 66. New York now has 76 stores, including many that are part of museums, libraries, and other institutions.

TWENTY LEADING BOOK CITIES IN 1945 AND NUMBER OF INDEPENDENT BOOKSTORES IN EACH[2]

City	*Stores*
New York	333
Chicago	88
Los Angeles	66
San Francisco	59
Philadelphia	54
Boston	46
Washington, D.C.	44
Baltimore	32
Seattle	26
Cincinnati	24
Detroit	23
St. Louis	23
Buffalo	20
Dallas	20
Minneapolis	19
Columbus	16
Indianapolis	11
St. Paul	11
Total	915

Independent bookstores used to offer an alternative to the uniform product of the mass media. The transformation of American bookselling began well before the chains arrived. Bennett Cerf, in his memoirs, dictated in 1967, described the problems that were already being created by new discount stores. Tellingly, all three of the stores he mentions have since disappeared:

> The discount stores, because they don't carry a complete stock but do carry the best sellers, have hurt the small bookseller. In New York, for example, such a store is right across the street from Brentano's on Fifth Avenue and right down the street from Scribner's, and as a result, Scribner's and Brentano's don't sell as many copies of the top best sellers as they used to, because people go to Korvette's. . . . [3]

Bennett goes on to describe how difficult it had become to place more complex books in the independent stores, which were suffering more from the competition with the discounters.

It was the decision to discount books—particularly best-sellers—that made the chains the phenomenon they are today. In many cities, the chains were the first to establish major bookstores, and there is no question that these stores now offer Americans greater choice than existed before. On the other hand, their progressive expansion has been harmful to the remaining independent stores. In a statement made to the *Financial Times* at the time of the Frankfurt Book Fair, the German minister of culture (and former publisher) Michael Naumann predicted that if discounting was allowed in Europe, 80 percent of Germany's four thousand bookstores would fold.

In recent years, the chains have grown dramatically in the United States and are now selling over 50 percent of all books available for retail. Independent bookstores are down to 17 percent, and that number is decreasing with every passing year. Price clubs and other discounters play an increasingly important role, as do Internet sellers such as Amazon. These factors have brought about a dramatic decline in the number of independent bookstores, from 5,400 stores in the early 1990s to 3,200 today.

The major chains focus their very considerable resources on best-sellers, to the neglect of other titles, which in turn affects the decisions of publishers. Further, because they control such an important part of the market for books, the chains are now able to demand almost whatever terms they wish from the major publishers, who are pressed to pay large amounts of co-op advertising money if they want their books to be placed prominently in the stores, a service traditional booksellers rendered as a matter of course without charge. Independent bookstores recently won a lawsuit against the major publishers for the way they help the chains. These policies have a negative effect on small publishers who are hard put to pay the extra amount for promotion.

To make matters worse, the chains have aggressively opened new stores close to the most successful independents, sometimes directly across the street (as Bennett observed). As a result, more independents are going out of business every day; in the center of New York only a handful remain—three more have closed in the months I have been working on this book.

Limiting outlets in this way compounds the difficulty faced by smaller publishers. The independent bookstore—which could be counted on to feature a new novel or volume of poems if the staff particularly liked it—is replaced by the large chain store using the most up-to-date marketing techniques. Chains have gone so far as to demand that publishers limit author tours to only their stores. Some authors, such as Stephen King, have refused to go along with such restrictions (King insisted on visiting only independents on his last tour). But important as such gestures are, the monopolistic trend of the larger stores cannot be underestimated.

The managers of chains often come from other fields of retailing, and they have no particular interest in books as such—only in the number of dollars each cubic foot of space can earn. The chains' return practices have also generated a host of problems. I once sat at an American Booksellers Association lunch with the chief buyer of popular fiction for one of the chains, hardly someone on the front lines in defense of high culture. Nevertheless, she was deeply unhappy. Her company guidelines mandated that if a book did not sell a certain number of copies per day during the first week on display, it would be moved to the back of the store and then returned. It did not matter if the reviews were late or the promised appearance on *The Today Show* were delayed. Alfred Knopf's old joke that books were "gone today and here tomorrow" has proved to be the rule.

Notes

1. From an interview with the author in 1990.
2. Book Industry Report of the Public Library Inquiry of the SSRC.
3. Bennett Cerf, *At Random* (New York: Random House, 1997).

8
UNFAIR TRADE PRACTICES IN BOOKSELLING

Wallace Kuralt

Wallace Kuralt, along with his wife Brenda, was the owner of The Intimate Bookshop, a sixty-year-old institution just across the street from the campus of The University of North Carolina in Chapel Hill. The Intimate grew into a small chain of nine bookshops throughout North Carolina. But when the large chain bookstores moved in, Kuralt was forced, one by one, to shutter his stores. In 1998, Kuralt filed suit against Borders and Barnes & Noble. He argued that the chain stores' bullying of publishers into giving them big discounts unavailable to the smaller stores violates the Robinson-Patman Act and antitrust legislation intended to deter businesses from leveraging high volumes of sales into discounted wholesale prices.

In the 1970s and 80s, the ABA (American Booksellers Association) counted some 7,000 independent bookshops as members, and many of these members had multiple store locations (we had nine, for example). Then, too, a good many of the very small independents did not join the ABA. I would guess that, just two decades ago, there were over 10,000 thriving independent stores out there. Today's figures show 3,000 existing independents, and many of these have made heavy adaptations (as have we), such as offering used, old, and rare books in order to distinguish their operations from those of the chains. The stores that remained are considerably weaker than those of the 1970s and 1980s, with perhaps fewer than 1,000 independents that can provide any meaningful competition to the national retailers.

The total retail space provided by the chains about equals the old space available, but prices have risen dramatically (even though discounted to some extent by the chains). Why? When manufacturers are squeezed for greater benefits by the chains, sooner or later they'll either give away all their profit or will have to raise prices. Thus the independent competitors, who must pay about twice as much for the same inventory as that purchased by the chains, can either discount at a loss or sell at the new higher price—and lose customers.

The chains have created a market situation that benefits only themselves—not thee nor me, not the authors, agents, publishers, sales reps, independent shops, or economy in general, and certainly not the literary value normally available through lawful trading.

Carl Person [Kuralt's attorney] has been battling for the integrity of the system, fair trading, preservation and maintenance of our civil rights, and court reform—all of which are matters addressed by the current lawsuit of *The Intimate Bookshop* v. *Barnes & Noble, Borders and others.* The Intimate has always been a large, general trade bookshop, grossing over $100,000,000 in sales in the 1980s and early 1990s before the attacks by the chains managed to overwhelm our resources and ability to compete against a corrupted system.

This is not merely an effort by a single, failed, bookselling group to recover their own damages. The efforts of almost ten years of work, including five years of legal motions and arguments and the examination of hundreds of thousands of papers supplied under subpoena by the defendants would hardly be expected to be justified for such minor compensation.

The validity of the law—antitrust, Robinson-Patman Act, and state and local law—must be upheld if the suit is to be truly successful, with a resulting demand for renewed effort by the regulators to demand strict observance of the regulation and the reinstatement of the "level playing field" in which real competition produces the best results for everyone.

If the power of money and the "buying power" and coercion of suppliers are permitted to continue to rule, if the things we produce are underpriced by the goods of other nations created through criminally cheap labor, we could well find ourselves a nation unable to produce goods that are made with consideration of quality, innovation, variety, beauty, value, or elegance, and that contribute, each in their small way, to the quality of life in this great country.

When the smaller retailers disappear, the downtowns go away, the civilizing society created by the brightness of the entrepreneur and the ideals they apply to business practice are simply lost. Prices should remain as low as reasonable through normal competitive practices, but not at the cost of variety and fresh ideas and efficient practices applied under legal requirements and legal protections.

We have to act now—all the wails of the damaged can't help after the deed has destroyed the infrastructure that would be required to rebuild a failed system.

9

THE MILITARY-INDUSTRIAL COMPLEX IS DEAD![1] LONG LIVE THE MILITARY-MEDIA-INDUSTRIAL COMPLEX!

Dee Dee Halleck

The Wrong Mac?

When antiglobalization protests are announced, one of the first responses by local authorities is to board up any nearby McDonald's. While activists in many locations have aimed their rancor at the fast-food chain, it is another "mac" that makes possible the widespread globalization that has ensured the extraordinary proliferation of McDonald's worldwide. That "really Big Mac" is McDonnell Douglas, a giant corporation (and subsidiary of Boeing) that is both a prominent member of the "military-industrial complex" and defender of the "free trade" of which fast-food king McDonald's is the iconic flagship. Although much antiglobalization activity has been directed at McDonald's and Starbucks, military profiteers have remained *sub rosa.* At the same time, military culture, from camouflage clothing to video games featuring military exercises and snipers, has triumphed at the mall. Christmas toy lists feature rocket launchers, tanks, and plastic M-16s. Meanwhile, on television and the pages of glossy magazines, war is glorified in many forms: from the heroic promotional spots for the aircraft corporations to the armed services' MTV-style recruiting ads.

The mass media corporations are now central to the U.S. military machine through their own Department of Defense contracts or through board members shared by defense industry suppliers and contractors such as Boeing and Halliburton. The Department of Defense has courted many Hollywood studios, offering free locations, consultants, and the use of equipment for films dealing with war themes in a positive light. A Web site, *The Hollywood Military Advisor,* offers free help to film production companies interested in using weaponry and military vehicles. The Military Industrial Complex, what President Eisenhower warned about in his farewell presidential address, is no longer a *potentially* troublesome threat, but an ominous reality, made more menacing by its increased size and power and by its ownership of such media outlets as NBC (by General Electric) and CBS (by Westinghouse). It's useful to think of this new stage in the condition Eisenhower described as the *Military-Media-Industrial Complex.*

The Art of Resistance

There are few examples of activism that address the *Military-Media-Industrial Complex.* The occasional guerrilla theater skit with generals clutching briefcases stuffed with money or poster featuring cartoon images of suited hogs gobbling up dollars point to the problem. There is little concerted attention paid to the corporations that reap the profits of the contemporary war regimes. Where is the twenty-first-century equivalent of John Heartfield, whose photomontages so clearly expressed the German government's collusion with military manufacturers and suppliers during the Nazi era?

During the Vietnam War, Dow Chemical's production of Napalm became a striking example of industry in service of the devil. Dow's funding of research at universities was denounced, and in some cases eliminated. Demonstrators hounded Dow executives and factories. In Germany, Harun Farocki made a short film, *Inextinguishable Fire* (1969), about Dow's production of Napalm B.

Is the militarization of our society so total that the role of these corporations is imperceptible? Or hidden in plain sight? And where is the cultural equivalent of Heartfield's or Farocki's work today? A rare example of someone who takes military issues as subject matter for her art is Australian cyberfeminist Francesca Da Rimini. Her Web site, *Liberation Range* <http://dollyoko.thing.net//subtle/>, documents and annotates 27 military contracts in clearly understandable terms: "McDonnell-Douglas contracts of $689 million to create kits for 2000-pound bomb. The University of Southern California was awarded almost $12.5 million to provide the 'MONARCH Cognitive Heterogeneous Information Processor.' " She accompanies these texts with scientific-looking images of weaponry, juxtaposed with images of war victims and blank-faced youths who stare out at the viewer in passive disbelief.

One of the Da Rimini's surprising discoveries is the prominence of universities among contract recipients. At the state and federal level, funding for most educational research is drying up. The exception is military research. As I mentioned in connection with Dow, such research contracts were a prime target for Vietnam War activists during the sixties. Since then, relatively little attention has been paid to the militarization of education. Military funding comes in many guises: Psychology and communication departments, for instance, collect funds for graduate students to conduct research on the effects of stress on mechanical response, or the efficacy of military recruiting Web sites.

For many, it's hard to criticize hard-pressed department heads who respond to the Department of Defense's RFPs (requests for proposals). Most universities have enacted a sort of "structural adjustment" similar to what is required by the World Bank or International Monetary Fund of debtor nations: Departments must "pay their own way" to the extent that funding for graduate programs must come from grants the department wins. Since sources for this sort of funding are drying up as foundations cope with diminishing endowment income or shifting funding priorities, the Department of Defense (DoD) research grants undoubtedly look quite attractive. The result is that few faculty members are willing to take a stand that would deprive their graduate students of funding.

Students themselves are less inclined to resist in ways that would put their graduation prospects and career plans at risk. Most students are now heavily in debt, both to educational institutions as well as to credit-card companies, which are quick to issue multiple cards to all freshman students. There are many students who receive their bachelor's degree along with a bill for over $100,000. Those who go on to graduate school are likely to more than double this amount. So don't expect them to turn down desperately needed DoD grants.

The Military R Us: Community Access Commandeered

Local public, educational, and governmental (PEG) access channels have been targeted by the military as useful vehicles for recruiting and promotion. Six hundred seventy local channels currently run *Army News Watch,* a weekly program produced especially for them. *Army News Watch* is upbeat about war: See the happy recruits and their shiny equipment! According to these shows, the military is simply in the business of testing new electronic gadgets and doing calisthenics in scenic locales. This isn't even reality TV. The unloading of coffins from Iraq or wounded amputees entering Walter Reed Hospital are nowhere to be seen.

Public-access channels are a unique resource, the result of negotiations between cable companies and municipalities. Spurred on by media activists over the last thirty years, cities have demanded cable corporations repay the public for the use of city resources such as streets and utility lines. This "payback" is in the form of channels for community use and funds to support the local infrastructure. The fact that several branches of the military are producing programs for these channels indicates that someone in the Pentagon, at least, thinks this is a useful way to reach the public. In addition to the weekly programs, the military also sends out public service announcements (PSAs) and video news releases to hundreds of community channels every week. Every branch of the military does this—the Army, the Coast Guard, the Marines, and the Navy.

Counter-programming

I have been working as a producer for Deep Dish Television Network, a pioneering grassroots network that has delivered programming to community channels nationwide since 1986. At Deep Dish, we believe there is a need for programming that promotes peace and gives a more realistic view of what the recruits and reservists currently face in the Middle East. During the past two years, we collected video footage from independent and community producers for the 12-part series, *Shocking and Awful: A Grassroots Response to War and Occupation.* This series takes a hard look at the U.S. invasion and occupation of Iraq.

The programs are organized by theme: military personnel and their families, the destruction of libraries and museums, the role of women, the economic background to the war and global resistance, among others. Community stations downlinked the series and cablecast it on their local channels. Deep Dish encourages local channels to program the series directly after or before *Army News Watch* or other military media productions. In many communities, this sort of counter-programming is the only opposition audiences have seen against the war, with the exception of Michael Moore's *Fahrenheit 9/11*.

There is no denying that the past twenty-five years has seen the successful realization of a campaign to reverse negative images of the military. The erasure of the "Vietnam media Syndrome" hardly began with September 11th. From the war against the "rogue state" of Nicaragua in the eighties, through the Gulf War of 1991, the image of "our heroes" has been polished and re-polished. Conversely, since the Vietnam War and the demise of the domino theory, "criminals" have replaced "communists" as the enemy at hand; the media-driven hysteria has led to the doubling of police department budgets, especially during the nineties and despite the actual diminishing of crime. September 11th ushered in a radically new mindset: The apolitical "criminal" has merged and converged with the "terrorist" as the cunning and ubiquitous enemy. Hello "embedded" media, good-bye freedom of the press. Welcome to the secure homeland.

Notes

1. This article was adapted from Part Two of the series of panel discussions, "Censorship in Camouflage," held at the New School University, in New York, in June 2003.

PART II

The Internet

Muntadas, *The File Room, Chicago Cultural Center,* 1994 (installation shot).

10

HIGH WIRE[D] ACT: BALANCING THE POLITICAL AND TECHNOLOGICAL

Robert Atkins

If the twentieth century was an ongoing celebration of technology and science—a giddy succession of remarkable developments ranging from the airplane and polio vaccine, to the moon landing and the splitting of the atom—one late-century phenomenon, the Internet, pointed the way to the electronic future. The decentralized, multicentered design of the U.S. Defense Department–initiated project precluded the possibility, in case of nuclear attack, of communications being intercepted. This project—along with advances in computing and the invention of the World Wide Web in 1989, helped make the 1990s the decade many of us began e-mailing, researching, shopping, archiving, and dating online. Although the transformation of the Web into a sort of cyber-shopping mall has disappointed many, the Internet continues to provide alternative, relatively uncensored space for art and activism to flourish, most recently in the form of blogs, or self-published, serialized journalistic or diaristic commentary. Nonetheless, as with every modern telecommunications advance, political pressures for control have quickly led to increasingly tight regulation of the new medium.

Clearly, the Utopian promise of a parallel, virtual world offering authentic community and genuinely free expression has been compromised. Stanford University law professor Lawrence Lessig, in *The Future Of Ideas: The Fate of the Commons in a Connected World,* from which "Creativity in Real Space" and "Innovations from the Internet" are excerpted in this section, protests the increasing privatization of information and governmental control of content. The new possibilities opened by new forms and media such as HTML books or MP3 players, Lessig argues, contrast with the closing of the commons (that is, information to which everyone shares access), which was, in fact, crucial to the development of digital media: "Closer to the world of ideas than to the world of things, [this new digital realm] has flourish[ed] as it has largely because of the commons it has built." Lessig offers the hopeful possibility that economic self-interest will yield to enlightened self-interest on the part of media magnates and the commons will once again be public property.

Like every new frontier, the favored metaphor for the Internet during the late 1980s and early 1990s, the Internet also had its cowboys and outlaws. First the geeks, then the hackers. They cracked code and broke laws, sometimes to dramatize the inadequacy of cyber-security on government and corporate computer systems, and almost always as a form of expressive behavior. The battle between the hackers and the powers that be was fought over the limits of expression and access: Would the Internet serve the public interest as libraries had served previous generations? Or only the private interests of those capable of subscribing to the information consolidators' high-priced products and services such as Lexus/Nexus? An information gap based on the scarcity of affordable hardware already separated the First World from the rest of humankind. Would the libertarian mantra of the hackers and geeks—"Information wants to be free"—prove to be a nostalgic reminder of twentieth-century Silicon Valley and the thwarted struggle that took place there? Or the *cri de coeur* of twenty-first-century Netizens everywhere?

In "Hacking Culture," the chapter excerpted from his book *The Evolution of the Hacker,* cultural historian Douglas Thomas attempts to ameliorate the criminal image of hackers. To do so, he examines three generations of hackers from the counterculture–connected late-sixties hackers to the cyberpunks of the nineties, all set against the backdrop of the shift from modernism to postmodernism, tellingly apparent in mass-media representations of hacking such as *War Games* (1983), a life-affirming film of the Reagan era, and the grimly dystopic *The Net* (1995). Thomas also points out that Bill Gates and Steve Jobs, the founders of Microsoft and Apple respectively, amassed their fortunes in large part by copyrighting—that is privatizing—software and systems that had been communally developed by groups of decidedly anti-capitalist geeks.

Before the Internet became a household word in the nineties, it had begun to attract artists and activists who believed that the twin problems of distribution and free expression—could you really have the latter without the former?—were resolved by the Internet *modus operandi* of self-publication and its DIY spirit. Giselle Fahimian, a San Francisco lawyer, chronicles the convergence of art and activism in her article, "How The IP Guerillas Won: ®™ark, Adbusters, Negativland, and the 'Bullying Back' of Creative Freedom and Social Commentary." Sympathetic to the social commentary, parody, and direct engagement with audiences and corporate targets that characterize the art of these well-established collectives, Fahimian presents an overview of legal issues—primarily trademark and copyright—raised by them. She is an able guide through this highly political yet slightly absurd realm in which art interacts directly with corporate culture and exemplifies the free space that the First Amendment carved out for such work.

The Internet has already generated more than its share of litigation and promises much more of the same. Cases involving musical file-sharing against Napster (in 2000) and Morpheus, KaZaA, and Grokster (all in 2003) embody copyright holders' economic concerns about the ease of disseminating copyrighted material. The courts have generally found for the copyright-holding plaintiffs, essentially terminating Napster in 2004, Grokster in 2005, and putting the others on notice that copyrights violated by technologies designed *primarily* to circumvent the payment of royalties will not be tolerated.

For hackers, or simply computer do-it-yourselfers, artist–theorist Alexander Galloway's and bio-technologist Eugene Thacker's essay, "The Metaphysics of Networks," will be troubling. They report a steadily increasing number of prohibitions to programming that range from limiting music sampling to digital rights–management agreements precluding the use of some newly purchased products. They term them deterrents to "freedom-to-use" and argue that the battle over them has already been won—and by the bad guys! "The future politics of expression," they write, "will turn on freedoms-of-use, rather than the antiquated and already-decimated category of freedom of expression."

It is difficult to deny that those who transgress this arguably "already-decimated" right to freedom of expression continue unabated, online or off. Or at least it's a reasonable supposition based on the number of submissions received by *The File Room,* an archive of censorship incidents spanning two millennia, to which site visitors may post cases and respond to those already online. The work of Antoni Muntadas, a Catalan conceptual artist living in New York, *The File Room* (1994) installation was produced with the Randolph Street Gallery in Chicago, and remains visible online at www.TheFileRoom.org under the auspices of the National Coalition Against Censorship. Muntadas, a conceptual art veteran, expresses cautious optimism about the politically transformative potential of online art in an interview with Svetlana Mintcheva, "Power, Politics, New Technology, and Memory in the Age of the Internet," conducted on the tenth anniversary of *The File Room:* "Every new medium appears and people use it at the same time they are learning *how* to use it," he observes. "[It is still too early to say] but there is potential for subversion in Internet art. And it is based on the blurring of the boundaries between fiction and reality that results in the questioning of reality."

As artists tease out the subversive potential of the Internet, politicians are under pressure to impose so-called moral standards on online content. Since 1996, a series of laws has criminalized the provision of minors with access to indecent—or even more difficult-to-define patently offensive—material online (see "Protection or Politics? The Use and Abuse of Children"). In addition, to receive federal funds for Internet connections or E-rate discounts, libraries must install filtering software on every computer, whether used by minors or not.

Of course, the subjectivity of such terms as "fitness for children" or "decency" is nearly total, but never more so than in the context of applying standards of conduct to global audiences. The international reach of Internet content is, potentially, one of its greatest strengths, but it also makes culture clash among nations inevitable when their local laws conflict.

One of the most closely scrutinized of these clashes went to trial in 2000. Yahoo! Inc. was sued by France's Union of Jewish Students and the International Anti-Racism and Anti-Semitism League for the sale of Nazi collectibles on its auction pages, in violation of French law. A French judge ordered Yahoo! to prevent French users from accessing the Nazi-related material, despite the technical impossibility of such a feat. Five years later, the case continues to bounce back and forth across the Atlantic in an (unlikely) quest for resolution. Along the way, it raises broad issues of jurisdiction, international standards, and First Amendment guarantees. Meanwhile, French fines against Yahoo! mount and the company long ago banned the traffic of Nazi memorabilia from its auction pages, claiming it did not want to profit from such material and, apparently, hoping to avoid further legal problems overseas.

Surely some sort of international court or commission will be created to assume jurisdiction over such matters. What other solution is possible? The European Union's 2005 attempts to ratify a continental constitution encompassing both economic and social integration are not encouraging, however. Once again, a familiar question arises: Can increasingly fractious societies spread across the globe muster the necessary harmony and resolve to establish such a body? Or, put another way, can humankind evolve to keep up with the technology it has created?

11
CREATIVITY IN REAL SPACE

Lawrence Lessig

Economics is the science of choice in the context of scarcity; it is a positive (if dismal) science that takes the world as it finds it. We can no more will a world where real-space printing presses were free than we can will a spacecraft that could fly as fast as the starship *Enterprise.*

So by contrasting this economy governed by layers of control with an economy governed by large swaths of the commons, I don't mean to criticize every system of control. Whether control is necessary for a particular good in a particular context depends upon the context—upon the technologies of that context and the character of the resource. Resources held in common in one context (among friends or in a small community) may need to be controlled in another (in a city or between tribes).

In particular, to the extent a resource is physical—to the extent it is rivalrous—then organizing that resource within a system of control makes good sense. This is the nature of real-space economics; it explains our deep intuition that shifting more to the market always makes sense. And following this practice for real-space resources has produced the extraordinary progress that modern economic society has realized.

A part, however, cannot speak for the whole, especially when changes in technology render the assumptions of the old obsolete. Even if the control model makes perfect sense in the world of things, the world of things is not the digital world. We may need fences and perfect control to assure that the world of things runs efficiently. That's what the prosperity of the market, property, and contract teach us.

But perfect control is not necessary in the world of ideas. Nor is it wise. That's the lesson our Framers taught us—in both the limits they placed on the Exclusive Rights Clause and the expanse of protection for free speech they established in the First Amendment. The aim of an economy of ideas is to create incentives to produce and then to move what has been produced to an intellectual commons as soon as can be. The lack of rivalrousness undercuts the justification for governmental regulation. The extreme protections of property are neither needed for ideas nor beneficial.

For here is the key: *The digital world is closer to the world of ideas than to the world of things.* We, in cyberspace, that is, have built a world that is close to the world of ideas that nature (in Jefferson's words) created: stuff in cyberspace can "freely spread from one to another over the globe, for the moral and mutual instruction of man, and improvement of his condition," because we have (at least originally) built cyberspace such that content is, "like fire, expansible over all space, without lessening [its] density at any point, and like the air in which we breathe, move, and have our physical being, incapable of confinement, or exclusive appropriation."

The digital world is closer to ideas than things, but still it is not quite there. It is not quite true that the stuff in cyberspace is perfectly nonrivalrous in the sense that ideas are. Capacity is a constraint; bandwidth is not unlimited.[1] But these are tiny flaws that cannot justify jumping from the largely free to the perfectly controlled. There are problems of coordination and constraints of scarcity. But the solution to these problems is not necessarily systems of control or better techniques of excludability. That cyberspace has flourished as it has largely because of the commons it has built should lead us to ask whether we should tilt more to the free in organizing this space than to the controlled that organizes real space.

Put differently: These imperfections in the capacity of cyberspace—that together may make it more rivalrous than ideas are—should not by themselves force us to treat the resources that cyberspace produces as we would treat real-space resources. If by resisting the model of perfect control we gain something important, then we should do so.

In the context of the media, we can be a bit stronger than this. Over the past twenty years, we have seen two changes in the media that seem to pull in different directions. On the one hand, technology has exploded the number of media outlets—increasing the number of television and radio stations as well as newspapers and magazines. On the other hand, concentration in the ownership of these media outlets has also increased. This increase in concentration especially should lead us to ask whether the control enabled in real space should carry over to cyberspace.

The statistics about increased concentration in ownership are undeniable and extraordinary. In 1947, 80 percent of daily newspapers were independently owned; in 1989, only 20 percent were independently owned. Most of the business of the nation's eleven thousand magazines was controlled by twenty companies in 1981; in 1988, that number had fallen to three.[2] Books are much the same. The independent publishing market was strong just thirty years ago; with Bertelsmann's purchase of Random House in 1998, the industry is now much more concentrated, dominated by just seven firms.[3] The significance of this concentration in books is no doubt less than that in film or other important media. There are still many independent publishers, and the range and diversity of book publishing are quite large. But the inertia is in the direction of concentration. And this inertia may be a source of concern.

Music is even more concentrated.[4] The five largest music groups in the United States account for over 84 percent of the U.S. market.[5] The same is true of radio. The top three broadcasters control at least 60 percent of the stations in the top one hundred U.S. markets.[6] The same is true in film. In 1985, the twelve largest U.S. theater companies controlled 25 percent of the screens; "by 1998, that figure was 61 percent and climbing rapidly."[7] Six firms accounted for over 90 percent of theater revenues in 1997; 132 out of 148 of the "widely distributed" films in 1997 were produced by "companies that had distribution deals with one of the six majors."[8] With this concentration, there has been a dramatic drop in foreign films. In the mid-1970s, foreign films accounted for 10 percent of box office receipts. By the late 1990s, the number had fallen to 0.5 percent.[9] Cable and television are no better. In 1999, Robert McChesney could write that "six firms now possess effective monopolistic control over more than 80 percent of the nation, and seven firms control nearly 75 percent of cable channels and programming."[10] Those numbers are now much more extreme.[11] Professor Ben Bagdikian summarizes the result as follows: "[D]espite more than 25,000 outlets in the United States, 23 corporations control most of the business in daily newspapers, magazines, television, books, and motion pictures."[12] The top firms in this set vastly outbalance the remainder. The top six have more annual media revenue than the next twenty combined.[13]

The reasons for this increase in concentration are many. I don't mean to argue, as many others have, that we should necessarily consider this increasing concentration inefficient or illegal. There are important efficiencies to be gained by the mergers of large media interests; important gains in coverage have also been realized. And while the conspiracy theories are many and practically unending in scope, we need not believe media conspirators are behind this radical change. The government has loosened its restrictions on concentration, sometimes for good economic reasons; technologies of transmission have changed to the great benefit of all; and the consequence has been an extraordinary concentration in media production.[14]

Something *has* mucked things up a bit. Something has entered the field in a way that could make these concentrations change—not the government or a regulation imposed by the government, but the architecture of the Internet we have been describing so far.

For the essence of this power in the handful of media companies that now dominate media internationally is control over distribution and the power it can promise artists.[15] Movies run in certain places only; getting films into those places is quite hard. CDs are distributed through predictable channels of distribution—including radio stations, whose choice of what to play or not to play determines which content is popular or not. Breaking into this distribution channel is likewise extremely hard.

The same is true with cable. While many thought that increasing the number of cable channels would mean more valuable competition, in fact, the fragmentation of channels simply induced more commercialization. Fragmentation makes it easier to "slice and dice people demographically" and "maximize . . . advertising revenues."[16] Cable has thus not been a source of new innovation (unsurprisingly, as we saw, because the physical, logical, and content layers are all controlled). Instead, as "one cable executive put it in 1998, 'Most entrepreneurs have already gotten the word that the cable field is closed.' "[17]

But the essence of the Internet that I've described so far is an architecture for distribution that admits of no controllers, architecture that neither needs nor permits the centralization of control that real-space structures demand. And while this lack of control won't on its own mean Hollywood will fail, it will mean that the success of any particular kind of content is more convincingly a function of the desire for that content. Or at least, as we'll see, this is what the traditional media fear.[18]

Innovation from the Internet

In both artistic and commercial contexts in real space, there are barriers that keep innovators out. These barriers, for the most part, have been economic and real: the real cost of resources is a real constraint for most who would create. These barriers are obviously not absolute; ours is an extraordinarily creative culture; plainly some overcome the limits I've described. Indeed, if markets were perfectly competitive, one might imagine the optimal number that overcomes the barriers I have described. But markets are not perfect, and costs can be regretted. Hence these barriers are enough to keep innovators away whom we would not otherwise want to exclude. The hassle, the uncertainty, the absolute cost: no doubt these together chill many.

These barriers in real space are a function of its nature or, we could say, its architecture. Not "architecture" in its ordinary sense—buildings and streets—but architecture in a much broader sense: architecture in the sense of the set of physical constraints that one finds, even if these are constraints that man has made. The constraints that are reflected through economics are constraints of architecture in this sense. You can't perfectly and costlessly copy a nutritious meal; that takes real resources. You can't costlessly and instantly move your car from one coast to another: that takes time and energy. The constraints of real space are built into the nature of real space, and though technology presses against this nature, it is only so effective. Real constraints remain.

Cyberspace has a different architecture. Its nature is therefore different as well. Digital content can be copied perfectly and practically freely. You can move a great deal of content almost freely and instantly. And you can replicate whatever good there is in one place in many places—almost instantaneously. The barriers of cyberspace in its natural state are radically different from the barriers in real space.

"In its natural state." I spent many pages in *Code* arguing against just this way of speaking. Cyberspace has no nature. How it is—what barriers there are—is a function of its design, its code. Thus, in this abstract sense, it makes no sense to speak about the nature of this system that is wholly designed by man. Its nature is as man designs it.

But cyberspace at its birth did have a certain character. I've described some of it here and more of it elsewhere.[19] The feature of its character at its birth that is most significant for our purposes here is an architecture that disabled the power of any in the middle to control how those at the ends interacted: this is the principle of end-to-end. This design choice of end-to-end assures that those with a new idea get to sell that new idea, the views of the network owner notwithstanding.

This principle can operate at very different levels. I described it initially in the context of a network design. I have argued that the same principle applies to open code. Spectrum organized in a commons would implement the principle in the physical layer. The same idea can operate within any social system. Within law, this is the principle of subsidiarity—decisions are made at the lowest level appropriate for the decision. Within politics, it is a principle embraced by libertarians, who urge not no control, but control by the individual.

We can argue about how far this principle should extend in politics. Tomes have been written about how far it should extend in law. But my aim is to push its embrace in the context of creativity. In this domain, at least, our presumption should be libertarian. And we should build that presumption into the architecture of the space.

As the dot.coms crash and the pundits ask whether there was anything really new in the new economy of the Internet, it is useful to frame just what this new space has given us so far. That is my aim in the balance of this essay. I want to show how we already have something new, or at least originally did. My hope is to link instances of innovation to changes in the layers of control that the Internet effected. This is not a survey; my examples are illustrative, not representative. But by the end we should have a clearer sense of the link between these different commons and the innovation these commons produced.

New Products from the Net

At the code layer, the Internet is a set of protocols. These protocols make new digital products possible. These are products that could not, or would not, have been built before the Net. Among these we could include the dynamically generated maps with driving directions;[20] massive translation engines, covering scores of languages, translating texts and Web sites on the fly;[21] and online dictionaries covering hundreds of languages that otherwise would not be available except in the largest libraries.[22]

But let's focus on a few of these products and their relationship to the architecture of the Net.

HTML Books: Physical books are extremely durable information sources. They are stable and preserve relatively well. They read well in many contexts; they will be a central part of culture for the next century, at least.

But there are things paper books can't do, and constraints on paper books that limit how far the knowledge they carry is carried. These limits thus suggest the place of a different kind of book—the "HTML book," or a book produced for the World Wide Web.

HTML books are the passion of Eric Eldred. Eldred was a computer programmer in the navy. In the mid-1980s, he became aware of the Internet. The Internet then, of course, was not the World Wide Web—the Web would not appear for another five years. Nonetheless, the Net facilitated an exchange of information long before the Web made that exchange hypertextual.

When the Web came online, Eldred wanted to experiment to see what the Web might do for books. Eldred's daughter had an assignment to read Hawthorne's *The Scarlet Letter.* He tried to locate the text online. What he found was essentially unusable. So Eldred decided to make a version that was usable. He cleaned up the text, added a few links, and created his first HTML book—a book designed to be read on the World Wide Web.

An HTML book can do things that a paper book cannot. The author of an HTML book can add links to aid the reader or to guide the reader to other related texts. It can be easily searched and copied into other texts. And because it lives on the Web, it is available to anyone anywhere—including to people who can't afford to purchase that particular work and to machines that index the work to be included within search engines.

An HTML book is a derivative work under copyright law. If the original text is protected by copyright, then to publish a derivative work, you would need the permission of the original copyright holder. *The Scarlet Letter,* however, is a work in the public domain. So Eldred was free to take that work and do with it as he wanted.

This started Eldred on a hobby that soon became a cause. With the publication of Hawthorne, Eldred began Eldritch Press—a free site devoted to publishing HTML versions of public domain works (http://

eldritchpress.org). With a relatively cheap computer and an inexpensive scanner, Eldred took books that had fallen into the public domain and made them available for others on the Net. Soon his site had pulled together an extraordinary collection of work, including a large collection of the works of Oliver Wendell Holmes (Sr., not the Supreme Court justice).

Eldred, of course, is not the only online publisher of public domain works. Michael Hart's Project Gutenberg has been publishing public domain texts on the Internet since 1971. But the point is not the uniqueness of Eldred's efforts. Indeed, the point is exactly the opposite: The physical and code layers of the Net enabled this kind of innovation—for Eldred and for anyone else. The physical layer was cheap; the code layer was open. His only constraint would come at the content layer—but more on that later.[23]

MP3: Internet texts are not the only innovation enabled by the Net. Much more dramatic is the innovation in audio and video technologies. MP3 technologies are at the core of the audio changes. They too can be considered a new product that the Internet has made available.

As I have described, MP3 is the name of a compression technology. It is a tool for compacting the size of a digital music recording. It works in part by removing parts of the file that are inaudible to humans. Dogs would notice the difference an MP3 file makes; most of the rest of us are blissfully ignorant.

Blissfully—because this deafness of ours means that music can be made available on the Internet in an efficient and simple way with relatively little loss in fidelity. A five-minute song can be compressed to a file just 6 megabytes in size. And as connection speeds increase, that 6 MB file can be shipped to someone else in less than a minute.

This means that the Net becomes a possible distributor for music, and therefore it inspires a new kind of production: music written and performed for sampling on the Internet. This is not just a substitute for CDs or audiotapes. The cheap distribution—at different levels of quality—makes it possible to sample music in a different way. This in turn expands the market for music, as more can be tried without the commitment to purchase.

Film: A similar change has happened with film. As I have previously suggested, the costs of production of film have dropped dramatically as digital equipment has become more powerful and less expensive. We are soon to enter a time when filmmakers will be able to produce high-quality film for digital devices at 1 percent of the cost of the same production with traditional tools. Apple Computer is fueling this demand, with cheap, high-quality digital film technologies bundled into its popular iMac computer. This same technology, costing a few thousand dollars today, would have cost $150,000 just five years ago.

This drop in the cost of production is due to changes in the physical layer that enables film production. It is also supported at the code layer by a wide range of tools for manipulating and editing digital images. These together create an important blurring of the line between amateur and professional. As a recent Apple ad put it, "And now you're the purveyor of, you're the generator of, you're the author of *great stuff.*"

How great, of course, is a matter of taste. In 2001, Apple proudly advertised the first iMac movie purchased by HBO—a short dealing with teenage pregnancy, produced by a fourteen-year-old kid.[24] This is not quite Hollywood in the den, but it points to a future that just ten years ago could not have been imagined—a broad range of film content produced by a wider range of creators and, in turn, potentially available to others.[25]

Lyric Servers and Culture Databases: Popular culture is diverse and expansive. Finding information about this culture, however, is often quite difficult. Fans may be many, but the systematic cataloging of data about such creativity has, so far, been quite lacking.

Think in particular about music lyrics. Music is an important part of our life. We grow up listening to songs on the radio; we buy records and listen to those songs over and over. Our ability to recall music is extraordinary; a few bars from a song we heard thirty years before will bring back memories of a certain party or an evening at a concert.

Our memory is of both songs and lyrics. But it is often extremely hard to locate either. You might remember a particular song, but recall only a few words. Or you might remember the name of the song, but be unable to find its author.

The Internet provided an obvious solution to this problem, and by the mid-1990s, there was an explosion of lyric sites across the Web. These sites had grown from earlier sites located on the Net. But they quickly became extremely popular locations where fans might find the words that were echoing around in their heads.

These sites did not make money. They were produced by fans and hobbyists. But though there was no money to be earned, thousands participated in the building of these sites. And these thousands produced a far better, more complete, and richer database of culture than commercial sites had produced. For a time, one could find an extraordinary range of songs archived throughout the Web.

Slowly these services have migrated to commercial sites. This migration means the commercial sites can support the costs of developing and maintaining this information. And in some cases, with some databases, the Internet provided a simple way to collect and link data about music in particular.[26]

Here the CDDB—or "CD database"—is the most famous example. As MP3 equipment became common, people needed a simple way to get information about CD titles and tracks onto the MP3 device. Of course, one could type in that information, but why should everyone have to type in that information? Many MP3 services thus enabled a cooperative process. When a user installed a CD, the system queried the central database to see whether that CD had been cataloged thus far. If it had, then the track and title information was automatically transferred to the user. If it had not, then the users were given a chance to contribute to the system by adding the records necessary to complete the database for that recording.

This meant that quickly, all but the most obscure music was entered into this large cooperative database. And this database itself then became a product that otherwise would not have been available generally.

Each of these new products grows out of the different economics of digital production and the ability of innovators to add value at the edge of the network. Some surprise; others are obvious extensions; and still others are ideas that are timeless but possible only in this time. But regardless of their character, they were enabled by the environment of innovation of the original Net.

New Markets

New products beget new markets. And new modes of distribution (including the removal of barriers to distribution) induce the creation of new markets for existing products as well.

Consider just one example: the production of poetry. The market for poetry is extremely small; the burden in getting poems published is exceptionally great. These real-space constraints translate into an extraordinarily difficult market for poets.

But using both the cheap distribution of the Internet and tools for better structuring the delivery of content, the market for poetry on the Internet has taken off. There has been an explosion of sites dedicated to producing and distributing poetry. Poetry Daily, for example, launched in 1997, receives over 150,000 visitors a month. At peak usage, 12,000 users come to the site per day. And over 16,000 subscribe to a regular content newsletter.[27]

These sites are not simply tools for delivering poems more cheaply. Their technology also enables better control over how that content is consumed. Some sites have technologies for guiding the reading of poetry—thereby making it accessible to or understandable by a much wider audience.[28] Others enable the audio reading of poetry, similarly enabling a market for the blind that otherwise would have been restricted.[29] These tools in turn expand the reach of this form of creativity to people who otherwise would not consume this poetry.

New Means of Distribution

The most dramatic potential for affecting creativity is, as Coase described earlier, the lowering of the transaction costs of distribution, and hence the expansion of the extent of the market. Here there are a number of well-known examples that we will consider again when we examine changes in copyright law and their effects on the Net.

My.MP3: The compression technique of MP3 is "free" in the sense I have described it: Anyone is allowed to develop technologies that use it.[30] And through the 1990s, thousands of such technologies developed. It was extremely easy to find a program on the Net that would "rip" the contents of your CDs—meaning copy the music in an MP3 format so that you could store the music on your machine. And many MP3 players were offered for free or for sale.

But though MP3 files were small relative to their original data file, they were still quite large to be sent across the Internet. While a fast connection could chomp through an MP3 song in a few seconds, on a standard telephone connection it could take twenty to thirty minutes.

This restriction in bandwidth gave birth to an important industry of streaming technologies. The idea was quite simple: Rather than downloading the full copy of music and then playing it, streaming technologies allow the user to stream the desired content and play it at the same time. No copies of the file must be made first, which means the user need not waste time waiting for the music to be delivered.

RealAudio was the innovator here, though its idea was soon mimicked by Microsoft and Apple. RealAudio sold tuners that enabled people to tune in to audio, and then video, content. That content was compressed and streamed across the Net.

MP3.com took this idea further. Started in 1997, MP3.com has no real relation to the technology MP3. It didn't invent the technology, and it had no exclusive license. Nor did its founder, Michael Robertson, have any real relation to the music industry. Robertson was simply an entrepreneur who saw the Internet as a great new opportunity. MP3.com was started to find new ways to use the technology to produce and distribute music.

MP3.com pushed production by encouraging artists to produce and distribute music across its site. This was not unique to MP3.com. It was the business model of companies like EMusic.com as well.

But more interesting were MP3.com's new ideas about how to push distribution. The existing labels had a clear idea about how the business worked. Their business, Robertson explains, "is making a bet. They make big bets on a small number of acts, hoping that one of them is the lottery ticket and pays off."[31] And to help make sure their bets paid off, as artist Courtney Love explains, "record companies controlled the promotion and the marketing; only they had the ability to get lots of radio play, and get records into the big chain stores."[32]

When representatives from the existing labels spoke to Robertson, they tried to convince him to follow the same model. "They were all about, okay, we gotta find the next U2 or Backstreet Boys, or whatever. . . . Try to find that one, and promote the heck out of him, and hope we break even." Owning the artist is key to this model; the traditional labels thus demand exclusivity.

But Robertson's model was different.

> I just said, that's not our model. Why don't we let somebody else make the music and produce the music and do whatever they do in the creative process? And we'll just pick up after that creation is already done, and worry about the delivery.[33]

So MP3.com rejected exclusivity (Robertson: "Exclusivity is a very bad thing for content owners") and worked instead on technologies to make it easier for customers to get access to music. And using subscriptions and advertising, the company expected to make this way of getting content pay.

A core feature of this technology was an "automatic" way for popular content to find its way to the top. As Robertson describes it, the key is collecting good data. For "data changes the balance of power." Consumers "listen to the good music, and we'll make sure the good music floats to the top."[34]

The floating follows the listening. The more users listen and download music, the more the music "floats"; and the more the system learns the patterns of who likes what, the more the system can make sure that the music you like is likely to float to the top of your screen.

MP3.com thus conceives of itself as a "service bureau."

> [Artists] can come and go as they please. . . . You don't even have to agree to exclusively give it to us. It defies all logic in the music industry. I can't tell you how many people came into my office and said, "You don't get it. You don't get the business. I don't know why you're not forcing these guys to give you a piece of their intellectual property. Because you're gonna make the next Madonna, and you're not gonna own the next Madonna."[35]

There was one innovation, however, that earned MP3.com more than the sucker scorn about Madonna. This was the My.MP3 service, launched in January 2000. Using this service, consumers could get access to their music in two different ways. First, through cooperating sites, they could purchase music. Those cooperating sites would then send a CD to the customer but immediately make the music purchased by the customer available in the customer's MP3 account. Once available in a user's account, the customer would be able to stream that music to his or her computer, wherever the customer was. MP3 would then keep a collection of music stored in that account, and give the customer access to it wherever he or she had access to the Web.

The second aspect of My.MP3 was a bit bolder. MP3.com released a program called Beam-it. If you (the customer) had Beam-it installed on your machine, you could insert a CD into the computer, and the

MP3.com service would then identify what the CD was. If MP3.com had that CD in its library, it would make that music available to you. Thus, you could take all the CDs you had at home, "beam" them to the MP3 server, and subsequently get access to your music anywhere else you happened to connect to the Web.

Plainly, consumers could do much of this without MP3.com's help. My former colleague at Harvard, Jonathan Zittrain, was an early online music fanatic. He bought a basic computer from Dell Corporation with a large hard drive, and proceeded to copy all his CDs onto the computer. He then connected the computer to his cable modem and designed the system so that wherever he was (and mainly in his office) he could listen to his music. Zittrain thus built a music server like MP3.com which distributed his music on demand.

The difference with MP3.com was that you didn't need to be Zittrain to get your music. Nor did you have to waste the time that Zittrain wasted to copy all of your music. The Beam-it service would recognize your disk in less than ten seconds; you would have access to your music after a few seconds more. There was no need for a large disk drive to store all your music. All the music was stored at MP3.com's servers.

This service by MP3.com made it easier for consumers to get access to the music they had purchased. It was not a service for giving people free access to music. Of course, people could borrow other people's CDs and hence "steal" the content of those CDs if they wanted. But that was possible before MP3.com came along. MP3.com's aim was simply to make it easier to use what you'd already bought.

Napster: No doubt the most famous story of musical "innovation" has been the explosion called Napster—a technology simplifying file sharing for MP3 files. The idea was the brainchild of Shawn Fanning and Sean Parker—in the eyes of many, children themselves.

Fanning and Parker's idea was just this: Individuals had music stored on their computers—think again about the hoarder Zittrain. Others would want copies of that music. Fanning devised a way to engineer a "meeting" between the copies and those wanting them. His system, Napster, would collect a database of who had what. And when someone searched for a particular song, the database would produce a list of who had that song and was on the line at that moment. The user could then select the copy he or she wanted to copy, and the computer would establish a connection between the user and the computer with the copy.

The system would function as a kind of music matchmaking service—responsible for finding the links, but not responsible for what happened after that.

Napster is an "aha" technology: you don't quite get its significance until you use it. The experience of opening a Napster search window, rummaging through your memories for songs you'd like to hear, and then, within a few seconds, finding and hearing those songs is extraordinary. As with the lyric database, you can easily find what is almost impossible to locate; as with the MP3 server, you can then hear what you want almost immediately. Music exchanged on Napster is free—in the sense of costing nothing. And at any particular moment, literally thousands of songs are available.

The innovation excited an immediate legal reaction. The Recording Industry Association of America (RIAA) immediately filed suit against Napster for facilitating copyright violation. That may have been a mistake. At the time the RIAA filed suit, the number of Napster users was under two hundred thousand; after the suit hit the press, the number of users grew to fifty-seven million.

What Fanning had done was to find a way to use the dark matter of the Internet—the personal computers connecting the Net. Rather than depending upon content located on a server somewhere—in this strict hierarchical client/server model of computing—Fanning turned to the many individual computers that are linked to the Net. They could be the place where content resides. Using the protocols of the code layer, he was able to find an underutilized asset at the physical layer. Hence the importance of these centralized servers would be reduced.

Many believe the central motivation behind Napster was to find a way to avoid "the copyright police." For some content (but not streaming content), centralized servers are more efficient places for storage. But they are also more efficient places to harbor illegal content. And if it is illegal content that is being stored, the efficiency of the storage gets outweighed by the risk of getting caught.

But if the content is located on many machines set up individually, then the content is hard to find and it becomes difficult to prosecute those harboring it. So Napster imagined that individuals would put up content that would be available for others, but the individuals holding the content would not be so regular as to be targets of prosecution.

These groups, however, would serve a separate function as well. They would induce the exchange of information about preferences among members of these groups. That information would induce an expansion of demand by consumers of this music. And that demand in turn could be satisfied by music from Napster or from the ordinary channels of distribution.

To the extent you view Napster as nothing more than a device for facilitating the theft of content, there is little usefulness in this new mode of distribution. But the extraordinary feature of Napster was not so much the ability to steal content as it is the range of content that Napster makes available. The important fact is not that a user can get Madonna's latest songs for free; it is that one can *find* a recording of New Orleans jazz drummer Jason Marsalis's band playing "There's a Thing Called Rhythm."

This ability competes with the labels, but it doesn't really substitute for the demand they serve. A significant portion of the content served by Napster is music that is no longer sold by the labels.[36] This mode of distribution—whatever copyright problems it has—gives the world access to a range of music that has not existed in the history of music production.

Once you taste this world of almost limitless access to content, it is hard to imagine going back. What Napster did more effectively than any other technology was to demonstrate what a fully enabled "celestial jukebox" might be.[37] Not just for the music that distributors want to push at any particular moment; not just for the music that a large market would demand; but also for practically any recording with any fans using the service anywhere, the music was available.

This represents the end of the progression that began when broadcast channels started multiplying. When television, for example, is just a few stations, then the producers of television have a great deal of power to guide the audience as the program director chooses. As the channels multiply, each channel becomes a competitor of all others. At any one time, the number of competitors for attention has increased, and the effective choice is much greater.

Napster represents the extreme of this trend. Channels here no longer *channel* consumers. Consumers have the broadest range of choices possible. Thus, just as it is for an avid reader in a very large library, the content of music becomes available for individuals to choose rather than available as disc jockeys choose.

Notes

1. Or at least not yet. George Gilder has repeatedly argued that a future infrastructure based on fiber optics would provide "infinite bandwidth." See George Gilder, *Telecosm: How Infinite Bandwidth Will Revolutionize Our World* (New York: Free Press, 2000); George Gilder, "Rulers of the Rainbow: The New Emperors of the Telecosm Will Use the Infinite Spectrum of Light—Visible and Invisible—to Beef up Bandwidth," *Forbes ASAP* (October 1998): 104; and George Gilder, "Into the Fibersphere (Fiber Optics)," *Forbes* (December 1992): 111.
2. Ben H. Bagdikian, *The Media Monopoly,* 6th ed. (Boston: Beacon Press, 2000), 4.
3. Robert W. McChesney, *Rich Media, Poor Democracy: Communication Politics in Dubious Times* (Urbana: University of Illinois Press, 1999), 18.
4. The reasons for this increased concentration are hard to track precisely. There are a number of changes that have certainly occurred. The relaxation of rules on ownership of radio stations, for example, has exploded concentration in radio station ownership. This, in turn, has led to an increase in the modern equivalent of "payola." See Douglas Abell, "Pay-for-Play," *Vanderbilt Journal of Entertainment Law & Practice* 2 (2000): 52. As Boehlert describes it:

   > There are 10,000 commercial radio stations in the United States; record companies rely on approximately 1,000 of the largest to create hits and sell records. Each of those 1,000 stations adds roughly three new songs to its playlist each week. The [independents] get paid for every one; $1,000 on average for an "add" at a Top 40 or rock station, but as high as $6,000 or $8,000 under certain circumstances.

   Eric Boehlert, "Pay for Play," *Salon,* March 14, 2001, http://www.salon.com/ent/feature/2001/03/14/payola/print.html, 2.
5. Allyson Lieberman, "Sagging Warner Music out of Tune with AOL TW," *New York Post,* April 19, 2001, 34. See also Charles Mann, "The Heavenly Jukebox," *Atlantic Monthly* (September 2000), 39, 53.
6. Boehlert, 2.
7. McChesney, 18.
8. Ibid., 17.
9. Ibid., 33.
10. Ibid., 18.
11. According to the National Cable Television Association's figures, the top seven "multiple system operators," or MSOs, controlled 90 percent of the national cable television market at the end of 2000. http://www.ncta.com/industry_overview/top50mso.cfm.

See also Richard Waters, "Appeals Court Overrules Curbs on Cable TV Ownership in U.S. Federal Rules," *Financial Times,* March 3, 2001, 7. As of March 2001, AOL–Time Warner's cable market share was about 20 percent, while AT&T's share stood at 42 percent (including AT&T's purchase of MediaOne Group and its 25.5 percent stake in Time Warner Entertainment). AT&T's 42 percent market share well exceeds the FCC's cap of 30 percent, leading AT&T to challenge the cap in court as being "arbitrary." See Edmund Sanders and Sallie Hofmeister, "Court Rejects Limits on Cable Ownership; Television: Controversial 30% Cap Is Deemed Unconstitutional, but Consumer Groups Call the Decision 'Devastating,' " *Los Angeles Times,* March 3, 2001, C1.

12. Bagdikian, 4.
13. Ibid., x.
14. See Mike Hoyt, "With 'Strategic Alliances,' the Map Gets Messy," *Columbia Journalism Review* (January–February 2000), at http://www.cjr.org/year/00/1/hoyt.asp; *Global Media Economics: Commercialization, Concentration and Integration of World Media Markets,* Allan B. Albarran and Sylvia M. Chan-Olmsted, eds. (Ames: Iowa State University Press, 1998), 19–31; Dennis W. Mazzocco, *Networks of Power: Corporate T.V.'s Threat to Democracy* (Boston, Mass.: South End Press, 1994), 1–8. Cf. Benjamin M. Compaine, "Distinguishing Between Concentration and Competition," in *Who Owns the Media?,* 3rd ed., Benjamin M. Compaine and Douglas Gomery, eds. (Mahwah, N.J.: L. Erlbaum Associates, 2000), 537; Douglas Gomery, "Interpreting Media Ownership," in *Who Owns the Media?,* 3rd ed., Benjamin M. Compaine and Douglas Gomery, eds. (Mahwah, N.J.: L. Erlbaum Associates, 2000), 507.
15. McChesney, 80, 179.
16. Ibid., 250.
17. Ibid., 148.
18. Ibid., 168.
19. See Lawrence Lessig, *Code and Other Laws of Cyberspace* (New York: Basic Books, 1999).
20. For examples of online mapping services, see MapQuest.com at http://www.mapquest.com; Maps On Us at http://www.mapsonus.com; and MapBlasti at http://www.mapblast.com.
21. For examples of online translation Web sites, see AltaVista World/Translate at http://world.altavista.com; FreeTranslation.com at http://www.freetranslation.com; and From Language to Language at http://www.langtolang.com.
22. A short list of many examples of online dictionaries includes Merriam-Webster On-Line at http://www.m-w.com; Cambridge Dictionaries Online at http://dictionary.cambridge.org; and AllWords.com at http://www.allwords.com. There are also sites that perform aggregate searches through multiple multilingual dictionaries, such as yourDictionary.com at http://www.yourdictionary.com.
23. This is not a slight constraint. Because his site was noncommercial, Eldred could include only work that had fallen into the public domain. When Eldred began, the content constraint meant that works published before 1923 were free, works published after 1923 were only possibly free. But in 1998, Congress changed that by passing the Sonny Bono

Copyright Term Extension Act. The Bono Act extended the term of existing copyrights by twenty years, meaning work that was to fall into the public domain in 1999 would now not fall into the public domain until 2019. This turned Eldred into an activist.

24. See http://www.apple.com/hotnews/articles/2001/03/imacdirector/.
25. There are skeptics, however, about whether diversity will increase. Le Duc, for example, argues that the real constraint on diversity in films is not the channels of distribution, but rather the limited attention viewers have for stars. There are only so many stars we can like; they are the true constraint on this mode of production; and as long as that limit remains, the range of film will be restricted as well. Don R. Le Duc, *Beyond Broadcasting: Patterns in Policy and Law* (New York: Longman, 1987), 128.
26. On the risk of liability, see Janet Kornblum, "Lyrics Site Takes Steps to Avoid Napster Woes," *USA Today,* Dec. 12, 2000, available at http://www.usatoday.com/life/cyber/tech/jk121200.htm.
27. Tom Parsons, "World Wide Web Gives Poets, Poetry Room to Grow," *Dallas Morning News,* July 30, 2000, 8J.
28. For example, a Web site devoted to Chaucer uses multiple frames to navigate quickly through *The Canterbury Tales* and define the medieval English terms. See Librarius at http://www.librarius.com/cantales.htm. Another site provides a high-tech multimedia companion to the printed *Anthology of Modern American Poetry.* See Modern American Poetry at http://www.english.uiuc.edu/maps.
29. See Favorite Poem Project at http://www.favoritepoem.org (featuring readings of famous poems read by individual Americans); Internet Poetry Archive at http://www.ibiblio.org/ipa (offering modern poetry readings by the poets); and e-poets.net at http://www.e-poets.net (featuring contemporary audio poetry).
30. Free in the sense that I have defined the term. The technology is offered under a nondiscriminatory license. The underlying technology is patented. See Brad King, "MP3.com Open to Friends," *Wired News,* January 19, 2001, at http://www.wired.com/news/mp3/0,1285,41195,00.html. "Vorbis" is an alternative to MP3 that is royalty free and compresses more than the MP3 format does. Vito Pilieci, "MP3 May Go Way of Eight-Track: Vorbis Audio File Players Would Be Free of Royalty, Patent Fees," *National Post,* June 29, 2000, C8. The licensing does, however, create problems for open code developers. See Wendy C. Freedman, "Open Source Movement Vies with Classic IP Model, Free Software Is Bound to Have a Significant Effect on Patent, Copyright, Trade Secret Suits," *National Law Journal* 22 (Mar. 13, 2000): B14.
31. Telephone interview with Michael Robertson, Nov. 16, 2000.
32. Courtney Love, "Courtney Love Does the Math," *Salon* (June 12, 2000): 5. Love has offered a slightly exaggerated but illustrative description of how the market for music now works:

> This story is about a bidding-war band that gets a huge deal with a 20 percent royalty rate and a million-dollar advance. (No bidding-war band ever got a 20 per-

cent royalty, but whatever.) This is my "funny" math based on some reality and I just want to qualify it by saying I'm positive it's better math than what Edgar Bronfman Jr. [the president and CEO of Seagram, which owns Polygram] would provide. What happens to that million dollars? They spend half a million to record their album. That leaves the band with $500,000. They pay $100,000 to their manager for 20 percent commission. They pay $25,000 each to their lawyer and business manager. That leaves $350,000 for the four band members to split. After $170,000 in taxes, there's $180,000 left. That comes out to $45,000 per person. That's $45,000 to live on for a year until the record gets released. The record is a big hit and sells a million copies. (How a bidding-war band sells a million copies of its debut record is another rant entirely, but it's based on any basic civics-class knowledge that any of us have about cartels. Put simply, the antitrust laws in this country are basically a joke, protecting us just enough to not have to rename our park service the Phillip Morris National Park Service.) So, this band releases two singles and makes two videos. The two videos cost a million dollars to make and 50 percent of the video production costs are recouped out of the band's royalties. The band gets $200,000 in tour support, which is 100 percent recoupable. The record company spends $300,000 on independent radio promotion. You have to pay independent promotion to get your song on the radio; independent promotion is a system where the record companies use middlemen so they can pretend not to know that radio stations—the unified broadcast system—are getting paid to play their records. All of those independent promotion costs are charged to the band. Since the original million-dollar advance is also recoupable, the band owes $2 million to the record company. If all of the million records are sold at full price with no discounts or record clubs, the band earns $2 million in royalties, since their 20 percent royalty works out to $2 a record. Two million dollars in royalties minus $2 million in recoupable expenses equals . . . zero! How much does the record company make? They grossed $11 million. It costs $500,000 to manufacture the CDs and they advanced the band $1 million. Plus there were $1 million in video costs, $300,000 in radio promotion and $200,000 in tour support. The company also paid $750,000 in music publishing royalties. They spent $2.2 million on marketing. That's mostly retail advertising, but marketing also pays for those huge posters of Marilyn Manson in Times Square and the street scouts who drive around in vans handing out black Korn T-shirts and backwards baseball caps. Not to mention trips to Scores and cash for tips for all and sundry. Add it up and the record company has spent about $4.4 million. So their profit is $6.6 million; the band may as well be working at a 7-Eleven.

Ibid. Compare Senator Hatch's very different account of music production outside the control of the labels:

I will quote him at length, because his experience is instructive. He said: "As a result of doing it on my own, I get about $7 for every CD that sells in a store. And

> about $10 per CD sold at concerts. In contrast, I've got a friend who is also a performer/songwriter who opted to sign with a . . . label. He recorded a CD that cost about $18,000 to make, which the label paid for. Now, when one of his CDs sells at a store or at a concert, he makes about $1. The rest of the $7–10 which I make on my CD sales goes to his label. On top of that, he has to pay back the $18,000 it cost to make the CD out of his $1-per-CD cut. In other words, he won't make a dime until he has sold 18,000 CDs. And then, he still won't own the CD, the label will. They maintain the copyright. It's kind of like paying off your mortgage and then having the bank still own your house.

Orrin G. Hatch, "Address of Senator Orrin G. Hatch Before the Future of Music Coalition," Future of Music Coalition, January 10, 2001, 2. Currently, the average album release is under twenty-five thousand per CD. Jon Healey, "Industry Seeks to Justify Huge Overhead on the Price of Compact Disks," *Knight Ridder Tribune Business News,* September 3, 2000.

33. Telephone interview with Michael Robertson.
34. Ibid.
35. Ibid.
36. See Testimony of the Future of Music Coalition on "Online Music and Copyright Law," submitted to Senate Judiciary Committee, April 3, 2001, 13 ("The fastest-growing demographic segment using Napster are adults over the age of 24. Research reports have confirmed that one of the major reasons that they are doing so is to access commercial recordings that are no longer commercially available.").
37. See Paul Goldstein, *Copyright's Highway: From Gutenberg to the Celestial Jukebox* (New York: Hill and Wang, 1994). There are two parts to this conception, of course. One is the "celestial" part—emphasizing universal access. The other is the "jukebox" part—emphasizing payment. Napster emphasized the first.

12
HACKING CULTURE

Douglas Thomas

> Fry Guy watched the computer screen as the cursor blinked. Beside him a small electronic box chattered through a call routine, the numbers clicking audibly as each of the eleven digits of the phone number was dialed. Then the box made a shrill, electronic whistle, which meant the call had gone through; Fry Guy's computer . . . had just broken into one of the most secure computer systems in the United States, one which held the credit histories of millions of American citizens.
>
> —Paul Mungo and Bryan Clough, *Approaching Zero*

This is the common perception of today's hacker—a wily computer criminal calling up a bank or credit card company and utilizing mysterious tools to penetrate simply and effortlessly the secure system networks that hold our most important secrets. However, any attempt to understand today's hackers or hacking that only examines the blinking cursors and whistling boxes of computing is destined to fail. The reason is simple: hacking has never been just a *technical* activity. Perhaps the most striking illustration of this is that William Gibson, who in his book *Neuromancer* coined the term "cyberspace" and who invented a world in which hackers feel at home, for nearly a decade refused to have an e-mail address. In fact, *Neuromancer,* the book that has been (rightly or wrongly) held accountable for birth of the "new breed" of hackers, is rumored to have been written on a manual typewriter.[1] Hacking, as Gibson's work demonstrates, is more about the imagination, the creative uses of technology, and our ability to comment on culture than about any tool, computer, or mechanism. The hacker imagination, like the literature that it is akin to, is rooted in something much deeper than microchips, phone lines, and keyboards.

The current image of the hacker blends high-tech wizardry and criminality. Seen as the source of many evils of high-tech computing, from computer espionage and breaking and entering to the creation of computer viruses, hackers have been portrayed as the dangerous other of the computer revolution. Portrayals in the media have done little to contradict that image, often reducing hackers to lonely, malicious criminals who delight in destroying sensitive computer data or causing nationwide system crashes.

In both the media and the popular imagination, hackers are often framed as criminals. As Mungo and Clough describe them, hackers are members of an "underworld" who "prowl through computer systems looking for information, data, links to other webs and credit card numbers." Moreover, hackers, they argue, can be "vindictive," creating viruses, for instance, that "serve no useful purpose: they simply cripple computer systems and destroy data. . . . In a very short time it has become a major threat to the technology-dependent societies of the Western industrial world."[2]

To answer the question, What is hacking? properly, we cannot simply examine the manner in which hacking is done, the tools used, or the strategies that hackers deploy—the instrumental forces that constitute hacking. Instead we must look at the cultural and relational forces that define the context in which hacking takes place.

Hackers and Hacking

Not long ago, being called a hacker meant only that one belonged to a group of technology-obsessed college or graduate students who worked tirelessly on the dual diversions of finding interesting ways around problems (often in ways that resembled Rube Goldberg machines) and perpetuating clever, but harmless, pranks. This "class" of technophile is characterized by a kind of "moral code," as documented by Steven Levy in his 1984 book, *Hackers.* The code, as Levy describes it, was "a philosophy, an ethic, and a dream," and it was constituted by six basic theses:

1. Access to computers—and anything which might teach you something about the way the world works—should be unlimited and total. Always yield to the Hands-On Imperative!

2. All information should be free.
3. Mistrust Authority—Promote Decentralization.
4. Hackers should be judged by their hacking, not bogus criteria such as degrees, age, race, or position.
5. You can create art and beauty on a computer.
6. Computers can change your life for the better.[3]

The hackers Levy refers to were the original champions of the information superhighway, and their ethic was utopian in nature. As Levy describes it: "To a hacker a closed door is an insult, and a locked door is an outrage. Just as information should be clearly and elegantly transported within the computer, and just as software should be freely disseminated, hackers believed people should be allowed access to files or tools which might promote the hacker quest to find out and improve the way the world works."[4]

The "old hacker" of the 1960s and 1970s is often characterized with no small amount of nostalgia and is frequently seen as a counterpoint to the emergence of the new breed of hacker, the "cyberpunk" or "cracker." The "old hackers," in this romanticized telling, were "a certain breed of programmers who launched the 'computer revolution,' but just can't seem to be found around anymore. . . . [A]ccording to these 'old-school' hackers, hacking meant a willingness to make technology accessible and open, a certain 'love affair' with the computer which meant they would 'rather code than sleep.' It meant a desire to create beauty with computers, to liberate information, to decentralize access to communication."[5] In short, the old-school hacker was dedicated to removing the threat of high technology from the world by making that technology accessible, open, free, and "beautiful." To the 1960s hacker, hacking meant rendering technology benign, and hackers themselves not only were considered harmless but were framed as guardians of technology—scientists with an ethic that resembled Isaac Asimov's "Laws of Robotics": above all else, technology may never be used to harm human beings. Moreover, these hackers effected a strange anthropomorphism—information began to be personified, given a sense of Being usually reserved for life-forms. The old-school hacker was frequently motivated by the motto "Information wants to be free," a credo that attributed both a will and an awareness to the information itself. Interestingly, it is these two things, will and awareness, that seem to be most threatened by the evolution of technology. In an era when the public is concerned both with a loss of freedom to technology and with a fear of consistently finding themselves out of touch with the latest technological developments, there is a transference of our greatest fears about technology onto the idea of information. The hacker ethic remedies these concerns through the liberation of information. The logic is this: If technology cannot even confine information, how will it ever be able to confine us? Within the framework of this initial question we can begin to trace out the history of hacking as a history of technology.

A Genealogy of Secrecy

One of the primary issues that hackers and hacker culture negotiates is the concept of secrecy that has evolved significantly and rapidly since World War II. Indeed, hackers' relationships to technology can be understood as a cultural phenomenon and cultural response to the evolution of secrecy, particularly in relation to the broader political and social climate, the birth, growth, and institutionalization of the computer industry, and the increasing import of multinationalism in industry. The concept of secrecy seems to change from generation to generation. What secrecy means and particularly its value shift as social, political, and economic contexts change over time, but what has always remained stable within hacker culture is the need to negotiate the relationship between the technical aspects of the machines themselves and the cultural value of secrecy.

One of the first connections between secrecy and machines arose during the Allies' work to break German codes during World War II. Until this point, most cryptography had utilized methods of simple substitution, meaning that letters in the alphabet would be substituted for other letters, scrambling a clear text message into a ciphertext. For example, substituting the letter *a* for the letter *r, b* for *e,* and *c* for *d* would produce the ciphertext "abc" for the word "red." The problem with such a system of simple substitution is that the English language tends to utilize letters with fairly regular frequencies, and for that reason, no matter what substitutions are made, it becomes fairly easy to guess what has been encoded just by knowing how often certain letters appear in the message. Machines that encoded or decoded substitution schemes only helped speed up the process of encoding and decoding; they didn't actually perform the act of encoding in a meaningful way. That would all change with the German Enigma Machine, the first machine that actively encoded messages. The Enigma Machine consisted of eight code wheels that would rotate each time they were used. That meant that each time a substitution was made, the wheel making that substitution would rotate forward so the next time that letter was to be used, the substitution would be different. To complicate things further, each of the eight wheels had a different set of substitutions. The only way to decode the message was to have an Enigma Machine on the other end, with the wheels set to the original position, and feed the message back through to decode it.

The process of World War II code-breaking spawned the first generation of computer scientists and committed the evolution of the machine to the interests of secrecy and national security. From World War II on, two of the primary functions of the computer would be code-making and code-breaking. Indeed, it is not too far a stretch to claim that the first computer scientists (including Alan Turing, the "father" of modern computer science) who broke the Enigma Machine's coding process were, in the most basic sense, the first computer hackers and that the origin of computers rests with the need to keep and, perhaps more important, break secrets.

The Hacker Imagination: From Sci-Fi to Cyberpunk

It should come as no surprise that the hacker tradition is grounded in the literature of science fiction and fantasy. The literature of cyberpunk teaches, or reflects, the value of information both as data and as a social fabric, a medium of exchange, and a relational concept. Cyberpunk represents a world where information has taken over, and the literature provides a sense of the fears, dangers, anxieties, and hopes about that new world. As opposed to the earlier hackers who sought to "liberate" information, hackers of the 1990s see themselves as trapped by information. As a result, the "hacker ethic," which took as its most basic tenet that "information wants to be free," needs to be radically transformed. While the spirit of the ethic remains intact, the letter of it must necessarily change. Where the hackers of the 1960s had a great deal of control over the information that they created and utilized, the hackers of the 1990s and the beginning years of the twenty-first century find themselves in a world so overwhelmed by information that control itself becomes the contested issue. Most important to the later hackers is the concept that information is now their home, and secrecy of information is the equivalent of confinement or prison. The original ethic is, for the most part, still intact, but its meaning, value, and application have been radically altered by the ways in which the world has changed.

The cyberpunk vision of the future has radically reshaped the vision of the latter-day hacker. In one document currently being circulated on the Internet, the "Declaration of Digital Independence," one hacker describes the Internet as the next battleground for the regulation of information, and hence freedom. "It [the Internet]," he writes, "should be allowed to make its own rules. It is bigger than any world you can and can't imagine, and it will not be controlled. It is the embodiment of all that is free; free information, friendship, alliances, materials, ideas, suggestions, news, and more."[6] The hackers of the 1960s, inspired by the utopian science fiction of their day, saw the battle in terms of free information and felt encouraged by that literature to experiment, learn, and develop. In contrast, the hackers of today, with the dystopic vision of cyberpunk, see this battle as already lost and as something that can only be rectified by revolution. In part, this is the result of the increasing commodification of information, which has created a media that they describe as "the propaganda vending machine of today," which, "as a whole, trip over themselves, feeding lies to the ignorant."[7]

These hackers hold that the commodification of information has led to an increasing investment of power in the media. Accordingly, they argue, a transformation has taken place. The media, who "enjoy the power of managing information" in an era of commodification of information, are no longer interested in the freedom of information, but, rather, are invested in the careful control and dissemination of information. As Paul Virilio argues, the commodification of information has had an ironic effect: "[T]he industrial media have gone the way of all mass production in recent years, from the necessary to the superfluous. . . . [T]heir power to denounce, to reveal, to flaunt has been growing endlessly to the detriment of the now precarious privilege of dissimulation—so much so that currently the real problem of the press and television no longer lies in what they are able to show as much as in what they can still manage to obliterate, to hide."[8] The point is not so much that the media do not break news or reveal secrets as much as it is that they are selective about which secrets can and will be revealed. As media power is increasingly consolidated, media outlets have a possessive investment in particular stories and a similar investment in keeping other stories quiet. The more centralized the media become, the more power they have to self-regulate what constitutes "news."

Today's hackers, who follow this dystopic vision, contrast the media's approach to the management of information with their own sense of boundless curiosity. As the "Digital Declaration of Independence" illustrates: "Everyone has the need to know, the curiosity of the caveman who invented fire, but some have been trained like monkeys, not ever knowing it's there. They simply accept things, and do what is expected of them, and this is sad. They are those who never fight back, and never open their minds. And they are, unfortunately, usually the governing bodies; the teachers, bosses, police, federal agents, congressmen, senators, parents, and more. And this, my friend, must change."[9] Such a call to action defines the problem in terms of curiosity and recognizes that such curiosity is problematic within contemporary culture. Curiosity becomes dangerous and even subversive not to any particular group or organization but in principle. Curiosity is precisely what threatens secrecy, and in doing so, it challenges the economic structure, the commodification, of information.

Blurring the Lines between Old and New

The new-school hacker was introduced into the popular imagination through the 1983 release of the film *WarGames,* featuring Lightman (played by Matthew Broderick) as a curious kid exploring computers and computer networks who unwittingly starts the U.S. military on the road to World War III by playing what he thinks is a game—global thermonuclear war.

WarGames opens, somewhat ominously, with a scene in which U.S. soldiers in missile silos are ordered to fire their weapons at the Soviet Union, beginning what they believe will be the third, and undoubtedly last, world war. The soldiers are uncertain as to whether the order is part of a training exercise or not. As a result, a large percentage of the soldiers, uncertain about the effects of their actions, choose not to fire their missiles. The orders are part of a simulation, designed to test U.S. military battle-readiness. Their failure results in the implementation of a new program, wherein humans are removed from missile silos and replaced by electronic relay switches and strategic decisions about nuclear warfare are to be made by a state-of-the-art computer named WOPR (pronounced whopper)—War Operations Planned Response. The machine is devoted to constantly replaying World War III in an effort to maximize the effectiveness of U.S. missiles and minimize U.S. casualties. In effect, its job is to figure out how to win a nuclear war.

The young hacker, David Lightman, stumbles across WOPR quite accidentally while searching for a game company called Protovision. Using a modem and computer program (since termed a WarGames dialer), the hacker scans every open phone line in Sunnyvale, California (in the heart of the Silicon Valley), looking for modem access to Protovision. He comes across a system and, through hours of research (principally learning about the system's designer, Stephen Falken) and hacking, gains access.

The initial game continues to run even after Lightman is disconnected from the system, and, as Lightman soon discovers, the computer is unable to distinguish the game from reality. In less than three days time, WOPR will calculate a winning strategy and fire its weapons. In the meantime, Lightman is arrested. On the verge of being charged with espionage, he escapes custody and searches out the system designer with the help of his girlfriend, Jennifer Mack (played by Ally Sheedy), to convince him to help persuade NORAD (North American Air Defense command) not to believe the information that the computer is sending them. Falken, the system designer, has become a recluse since the death of his son, Joshua (whose name is the secret password that gains Lightman access and the name that Lightman and Falken use to refer to the WOPR computer). Eventually, after several incidents that put the world on the brink of a nuclear holocaust, Lightman manages to teach the computer (now Joshua) the meaning of futility by having it play ticktacktoe in an infinite loop sequence. The computer concludes, after exhausting the game of ticktacktoe and learning from it, that nuclear war is also unwinnable and that "the only winning move is not to play."

The film demonstrates a tremendous anxiety about technology, represented both by the missiles that threaten to destroy the United States and the Soviet Union and by the machines that control those missiles.[10]

The hacker, however, is represented in a more ambivalent manner. On the one hand, the harmlessness of Lightman's actions early on (using his computer to make faux airline reservations or even finding a bank's dial-in line) is made clear by his good nature and curiosity. That sense of "playing a game" is radically transformed when the machine he hooks up to (the WOPR) is unable to distinguish between a game and reality. On the other hand, Lightman and his understanding of "playing a game" (in this case ticktacktoe) ultimately are able to save the day.

In the film, the hacker is positioned as dangerous because he is exploring things about which he has little or no understanding. It is easy in a world of such great technical sophistication, the film argues, to set unintended and potentially disastrous effects into motion even accidentally. But equally important is the characterization of the hacker as hero. WOPR, above all else, is a thinking machine, an artificial intelligence, and that thinking machine needs guidance and instruction in its development. Technology is infantilized in the film (underscored by the use of the name of Falken's deceased son, Joshua), and the message of the film is that Lightman, the hacker, is the most appropriate educator for the technology of the future. Not the generals, the system administrator, or even the system designer himself is able to teach the machine, but Lightman, the hacker, can. The hacker stands at the nexus between the danger and the promise of the future of technology.

Films about hackers almost always deal with the question of secrecy. If we are to take *WarGames* as the prototypical hacker film, it is easy to see exactly what this means. *WarGames* begins with David Lightman trying to break into Protovision in an effort to play the latest games before they are publicly released. In essence, Lightman seeks to break Protovision's corporate secret in order to have access to "secret" games. As the name suggests, Lightman wants to see something before anyone (or, more to the point, everyone) else does. While searching for Protovision's phone number, Lightman comes across a more interesting system, one that "doesn't identify itself." Thinking that this is Protovision's dial-in number, Lightman attempts to hack into the system, even after he is warned by two system programmers that the system is "definitely military."

The crucial point about the basic theme underwriting the film is that these two cultures of secrecy, Protovision's and NORAD's, are virtually identical. The structure of *WarGames* depends on our understanding and acceptance of the confusion of a corporate computer-game manufacturer's notion of secrecy with that of NORAD. In other words, corporate and military secrets are, at some level, indistinguishable. In the films that followed *WarGames,* this theme was renewed and expanded upon. In *Sneakers* (1992), the confusion between corporate and government secrecy is complete when it is revealed that the only real governmental use for the "black box" agents have been sent to recover is to snoop on other U.S. governmental departments, rather than on foreign governments. What we witness throughout the film, however, is that as a corporate tool, that black box is capable of everything from corporate espionage to domestic terrorism. Indeed, the project "SETEC ASTRONOMY" which is at the center of *Sneakers,* is an anagram for "TOO MANY SECRETS." And while it is a government project (funded by the NSA in the film), it is revealed in the film's epilogue that the box will not work on other countries' cryptographic codes, only on those of the United States. Accordingly, the message is clear: domestically, there are to be "no more secrets" kept from those in power.

In two films of the 1990s, *Hackers* (1995) and *The Net* (1995), secrecy plays a major role as well. In these films, however, secrecy is what allows criminality to function in both the government and corporate worlds. In the case of *Hackers,* two employees (one a former hacker) of a major corporation are running a "secret worm program" to steal millions of dollars from the corporation. They are discovered when a hacker unwittingly copies one of their "garbage files" that contains the code for the worm's program. The same plot is played out in *The Net,* but from a governmental point of view. Angela Bassett (played by Sandra Bullock) accidentally accesses and copies secret governmental files that reveal wrongdoing on the part of governmental officials, again demonstrating the manner in which the culture of secrecy is able to hide and allow for a deeper sense of criminality to ferment and function. In both cases, hackers, by violating the institutions' secrecy, expose criminality by enacting criminality. The message from the later films is that secrecy creates a space for the worst kinds of criminality, which, because of the culture of secrecy, can only be exposed by another type of criminality—hacking.

Hackers of Today

As Steve Mizrach has noted, the split between the hackers of the 1960s and those of today is cultural and generational rather than technological:

> The main reason for the difference between the 60s and 90s hackers is that the GenXers are a "post-punk" generation, hence the term, "cyberpunk." Their music has a little more edge and anger and a little less idealism. They've seen the death of rock n' roll, and watched Michael Bolton and Whitney Houston try and revive its corpse. Their world is a little more multicultural and complicated, and less black-and-white. And it is one in which, while computers can be used to create beauty, they are also being used to destroy freedom and autonomy. . . . [H]ence control over computers is an act of self-defense, not just power-hunger. Hacking, for some of the new "hackers," is more than just a game, or means to get goodies without paying for them. As with the older generation, it has become a way of life, a means of defining themselves as a subculture.[11]

Born in the world that the 1960s hackers shaped, this new generation has been jaded precisely by the failure of the old-school hackers to make good on their promises. Technology has not been rendered benign, and information, while still anthropomorphized and personified, reveals that we are more like it—confined, coded, and organized—than information is like us. The cautionary tales, like Asimov's, that guided the 1960s hackers have been replaced with tales of a dystopian cyberpunk future that features technology no longer in the service of humankind, but humankind fused with technology through cybernetics, implants, and technological modifications to the body.

There seem to be two reasons for the shift. The first is that the rate of technological growth has outstripped society's capacity to process it. A certain technophobia has emerged that positions technology as always ahead of us and that produces a fear that is embodied by the youth of contemporary culture doing things with computers that an older generation is unable to understand. Hacking promotes fear, but it is about a contained kind of fear, one that is positioned as a form of "juvenile delinquency" that these youth will, hopefully, grow out of. In that sense, hackers emerge as a type of "vandal," a criminal who is often malicious, who seeks to destroy things, yet is terribly elusive. The threat, like the technology that embodies the threat, is decentralized, ambiguous, and not terribly well understood, but it doesn't need to be. We feel we can trust our information networks, for the most part, the same way we can trust our trains and buses. Occasionally, someone may spray-paint them, flatten a tire, or set a fire on the tracks, but these things are inconveniences, not disasters. Hackers pose a similar type of threat: They may deface the surface of things, but the underlying faith in the system remains intact. Just as one does not need to understand how internal combustion engines work to trust that a car will function properly, one does not need to understand how information networks function in order to use them. The second reason for a fear of hackers is the result of a displacement of anxiety that the hackers of the 1960s have identified—namely, the increasing centralization of and lack of access to communication and information.

Hacking is about technology; arguably it is about nothing but technology. Hackers and hacking constitute a culture in which the main concern is technology itself and society's relationship to the concept of technology. Accordingly, I adopt the term "culture of technology" as a way to understand the cultural implications of technology from the hackers' point of view as well as from a broader cultural standpoint.

Hackers themselves rarely, if ever, talk about the tools they use. Indeed, their activity demonstrates that computer tools are above all mere vehicles for activity. In many cases, today's hackers utilize common UNIX servers as their goals, targets, and mechanisms for hacking—that is, they utilize other people's resources as a means to accomplish their goals. Even the most high-powered PC is little more than a dumb terminal that allows the hacker to connect with a more powerful corporate or university machine, an act that can be accomplished just as effectively with a fifteen-year-old PC or VT100 terminal as it can with the fastest, highest-end multimedia machines on the market today.

Hacking is not, and has never been, about machines, tools, programs, or computers, although all of those things may appear as tools of the trade. Hacking is about culture in two senses. First, there is a set of codes, norms, values, and attitudes that constitute a culture in which hackers feel at home, and, second, the target of hackers' activity is not machines, people, or resources but the relationships among those things. In short, hacking culture is, literally, about *hacking* culture. As culture has become dependent on certain types of technology (computers and information-management technology, particularly), information has become increasingly commodified. And commodification, as was the case with the first personal computer, is the first step in the revaluing of information in terms of secrecy. As Paul Virilio maintains, along with commodification comes a new way of valuing information—in "the maelstrom of information in which everything changes, is exchanged, opens up, collapses, fades away, gets buried, gets resurrected, flourishes, and finally evaporates in the course of a day," duration no longer serves as an adequate means of valuation. Instead, he argues, "speed guarantees the secret and thus the value of all information." Accordingly, American, and perhaps all of Western, culture's relationship to information has been undergoing radical change, moving from a culture that values duration to one that values secrecy. That transformation also marked the moment of emergence of the hacker, a moment Virilio situates as a "data coup d'etat" that originated with the "first military decoders to become operational during the Second World War." It was those machines, the "ancestors of our computers and software systems," that produced the merging of "information and data processing" with the "secret of speed."[12] And, indeed, Virilio is right in the sense that World War II produced the first machines that were capable of what we currently think of as cryptography and that were, perhaps, the beginning of the union of information and speed to produce secrecy. The employment of machines that were, in essence, rudimentary computers made complex coding and decoding efficient. This allowed for the production of codes that were much more complex and, therefore, much more difficult to break. As speed and information merge, secrecy becomes an increasingly important component of the culture in which we live. However, such secrecy is precisely what hacker culture abhors.

Secrecy is not limited to encryption schemes but begins, as Virilio points out, with the process of commodification. In 1975, when hobbyists were busily programming the Altair, coding was done on paper tape and had to fit in 4K of memory. One of the first successes was Altair BASIC, a programming language written by two college students, Paul Allen and Bill Gates, that would allow others to develop software for the Altair. The difference between Allen and Gates's Altair BASIC and just about every other program written for the Altair was that Allen and Gates sold their program, rather than giving it away. This difference was enormous, since for computer hobbyists, the question was never one of profit, but one of access. Dan Sokol, the person who had obtained and copied the original version of Allen and Gates's BASIC, distributed the program at the next meeting of the Homebrew Computer Club and "charged what in hacker terms was the proper price for software: nothing. The only stipulation was that if you took a tape, you should make copies and come to the next meeting with two tapes. And give them away."[13] In no time, everyone had a copy of Allen and Gates's program. Bill Gates responded by sending an "Open Letter to Hobbyists," which was published both in the Altair users' newsletter and in the Homebrew Computer Club newsletter. "As a majority of hobbyists must be aware, most of you steal your software," Gates wrote, accusing hobbyists of being "thieves." "What hobbyist," Gates continued, "can put 3 man-years into programming, finding all the bugs, documenting his product and distributing for free?"[14]

In essence, Allen and Gates treated the BASIC interpreter as a secret that could be purchased. Most other hackers didn't see it that way. And for them, ownership was precisely what was at stake. To violate the principle that "computer programs belonged to everybody" undercut every tradition of programming.[15] For the first generation of hackers, programming meant passing your work on for others to rewrite, rethink, debug and, generally, improve on. Secrecy and ownership, even at the level of commodification, made that impossible.

This sense of secrecy that developed along with the evolution of the PC changed the climate in which hackers operated. Part of the transformation from duration to speed is also a distancing of information. As information is made secret, language adapts, and, increasingly, language reflects the need for secrecy. Accordingly, as the technology of language accommodates the possibility of secrecy, it too grows more distant. The result is not simply a feeling of being misunderstood or of alienation. Rather, this distance produces a more radical sense of being out of sync with the world, insofar as while one may speak or be able to speak the language of the world, it is not your first language; it is not your home language. In a culture of technology, the technology of language and the language of technology itself become more distant. But, for hackers, a subculture has emerged where the language of technology has taken over, where the language of technology is not distant but immediate. It is in this space that the hacker feels "at home." For example, Warren Schwader, after spending over eight hundred hours working on a program, "felt that he was inside the computer. . . . His native tongue was no longer English, but the hexadecimal hieroglyphics of LDX #$0, LDA STRING, X JSR $FDF0, BYT $0, BNE LOOP."[16] Hacker culture emphasizes the degree to which technology defines culture. For hackers, the process of hacking exposes the manner and way in which culture relies on technology and the ways in which technology is constitutive of culture itself. In this sense, technology is the hacker's home culture, and, as a result, the hacker is at home speaking the language of technology.

Notes

1. See Scott Bukatman, "Gibson's Typewriter," *South Atlantic Quarterly* (fall 1993): 627.
2. Paul Mungo and Bryan Clough, *Approaching Zero: The Extraordinary World of Hackers, Phreakers, Virus Writers, and Keyboard Criminals* (New York: Random House, 1992), xvii–xviii.
3. Steven Levy, *Hackers: Heroes of the Computer Revolution* (New York: Anchor/Doubleday Press, 1984), 27–33.
4. Ibid., 91.
5. Steve Mizrach (aka Seeker1), "Old Hackers, New Hackers: What's the Difference?"; electronic publication available at http://www.eff.org.
6. Anarchy and AoC, "Declaration of Digital Independence."
7. Ibid.
8. Paul Virilio, *The Art of the Motor,* trans. Julie Rose (Minneapolis: University of Minnesota Press, 1995), 3.
9. Anarchy and AoC, "Declaration of Digital Independence."
10. For an extensive discussion of technology and Cold War politics, see Paul Edwards, *The Closed World: Computers and the Politics of Discourse in Cold War America* (Cambridge, MA: MIT Press, 1996), 325–27.
11. Mizrach, "Old Hackers."
12. Virilio, *Art of the Motor,* 52–53, 33.
13. Levy, *Hackers,* 224.
14. Quoted in ibid., 224–25.
15. Ibid., 225.
16. Ibid., 342.

13

HOW THE IP GUERRILLAS WON: ®™ARK, ADBUSTERS, NEGATIVLAND, AND THE "BULLYING BACK" OF CREATIVE FREEDOM AND SOCIAL COMMENTARY

Giselle Fahimian[1]

When the Internet first emerged as a tool for the relatively inexpensive mass dissemination of information and images, some scholars embraced it as a potential harbinger of *semiotic democracy,* a society in which all persons are able to participate in the generation and circulation of cultural meaning-making. However, it quickly became apparent that the true power of meaning-making actually remained concentrated in the hands of the relatively few goliaths of the corporate world who could afford to threaten and prosecute anyone who used his trademarks or copyrights in ways they found objectionable. Despite provisions for fair use and parody, the intellectual property regimes that serve to protect the copyrights and trademarks of these goliaths (which include Coke, Nike, Barbie, Blockbuster, and McDonald's) leave little room for the type of social commentary, criticism, and artistic reworking of protected works that a true semiotic democracy would facilitate and support.

Recently, a number of Web sites run by artists and activist groups such as ®™ark (pronounced "artmark"), Adbusters, and Negativland have sprung up on the Internet to battle these goliaths guerrilla style. These cultural activists push the boundaries of intellectual property protection, inviting their members to engage in mass civil disobedience in order to highlight the constrictive and seemingly arbitrary nature of current intellectual property regimes and push for doctrinal change. This paper examines the various projects undertaken by these organizations and the range of tactics utilized by these Internet-based groups in their quest for "cultural dividends."[2] Specifically, this paper discusses the long-term goals and organizational styles, the use of technology to mobilize forces for large-scale international projects, and the strategies these groups employ to skirt the law and protect both themselves and their members from liability for their (often illegal) actions.

"It's More Fun to Compute": Technology and the Internet

The increasing popularity of the Internet and the resulting ease of mass communication via the use of related technologies such as email have greatly influenced the mobilization of groups that are formed in order to challenge the status quo. Historically, technological developments have often bolstered social movements by aiding in the faster and broader dissemination of information and images. Examples are as numerous and varied as the movements themselves: Johannes Gutenberg's invention of the printing press (circa 1455) marked Western culture's first viable method of spreading ideas and information from a single source to a large and far-ranging audience[3], national television networks gave force to the use of civil disobedience by Civil Rights activists during the 1950s and 60s[4]; photocopiers and desktop publishing programs fostered the development of alternative "zines"[5] and the Riot Grrrl movement in the 1980s and 90s.[6]

Better, faster, and cheaper methods of disseminating information have made more effective the mobilization efforts for, as Justice Black phrased it many years ago, "the poorly financed causes of little people."[7] Today, publicizing a cause does not even require owning a computer. For a nominal price, the neighborhood Kinko's will provide both computer access and photocopying equipment, making the design, printing, and copying of flyers a quick and simple undertaking. For students, mass dissemination of information is even easier, as university facilities allow a student to email an announcement to the entire student body for free.

Freedom of the press is no longer guaranteed "only to those who own one."[8] In many ways, the Internet functions as an equalizing force, providing even the "little guy" with a forum to speak. Whether the "little guy" is a freckle-faced thirteen-year-old posting to a listserv about hacking Windows 95 or a high-powered corporate attorney airing his grievances about lock-step compensation schemes on the Greedy Associates bulletin boards, he is given the same opportunity to communicate in these online environments. Using handles, screen names, and madeup@yahoo.com email addresses, users can easily correspond with others who are passionate about the same topics they are without ever revealing their real names.[9]

The Organizations

The Incorporated Anti-Corporate Warriors: ®™ark

Internet-based organizations such as ®™ark, in their ongoing quest for cultural dividends, have capitalized on the potential anonymity and power of mass mobilization of the Internet.[10] The use of Internet Web sites and email has helped groups like ®™ark organize almost all of their subversive activities (both offline and online) for little, if any, financial cost.[11] For example, ®™ark's Archimedes Project, hatched through a combination of threaded-message discussion board postings and anonymous international email correspondence, brought together one thousand activists in Genoa, Italy in July 2001 to protest a World Bank meeting.[12]

®™ark is an anonymous collective of media provocateurs and corporate saboteurs who have pulled some of the best-known cultural pranks of the past ten years. These include swapping the voice boxes of hundreds of talking Barbie and G.I. Joe dolls at a New York Toys 'R' Us and launching satirical "G.W. Bush" and "GATT" Web sites. On its own Web site, international projects are divided into fifteen different topics ("mutual funds"), including Biological Property, Media, Intellectual Property, Communications, and Corporate Law,[13] each providing a list of projects under that particular subject heading and identifying how much capital (both human and financial) is needed for each project.

Specific projects are given four-letter NYSE/NASDAQ style abbreviations akin to publicly traded stocks. For example, project BABY from the Corporate Law fund seeks an initial capital investment of $6,000 in order to "get a famous sportswear manufacturer (or any other giant corporation) to agree, on broadcast or other public media, to sponsor the high-quality education, health care, etc., of a U.S. baby who would otherwise not have access to same—in exchange for having the baby tattooed with the company's logo in the womb or at birth."[14] Project MP3S from the Intellectual Property fund aims to "create a web site that lets people select from a list of MP3s which MP3s they've 'stolen.' A form should allow them to write a little apology to the [Recording Industry Association of America, "RIAA"] with their name and email;

the script should then attach the selected MP3 and send it along with the apology."[15] Of course, sending hundreds of large MP3 files to the RIAA at once could flood the RIAA's email inbox and even cause their servers to crash; perhaps this sort of "email bombing"[16] is an intended side effect of project MP3S.

In order to limit the legal liability of its members, ®™ark is structured in the most decentralized and anonymous manner possible. Its members are scattered across the world, and the organization itself is funded by anonymous private donors. The entire participatory process can be as anonymous or as transparent as a member wants. Subscription to the general ®™ark email list requires only the provision of an email address. Revealing one's name, real or phony, is optional. This sense of anonymity and decentralization is all-encompassing. There is no detailed contact information available on the ®™ark Web site. The names of founders, organizers, directors, and members are not listed. There is no phone number, mailing address, or physical location mentioned anywhere. There are no headquarters. My attempts to get in touch with the "people in charge" began with emails sent to the generic admin@ and info@rtmark.com addresses. I finally received a friendly response from Ray Thomas—admin@rtmark.com—and began corresponding with him. Only after stumbling upon some newspaper articles did I realize that the Ray Thomas I was corresponding with did not really exist. Neither did "frank guerrero," my other helpful email contact. It turns out that the group's three current managing members, spokesman Ray Thomas, CFO Frank Guerrero, and legal assistant Max Kaufman—rumored to be a San Francisco lawyer, New York financial analyst, and Snuffleupagus-like man of mystery, respectively—refuse to reveal their real names and communicate almost exclusively via email. Some of the group's core members have never even met each other face to face. The identities of investors in the mutual funds and projects are also unknown.

Why the strong emphasis on anonymity? ®™ark operates under the assumption that the same legal structure and protections that allow some corporations to "maim with impunity" also protect ®™ark's clients, both the initiators/plotters of sabotage and the investors in the mutual funds that finance the actual sabotage, from punishment.[17] CFO Frank Guerrero notes, "[o]ur investors are protected by the same limited-liability status that lets officers of other corporations avoid responsibility for their companies' wrongdoing. . . . We *are* a for-profit organization—although we don't see capital as profit; our profits are cultural dividends [not money]."[18] At one point, ®™ark was registered as a Delaware S-corporation, but its current corporate status is unclear. It deregistered when it couldn't figure out how to declare "cultural profits" on corporate tax forms.[19]

It could be argued that ®™ark is simply a matchmaker or middleman, a true "broker" in the traditional sense of the word, providing a service that brings together individuals with ideas and individuals with the necessary funding to carry out those ideas. For example, a San Francisco computer programmer was paid $5,000 in anonymously donated ®™ark funds for reprogramming the SimCopter video game. Instead of rewarding the player/hero with images of scantily clad women, the screen showed boys in swimsuits kissing each other. Fifty thousand copies of the game were shipped before the hack was discovered.[20]

Ultimately, ®™ark's goal is to attack—without ever causing physical injury—in order to raise public consciousness about the wrongs that corporations are capable of getting away with every day. Ray Thomas notes, "[w]e're not corporate in our hearts, we just use the corporate structure in order to illustrate its nature: *We* can do this sometimes illegal sabotage stuff because we have corporate protections; imagine what really nasty-minded corporations are doing."[21] More broadly, ®™ark seeks to teach the public how to protest the acts of corporations and to show individuals that they possess the power to affect institutions and institutional behavior. "People know how to protest the government—there's a huge history to that, a lot written, a lot of examples—but not how to protest corporations."[22]

®™ark's Web site is currently accessed by approximately 2,300 distinct visitors per day. A few years ago, the number was closer to 1,000.[23] Although the average number of daily page requests fluctuates (in part based on press coverage about various projects), the general trend has been upward: December 2000—4,657 pages, June 2000—29,813, December 2001—6,541, and April 2002—6,481.[24] The surge in Web site traffic in June 2000 was probably a result of publicity surrounding ®™ark's inclusion in the Whitney Museum of American Art's Biennial Exhibition, which ran from March 23 through June 4, 2000.[25] ®™ark's international influence is surprisingly broad. In one randomly selected twenty-four-hour time period in April 2002, Internet users from over fifty different countries visited the Web site. Their locations ranged from Trinidad & Tobago in the Caribbean to Tuvalu in Oceania to Mauritius, an island off the coast of Southern Africa.[26] Over 3,000 members participate in the online discussion forums, and approximately 30,000 people subscribe to the main ®™ark email list.[27]

This begs the question: Could ®™ark continue to exist and function effectively without the aid of the Internet? "It would be more expensive, but it could exist," explains Thomas. He notes that, as ®™ark's primary activities are disseminating information about and seeking publicity and funding for its many projects, most of its press-release type work could be accomplished simply by using traditional media public relations tools such as envelopes, packages, press conferences, and video news releases. Still, Thomas admits that use of the Internet saves the organization a lot of time and money: "[E]mailing press releases is much easier and cheaper for us."[28]

The Marketing Parodists: Adbusters

Adbusters Media Foundation defines itself as a "global network of artists, activists, writers, pranksters, students, educators and entrepreneurs who want to advance the new social activist movement of the information age," in order to "topple existing power structures and forge a major shift in the way we will live in the 21st century."[29] It is structured as a nonprofit organization with three main activities: the publication of *Adbusters* magazine, the operation of PowerShift (an "advocacy advertising agency"), and the maintenance of adbusters.org, home of the Culture Jammers network. The Adbusters Web site states that it is designed to help visitors participate in worldwide activism, to help "turn the drab number cruncher you're staring at right now into the most versatile activist tool ever reckoned with."[30] As one Adbusters representative explained, many people erroneously assume that Adbusters' social commentary is limited to the publication of their popular magazine, but the magazine is only a starting point: "[W]e're not a magazine as much as a movement."[31]

In addition to the print magazine and Web-based cultural activist campaigns such as "Buy Nothing Day" and "TV Turnoff Week," Adbusters is well-known for its "spoof" ads, which mock the slick advertising campaigns staged by the tobacco, alcohol, fashion, and food industries. Targets of spoof ads have included Calvin Klein, The Gap,

McDonald's, and Absolut Vodka.[32] One popular series parodied Joe Camel, the fun-loving cigarette advertisement character. In the Adbusters spoof ads, he is no longer smiling, dancing, smoking, and schmoozing with attractive women. Instead, the "Joe Chemo" series shows him wheeling around an IV in a hospital corridor, sitting in a hospital bed looking sad, sick, and lonely, and finally, dead in a coffin.[33] In another campaign, a group of street jammers[34] changed a McDonald's billboard advertising the Big Mac sandwich from "[f]eeling hungry all of a sudden?" to "[f]eeling *heavy* all of a sudden?"[35] The Adbusters street jamming network also handed out bright McDonald's-red colored stickers saying "GREASE," with each of the "E"s depicting a sideways golden arch.[36]

Adbusters' international presence is impressive. An estimated 70,000 people subscribe to the Culture Jammers Headquarters email list, which provides "news releases, fresh news form the front and strategic updates" approximately twice per month. The Adbusters print magazine, which publishes six issues per year, has a total print run of 85,000 copies, including over 22,000 subscribers in over sixty countries, and solid newsstand sales.[37] Although it is admittedly difficult to measure responses to specific Internet-based projects, the Adbusters Web site averages between 7,000 and 11,000 unique visits daily and experiences far more during campaigns. For example, there were almost 20,000 hits on the last Buy Nothing Day. Like ®™ark, the online presence of Adbusters is growing, daily visits have been increasing substantially every year.[38]

Unlike the elusive ®™ark, however, Adbusters is structured with nearly complete transparency. Contact information abounds. Anyone is invited to "drop by" their headquarters in Vancouver, B.C., for a cup of coffee.[39] The street address is listed on the Web site, and there is even a worldwide toll-free 800 number. The founder regularly gives speeches around the world. Adbusters managers and staff work in the office from nine to five, Monday through Friday. The managers, founder, employees, and volunteers actually use their real names. Like for ®™ark, the Internet has been instrumental in bringing the Adbusters network of activists together. Adbusters founder Kalle Lasn echoes ®™ark's communications concerns:

> [The Internet has] been the key fact. We communicated as best we could for many years without the Internet. We had 300 organizers around the

> world for Buy Nothing Day. We had to send them expensive packages through the mail. And . . . as soon as we went on the Internet, things really took off for us on many of our campaigns. And the 300 or 400 people we used to deal with . . . it's grown to 35,000, and we are now a different kind of organization. And we are global.[40]

As for their attitudes toward current intellectual property laws, Adbusters thinks that they "are not merely too restrictive, they shouldn't exist."[41]

Civil Disobedience/Hacktivism

While the founders of ®™ark are content with feeding the corporate system's dissociative effects back on itself (and perhaps eliciting a few laughs and widespread publicity in the meantime), Adbusters founder Kalle Lasn wants to "dismantle the corporate system altogether."[42] Both organizations strongly support the use of "semiological guerrilla warfare"[43] and modern-day civil disobedience to achieve their anti-corporate power ends.

The term "civil disobedience" was originally coined by American philosopher Henry David Thoreau in reference to his refusal to pay a state poll tax enacted to finance enforcement of the fugitive slave law. It can be defined as unlawful public conduct designed to appeal to the sense of justice of the majority in order to change the law without rejecting the rule of law. Nonviolence and nonrevolutionary intent, as well as a willingness to accept lawful punishment, are often treated as defining conditions of civil disobedience.[44]

Electronic Civil Disobedience

The Internet has made "electronic" forms of civil disobedience and "hacktivism" possible:

> Acting in the tradition of non-violent direct action and civil disobedience, proponents of Electronic Civil Disobedience ["ECD"] are borrowing the tactics of trespass and blockade from these earlier social movements and are applying them to the Internet. A typical civil disobedience tactic has been for a group of people to physically blockade, with their bodies, the entranceways of an opponent's office or building or to physically occupy an opponent's office—to have a sit-in. Electronic Civil

> Disobedience . . . utilizes virtual blockades and virtual sit-ins . . . an ECD actor can participate in virtual blockades and sit-ins from home, from work, from the university, or from other points of access to the Net. Further, the ECD actor can act against an opponent that is hundreds [or] thousands of miles away.[45]

One popular form of electronic civil disobedience is accomplished through denial-of-service ("DoS") attacks, also referred to as virtual or electronic sit-ins. These attacks flood web servers or networks with false requests for information, which result in overwhelming the system, preventing legitimate network traffic, and ultimately crashing the server.[46] The effects are similar to what would happen if hundreds of people kept repeatedly dialing the same phone number to keep the line busy. An effective DoS attack is relatively simple to organize, requiring only the coordinated effort of a group of individuals simultaneously reloading a specific Web site repeatedly. For Web-based cultural activists, however, the appeal of such attacks is not only the slowing (and sometimes complete crippling) of targeted Web sites, but also the high-profile publicity that will inevitably result from DoS attacks on popular Web sites such as CNN, eBay, and Yahoo![47] There is also a David-versus-Goliath type enthusiasm surrounding these attacks, since they allow a few "little guys" sitting at their computers to disable the Web sites of the largest corporations and most important government agencies.

Recent technology has made denial-of-service attacks even easier to accomplish; for example, with funding and support from ®™ark, the Electronic Disturbance Theater developed software called FloodNet, a Java applet that automatically reloads a Web site every few seconds.[48] This is a valuable time-saving device because it eliminates the need to manually keep reloading the Web site.[49] The software also allows protesters to leave personal statements on the targeted servers' error logs. For example, instructing the browser to load a file called "human_rights," when such a file does not exist on the target server, will return and log the message, "human_rights not found on this server."[50]

Another form of electronic civil disobedience occurs when people spread (or encourage spreading) programs that are arguably illegal in the first place. An example of this type of electronic civil disobedience is what happened with the DeCSS DVD-decryption program. CSS, or "Content Scrambling System," is the main type of encryption used to prevent the copying of DVDs. DeCSS is an illegal program that allows the copying and reading of DVDs that are encrypted with CSS. After Universal Studios and the MPAA obtained an injunction prohibiting 2600.com from posting copies of the DeCSS decryption program on its Web site, both 2600.com's magazine and Web site provided the addresses of hundreds of other Web sites around the world that had DeCSS available for download.[51] After another legal injunction forced those Web sites to stop sharing the program, a number of programmers stepped up to continue the battle. One programmer decided, "If I couldn't distribute [the decryption program] DeCSS. . . . I could distribute *another* piece of software called DeCSS that is perfectly legal in every way, and would be difficult for even the . . . lawyers to find fault with." And he did. He wrote a different—and completely legal—program called DeCSS, a program having nothing to do with breaking DVD encryption, and asked website operators to link to it in order to provide "a convenient layer of fog over the *other* DeCSS."[52] A different Web site with the aim of highlighting the "absurdity" of the judge's reasoning behind granting the injunctions—that source code can be legally differentiated from other forms of written expression—featured creative ways of getting around the injunction. Projects ranged from having the program embedded in the code of a portrait to printing the source code on a necktie and describing the descrambling algorithm in a humorous haiku format.[53]

Cultural Activism or Commercial Terrorism?

Some legal commentators are not amused. In fact, a group of attorneys recently proposed a new federal criminal statute addressing the "solicitation of commercial terrorism" through the Internet, arguing that "in its present infant stage," the Internet resembles the lawless "Wild West" and needs far more regulation.[54] The author's definition of "commercial terrorist" specifically includes "inflammatory" organizations such as ®™ark, who "not only provide a blueprint for readers to perform acts of sabotage and destruction, but also actively encourage such acts."[55] They argue that since the operators of these types of websites currently have little reason to fear prosecution, new criminal laws are needed to specifically address the "type of destruction caused by Internet terrorism."[56] The proposed statute requires jail time for the solicitation of a felony through the Internet or other online means. In an attempt to cover the bulk of the activities organized by online activist (or, in the drafters' words, "terrorist") groups, the proposed statute's definition of felony was drafted to include false advertising, solicitation of theft, and computer sabotage. For example, altering billboards is false advertising, and coordinating a virtual sit-in constitutes computer sabotage.

Conclusion

Most online copyright and trademark disputes fizzle out quickly, with Web site owners taking down the potentially infringing material and corporate attorneys smugly chalking up another victory for their clients. Some might argue that the "bullying back" victories of groups such as Adbusters, Negativland, and ®™ark are few and far between, occasional heroic (and folkloric) battles won by the Davids of the online world. Others might view this sort of collective action by "virtual communities"[58] as the only force that is effectively pushing back against the chilling effects of those who seek overbroad intellectual property protection.

If the "problems" with current intellectual property doctrines—and their enforcement—are defined as the arbitrariness of courts in handling intellectual property issues, the lack of adequate protection for fair use and parody, and the chilling effects of litigation threats via cease-and-desist letters, there are a variety of possible solutions. There is often a push in legal academic writing for "*the* solution". I strongly believe that any attempt to provide such a solution would be not only pretentious but also rather arbitrary. Instead, I offer this paper as a necessary *part* of any solution: increased awareness of the problem and an exploration of what is currently being done about it.

Perhaps a broader solution is best framed as a *bricolage,* a collage constructed from the various materials at hand. Such a solution would include the work of the Chilling Effects Clearinghouse, which aims to inform recipients of cease-and-desist letters about their legal rights and protections. It would include the work of copyright-aware musicians such as Negativland, who provide detailed information about intellectual property laws and resources on their website and speak regularly about these topics. It would include all the online activist individuals and groups, such as Detritus.net and those who put up DeCSS and Napier's Distorted Barbies mirror websites, who continue to embrace the battles of the "little guys" via electronic civil disobedience. It would include scholars and law professors such as James Boyle, who has proposed that courts and scholars should look more critically at the consistency of intellectual property rules with the First Amendment in the future, and Jessica Litman, who has suggested that copyright laws should be "sufficiently intuitive to appeal to school children."[59] It would include continued pranks, spoofs, civil disobedience, and culture jamming by Adbusters, ®™ark, and the Billboard Liberation Front.

A solution would also include hoping that the present and future intellectual property lawyers reading this—yes, you, the ones who represent Disney and Mattel and Blockbuster and Microsoft, the ones that I and my law school classmates have recently joined—are a bit more aware of these challenges and battles, a bit more appreciative of the importance of parody, artistic reworking, and social commentary in shaping a diverse and creative culture, and a bit more concerned with balancing zealous client advocacy with respect for creativity and free speech.

Notes

1. [cc] This paper is counter-copyrighted, which means that readers may freely use and build upon it, adding whatever links, modifications and commentary they wish directly to the original document. See http://cyber.law.harvard.edu/cc/cc.html for details about the counter-copyright campaign.
2. Ray Thomas from ®™ark explains cultural dividends as: "Projects can be seen as stocks, and when you support a project you're investing in it. When you contribute, say, $100 to a project that you would like to see accomplished, you are sort of investing in the accomplishment of the project. What you want to see out of that project is cultural dividends; you want to see a beneficial cultural event take place because of your money, as a reward. What you're doing is you're investing in the improvement of the culture; that's why we've modeled it after the financial sector because really these words like 'profit,' and 'investment,' and 'dividends,' and so on, they've really contaminated the language and we want to reclaim those words and use the power in those words. And so we talk about cultural dividends; we talk about for-profit companies are really . . . RTMark is a for-profit company, we're for cultural profit," at http://www.abc.net.au/arts/headspace/tn/bbing/trouble/b.htm.
3. *Jones Telecomm. & Multimedia Encyclopedia,* at http://www.digitalcentury.com/encyclo/update/print.html
4. *See* American Studies Today Online, "Civil Rights and Black Raditalism," at http://www.americansc.org.uk/Conferences/Civil_Rights.htm (Oct. 31, 2001).

5. Mark Frauenfelder, "Cheap Memes: Zines, Metazines & the Virtual Press," *The Zine & E-zine Resource Guide* at http://www.zinebook.com/resource/memes.html (last visited June 12, 2003).
6. *See* Seth F. Kreimer, "Technologies of Protest: Insurgent Social Movements and the First Amendment in the Era of the Internet," 150 *U. Pa.L. REV.* 119, 120 (2001).
7. *Martin v. Struthers,* 319 U.S. 141, 146 (1943).
8. Kreimer, *supra* note 6, at 121–22. (commenting upon A.J. Liebling's observation before the advent of the Internet that "freedom of the press is only guaranteed to those who own one.").
9. A major area of debate that I will not be addressing in this paper is the so-called "digital divide" problem. As the Digital Divide Network notes:

> We use the term "digital divide" to refer to [the] gap between those [people and communities] who can effectively use new information and communication tools, such as the Internet, and those who cannot. While a consensus does not exist on the extent of the divide (and whether the divide is growing or narrowing), researchers are nearly unanimous in acknowledging that some sort of divide exists at this point in time.

Digital Divide Network, "Digital Divide Basics," at http://www.digitaldividenetwork.org/content/sections/index.cfm?key=2 (last visited June 12, 2003). The "Open Economies" project sponsored by the Berkman Center for Internet & Society is currently working on finding solutions to the digital divide problem. *See Open Economies,* at http://cyber.law.harvard.edu/openeconomies (last visited June 12, 2003).

10. Andy Dworkin, " 'Mutual Fund,' Skewers Big Business," *Dallas Morning News,* May 30, 1999, at 1H, available at http://www.rtmark.com/more/articles/dallas1990530.htm.
11. Of course, ®™ark is not the only organization that takes advantage of Internet resources for organizing and publicizing these types of protest activities. *See, e.g.,* Rene Sanchez & William Booth, "Protest Movement Loses Its Steam in Heat of L.A." *Wash. Post,* Aug. 20, 2000, at A3 (discussing demonstrations that were organized by "small leaderless groups on shoestring budgets, spreading the word of their causes largely through the Internet.").
12. *RTMark: Archimedes Project,* at http://www.rtmark.com/archimedes.html (last visited June 12, 2003).
13. *RTMark: The Mutual Funds,* at http://www.rtmark.com/funds.html (last visited June 12, 2003).
14. *RTMark: The Corporate Law Fund,* at http://www.rtmark.com/fundcorp.html (last visited June 12, 2003). In July 2001, a New York couple put up for auction (on eBay and Yahoo!) the naming rights to their newborn son, hoping that a corporation would bid at least $500,000 for the advertising opportunity of a lifetime. *See* Paul Eng, *Bidding on a Boy's Name Couple Seeks Corporate Sponsor for Their Baby Boy,* (July 26, 2001) at http://abcnews.go.com/sections/scitech/DailyNews/babynameaue010726.html.

15. *RTMark: The Intellectual Property Fund,* at http://www.rtmark.com/fundintel.html (last visited June 12, 2003).
16. Mailbomb means "[t]o send, or urge others to send, massive amounts of email to a single system or person, [especially] with intent to crash or spam the recipient's system." *See* DICTIONARY.COM, at http://www.dictionary.com/search?q=mailbomb (last visited June 12, 2003).
17. Doug Harvey, "Tactical Embarrassment: The Subversive Cyber Actions of RTMark," *LA Weekly,* Mar. 24–30, 2000, 16.5(a) available at http://www.laweekly.com/ink/00/18/art-harvey.shtml.
18. Ethan Smith, "Mischief Executives," *New York* magazine, Sept. 6, 1999, http://rtmark.com/more/articles/newyorkmag19990906.html.
19. Dworkin, *supra* note 10, at 1H.
20. *See* Steve Silberman, "Boy 'Bimbos' Too Much for Game Maker" *Wired,* Dec. 3, 1996, http://www.wired.com/news/culture/0,1284,775,00.html.
21. Glen Helfand, Q&A with RTMark, SFGATE.COM, June 12, 2001, at http://www.sfgate.com/cgi-bin/article.cgi?f=/gate/archive/2 001/06/12/rtmark.DTL.
22. Ellen Barry, "The Dilbert Front," *Boston Phoenix,* Jan. 22–29, 1998, at http://www.bostonphoenix.com/archive/features/98/01/22/ARTMARK.html.
23. Email from Ray Thomas, Spokesman, ®™ark (Apr. 5, 2002) (on file with author).
24. These numbers indicate traffic during random twenty-four hour snippets. All statistics are from *Web Server Statistics for rtmark.com* (on file with author); *see also* email from Ray Thomas, spokesman, ®™ark (Apr. 5, 2002) (on file with author).
25. ®™ark actually caused quite a stir when, without notifying the Whitney Museum, it altered its Web site (chosen to appear as an example of Internet art in the Whitney's prestigious Biennial Exhibition) so that museum visitors who tried to view it at exhibition kiosks instead found a series of rotating Internet pages submitted by the public, ranging from pornography to a mirror of the Whitney museum's own homepage. ®™ark also auctioned its tickets to the Whitney Biennial's opening reception (which was supposed to be only for patrons, curators, and artists) on eBay, with the proceeds going to finance more projects. As Ray Thomas noted, "[w]e actually didn't want to go. . . . We might be able to make some money schmoozing people at an art reception, but people in that context aren't used to being asked for cash to finance sabotage." In fact, the winning bidder gave the tickets away to the next highest bidders for free and specifically requested that the money be used by ®™ark for project BABY, which is mentioned earlier in this paper. *See* Harvey, *supra* note 17, http://www.laweekly.com/ink/00/18/art-harvey.shtml.
26. *Web Server Statistics for rtmark.com: Domain Report* 5–6 (on file with author).
27. Email from Ray Thomas, spokesman, ®™ark (Apr. 5, 2002) (on file with author).
28. Helfand, *supra* note 21, *at* http://www.sfgate.com/cgi-bin/article.cgi?f=/gate/archive/2001/06/12/rtmark.DTL.

29. Adbusters Media Foundation, at http://adbusters.org/information/foundation (last visited June 12, 2003).
30. *Id.*
31. Telephone interview with Jules Killam, Computer Consultant, Adbusters (Apr. 4, 2002).
32. Adbusters: Spoof Ads, at http://adbusters.org/spoofads/ (last visited June 12, 2003).
33. Adbusters: Spoof Ads—Tobacco, at http://adbusters.org/spoofads/tobacco/ (last visited June 12, 2003). "Joe Chemo" first appeared in the Adbusters print magazine in 1996. *See* http://www.joechemo.org/about.htm.
34. The term "street jamming" is an offshoot of "culture jamming," which has been defined as: "media hacking, information warfare, terror-art, and guerrilla semiotics, all in one." The term "cultural jamming" was first used by the musical collage group Negativland to describe billboard alteration and other forms of media sabotage. *See* Mark Levy, *Culture Jamming: Hacking, Slashing, and Sniping in the Empire of Signs,* at http://www.levity.com/markdery/culturjam.html (last visited June 12, 2003).
35. Adbusters: Jammer's Gallery, at http://adbusters.org/creativeresistance/jamgallery/street/ (last visited June 16, 2003). This sort of guerilla billboard commentary is reminiscent of the San Francisco–based Billboard Liberation Front ("BLF"), which credits itself with "26 years of outdoor advertising improvement." Billboard Liberation Front, at http://www.billboardliberation.com/home.html (last visited June 16, 2003). Like ®™ark, the BLF operates under a veil of secrecy. Founder Jack Napier (another pseudonym) is rumored to have a day job in advertising.
36. Donella H. Meadows, *The Global Citizen: Kalle Lasn Is Mad as Heck,* AlterNet.org, Mar. 15, 2000, at http://www.alternet.org/story.html?StoryID=9147.
37. http://adbusters.org/information/foundation; *see also* email from Brant Cheetham, Office/Production Manager, Adbusters Apr. 4, 2002 (on file with author).
38. Email from Brant Cheetham, Office/Production Manager, Adbusters (Apr. 4, 2002) (on file with author).
39. Adbusters: Information—How to Contact Us, at http://adbusters.org/information/contact/ (last visited June 16, 2003).
40. *Grant Rosenberg Interviews the Founder of* Adbusters, Gadfly Online at http://www.gadflyonline.com/lastweek/kale%20lasn.html (last visited June 16, 2003).
41. Email from Paul Dechene, Campaigns Manager, Adbusters (Feb. 13, 2002) (on file with author).
42. Alex Burns, "RTMark: No Deconstruction Necessary," *Disinformation,* May 30, 2001, http://www.disinfo.com/pages/dossier/id561/pg1/.
43. This phrase was used to explain the communication revolution envisioned by Umberto Eco in 1967. Eco urged the receiver of the message (i.e., the audience) to embrace the freedom to interpret the meaning on the message in a completely different way than what the sender of the message originally intended. *See* UMBERTO ECO, "Towards a Semiological Guerrilla Warfare," in TRAVELS IN HYPERREALITY (1986), http://www.newstrolls.com/news/dev/downes/column052799-7.htm.
44. *Oxford Companion to Philosophy* 136 (Ted Honderich ed. 1995).

45. Stefan Fray, "The Electronic Disturbance Theater and Electronic Civil Disobedience," *The Thing,* June 17, 1998, at http://www.thing.net/~rdom/ecd/EDTECD.html.
46. CNET News.com "How a Denial of Service Attack Works" (Feb. 9, 2000), at http://news.com.com/2100-1017-236728.html?legacy=cnet.
47. CNN.com, "Cyber-attacks Batter Web Heavyweights," (Feb. 9, 2000), at http://www.cnn.com/2000/TECH/computing/02/09/cyber.attacks.01/index.html.
48. RTMark Press Release: *Floodnet,* at http://www.rtmark.com/zapfloodpr.html (Sept. 9, 2000). The Electronic Disturbance Theater first used FloodNet in a series of DoS attacks against the U.S. Department of Defense, the Frankfurt Stock Exchange, and Mexican President Ernesto Zedillo to gain publicity for their support of the Zapatista rebels fighting against the Mexican government in Chiapas. *See* Wired News, "Pentagon Deflects Web Assault," (Sept. 10, 1999), at http://www.wired.com/news/politics/0,1283,14931,00.html.
49. *See* Brett Stalbaum, "The Zapatista Tactical Floodnet," at http://www.thing.net/~rdom/ecd/ZapTact.html.
50. Dorothy E. Denning, *Activism, Hacktivism, and Cyberterrorism: The Internet as a Tool for Influencing Foreign Policy, available at* http://www.nautilus.org/info-policy/workshop/papers/denning.html (last visited June 16, 2003).
51. Due to a later legal injunction against linking to any websites that provided DeCSS, 2600.com now lists hundreds of websites that *used* to have the DeCSS program available for download. *See* 2600 News (Dec. 1999) at http://www.2600.com/news/1227-help.html.
52. Mr. Bad, "Pigdog Journal DeCSS Distribution Center," *Pigdog Journal,* Feb. 16, 2000, at http://www.pigdog.org/decss/.
53. Gallery of CSS Dascramblers, at http://www-2.cs.cmu.edu/~dst/DeCSS/Gallery/ (last visited June 16, 2003).
54. See Bruce Braun et al., Model Statute: www.commercial_terrorism.com: "A Proposed Federal Criminal Statute Addressing the Solicitation of Commercial Terrorism through the Internet," 37 *Harvard Journal on Legislature* 159, 160 (2000). The accuracy of the authors' initial assertion—that the Internet was still in its "infant stage" in the year 2000—is questionable. I would argue that the Internet's "infant stage" was actually in the early 1990s. The following chart shows the exponential growth in the number of host computers on the Internet since August 1981:

Date	Hosts
08/81	213
08/83	562
10/85	1,961
12/87	28,174
10/89	159,000
10/90	313,000
10/91	617,000

10/92	1,136,000
07/93	1,776,000

55. Bruce Braun et al., supra note 54, at 160–61.
56. *Id.*
57. *Id.* at 172.
58. Rosemary J. Coombe & Andrew Herman, "Trademarks, Property, and Propriety: The Moral Economy of Consumer Politics and Corporate Accountability on the World Wide Web," 50 *De Paul Law Review* 597, 614 (2000).
59. James Boyle, "The First Amendment and Cyberspace: The Clinton Years," 63 *Law & Contemp. Probs,* 337, 350 (2000); Jessica Litman, "Copyright in the Twenty-First Century: The Exclusive Right to Read," *13 Cardozo arts & Ent. l.j.* 29, 53 (1994).

14

THE METAPHYSICS OF NETWORKS[1]

Alexander Galloway and Eugene Thacker

Freedom of expression is no longer relevant, freedom of use has taken its place. Consider two categories: the computer user and the computer programmer. One designates the mass of computer society, while the other a clan of technical specialists. Or not? The user and the programmer are also two rubrics for understanding one's relationship to technology. User is a modern synonym for "consumer." Conversely, programmer is a synonym for "producer." Thus, "user" is a term for any passive experience with technology, while "programmer" means any active experience with technology. Taken in this sense, anyone can be a programmer if she so chooses. If a person installs a game console modchip, he is programming his console. If she grows her own food, she is programming her biological intake.

The unfortunate fallout of this is that most legal prohibitions today are migrating away from prohibitions on being (the "user" model) toward prohibitions on doing (the "programmer"). There are more and more threats to programmers everyday: digital rights management agreements prohibit specific uses of one's purchased property (such as sharing files), while sampling music has become a criminal act, to name just two. The future politics of expression will turn on freedoms-of-use, rather than the antiquated category of freedom of expression.

For the last decade, network discourse has proliferated with epidemic speed and intensity: Consider peer-to-peer file-sharing networks, wireless community networks, terrorist networks, contagion networks of biowarfare agents, political swarming and mass demonstration, economic and finance networks, massively multiplayer online role-playing games, Personal Area Networks, grid computing, "generation txt," and on and on.

Often the discourse surrounding networks tends to be aimed, both morally and architecturally, against what its participants see as retrograde structures such as hierarchy and verticality and the concomitant techniques for keeping things under control: bureaucracy, the chain of command, and so on. The concept of the network has infected, however, broad swaths of contemporary life beyond the fields of technology and philosophy. Even the U.S. military, a bastion of vertical, pyramidal hierarchy, is redefining its internal structure around network architectures. RAND researchers John Arquilla and David Ronfeldt have suggested that the military concept of "netwar" is defined in topological terms: "Hierarchies have a difficult time fighting networks. [. . .] It takes networks to fight networks. [. . .] Whoever masters the network form first and best will gain major advantages."[2] In short, the current global crisis is an asymmetrical crisis between centralized, hierarchical powers and distributed, horizontal networks.[3]

Today's conventional wisdom cajoles us into thinking that everything can be subsumed under the warm security blanket of interconnectivity. However, it hasn't yet told us quite what this means, nor how one might draft a critique of networks. This "network fever"[4] is characterized by a delirious tendency, a general willingness to ignore politics by masking it inside the so-called black box of technology. What is needed, then, is a political analysis of networks at the micro-technical level of nonhuman, machinic practices. To this end, we suggest *protocol* as the principle of political control most helpful for thinking about technological networks.

Protocol is a concept derived from computer science, which also resonates in the life sciences. It describes the action within a network, which can be deliberately guided by human actors or accidentally affected by nonhuman actors (a computer virus or emerging infectious disease, for example). As we shall see, protocological control brings into existence a certain contradiction, at once distributing agencies in a complex manner, while at the same time concentrating rigid forms of management and control. Often an intentionally or unintentionally misused protocol reveals the political fissures in a network. We suggest that such instances, while often politically ambiguous when taken out of context, can also serve as the basis of a more critical, more politically engaged "counter-protocol" practice.

The Politics of Algorithmic Culture

What is the principle of political organization or control that stitches a network together? Writers including Michael Hardt and Antonio Negri have helped answer this question in the socio-political sphere using the concept of "empire." Like a network, empire is neither reducible to any single state power nor does it organize itself as an architecture of pyramidal hierarchy. Empire is fluid, flexible, dynamic, and far-reaching. In this sense, the concept of empire helps us think about political organization within networks. We are concerned, though, that no one has yet adequately answered this question for the technological sphere of bits and atoms.

"Protocol" abounds in techno-culture. It is a totalizing control apparatus that guides both the technical and political formation of computer networks, biological systems, and other media. Put simply, protocols are all the conventional rules and standards that govern relationships within networks. Quite often these relationships come in the form of communication between two or more computers, but "relationships within networks" can also refer to purely biological processes as in the systemic phenomenon of gene expression. Thus by "networks" we want to refer to any system of interrelationality, whether biological or informatic, organic or inorganic, technical or natural—with the ultimate goal of undoing the polar restrictiveness of these pairings.

Research in molecular biotechnology frequently makes use of protocol to interpret biological life as a network phenomenon, be it as gene expression networks, metabolic networks, or the circuitry of cell signaling pathways. In such instances, the biological and the informatic become increasingly enmeshed in hybrid systems that are more than biological: Proprietary genome databases, DNA chips for medical diagnostics, and real-time detection systems for biowarfare agents. Protocol is twofold; it is both an apparatus that facilitates networks and also a logic that governs how things are done within the apparatus.

From the lengthy technological discourse documented in white papers, memos, and manuals, we can identify some of the basic qualities of the organizational apparatus of we call *protocol:*

- protocol facilitates relationships between interconnected, but autonomous, entities;

- protocol's virtues include robustness, contingency, interoperability, flexibility, and heterogeneity;
- a goal of protocol is to accommodate everything, no matter what source or destination, no matter what originary definition or identity;
- while protocol is universal, it is always achieved through negotiation (meaning that in the future protocol can and will be different);
- protocol is a system for maintaining organization and control in networks.

"Networks are the emerging form of organization of our time," Geert Lovink and Florian Schneider note, and go on to observe that due to this emerging form of organization, "networking has lost its mysterious and subversive character."[5] We agree wholeheartedly.

Yet they also note that, despite being the site of control and organization, networks are also the very medium of freedom, if only a provisional or piecemeal liberation. They write that networking is able "to free the user from the bonds of locality and identity," and later they describe networking as "a syncope of power."[6]

In this sense, Lovink and Schneider posit *power* as the opposite of *networking,* as the force that restricts networking and thus restricts individual freedom:

> Power responds to the pressure of increasing mobility and communications of the multitudes with attempts to regulate them in the framework of traditional regimes that cannot be abandoned, but need to be reconfigured from scratch and recompiled against the networking paradigm: borders and property, labour and recreation, education and entertainment industries undergo radical transformations.[7]

Our point of departure is this: Lovink and Schneider's "Info-Empire" should not be defined in terms of either corporate or state power, what they call "the corruption of state sovereignty." Instead it must be defined at the level of the medium itself. (Otherwise we are no longer talking about Info-Empire but about more familiar topics including corporate greed or incipient fascism.) Informatic control is different. It must be defined in connection with the actual technologies of control that are contained within networks, not the content carried by those networks, or the intentionality of those using them.

Networks are often seen as advantageous during political struggles. There is presumed to be something about the structure of networks that enables forms of resistance to emerge in the face of more centralized power structures. The characteristics of multiple sites of locality, many-to-many communications channels, and a self-organizing capacity (local actions, global results) are cited as part of the network structure. Indeed, analyses of computer virus attacks, distributed political protests, and other forms of so-called "netwar" invariably mention these aspects of networks.

But we find it curious that networks in this characterization are rarely contextualized—or rendered historical or archaeological. On the one hand, the centralized structure of empire is assumed to emerge out of a long history of economically driven imperialism and colonialism. On the other hand, the various "networks" which resist empire seem to suddenly appear out of nowhere, despite the fact that the technologies, which constitute these networks, are themselves rooted in governmental, military, and commercial developments. We need only remind ourselves of the military backdrop of World War II–era mainframe computing and the Cold War context of ARPAnet to realize that networks are not ahistorical entities, but given meaning by surrounding complex interactions among institutions, businesses, "subjected" individuals, and social groups.

Thus, in many current political discussions, networks are seen as the new paradigm of social and political organization. The reason is that networks exhibit a set of properties that distinguishes them from more centralized power structures. Those properties are often taken to be merely abstract and formal; the network itself is characterized as a kind of meta-structure. We see this in "pop science" books discussing complexity and network science, as well as in the political discourse of netwars and so forth. What we end up with is a *metaphysics of networks.* The network appears as a universal signifier of political resistance, whether in Chiapas, Seattle, Geneva, or online. We question not the concept of the network—a number of network examples, such as that of Indymedia, the Zapatistas, or the "Battle of Seattle," unquestionably demonstrate their effectiveness as modes of political struggle. What we question is the obsessive focus on the metaphysics of the network, as if this ahistorical concept is self-legitimizing.

A politically engaged understanding of networks will not only pay attention to networks in general, but to networks specifically. Networks can be engaged with at the general level, but they always need to be qualified—and we mean this in technical as well as socio-political terms.

Biological or computational, the network is always configured by its protocols. We stress this integrative approach again because we cannot afford naively to view "information" as solely immaterial. Negri notes that "all politics is biopolitics," and to this, we would add that all networks are not only biopolitical but biotechnical as well. Protocological control in networks is as much about networks as *living networks* as it is about the materiality of informatics.

How then to understand political change within networks? What follows might be thought of as a series of challenges for "counterprotocological practice," designed for anyone seeking progressive change inside of biotechnical networks.

First, oppositional practices will have to focus not on a static map of one-to-one relationships, but a dynamic diagram of many-to-many relationships. This is a nearly insurmountable task. These practices must also avoid the dangerous mistake of regarding many-to-many as synonymous with total or universal. There will be no universals for life. This means that *the counterprotocols of current networks will be pliant and vigorous* where existing protocols are flexible and robust. Instead of being predominantly concerned with managing or delimiting a network, counterprotocols will be concerned with the generative, productive capacity of networks, the ways that networks always open onto other networks—the way that "networking" is a process of opening. Counterprotocols will attend to the tensions and contradictions within such systems, such as the contradiction between rigid control implicit in network protocols and the liberal ideologies that underpin them. Counterprotocological practice will not avoid downtime. It will restart often.

The second point concerns tactics. In reality, counterprotocological practice is not "counter-" anything! The idea that politics is an act of "resistance" was never true, except in the most literal interpretation of conservatism. We must search-and-replace all occurrences of "resistance" with "impulsion" or perhaps "thrust." Thus *the concept of resistance in politics should be superceded by the concept of hypertrophy.* Resistance is a Clausewitzian mentality; the strategy of maneuvers teaches us instead that the best way to beat an enemy is to become a better enemy. One must push through to the other side, rather than drag one's heels. There are two directions for political change: resistance implies a desire for stasis or retrograde motion, but hypertrophy is the desire for pushing beyond. The goal is not to destroy technology in some neoluddite delusion, but to push technology into a hypertrophic state, further than it is meant to go. We must scale up, not unplug. Then, during the passage of technology into this injured, engorged, and unguarded condition, it will be transformed into something better, something in closer agreement with the real desires of its users.

The third point has to do with structure. Because networks are (technically) predicated on creating possible communications between nodes, *oppositional practices will have to focus less on the characteristics of the nodes, and more on the quality of the interactions between nodes.* In this sense the node-edge distinction will break down. Nodes will be constructed as a byproduct of the creation of edges, and edges will be a precondition for the inclusion of nodes in the network. Conveyances are key. The basic node-edge distinction will have to be considered as a dynamic, temporal phenomenon: a given node—be it a Web site or a person with a mobile phone—may be a key "connector" from one subnetwork to another (the "weak ties"). From the oppositional perspective, nodes are nothing but dilated or relaxed edges, while edges are constricted, hyperkinetic nodes. Nodes may be composed of clustering edges, while edges may be extended nodes: dense information traffic may be considered a "node," while a Web site or mobile phone whose main function is to be a "connector" can be considered an "edge." Action and reaction would be the main unit of analysis, not whether something is a server or a cable.

Using various protocols as their operational standards, networks tend to combine large masses of different elements under a single umbrella. The fourth point we offer, then, deals with motion: *Counterprotocol practices can capitalize on the homogeneity found in networks to resonate far and wide with little effort.* Again, the point is not to do away with standards or the process of standardization, for there is no imaginary zone of nonstandardization, no zero-place where there is a ghostly, pure flow of only edges. Protocological control works through inherent tensions, and as such, counterprotocol practices can be understood as tactical implementations and intensifications of protocological control.

Rhetorics of Freedom

As a political program, open source software—that is, software programs whose code is available free to anybody—is ultimately flawed. (It is tactically valuable in the fight against proprietary software, however.) Open source focuses on computer code in isolation. It fetishizes all the wrong things: language, originality, source, the past, stasis. To focus on inert code in isolation is to ignore code in its context, in its social relation, or actual dynamic relations with other code and other machines. Debugging never happens by reading the source code, but only by running the program. *Open runtime* might be a better term than open source: it would prize all of open source's opposites: open articulation, open iterability, open practice, open becoming.

However, the notion of open runtime may also mislead, given its basis in rhetoric of the relative openness and closure of technological systems. This rhetoric operates as follows: technological systems can either be closed or open. Closed systems are generally created by either commercial interests or the state—courts regulate technology, companies control their proprietary technologies in the marketplace, and so on.

Open systems, on the other hand, are generally associated with the public interest and with freedom and political transparency. Geert Lovink contrasts "closed systems based on profit through control and scarcity" with "open, innovative standards situated in the public domain."[8] Later, in his elucidation of Manuel Castells, Lovink writes of the opposite, a "freedom hardwired into code."[9] This gets to the heart of this problematic rhetoric. (Lessig and many others rely heavily on this rhetoric of freedom.) If it's hardwired can it still be freedom? Instead of guaranteeing freedom, the act of "hardwiring" suggests limiting it. And in fact this is precisely the case with the Internet, where strict universal standards of communication have been rolled out more widely and more quickly than in any other medium in history.

This opposition between closed and open is deeply flawed. It unwittingly perpetuates one of today's most insidious political myths, that the state and capital are the two sole instigators of control. *Instead of the open/closed opposition we suggest the pairing physical/social.* The so-called open logics of control, those associated with (nonproprietary) computer code or with the Internet protocols, operate primarily using a physical model of control. For example, protocols interact with each other by physically altering and amending lower protocological objects (IP prefixes its header onto a TCP data object, which prefixes its header onto an HTTP object, and so on). On the other hand, the so-called closed logics of state and commercial control operate primarily using a social model of control. For, example, Microsoft's commercial prowess is renewed via the social activity of market exchange. Or, using another example, Digital Rights Management licenses establish a social relationship between producers and consumers, a social relationship backed up by specific legal realities (DMCA).

Viewed in this way, we find it self evident that physical control (such as protocol) is as powerful as social control, if not more powerful. We hope to show that if the issue is control, then the descriptors "open" and "closed" further confuse matters. Instead we would like to speak in terms of alternatives to control, whereby the controlling logic of both "open" and "closed" systems is made transparent, brought out into the light of day.

Notes

1. This article was adapted from Part Two of the series of panel discussions, "Censorship in Camouflage," held at the New School University, in New York, in June 2002.
2. John Arquilla and David Ronfeldt, *Networks and Netwars: The Future of Terror, Crime, and Militancy* (Santa Monica, CA: RAND, 2001), 15; emphasis removed from original.
3. There are several sides to the debate. The technophilic perspectives, such as those expressed by Howard Rheingold or Kevin Kelly, are expressions of both a technological determinism and a view of technology as an enabling tool for the elevation of bourgeois humanism in a general sense. The juridical/governance perspective, seen in the work of Lawrence Lessig, Yochai Benkler, and others, posits a similar situation whereby networks will bring about a more just and freer social reality via legal safeguards. The network science perspective, expressed in popular books by Mark Buchanan and Albert-László Barabási, portrays networks as a kind of apolitical natural law, operating universally across heterogeneous systems, be they terrorism, AIDS, or the Internet. And, further, this dichotomy (between networks as political and networks as technical) is equally evident in a variety of other media, including news reportage, defense and military research, and the IT industry.
4. See Mark Wigley's recent essay of the same name in *Grey Room* 4 (summer 2001): 80–122.

5. Geert Lovink and Florian Schneider, "Notes on the State of Networking," *nettime,* Feb 29, 2004.
6. Ibid.
7. Ibid.
8. Geert Lovink, *My First Recession* (Rotterdam: V2, 2003), p. 14.
9. Ibid., p. 47.

15

POWER, POLITICS, NEW TECHNOLOGY, AND MEMORY IN THE AGE OF THE INTERNET

Antoni Muntadas in conversation with Svetlana Mintcheva

In 1994 Antoni Muntadas, a Spanish artist based in New York, initiated *The File Room,* an interactive archive of global censorship incidents. The project was produced, both online and as an installation within a gallery, by the Randolph Street Gallery in Chicago, and continues to operate online under the auspices of the National Coalition Against Censorship.

"*The File Room* began as an idea: an abstract construction that became a prototype, a model of an interactive and open system," wrote Muntadas in his introduction to the original insallation of *The File Room* more than a decade ago. "It prompts our thinking and discussion, and serves as an evolving archive of how the suppression of information has been orchestrated throughout history in different contexts, countries and civilizations. . . . The interactive technology is being utilized to add new points of view, complete missing information, challenge notions of authorship, and to reflect direct voices and opinions wherever possible."

Ten years after the initiation of *The File Room,* Svetlana Mintcheva, Director of the Art Program at the National Coalition Against Censorship, talks to Muntadas about the changes brought about by the rapid expansion of the Internet, the abundance of available information, and the changing nature of censorship itself.

September 2004–March 2005

Svetlana Mintcheva: *The File Room* was launched just as the Internet began to emerge as the unlimited source of information it is today. There was widespread optimism that the Internet presented a space of grassroots communication, unmediated connections, freedom from power hierarchies, and wider availability of alternative information. And *The File Room* was one of these alternatives—a forum where people could come together, share information, and respond to it. And then, in the late 1990s, with the increase of Internet commerce, it came to resemble more a shopping mall than a town commons. Did that change the way you think about the project now?

Antoni Muntadas: This is a two-part issue. The first part concerns the evolution of a medium; the other part concerns the history of a practice such as net-art, which uses a medium. When a new medium appears, people use it at the same time they are learning *how* to use it. In the beginning of the Internet, there were some intuitions, some possibilities, and some hopes.

Initially I was not even thinking of using the Internet for *The File Room;* I was thinking of using some kind of computer language—like hypertext—as well as certain computer systems of archiving the information the project would generate. At that moment Mosaic, the first web browser, was being developed in Illinois, where *The File Room* was realized, and I had the chance to work with this research group. And I also saw the potential of interactivity in the medium. So, yes, certain expectations were created and then the reality of the medium and how it was used had an effect. Some things were transformed, some disappeared and some never happened the way we thought they would.

SM: Can you elaborate on that?

AM: The Internet was conceived as a medium with the full capability for interactivity; it was assumed that the "viewer" would be an active participant. (The power of television in terms of two-way participation is practically zero.) Yet, we see from *The File Room* that, even though the capacity is there, participation is limited. Not everybody is willing to send a letter to a newspaper, join a chat room, or submit a case to *The File Room.* Faced with a long questionnaire, I might not submit a case, simply because I don't have the time. And then there are some other unforeseen developments: some sites, which host open discussion boards, become very successful in terms of interactivity; however, they also become very gossipy, even destructive, like the tabloid press. I believe this is a result of the anonymity of users. *The File Room* has been lucky in that it has kept a serious approach.

With the Internet people expect to be heard, but the overuse of the medium sometimes leads to the opposite—individual voices are not heard anymore. If you have a newspaper with four pages, a lot of people will read the long editorial; this is not the case with the 150 pages of *The Village Voice,* which is mostly advertising. With all this information one thing keeps you from seeing another thing. Thus, with search engines directing you, you'll encounter things that are already, as the French say, *ciblé,* things are already targeted, or pointed at. This is part of the nature of the medium. And, in a way, this has been the medium since the beginning. Searches are a system of editing.

SM: When *The File Room* was launched, one of the things it aimed to accomplish was visibility: censorship incidents were categorized, archived, and made available to anybody with access to a computer and Internet connection. The assumption was, that visibility would generate a lively debate and foster a new awareness. Today, it seems that even if we are arguably successful in getting visibility for key political issues, little changes tangibly. Think of the revelations about the Bush administration and how little a difference this information seems to have made. We now probably have too much information—if you are an interested citizen you have unprecedented access to information.

AM: The history of information is also a history of disinformation. At this moment if you want to be informed this is not difficult: through the Internet you have access to practically all the newspapers in the world. But the question is how is all this information—both local and global—is orchestrated; how our interest as citizens and readers is engaged.

The way this country functions, it seems people are interested in politics every four years for only two or three weeks. Advertising and media companies are orchestrating strategies and techniques, which, to me sometimes appear naïve, but not for people who are unaccustomed to analyzing media and reading between the lines.[1] Even with the rise of the Internet advertising in politics is still very much conducted on television. There are not only strategies of production, but also of distribution—most election campaign ads air not in New York and California, but in the so called "swing" states where they target undecided voters.

This is pure marketing—they are trying to sell a product in places where they can create a market for it. Internet advertising has added some additional strategies in the last few years, but people still watch at home, at the end of the day, during the two months before the elections, and this is the way to get information to the undecided voters. Passing along genuine information is crucial but I don't think the Democrats are very successful in breaking the barriers of lies, corruption, and manipulation typical of this administration.

I feel that we are at a moment in history when we need to give the citizen the right to make decisions again. A lot of people have lost faith in politics and find that there are more interesting things to do. Citizen participation is important everywhere but even more important in the United States, because this is what happens here affects what happens in, say, Pakistan, Brazil, or South Africa.

SM: Maybe the Republicans know their passive electorate better than the Democrats, who seem to be depending more on active citizenship.

AM: Yes, it is sad to say but the Right is much more sophisticated than the Left. In the history of rightwing and authoritarian regimes, as well as in the Fascist governments of Spain, Italy, and Germany, one can see expert manipulation. In the U.S., the Republicans have the best advisors. Kerry ads are really boring, but the Bush ads are quite appealing, although perverse and sinister at the same time.

SM: It seems, from what you are saying, that the problem of the media is not so much problems like CBS's refusal to air a Moveon.org political ad.[2] Many people saw that ad because it was rejected. It is rather those slight manipulations in the news—a change in emphasis here, a subtle or not so subtle spin there—that have a much stronger effect than banning a program outright. Overt censorship guarantees publicity. So rather than visibility and invisibility, the issue seems to be more about the nature of the visibility itself. The Democrats can say whatever they wish; the Republicans are going to repeat the same less-than-truthful messages over and over and over again. And that is a powerful strategy—it is not outright censorship—it is just turning up the volume of one message and, as a result, drowning out everything else. Iron out every complexity, reduce everything to black and white oppositions and you can quickly train a passive audience.

It is quite obvious what we no longer have the bureaucratic figure of the censor with the red stamp. Information is out there—somewhere—but finding information, how it is presented, and its targeted visibility is what matters. How does this change the meaning of censorship?

AM: I have a very strong conviction that economics is one of the main reasons that everything is changing. Once politics is subordinate to economics, decisions are made from another perspective. Economics is basically about selling. Selling has used advertising from the beginning; at the beginning it was information and then information mutated into strategies of seduction. Today information isn't even part of it: Advertising is solely a way to convince you to go and buy something. And that has become also part of political advertising.

Censorship is part of these sophisticated strategies of publicity and propaganda. It might be necessary today to try to find another word because "censorship" is very narrowly defined. I always refer to gentrification—there are societies where gentrification does not exist as a word, not that the process is not there, but the word does not yet exist to describe it. In the same way there is a whole spectrum of strategies of censorship, which are undefined.

SM: With this in mind, does the Internet still offer some kind of utopian space?

AM: Of course, technology is crucial in revolutions. Look at what happened in Spain with the elections. You see how fast you can dismantle a system. In the 2004 Spanish elections, all the organization was done through a network of cell phones as well as through the Internet. With Tiananmen Square, it was the fax. Certain mediums are connected to certain revolutions. Spanish television was totally controlled by the government, so people were text messaging with dates and times of meetings and actions. People were getting information from French and British television and then they were disseminating it. The Spanish government—by controlling the media—was trying to win time. And we rarely talk about time, but time is crucial: Something happens at a certain moment, not before and not after.

SM: What aspect of the Internet seems to you, today, to be the most valuable one from the point of view of artistic and political practices?

AM: I think the most important aspect of the medium today is its capacity to put people together. People are talking to each other in person less and less. They do have long conversations on the telephone though and the Internet is type of technologically mediated communication brought to another level. And, of course, there is the counter-information the Net offers, i.e., information that is not official information.

As to art, the possibilities are just beginning to be explored. With photography, more than a hundred and fifty years after its invention, new artistic uses are still being discovered. It is too early to judge the artistic potential of a twenty-year-old medium. However, there is a potential for subversion in Internet work that is based on the blurring of the boundaries between fiction and reality, which result in the questioning of reality. The potential is there, but there are things that yet need to be invented. At this moment, the medium presents an open challenge. It's a wide-open situation.

Notes

1. Since 1984, in collaboration with Marshall Reese, Muntadas has been collecting electoral campaign ads and editing them for inclusion in *Political Advertisement,* a series the artists update every four years.
2. In early 2004, CBS rejected a Super Bowl advertisement from MoveOn.org, saying the ad violated its advocacy rules. The ad uses images of children working at adult blue-collar jobs to point at the possible long-term consequences of the federal budget deficit. Executives at CBS, which is owned by Viacom Inc., said the rejection stemmed from a 1950s policy prohibiting the showing of advertisements that take stands on controversial public-policy issues.

PART III

Protecting Children

Kim Dingle, *Wild Girls (girl wielding baby),* 1993. Oil and charcoal on linen, 72" x 60". Courtesy of Sperone Westwater, New York.

16

PROTECTION OR POLITICS? THE USE AND ABUSE OF CHILDREN

Svetlana Mintcheva

Over the past several decades, the protection of children has surpassed obscenity and blasphemy as the leading rationale for censorship. While the idea that children are a vulnerable population that should be shielded from moral corruption can be traced back at least as far as Victorian England, it seems to have gained ground in direct proportion to ground lost by other justifications for censorship. With blasphemy no longer a universally acceptable reason to ban a film or burn a book, with the legal standard of obscenity defined narrowly enough to allow for most kinds of sexual expression, children remain the last sure-fire refuge of the censor.

The "need" to "protect" children is summoned when a gallery chooses not to display nudes, when the federal government forces libraries to use filtering software on computers, when parents organize to ban literary classics in schools, or when the Federal Communications Commission caves in to groups that want TV broadcasting content to conform to their particular sensitivities.

The protection of children is, of course, a political goldmine. No politician or public official can afford to be on record as refusing to act on behalf of children. (This was clear in 2005, when an overwhelming bipartisan house majority [of 389 to 38] voted to increase penalties for "indecency" in public broadcasting so that children would not be exposed to explicit language or sexual content.) Yet, the very notion of "protection" is highly subjective. In fact, the actual—that is, quantifiable—condition of U.S. children is disturbing. Despite its wealth, the U.S. has one of the highest rates of relative child poverty on the planet according to two recent studies, by UNICEF and Free the Children (an international group founded by children to promote children's rights).

The latter reported that nearly 15 million American children live in poverty and account for 25 percent of the homeless population!

With poverty, homelessness, lack of health care, and the diminishing quality of public education threatening children's well-being, it is striking that so much political energy should be harnessed shielding children from the sight of a bare breast, the sound of a four-letter word, or time spent playing video games with animated images of violence. It is true that in our media-saturated world, words and images have unprecedented cultural influence. But are the effects of exposure to words and images really so harmful?

Some researchers claim to have proven that children exposed to depictions of violence imitate them in real life or become more aggressive in their behavior. Most of this research, however, is questionable, according to First Amendment lawyer Marjorie Heins. Isolating cause and effect from other contextual factors in psychological development is notoriously difficult, she argues in *Media Effects*—especially in this case, because notions of what constitutes harmful violence vary so greatly. Think of the violence of fairy tales, of movie Westerns, or even of playing soldiers in the backyard. How can one draw a line between this acceptable violence and the, presumably, unacceptable violence of a video game like "Grand Theft Auto"?

Such ambiguities have not slowed the momentum of state-level legislation to ban the sale of violent games to minors. And, in spite of the repeated legal failure to assign responsibility for look-alike crimes to the creators of media and entertainment products, a bill was recently introduced in Congress allowing just such claims against manufacturers and retailers of video or computer games, who sell or rent these games to minors, if "the game was *a factor* in creating *conditions* that assisted or *encouraged* the person to cause injury or death to another person."[1] (ital. added) Such vague legislation would make it possible to go after the video game industry just because some kid, who happened to play video games, also commited a violent act. Of course, most teenagers who play those games do not become violent.

Nevertheless, in the effort to explain high-profile school shootings, representations of violence—in games, music, or film—have been assigned a larger share of the blame than any other factor. Yet, the number of juvenile offenders convicted of violent crime has markedly decreased over precisely the same period that violent video games have proliferated. Ignoring the statistics, school administrators anxious to do something (anything!) to prevent another Columbine, have suspended students because their writings or drawings appeared to be violent. In one case, criminal charges were filed against a fifteen-year-old California student for writing a disturbingly "dark" poem and sharing it with his peers. (The student, "George T," was convicted, but the California Supreme Court overturned the conviction in 2004.)

Hard as it is for researchers to prove a connection between the consumption of violent images and violent behavior, the effects of viewing "indecent" material on children have not even been seriously studied and exist, at this point, mainly in the imagination of adults. Nonetheless, the argument that children might see a drawing of a nude, hear a "dirty" word, or read about sex is used to limit what galleries show, which subjects can be represented in public art, which programs can be shown on TV, and what books are available in libraries.

What do young people think of all these efforts to shield them from "dangerous" material? Seth Killian, an expert video game player, offers witty commentary from inside a video gaming tournament in his essay, "Violent Video Game Players Mysteriously Avoid Killing Selves, Others," and a group of New York–area teenagers, interested in censorship, discuss its role at school and at home in "Taboos, Trust, and Titillation." As we learned, among the things from which teens need protection images and ideas occupy an insignificant position. Rarely heard in this debate, we found these teenagers far more thoughtful than the adults who try to preserve childhood innocence by keeping children ignorant.

The lack of clear understanding as to what exactly might hurt them, coupled with an (adult) consensus that children are vulnerable to images and need to be protected, makes them an invaluable pretext for limiting what adults can see or hear. The threat of decency regulations has already prompted broadcasters to sanitize everything from Masterpiece Theater to a documentary on *Down These Mean Streets* author Piri Thomas, and even to refuse to present at all celebrated, largely unobjectionable films such as *Saving Private Ryan*.

Initiatives presumably designed to protect children not only frequently violate the rights of adults, they have the potential to actually harm children. Government-funded, "abstinence-only" sex education, for instance, both urges abstinence and bans teachers from distributing information about contraception or safe sex. Unfortunately, sexual ignorance insures against neither STDs nor teen pregnancies; both occur at far higher rates in the United States than in European countries with comprehensive sex education programs.[2] Internet filtering software mandated by government for schools and public libraries often blocks Web sites containing valuable information about lesbian and gay relationships or about breast cancer.[3] At the same time, filtering software is frequently ineffective vis-à-vis its real target—pornography—and incapable, of course, of preventing any determined teen (or even pre-teen) from finding porn in the "real" world.

Proponents of media literacy suggest a different approach to help children navigate our image-saturated—and frequently crass, violent, and unjust—society. They argue that, rather that making futile and frequently counterproductive efforts to sanitize what kids see and hear, adults should direct their efforts into teaching children how to think critically about the images around them.

Even though the media literacy movement has gained significant traction in academia, it has little grip on the culture-at-large. Perhaps because, in its utter reasonableness, it fails to take into account the likelihood that childhood sexuality (and sex in general) threatens adults more than children. Such a likelihood helps explain panic responses to any association between sex and children, including a book aimed at adults that merely suggests that our attitudes to childhood sexuality ought to be reconsidered. Judith Levine's *Harmful to Minors: The Perils of Protecting Children from Sex* (excerpted in this section) was published by the University of Minnesota press after years of Levine's inability to find a publisher and then not until after it had undergone an extensive peer review. Nevertheless, the scathing attacks on the university press in the state legislature resulted in the establishment of an external review committee to evaluate publishing criteria and processes and has undoubtedly contributed to a chilling effect on the future publication of such books.

Anxieties about childhood sexuality are fed by the relatively novel attention on sexual abuse and child pornography. Sexual abuse is, in spite of its prominence in the cultural consciousness, a relatively minor problem compared to other types of child abuse. The Children's Bureau in the Administration on Children, Youth and Families estimated that, in 2002, only ten percent of the 896,000 victims of child abuse were sexually abused. Of the sexual abusers, it seems that only a tiny minority take sexually explicit pictures of children (of 400 federal child pornography prosecutions between 2000 and 2005, only about 25 involved the production of child pornography, the rest targeted distributors, the majority of whom traffic in older images).

Surely, using children to produce pornographic images is despicable. With alarming frequency, however, charges of producing child pornography target the wrong people and the wrong images. A photograph of a naked child is a red flag for photo labs, whose employees summon the police, who, in turn, pore over a picture to determine whether it might be sexually arousing to a pedophile. Photographers shooting children in the nude—frequently their own children or grandchildren—are the usual suspects. Although the charges filed against them are usually dropped, such charges disrupt lives and promote the unacceptability of photographs of nude children. Several mothers and one grandmother relate the harrowing stories of lives forever altered in a chapter called "Not a Pretty Picture." One of these women lost her job, another lost custody of her child, the third one is too afraid to photograph her grandchildren nude anymore, and the fourth cannot think of exhibiting in the United States.

It was only in 1982 that child pornography was criminalized, but since then the scope of the law has expanded to include even the images of fully clothed children when they are deemed arousing to pedophiles. No wonder innocent images of nude children are caught in so wide a net. Judges must now decide whether a snapshot of a three-year-old, for instance, contains a "lascivious exhibition of the genitals"—a central term in the legal definition of child pornography. In *Child Pornography Law and the Proliferation of the Sexualized Child,* New York University law professor Amy Adler argues that, rather than resolving the problem, the law forces us to look at images of children from the point of view of the pedophile, thus *creating* and expanding the idea of the sexualized child.

The panic around child pornography has reached such proportions that the rationale for criminalizing it—that children are abused while producing the images—has been forgotten. The Child Pornography Prevention Act of 1996 banned any image that *appeared* to be a minor engaged in a sexual act. In April 2002, the U.S. Supreme Court ruled that the law was too broad—potentially applying to works such as *Romeo and Juliet*—and violated free speech protections. Only two months later, The House of Representatives approved the "Child Obscenity and Pornography Prevention Act of 2002" (COPPA), which narrows the definitions of the law by banning only those computer images that are "indistinguishable" from real child porn images. In this, narrower form, the restriction on sexually explicit images of children that *appear* real became law in 2003 as part of an extensive "Act to prevent child abduction and the sexual exploitation of children." The same act bans the production of obscene cartoons, drawings, paintings, etc., of what appears to be a minor. In essence, the bill rendered the representation of some fantasies illegal, even in the privacy of one's own home, even when no real children are involved. Such is the political power of evoking children.

The intensity of public sentiment about pedophilia and child pornography, fed by a sensationalizing media machine, has heated up to the point where it far exceeds the relative weight of the problem. In "Invasion of the Kiddyfiddlers," Mike Wilson applies the concept of "moral panic," coined in the sixties, to the "pedophile scare." In periods of moral panic, a condition, person, or group "emerges to be defined as a threat to societal values and interests." Moral panics can serve different purposes: They can provide a sense of community that compensates for a pervasive sense of political powerlessness or they can displace and obscure a range of abuses.

Could it be that the cultural fear of children's sexuality and the vehemence of attacks targeting violent film and video conveniently displace the much more tangible problems of gun control, homelessness, urban poverty, or the generally lamentable condition of public schools? And could it be that under the guise of protecting childhood innocence adults are using children as weapons in the culture wars? Evidently it is time to ask: Who is really being protected when the idea of "protecting children" arises?

Notes

1. House Bill 2178. Introduced by Representatives Dickerson, McCune, and McDermott. Read first time 02/22/2005.
2. Cf. "Adolescent Sexual Health in Europe and the U.S.—Why the Difference?" A report published by Advocates for Truth, 2000.
3. For information about sites unintentionally blocked by Internet filters, go to peace fire.org.

17
MEDIA EFFECTS

Marjorie Heins

While European Union officials exude skepticism about the actual harm to minors from controversial expression, in the United States by the 1990s it was politically almost untenable to question the claim that media violence has been proven to have dire effects on youth. Yet from Dr. Tissot's influential 1758 work, *L'Onanisme: Dissertation Sur les Maladies produits par la Masturbation,* to campaigns against comic books in the 1950s and TV violence studies a generation later, those favoring censorship have invoked science to bolster their claims. Have the more quantitative studies of recent decades actually added any new knowledge to this endless debate?

Part of the problem has been that the issue of media effects is too often posed in "either/or" terms. Statistical correlations between exposure to films classified as violent by experimenters in a laboratory setting and subsequent behavior deemed aggressive by the experimenters are said to prove that all or a great percentage of children imitate what they see in the media. Catharsis—the therapeutic or "drive reduction" effect of entertainment—has supposedly been disproved by these social science experiments. Rarely do the debaters note that the same work may induce imitation in some viewers and catharsis in others—or that the same person may respond differently to different violent or sexual content. Psychology is "still largely a speculative discipline";[1] it is not the same as physical science.

What, then, do studies of media violence or sex actually show? A few preliminary observations about social science research are useful before attempting an answer.

First, it's important to identify *what type of effects* social scientists have tried to measure. Researchers differ markedly in describing the effects that they think art, entertainment, and other expression have on youngsters. Some believe that violent content directly inspires imitation. Others say that its primary impact is to desensitize viewers, making them more callous about antisocial or dangerous behavior. Still others advocate an "excitation" theory which posits that physiological arousal—whether from violent entertainment or other sources—can be transferred into aggressive behavior if a person is provoked. Finally, there are champions of the "mean world" effect—a fear of being victimized and a perception that real-world brutality is more pervasive than it actually is.[2]

Many experts acknowledge that not all violent content has any of these possible negative effects. It all depends on context, they say—for example, whether the perpetrator in a violent story is punished. Prominent contributors to a 1998 report identified eleven separate "contextual factors" that they thought influenced a work's impact—among them humor, which they said trivializes violence and "generally contributes to the learning of aggression." (They gave the Three Stooges as an example.)[3]

The variety of different effects posited by social scientists demonstrates the impossibility of pinpointing the overall impact of sexual or violent content in entertainment. Excessive timidity caused by the mean world syndrome is a quite different effect from increased aggression. Different viewers will interpret such "contextual factors" as humor in different ways. One child may think—however fleetingly—that violence is the way to solve problems or gain social status after watching a John Ford Western; another may become fearful, while still a third may interpret the film as pure fantasy without any particular lesson about real-world behavior. As an expert witness in A.S. Byatt's novel *Babel Tower* observes, any mother "knows that some children can take *anything* and some cry and cry over the death of a seal or Bambi and never quite recover."[4]

Sexual material presents the same dilemma. While some children may be frightened or aroused by it, others will be uncomprehending or bored. Even scholars whose work favors media effects have observed that the same content "may create nightmares for one child and be the source of coping skills for another."[5] Dr. Victor Strasburger, a prominent advocate of media effects, agrees that sexual explicitness "could be extremely scary or confusing" for some children and "absolutely harmless" for others.[6]

If pinpointing effects is difficult, then *defining what is supposed to cause them* is equally so. Social scientists—not to mention politicians, advocacy groups, and individual parents—may mean many different things when they excoriate "media violence" or (in the words of Congress in its 1996 V-chip law) "casual treatment of sexual material."[7] Definitions in the experimental literature vary from one study to the next, when they are offered at all. And since even media effects enthusiasts tend to agree that expression touching on huge subjects like sexuality or violence is likely to have very different effects depending upon its style, context, and theme, defining what it is that researchers are trying to measure becomes even more treacherous. Thus, the same violent act can be "seen as treason or heroism. Physical discipline of a child may be viewed as appropriate or abusive, depending on viewpoint and culture," and "assault may be viewed as reprehensible conduct or as an appropriate part of a sport or entertainment, like hockey or boxing."[8] The same can be said of hitting Bobo dolls or other violence observed in lab experiments.

Some researchers have attempted to distinguish "good" from "bad" or "gratuitous" media violence. The British Board of Film Classification did so in 1999 when it justified a 15+ rating for *Saving Private Ryan* because "the examiners felt strongly that young people should be able to see this [extremely realistic portrayal] of war."[9] But distinctions based on whether cinematic violence is educational or gratuitous are so subjective, and turn so critically on interpretations that are colored by viewers' psychological, emotional, and cultural background, that quantitative measurement becomes ludicrous. Among other things, trying to shove creative expression into neat categories of "good" and "bad" violence fails to account for such common characteristics as ambiguity, satire, and irony. And there has been no consensus among social scientists on these contextual questions. Some think that depictions of justified violence by heroes who are rewarded, not punished, are in fact far worse than gruesome violence by villains who get their comeuppance in the end.

Other media effects researchers do not even attempt to identify content that they suspect is harmful; they simply examine the effects of TV viewing in general. Their conclusions range from nonempirical predictions that the "idiot box" has fundamentally altered our brains and will lead to the end of literacy to assertions that the very existence of television is responsible for increased rates of violent crime. Whatever their accuracy, studies of this type do not support claims that particular media content is traumatic or causes imitation. Yet even this basic distinction is sometimes lost by those arguing that bad behavior results from bad messages in art or entertainment.

The concept of bad behavior likewise suffers from vagueness and variability. Researchers use widely differing descriptions of the effects they are seeking, ranging from insensitive attitudes or incivility to risky conduct, from violent play with Bobo dolls to violent crime. As the psychologists Kenneth Gadow and Joyce Sprafkin note with considerable understatement, "the term aggression as it is used by researchers in this area is not a unitary concept." In some studies, "a distinction was made between playful and hurtful aggression and in others both peer and adult-directed aggression was studied."[10] The New York City Bar likewise pointed out that "most psychological studies of the effects of television are studies of aggression or aggressive attitudes, not violence. The distinction is significant: many behaviors which few would deem 'violent' may be counted and measured by psychologists as aggressive."[11]

The definitional problems are equally formidable when it comes to sex. If the Supreme Court has had trouble defining obscenity for the legal purpose of distinguishing it from constitutionally protected speech, the problems are truly mind-boggling when terms such as "offensive," "inappropriate for minors," or "casual treatment of sexual material" are deployed. Social scientists Edward Donnerstein, Daniel Linz, and Barbara Wilson offered a good illustration of the point in comments sent to the FCC to correct misstatements in a submission by the American Family Association (AFA) regarding alleged harm to minors from "indecent" radio or television broadcasts. In addition to misrepresenting the results of several studies and confusing youngsters with adults, the scholars said, the AFA confused violent pornography with "indecency." They concluded: "the available social science research does not show that exposure to 'indecent' materials has any effect on children."[12]

Thus, Donnerstein and Linz may have believed in adverse effects from viewing violent pornography, but "indecency" was a far broader and vaguer category that included not just "patently offensive" descriptions of sex but four-letter words, innuendos, and bathroom jokes. And even with respect to violent pornography, as Linz and Donnerstein acknowledged, "no one yet has been able to come up with either an acceptable operational definition of aggressive behavior on the part of the subject who is supposedly reacting to the film or other media event, or an acceptable definition of what actually constitutes violence in the media depiction itself."[13]

Another big question in social science research is *scientific validity.* At least since the days of *L'Onanisme,* scientific proof has been claimed for what are really just clinical or anecdotal reports of individual cases. Thus, Victor Cline, an early critic of the 1970 Lockhart Commission (a national commission on obscenity and pornography appointed by Congress in 1967), has concluded from his clinical experience that adolescent males are "particularly vulnerable" to the "negative and addictive effects" of pornography, which include "having their lives consumed by it: sitting for hours masturbating to adult material and needing progressively stronger, heavier, harder material to give them a bigger kick."[14] Cline offers a number of case histories to support his assertion, but no studies indicating whether it is fair to generalize from his observations. For every case he encountered of a person in need of therapy, there were probably many more who never came to the attention of clinicians and who consumed pornography in moderate doses with no ill effects. A witness in the 1994 "heinous crimes" trading card case made the same point about the evidence adduced by Fredric Wertham in the 1950s against comic books. Wertham interviewed juvenile offenders, she said,

> and asked them if they had read comic books. And they said they had. And he therefore concluded that reading comic books made them into juvenile delinquents. His study is now cited in courses on mass communication as a form of error . . . because you see, had he asked all children of New York City, have you read comics, he would have found that 93 percent of all children had read comics. And they were not all juvenile delinquents.[15]

Judith Harris pithily summarized the problem: "the plural of anecdote is not data."[16] People in therapy (or prison) are not a random cross section of society, and there are not ordinarily control groups when one draws inferences from clinical cases. Although case histories may be both suggestive and compelling (indeed, Freud built a monumental theory around them), they cannot lay claim to proof.

Related to the problem of scientific validity is the meaning of *statistics.* In studies that aren't simply anecdotal, researchers rely on statistical correlations to demonstrate imitative effects from violent media. But such correlations may actually be quite small. Statistical significance in social science generally means a result that would occur no more than once in twenty times by chance. But this doesn't necessarily mean the result occurs very often. In other words, " '[s]ignificant' in the statistical sense does not mean 'important.' It means simply 'not likely to happen just by chance.' "[17]

Thus, a "causation" hypothesis may be borne out, for social science purposes, by an experiment in which the great majority of subjects are unaffected by the particular book, film, or TV show being studied. As Frederick Schauer, the legal expert of the 1985 Meese Commission on Pornography, explained, causation in social science is not "deterministic," but "attributive" and "probabilistic."[18] The "identification of a causal relationship under a probabilistic account does not entail the conclusion that the identified cause produces the effect in all, a majority, or even a very large proportion of cases."[19] In the words of one contributor to the 1982 National Institute of Mental Health report, causal inferences in the social sciences "are, at best, approximations."[20]

Obviously, countless violent and sexual acts throughout history have occurred in the absence of any stimulus from television, books, or pornography; likewise, teenage girls became pregnant long before soap operas portrayed illicit sex; and children misbehaved before the introduction of crime comics or Tom and Jerry cartoons. But under the concept of "probabilistic causation," a causal relationship merely means *some* increase, no matter how small, in "the incidence" or "probability" of the effect. Probabilistic causation is not proof and indeed, as Victor Strasburger acknowledged, trying to "tease out the effects of television on human behavior can be a methodologic 'mission impossible' because television is ubiquitous and human behavior is complex."[21]

Researchers differ, moreover, regarding which statistical methods are most reliable: multiple regression analysis, cross-lagged correlations, and many other sophisticated ways of massaging numbers can produce quite different results.[22] Judith Harris describes instances in which social scientists have manipulated data relentlessly to find some sort of positive correlation to support their hypotheses.[23]

Even those who believe that art and entertainment have widespread imitative impact usually acknowledge that social factors such as family environment are far more important influences on children than the media, and have not claimed a "media effect" on attitudes and behavior of more than 5 to 15 percent.[24] "No reputable scholar," writes Sissela Bok, "accepts the view expressed by 20 percent of the American public in 1995, blaming television more than any other factor for teenage violence."[25] The National Research Council's 1993 report, *Understanding and Preventing Violence,* does not consider the media a serious factor.[26] Yet politicians, advocates, journalists, and even social scientists have repeatedly used imprecise language in talking about media effects, suggesting that they are large, uniform, and scientifically proven.

With these caveats in mind, what have social "science" media effects studies actually shown? Laboratory, field, and correlational work—the three main types of studies—each has its own large literature and separate strengths and weaknesses. What follows here cannot possibly be a complete description of the vast media effects literature. I have endeavored to put the studies in perspective, describe the highlights, and bring some coherence to what is obviously a daunting and voluminous body of often technical social science work. What must strike any open-minded student of the subject, though, is that despite widely publicized claims that adverse effects have been proven, the studies are ambiguous, disparate, and modest in their results. As Jonathan Freedman described his and his colleagues' eye-opening experience after reviewing what they assumed had been definitely established, "We were initially surprised, then amazed, and finally appalled at the discrepancy between what we found in the research and the way it was generally described."[27] Joyce Sprafkin had a similar experience after her own experiments with emotionally disturbed youths found either no effect of violent television or more aggressive behavior associated with *nonviolent* shows. "I decided to look back carefully at the field and say, well, what have other people really found?" For preschool children, the field studies simply "did not support a special significance for aggressive television."[28]

Despite the ambiguities, contradictions, and deficiencies of media effects studies, however, there ought to be little doubt that art, entertainment, and other forms of expression do have real psychological effects, including, in some cases, imitation. The point is that ultimately these effects are vast and various, and not amenable to quantitative measurement. The basic problem with social scientists' attempts to quantify aesthetic experience is that they "have been looking for simplistic explanations of extremely complex phenomena"; they seek to measure not "chemical bonds or electrical voltage" but "the most subtle human characteristics—the sentiments described so finely by Henry James."[29]

Kids, Ambiguity, and the Social Cognition Approach

By the 1980s, a more nuanced "humanistic" or "social cognition" approach to media effects had emerged, centering on "children's appropriation of cultural tools, goals, and activities" as they learn.[30] Even the 1982 NIMH report had noted "a change in psychology since the 1960s when the stimulus-response models of learning began to give way to a broader-gauged cognitive orientation," which understands human beings to respond to new information in varying ways, based on "preestablished schema" that are "built up by many previous interactions with the environment."[31] As psychologist Kevin Durkin put it, broad generalizations about simple, direct effects of art or entertainment on human psyches "do not carry us very far"; television "may be implicated" in child development, but "in different ways at different points in the lifespan." As much depends "upon what the child brings to TV viewing as upon what it extracts."[32]

The social cognition perspective recognizes that different types of expression have different intentions, meanings, and effects. Violence in action movies will be processed by viewers, depending on their ages, temperaments, and other contextual factors, differently from violence in cartoons, Stephen King novels, or interactive Web sites. The same is true of persuasion. Those who cling to a narrowly imitative view of media effects often make an analogy to advertising: corporations, they say, would not invest heavily in TV ads—particularly ads targeting children—unless they were effective. What they overlook is that advertising, like propaganda, is not the same as fantasy, satire, eroticism, pop music, or soap opera. It is a giant leap from acknowledging the power of advertising to accepting the notion that all forms of expression have easily predictable persuasive or imitative effects.

The inability of social science to quantify the impact of art or entertainment obviously does not preclude the existence of a wide range of psychological and behavioral effects, or obviate the need, in a democratic society, for interpretation and critique of media messages. As Victor Strasburger has said, lack of quantitative proof does not mean that objections to TV content cannot exist "on 'purely aesthetic, humanistic, and philosophical grounds.' "[33] Another expert likewise threw up his hands on the causation issue during congressional hearings in 1997 on rock music and teenage angst. Admitting that no studies had established a cause-and-effect relationship, he nevertheless said we should acknowledge "the overall effect music has on people, including adolescents and children."[34]

But as we acknowledge that overall effect, we should also be wary of oversimplifying. The critic Wendy Steiner has bemoaned the literalism, "the collapse of paradox," that in the late 20th century so often reduced art and literature to scripts for indoctrination. There is nothing new about the censorship impulse and the fear of ambiguity in art, Steiner says, noting that it goes back to Plato; but such frightening events as the *fatwa* announced by Iran against Salman Rushdie for insulting Islam in his novel *The Satanic Verses* dramatized the extent to which literalism and reductionism were overwhelming any appreciation for ambiguity. "We will not be led into fascism or rape or child abuse or racial oppression through aesthetic experience," Steiner writes. On the contrary, "the more practiced we are in fantasy the better we will master its difference from the real."[35]

Notes

1. Andrew Hacker, "The Unmaking of Men," *New York Review of Books,* Oct. 21, 1999, p. 25.
2. See University of Oxford Programme in Comparative Media Law & Policy, *Final Report: Parental Control of Television Broadcasting* (1999), ch. 3, "Media Theories Background," http://europa.eu.int/comm/dg10; Stacy Smith *et al., National Television Violence Study 3* (Thousand Oaks, CA: Sage, 1998), p. 10, Mike Allen & Dave D'Alessio, "A Meta-Analysis Summarizing the Effects of Pornography II Aggression After Exposure," *33 Human Comm'ns Rsrch* 258 (1995); George Gerbner & Nancy Signorielli, *Violence and Terror in the Mass Media* (Paris: UNESCO, 1988); George Gerbner *et al.,* "Living with Television: The Dynamics of the Cultivation Process," in *Perspectives on Media Effects* (Jennings Bryant & Dolf Zillmann, eds.) (Hillsdale, NJ: Lawrence Erlbaum, 1986); George Gerbner *et al.,* "The 'Mainstreaming' of America: Violence Profile No. 11," *J. Comm'n* 10–29 (Summer 1980); *Pornography and Sexual Aggression* (Neil Malamuth & Edward Donnerstein, eds.) (New York: Academic Press, 1984); Daniel Linz *et al.,* "The Attorney General's Commission on Pornography: The Gaps Between 'Findings' and Facts," 4 *Am. Bar Fdtn Rsrch J.* 713, 720–26 (1987); Daniel Linz & Edward Donnerstein, "The Effects of Violent Messages in the Mass Media," in *Message Effects in Communication Science* (J. J. Bradac, ed.) (Newberry Park, CA: Sage, 1989); Daniel Linz *et al.,* "Effects of Long-Term Exposure to Violent and Sexually Degrading Depictions of Women," 55 *J. Personality & Soc. Psych.* 758–68 (1988); Denise Caruso, "Linking Entertainment to

Violence," *New York Times on the Web,* Apr. 26, 1999, http://www.nytimes.com. library/tech/99/04/biztech/articles/26digi.html.

3. *Nat'l Television Violence Study, supra* n. 2, pp. 11–20.
4. A. S. Byatt, *Babel Tower* (New York: Vintage, 1996), p. 581.
5. Aletha Huston & Dolf Zillman, "Media Influence, Public Policy, and the Family," in *Media, Children, and the Family* (Dolf Zillmann *et al.,* eds.) (Hillsdale, NJ: Lawrence Erlbaum, 1994), p. 6.
6. Author's telephone interview with Victor Strasburger, Jan. 13, 1997.
7. Telecommunications Act of 1996, PL 104–104, §551(a), 110 Stat. 56 (1996), published in the Historical and Statutory Notes to 47 U.S.C. §303(w) (announcing Congress's "findings" that "children exposed to violent video programming at a young age have a higher tendency for violent and aggressive behavior later in life than children not so exposed," and "are prone to assume that acts of violence are acceptable behavior"; and that "children are affected by the pervasiveness and casual treatment of sexual material on television, eroding the ability of parents to develop responsible attitudes and behavior in their children").
8. Committee on Communications & Media Law, "Violence in the Media: A Position Paper," 52(3) *Record of the Ass'n of the Bar, City of New York* 273, 283–86 (1977), p. 284; see also *Final Report, supra* n. 2, ch. 3, "Media Theories Background" (without attending to style, genre, quality, nuance, and context, "a children's cartoon or a Shakespearean drama are rated as depicting the same level of violence as an action or horror film").
9. M. L. Poulter, "Report from BBFC's Consultation Evening, The Watershed, Bristol, 15 Nov. 1999," e-mail distributed from plmpl@eis.bris.ac.uk, Nov. 19, 1999.
10. Kenneth Gadow & Joyce Sprafkin, "Field Experiments of Television Violence with Children: Evidence for an Environmental Hazard?" 83(3) *Pediatrics* 399, 401 (1989).
11. "Violence in the Media," p. 296; see also Willard Rowland Jr., *The Politics of TV Violence* (Beverly Hills: Sage, 1983), p. 125 (noting experimenters' confusion between laboratory-induced or play aggression and real-world violence); Federal Trade Comm'n, *Marketing Entertainment Violence to Children: A Review of Self-Regulation and Industry Practices in the Motion Picture, Music Recording, and Electronic Game Industries,* appendix A, "A Review of the Research on the Impact of Violence in Entertainment Media" (Washington, DC: FTC, Sept. 2000), http://www.ftc.gov/reports/violence/vioreport.pdf (noting the wide variety of different effects posited by social scientists, and the weakness of the empirical evidence).
12. Edward Donnerstein, Daniel Linz, & Barbara Wilson, *Comments on the Submission to the FCC by the American Family Association et al.,* MM Docket No. 89-494 (FCC, undated).
13. Linz *et al., supra* n. 2, 4 *Am. Bar Fdin Rsrch J.* at 722.
14. Victor Cline, *Pornography's Effects on Adults and Children* (New York: Morality in Media, 1994), pp. 15, 3.
15. Testimony of Catherine Yronwode in *Eclipse Enterprises v. Gulotta,* CV-92-3416 (ADS), Transcript, May 23, 1994, pp. 92–93.
16. Judith Rich Harris, *The Nurture Assumption: Why Children Turn Out the Way They Do* (New York: The Free Press, 1998), p. 214.

17. David Moore, *Statistics: Concepts and Controversies* (4th ed.) (New York: W. H. Freeman, 1997), pp. 486–90. Sometimes, more rigorous measures of once in 100 times are used.
18. Frederick Schauer, "Causation Theory and the Causes of Sexual Violence," 4 *Am. Bar Fdtn Rsrch J.* 737 (1987).
19. Schauer, "Causation Theory," *supra* n. 18, at 752–54, citing Hubert Blalock, Jr., "Multiple Causation, Indirect Measurement and Generalizability in the Social Sciences," 68 *Synthese: An International Journal for Epistemology, Methodology, and Philosophy of Science* 13 (1986); Paul Humphreys, "Causation in the Social Sciences: An Overview," 68 *Synthese* 1 (1986).
20. Eli Rubenstein, "Introductory Comments," in *Television and Behavior: Ten Years of Scientific Progress and Implications for the Eighties* (Washington, DC: U.S. Dep't of HHS, 1982), Vol. 2, p. 104.
21. Victor Strasburger, *Adolescents and the Media: Medical and Psychological Impact* (Thousand Oaks, CA: Sage, 1995), p. 13; Victor Strasburger, "Children, Adolescents, and Television—1989: II. The Role of Pediatricians," 83 *Pediatrics* 446–48 (Mar. 1989). Dolf Zillmann, a prominent champion of media effects, also acknowledged that the "research on many potentially significant aspects of the influence of pornography on beliefs, attitudes, and behaviors cannot be definitive"; it "leaves us with considerable uncertainty about exposure consequences at the societal level." Dolf Zillmann, "Pornography Research, Social Advocacy, and Public Policy," in *Psychology and Social Policy* (Peter Suedfeld & Philip Tetlock, eds.) (New York: Hemisphere, 1991), p. 185; see also Jonathan Kellerman, *Savage Spawn: Reflections on Violent Children* (New York: Ballantine, 1999), pp. 72–73 (establishing a causal link is methodologically almost impossible because virtually every child in Western society "watches oodles of TV, so it is difficult to come up with control groups and to otherwise tease out specific effects of media violence"). A senior researcher at the University of Pennsylvania put it more boldly: "You can never prove anything in social science." Statement of Dr. Amy Jordan, senior researcher at Penn's Annenberg Public Policy Center, at a meeting of the Free Expression Network, Washington, DC, Mar. 22, 2000 (author's notes). Dr. Jordan may have spoken too broadly: many social science measurements are not empirically problematic. It is the subjective nature of judgments about media content and human attitudes that make them impossible to quantify.
22. See Schauer, *supra* n. 18; Rubenstein, *supra* n. 20, p. 2; Jonathan Freedman, "Effect of Television Violence on Aggressiveness," 96 *Psych. Bull.* 227 (1984).
23. Harris, pp. 18–23, 215; see also Hubert Blalock, Jr., *Casual Inferences in Nonexperimental Research* (Chapel Hill: U. of North Carolina Press, 1964), p. 5 ("causal inferences [in social science] are made with significant risk of error").
24. See, *e.g.*, Victor Strasburger, "Television and Adolescents: Sex, Drugs, Rock 'n' Roll," 1 *Adol. Medicine—State of the Art Reviews* 161, 172–73 (1990); Bok, p. 85 (repeating the 5–15 percent figure but noting that such estimates "are rarely specific enough to indicate whether what is at issue is all violent crime, or such crimes along with bullying and aggression more generally").
25. Bok, pp. 85, 5, 57 (identifying "more direct" causes of violent conduct to include fam-

ily breakdown, child abuse, firearms availability, and overindulgence in drugs and alcohol; and acknowledging that "it will always be difficult to disentangle the precise effects of exposure to media violence from the many other factors contributing to societal violence"); see also Nat'l Research Council, *supra* n. 41 (emphasizing genetic, social, and family influences on violent behavior–including alcohol abuse and availability of guns).

26. National Research Council, *Understanding and Preventing Violence* (Albert Reiss, Jr., & Jeffrey Roth, eds.) (Washington, DC: Nat'l Academy Press, 1993); see also Franklin Zimring & Gordon Hawkins, *Crime Is Not the Problem: Lethal Violence in America* (New York: Oxford U. Press, 1997) (availability of firearms—not media imagery or even the general crime rate—accounts for the high rate of lethal violence in America); Kellerman, *supra* n. 21 (focusing on psychopathology, produced by a combination of hereditary and environmental factors, and excoriating pundits who predictably blame the media after every senseless crime).
27. Jonathan Freedman, "Viewing Television Violence Does Not Make People More Aggressive," 22 *Hofstra L. Rev.* 833, 836 (1994), at 837. See also Jib Fowles, *The Case for Television Violence* (Thousand Oaks, CA: Sage, 1999), pp. 20–50 (summarizing the dubious results of media-violence research).
28. Testimony of Joyce Sprafkin in *Eclipse v. Gulotta,* Mar. 28, 1994, pp. 112–13.
29. David Buckingham, *Moving Images: Understanding Children's Emotional Responses to Television* (Manchester, UK: Manchester U. Press, 1996), p. 8; Howard Gardner, "Do Parents Count?" *New York Review of Books,* Nov. 5, 1998, p. 20.
30. Sara Meadows, *The Child as Thinker: The Development and Acquisition of Cognition in Childhood* (London: Routledge, 1993), p. 344.
31. *Television and Behavior,* Vol. 1, pp. 87–91, 20.
32. Kevin Durkin, *Television, Sex Roles and Children: A Developmental Social Psychological Account* (Milton Keynes, UK: Open U. Press, 1985), p. 3; see also Henry Jenkins, "Lessons from Littleton: What Congress Doesn't Want to Hear About Youth and Media," http://web.mit.edu/cms/news/nais9912 (because consumers respond to the same media in different ways, "universalizing claims are fundamentally inadequate in accounting for media's social and cultural impact"); Nat'l Research Council, pp. 101–2 (media effects theories are oversimplistic because they fail to consider either how different individuals respond to identical stimuli or how various factors—psychosocial, neurological, and hormonal—*interact* to produce particular behavior).
33. Strasburger, "Children, Adolescents, and Television," 83 *Pediatrics* 446–48 (quoting Gadow & Sprafkin, p. 404).
34. David Stout, "A Hearing Focuses on Lyrics Laced with Violence and Death," *New York Times,* Nov. 7, 1997, p. A21, quoting Frank Palumbo's testimony for the American Academy of Pediatrics.
35. Wendy Steiner, *The Scandal of Pleasure: Art in an Age of Fundamentalism* (Chicago: U. of Chicago Press, 1995), pp. 117–18, 211.

18

TABOOS, TRUST, AND TITILLATION: TEENS TALK ABOUT CENSORSHIP

A roundtable discussion with high school and college students moderated by Stephanie Elizondo Griest and Svetlana Mintcheva

Stephanie Elizondo Griest, discussion moderator, is the founder and director of the Youth Free Expression Network, a national coalition of teens and adults committed to defending the free expression rights of youth. Faced with Internet filters, "abstinence-only" sex education, and other restrictions on young people's access to ideas, YFEN's goal is to empower youth to advocate on their own behalf.

Svetlana Mintcheva, discussion moderator, is the Arts Advocacy Project Coordinator at the National Coalition Against Censorship, an alliance of national nonprofit organizations, including literary, artistic, religious, educational, professional, labor, and civil liberties groups united by the commitment to defend freedom of thought, inquiry, and expression.

Stephen Opong, seventeen, is a senior at Columbia Prep, a private school. He lives with a fourteen-year-old sister and his parents. Stephen is looking forward to studying business at Georgetown University.

Damali Slowe, fourteen, is a sophomore at Westminster School in Simsbury, Connecticut. She lives alternately with her older sister, who is a schoolteacher (27), and her brother (25). Her family is from Guyana, and she is a second-generation American.

Ife Collymore, sixteen, is a senior vocal major at LaGuardia High School. Ife has a twelve-year-old brother. Her father is a retired teacher and her mother is a retired musician.

Christopher Davis, sixteen, is a senior art major at LaGuardia High School. He works in painting, sculpture, drawing, and computer graphics. Chris has a twin brother and lives with his mother, who works in social services. His father, a retired NBA basketball player, lives in Manhattan.

Stephen, Damali, Ife, and Christopher all work for Harlem Live, a Web-zine produced by teens from New York.

Stephanie Elizondo Griest: Who has a good definition of censorship? What does it mean to you?

Stephen Opong: Censorship is something that people don't want other people to see—on TV, for instance—maybe because of their age, or the time of day, or whatever. It is banning things. It has a negative connotation for me because you are stopping people from seeing things without their consent. People should be exposed to everything.

Christopher Davis: Censorship is whatever a certain majority of people believes that children should see—or should not see. And whatever the majority says goes.

Damali Slowe: I don't think censorship comes from a majority; it comes from certain people. It can come from a government. It can come from a radio station that chooses to ban a certain song.

Ife: Censorship is negative because it might mean something is hidden, covered up—some truth that they don't want the public to know about. That could be detrimental, because people won't know the whole story—it hasn't been revealed to them.

Damali: A lot of the time, people want to see what they are told they are not allowed to see. The scary thing is that a lot of times, people just don't know what they're not being allowed to see. And with big media conglomerates buying everything under the new regulations of the FCC, only a handful of companies will soon be controlling what we see. If people don't know what's happening, how will they know to complain?

Ife: The protests before the war in Iraq really made me upset, because people were protesting about these things and I could tell that they didn't have the whole story. They were just repeating the same thing over and over again. It seemed that they didn't have enough background. The media kinda twisted things around.

Stephanie: Have you had any experiences with censorship at your school?

Damali: There are certain books that my school library won't lend me: These are books on subjects such as how to make bombs or pornography and material along those lines; otherwise my school library is pretty open about the material they lend us.

Chris: We don't get censored much in my school. It's very open; we have the Gay/Straight Alliance. We're given everything that we need in terms of artistic exposure. We have a lot of opportunities in my school. Kids in my school have a totally different outlook on life than those in other schools because we didn't grow up with the same [limited] opportunities. I think other schools should be more like my school. The openness comes from being an art school. The school is also very diverse—students come from every borough and even from upstate New York.

Ife: They tried to put a dress code in our school, but it was just not going to happen. You can't do that to artistic people. It was written about in the newspaper, and everyone was so against it.

Damali: In private schools, parents pay money for their kids to not break the rules. Which is ironic because the craziest kids will do anything just because Mommy and Daddy don't want them to. There is censorship against raunchy stuff, but there is also censorship against really important stuff that people don't want you to see. When kids at my school aren't allowed to see certain things or certain people because "it's bad," they just want to see it more. Unfortunately, they are paying attention to the wrong things, like the rules, "Oh, I'm not supposed to drink, oh, I'm not supposed to smoke"—so they go and do it. Most kids don't think "Well, since they don't push the history of Africans or Indians in our faces, I want to go out and learn about that."

Stephanie: Let's talk about the Internet. What is your experience with computer filters?

Stephen: When I first got AOL, I was creating my screen name and the parental controls came up. My mom said to put the control on "teen."

So I had it on "teen" for like two years. It wouldn't let me send instant messages; it blocked certain emails. I couldn't visit regular Web sites. It filtered everything.

Damali: Filters are really annoying, especially because kids will just find another Internet connection to use.

Ife: When I first got on the Internet, both my parents wanted me to put the Internet control on "kid," I asked why. I told them, "I'm getting older—what don't you want me to see?" My father said that they didn't want me to see naked people. I thought, "So what? They're naked." I didn't understand. So one day I secretly switched to general and went to the wrong Web site and saw porn. And then I understood that there was something wrong with it.

Svetlana: It seems that what everyone is afraid of is kids accessing porn and that is why they are pushing for filters.

Damali: I found porn when I was searching for black walnuts. We were studying the Middle East and I was looking up foods in the Middle East. I looked up dates, figs, and black walnuts. The computer froze and the teacher came into the room and asked what was going on—and I was trying to figure out how I was going to explain it. Luckily, someone else's computer froze, too. Another time I was watching television and I thought I was going to watch the "Blair Witch Project," but instead it was the "Bare Wench Project."

Stephen: European countries barely censor anything. Even on TV, they swear and show naked people. And their kids turn out less violent and smarter than us. I think that not banning things would open kids' minds.

Stephanie: How have Internet filters affected your online research?

Stephen: I remember I had to do a report on the *Titanic* and I couldn't type in the word because it started with "tit." A window came up that said "Parental Advisory: Restricted."

Stephanie: What about V-chips?

Stephen: I never had a V-chip, but my mother would not let us watch any television.

Ife: I remember when *TV Guide* came out with ratings like "T" for teen, and my mother would tell me that I couldn't watch certain things. It bothered me, but it hasn't been a problem because I've never had cable and most sexual and reality shows are on cable.

Stephanie: If you had children, do you think you would get a V-chip installed, or let it be a free-for-all?

Damali: First of all, I would want to trust my kids enough to know that they weren't watching things that they shouldn't watch. I wouldn't want my four-year-old to come across this stuff while trying to find Barney on television, but by the time they are ten to twelve, I would like to talk to them about these issues. But most of all, I would rather my children entertain themselves instead of being entertained by other people.

Stephanie: What do you think about parental advisory stickers on CDs?

Stephen: I remember when I first got into rap music in fifth grade and my father brought home a Notorious B.I.G. CD and I listened to it all the time. Then my mom comes in and asks, "What are they saying, turn it off!" Of course, I still listen to it anyway. In the store, when you want to buy a CD, they don't care if it has a parental advisory sticker on it.

Chris: I wanted to buy an OutKast CD. My mother saw that it had a parental advisory sticker on it and she said, "No, no, no!" Every other word was a curse and the cover of the CD had a naked woman on it, so she took it away from me. But I can hear curses on the radio and nobody gets in trouble. I'm going to hear it no matter what.

Ife: When I first got a CD with a parental advisory label on it, my mother took it away. My brother, who is twelve years old, has to get the edited versions of CDs or my father won't approve. A friend of mine couldn't buy a CD at Tower Records because she was under eighteen. I thought that that was ridiculous.

Stephanie: How does violent music affect you?

Chris: Sometimes if you're going through a certain situation and a song comes on, it might cheer you up or make you sad. But I have never listened to a song and then wanted to go out and be violent.

Ife: When I was ten years old, I listened to a lot of rock music and my mother thought that it was really violent and gave her a headache. But I was kind of angry at that time; there were a lot of things going on in my life. These musicians were angry and I was angry, so we had something in common. But I didn't want to go out and do crazy stuff.

Damali: The media definitely pushes stereotypical images in our faces, especially the image of the "black thug." It seems like every black kid is supposed to grow up and be a black thug. If not—you're an Oreo or a sellout. We can't blame it on rap music though—we should blame it on the people who own these music companies. They are rich white people who want little black kids to think that this is how they are supposed to be. There are a lot of good rap artists who are warning kids about drinking and using drugs. That is what rap is really about. But those artists don't make it big because they aren't selling the image that people want them to sell.

Chris: Like Malcolm X once said, the media is the most powerful entity on Earth. Anything they say, people will believe. Right now, the radio plays 50 Cent every five minutes, and that's why he's hot.

Damali: I've heard a lot of people say that they didn't really like 50 Cent, but they've heard his songs so many times, they finally began to like him. It's a cycle: People buy what you sell them because you're pushing it in their face.

Chris: African American children start adopting these [stereotypical, racialized] images at a very early age. I've seen babies wearing du-rags, gold chains, and jerseys. I've seen little kids cursing and trying to drink liquor because their parents are doing it and their big brothers and sisters are doing it. Little girls wear short skirts because their parents think it's cute. It's all part of a certain attitude and a way of life. It is all that they know. If the parents like it, the teenagers will like it and the babies will like it. If parents listen to jazz, the kids will listen to jazz. If they listen to gangster rap, their kids will like that.

Stephanie: Can playing violent video games make people act violently?

Stephen: I have been playing video games since I was four years old. Games weren't that violent back then, like *Mario Brothers,* where you would just jump on a guy's head to kill him. Then when games like *Mortal Combat* came out, it got more controversial because there was so much blood. My parents never saw me play video games so they didn't know to censor me. They bought them but they didn't know what was in them and that you could buy two versions—with or without blood; you could turn the gore content off.

Svetlana: Do you all play *Grand Theft Auto?*

Stephen: I like *Grand Theft Auto* because it's so real. You can go around the streets shooting people, taking cars, and buying prostitutes. You walk around the streets, and then steal a car, and the police start chasing you and you can shoot back at them. It's a fun game because it's so real.

Chris: I like *Grand Theft Auto* because there are no restrictions; it lets you do whatever you want to do. It's kind of like another life. You can go around exploring. You can just drive around for a while and pick up passengers.

Ife: My brother likes video games. He tries to get my father to buy him army and military games, but my father says no. He says it's just another way to train a child for the army, to go around shooting people. That is the one type of game that my brother is not allowed to play. So usually he just plays racing games.

Stephanie: Do you think there should be age restrictions placed on video games?

Stephen: I first began playing video games when I was five or six years old and there weren't that many restrictions because the graphics weren't as realistic. Now they have different ratings for each game—like Mature or Adults Only.

Chris: I think the ratings are more for difficulty. Some games are too hard and too complex for kids to learn how to play. Games like racing games are really easy to play, while *Grand Theft Auto* is too hard.

Stephen: When I was five, I wouldn't even know how to play *Grand Theft Auto.* Games were more simple back then. In *Mario Brothers,* all you did was cross the screen. I don't know how kids nowadays play these complex video games.

Svetlana: Do you think it's possible for someone to confuse real life and a video game?

Damali: If you can't tell the difference, you must have a mental disability.

Chris: I don't see any relation. How could you not tell the difference?

Damali: I can kind of see how someone can see violent movies and violent TV shows and can hypothetically see themselves killing someone. But there is a huge gap between that and actually picking up a knife or a gun and pulling the trigger. When you pull the trigger of a gun, you know what you're doing.

Tynesha McHarris and **Kehinde Togun** enter the discussion.

Kehinde Togun, nineteen, is a sophomore at Rutgers University. He has been on the board of YFEN since 2002. From 2000 to 2002 he was on the editorial board of Sex ETC, *a national newsletter written by teens for teens. Kehinde was born in Nigeria and now lives with his mother, who is a nurse.*

Tynesha McHarris, eighteen, is a freshman at Rutgers.

Tynesha and Kehinde are co-founders of Breaking the Chains, an after-school mentoring program in Westside Newark, NJ. The program provides youth mentoring and an afterschool shelter to about forty to fifty locals.

Svetlana: What about nudes—can you draw nudes in school?

Chris: They allow nude drawing in my school. We have models who pose for us who are in their twenties and thirties. On the first day, everybody is usually laughing for the first five minutes but if anyone jokes around later, they just look stupid. We are allowed to hang our nudes in the hallway.

Damali: We don't have an elective like that, but I don't think my school would ban it.

Svetlana: Well, in quite a few schools, we have had incidents where students were not allowed to show their drawings when they included nudity. Why do you think people censor images of nudes?

Damali: I think they think that kids will see nude images and want to go out and have sex. But I don't think kids look at it that way. If anything, they'll be like, "Ewww, he's forty-five years old!"

Svetlana: When you went to art museums as a child and saw nudes, did that affect you in any way? Were you embarrassed?

Tynesha: When I was a little kid, my mother took me to museums and I liked what I saw. It wasn't about sexuality but about art. It never bothered me.

Chris: When I saw nude art, I never made a connection with sex; I never got turned on or anything like that. In truth, I sometimes find drawings of nudes to be boring. It's just art . . . unless an adult has made you feel like you shouldn't want to see it.

Damali: I don't know if anyone else has realized this, but the women who are often painted nude are kind of chunky. But they are still very beautiful. I think it's healthy to see that their body is beautiful, and they celebrate their being chunky. Nowadays on TV, all we see are skinny models who look like they will break. They are clothed, but they are *much* more harmful than paintings of full-figured women. If anything, they should stop these harmful images of skinny women, because they are the ones who are making people vomit every day.

Chris: What I really hate are those reality shows, like the one that tries to see if you are "hot or not." Every person that they picked out as hot was blond and had fake breasts and was wearing a pink bikini. Every single one of them!

I saw plastic surgery on MTV on a show called *True Life Stories.* It's nasty. The girls on this show had plastic surgery. They had their noses done, their lips done, and they were never satisfied. They continued going back to the doctor. They looked fine in the first place, they look fine now, but they kept wanting to get more done. And the doctor was just cashing in, saying, "I see this little pocket of fat here." One guy on the show was really muscular and he wanted calf implants. Why would you want calf implants? If someone is so insecure about their body, they are never going to be satisfied. It's a lot worse for women, but it also affects men.

Svetlana: Do you think keeping controversial topics out of school protects children? For instance, under pressure from some religious leaders in the community, a Cincinnati theater cancelled the production of a play about the Palestinian teenager who became a suicide bomber. The play was supposed to be performed at schools in the area and the fear was that bringing up the controversial topic of Palestinian-Israeli relations—no matter how carefully and sensitively—would make some kids feel bad.

Damali: How is that any worse than showing films of black people getting lynched during slavery times? Have you ever been to The Great Blacks in Wax Museum? It's really graphic. I wouldn't say I was traumatized when I saw it in sixth grade, but a lot of people came out crying. It shows the chronological history of black people in America. It showed the fact about how women were raped, not allowed to have children, how they were all stacked on top of each other, how many died. It was all so real, like walking into a slave ship. They also had pictures of what the people looked like after they were whipped. I think it's really healthy—even if people came out crying. It's healthy for kids to see that and realize what happened in their past. You realize why you are here; you realize, hey, I'm something special because my ancestors went through something so incredible. And only the strong survived.

Svetlana: Should there be an age limit for kids to be admitted to such museums?

Kehinde: If I had a seven-year-old, I wouldn't take them to the Wax Museum. There should be some sensitivity toward a child's level of maturity and development. Children cry for a reason, and they shouldn't be made to cry just because they don't understand something. If you're twelve or thirteen years old, and your parents think you're old enough to see that, then you should see it.

Stephanie: Who do you think has the right to censor?

Kehinde: I think parents have the right. If I had a seven-year-old child, I wouldn't want them watching BET, MTV, or any of those stations. As children grows older though, their parents can judge how mature they are.

Damali: I can see why parents should have the ability to censor, but at the same time, their children must go out into the real world. The school system should have a right to step in at a certain age and say, "Your kid needs to learn about this." Kids need to know what's out there.

Kehinde: On the flip side, there are some parents who can't be so involved with their kids' lives because they have so many other issues to deal with. If I'm worrying about my crack addiction, the last thing I'm going to think about is my kid's sex education.

Chris: That's where schools should come in with programs, so that kids will know these things about human life and be able to protect themselves. I don't see why this is even an argument.

Stephanie: What does political correctness mean to you?

Stephen: P.C. is just being polite, like, don't call someone "black," call them "African American." You can't call Asians "Orientals."

Stephanie: Who is allowed to use the word "nigger"?

Everybody: Nobody!

Kehinde: Nobody is allowed to use that term. I don't care if you're black or white.

Stephanie: So you all think that term should just be abolished from our vocabulary?

Everybody: Yes!

Chris: I don't like that word period; it's the only word that I actually hate. I've been talking to my friend about that since we were little. I remember seeing this old *Webster's Dictionary* and I looked up black and it said "evil," and I looked up white and it said "pure as snow." It must have been fourth grade, I took the dictionary to school and told everybody and I kinda lost the battle, everyone told me to forget it.

Stephanie: It seems like in all the instances we've brought up, you've said censorship is bad. But in this case, do you think censorship is good?

Kehinde: It's not censorship. The word itself is just a bad word. I have no problem taking it out of the English language.

Svetlana: What about the word "gay" or "faggot" being used in a derogatory way?

Chris: I find myself guilty of saying those things. But like when Eminem says it, he doesn't mean it as in: "I don't like gay people." Of course, it's bad if you use it in a bad way. When you say someone is a "faggot," it's different if you say it to hurt them, and different if you say it to your friend. Then it's more like a joke. There is no relation to gay people whatsoever.

Kehinde: People may say that it's okay to call someone gay if you don't mean it in a derogatory way, but I don't agree.

Chris: I still don't think it's okay to say "gay" or "faggot" or anything, but I just know that people don't mean it to be derogatory.

Damali: But it *is* what people mean. It's like a white person saying, "Oh, you're such a nigger." You may not be saying it to a person to hurt their feelings, but we both know where the word originates. So why use it at all?

Kehinde: With "nigger," people say it's empowerment, a term of endearment.

Chris: I think sometimes that putting words out there makes them a joke. I think that is the only defense that people have. The word loses its value. If someone calls you the "n" word, you wouldn't get mad, it's just a joke. When your friend calls you that, it takes the hate out of the word. You don't think twice about it; you use it in every other sentence.

Damali: But isn't it bad to put minstrel shows on TV so we can laugh at it, so that we don't remember how degrading it was for people? Back then, when someone called you a nigger, you couldn't answer back—or they would have beaten you. It's sad to know that people are looking at it half-heartedly so they can laugh at it. Pretty soon, no one will remember how horrible it was before.

Chris: But do you really want people to go through that again—being hurt by those words?

Damali: It should be a word that you don't use as a joke. You shouldn't be saying, "Oh, it's not that bad anymore."

Chris: It's like taking the word away—period.

Stephanie: How is that not censorship?

Damali: I think censorship in this case is fine. It is just a word that we should no longer use. Diluting it or making the word "not that bad" is still a bad thing.

Chris: How is keeping it a bad word, like "nigger" always was, a good thing?

Damali: If not, people will forget what other people had to go through.

Chris: People will never forget that.

Damali: People should know not to use that word. They should know what the meaning was. It shouldn't be thrown around as a joke. It should be the same as a curse word, like—Oh! You just said a bad word. Don't!

19

VIOLENT VIDEO GAME PLAYERS MYSTERIOUSLY AVOID KILLING SELVES, OTHERS

Seth Killian

Maybe the next time a social scientist or politician is interested in making pronouncements about the effects of violent video games, they should actually check out the players.

I'm a lifelong video game player and a former national champion at "Street Fighter" (one of the world's most popular video games), for which I now organize international tournaments. I'm no social-science researcher, and my experiences are clearly anecdotal. However, I've seen the effects of violent video games—and on a scale far broader than any laboratory experiment. The advocates who claim there is a link between violence and video games should test their hypotheses at our events.

The tournaments take the games that invite you to punch, kick, shoot, and slash your way to domination, and put them into a testosterone-soaked crucible of competition. Add a discourse of insults and bragging, an almost maximal culture clash, and members of rival street gangs. Stir the pot with incessant noise, emotional stress, sleeplessness, and terrible food. What do you get? According to attendees, the best time they've had, with zero physically violent incidents in the ten years of these events.

Players scream, curse, and even hit the machines in disgust, but not each other. At events that include a wide spectrum of races, creeds, ages, and socioeconomic backgrounds, battles are left strictly in-game. Stepping outside to share cigarettes, a pizza, or to buy Cokes, they ask "Where you from?" Answers range from Long Island to Peru; Kuwait to Korea.

The universities that host our tournaments would kill to have the kind of diversity Street Fighter attracts. Far outnumbering the stereotypical pasty white geeks are black guys in cowboy getups, hip-hop Arabs, ex-Marines, and Vietnamese gang members.

So here's a situation where you've got thousands of unruly people playing some of the most purely violent games. They've been maximally exposed to these games, many from childhood. They are overwhelmingly young and male. They're being tested in front of their friends, with pride and money on the line, against people they may be prejudiced against. So where's the violence?

There's no evidence that these players are more violent in other settings than any other cross-section of the population, either. Connected by chat rooms and message boards, the community is close-knit and heavily into gossiping. A lot of these players are also friends of mine. If they were in to violent behavior, the other players and I would know.

If you can set aside your amazement at our failure to slaughter one another, you might even notice something else: a vibrant, diverse, and even democratic community. These tournaments are entirely grassroots, sponsorless, player-produced productions. Those who can, help out as translators; DJs and stage crew geeks set up the lights and sound; and people with arcade experience keep the equipment in good repair. Everyone's a player, no one is paid, and all the entry fees go directly into the prize pool. Apart from the swearing, insults, and virtual violence, it's kind of like an Amish barn raising.

Whether by allowing them a measure of control over an otherwise chaotic life, a venue to find respect, or a way of defusing daily frustrations, these games and the community have been credited by players with everything from helping them find jobs to getting them out of gang life. They make lasting friends of people from cultures and backgrounds they would otherwise have never met.

The existing research on violent video games can't explain this reality, because most of it is flawed. Sample sizes are ludicrously small, comparisons are made between radically different games, and multiple and poorly defined variables are often invalid. Studies invariably conclude by glossing over these evidentiary gaps to reach the desired conclusion, linking barely measurable, innocuous laboratory behaviors with an appetite for real-world destruction.

These failings are well documented by researchers like Henry Jenkins and Jonathan Freedman, who have called for rigor to replace the rhetoric, though largely to no avail. As a result, there is less a miscommunication between players and psychologists, politicians, and parents than no communication at all. Pundits predictably spout contrived, even laughable conclusions, while remaining pointedly oblivious to the routine experiences of millions and millions of actual players.

Science doesn't have to be politicized to be bad, but it sure helps.

20

CENSORSHIP: THE SEXUAL MEDIA AND THE AMBIVALENCE OF KNOWING

Judith Levine

> The twin concepts of innocence and ignorance are vehicles for adult double standards. A child is ignorant if she doesn't know what adults want her to know, but innocent if she doesn't know what adults don't want her to know.
>
> —Jenny Kitzinger,
> *Children, Power, and the Struggle Against Sexual Abuse*[1]

Around the turn of the twenty-first century, America was inundated by censorship in the name of protecting "children" from "sex." Among the most frequent targets was Maurice Sendak's classic *In the Night Kitchen,* because its main character, a boy of about five named Max, tumbles through his dream with his genitals bare. Paul Zaloom, the star of the children's TV science program *Dr. Beekman's Universe,* was forbidden by his producers to answer his viewers' most-asked question: What is a fart?[2] Even sex educators were not allowed to speak about sex. In 1996, when author Robie Harris went on the radio in Oklahoma to promote her children's book, *It's Perfectly Normal: Changing Bodies, Growing Up, Sex & Sexual Health,* the host requested that she not mention the S-word. Harris was obliged to refer to sex as "the birds and the bees."[3]

The cultural historian Michel Foucault said that sex is policed not by silence but by endless speech, by the "deployment" of more and more "discourses" of social regulation—psychology, medicine, pedagogy. While producing plenty of regulatory chatter from on high, our era also saw an explosion of unofficial, anarchic, and much more exciting discourses down below. When the sexual revolution collided with the boom in media technologies, mediasex mushroomed. Sexual imagery proliferated like dirty laundry: The minute you washed it and put it away, there was more. In Times Square, whose streets were transformed into a Disney-Warner "family-friendly" mall, the neon signs from shut-down peep shows were put on exhibit in a sort of Museum of the Smutty Past at the back of the tourist information office. Meanwhile, looming over the heads of camera-toting tour groups from Iowa, half-block-long billboards advertised Calvin Klein underwear, inside of whose painted shadows lurked penises as large as redwood logs.

As the ability to segregate audiences by age, sex, class, or geography shrank, we arrived at a global capitalist economy that—despite all our tsk-tsking—found sex exceedingly marketable and in which children and teens served as both sexual commodities (JonBenet Ramsey, Thai child prostitutes) and consumers of sexual commodities (Barbie dolls, Boyz 2 Men). All this inspired a campaign with wide political support to return to reticence,[4] especially when the kids were around.

History gives the lie to the notion that we live in a world of sexual speech at the turn of the twenty-first century and we did not, say, three centuries ago. There was plenty of dirty song-singing and breast- and buttock-grabbing that a child could witness in any sixteenth-century publick house. Still, there is a reason, particular to the last several decades, to be concerned about the world of unfiltered, unfettered sexual knowledge. *Pictures and words have attained unprecedented cultural influence in our time.* Our marketplace produces few actual widgets; we make almost nothing but digitized ideas and the media to send them from place to place. As the economy moves from the Steel Belt to Silicon Alley, the boundary between the symbolic and the real is disappearing. In many cases, representation is no longer just a facsimile of a thing. It is a thing itself.

Nobody lives more in the "hypermediated"[5] environment than the young. At the end of the twentieth century, a quarter of kids had their own TVs by the time they were five years old.[6] It was no use telling kids to go outside and get a "real" life. Why play sandlot baseball when you can pitch to Sammy Sosa from a virtual mound? Even technologized sexual speech no longer just stands for sex, it *is* sex. Sherry Turkle, a social analyst of computer communication at the Massachusetts Institute of Technology, described the onscreen erotic exchanges that Netizens call "tinysex": "A thirteen-year-old informs me that she prefers to do her sexual experimentation online. Her partners are usually the boys in her class at school. In person, she says, it is "mostly grope-y." Online, "they need to talk more."[7]

Where do you learn about sex? a TV interviewer asked a fifteen-year-old from a small rural town. "We have eighty-two channels," the girl replied.

Oversophisticated

The chat on any post-sexual revolution Internet site might make Alice Cramden blush. But public steaminess was around long before the Summer of Love, and for centuries there were Tipper Gores and Dan Quayles at hand to decry it. "It is impossible to prevent every thing that is capable of sullying the imagination," lamented the anonymous author of *Onania, or the Heinous Sin of Self-Pollution, And All its Frightful Consequences, in Both Sexes consider'd,* a best-selling antimasturbation treatise published in England around 1700 and exported to America soon after. *"Dogs* in the Streets and *Bulls* in the Fields may do mischief to Debauch's Fancy's, and it is possible that either Sex may be put in mind of Lascivious Thoughts, by their own *Poultry."*[8]

In the late 1800s the New York Society for the Prevention of Cruelty to Children "kept a watchful eye upon the so-called Museums of the City," whose advertisements were "like magnets to curious children." According to one of the society's reports, a play featuring "depravity, stabbing, shooting, and blood-shedding" so traumatized a ten-year-old girl that she was found "wander[ing] aimlessly along Eighth Avenue as if incapable of ridding herself of the dread impressions that had filled her young mind."[9]

By 1914, Agnes Repellier, a popular conservative essayist, was inveighing against the film and publishing industry "coining money" by creating a generation hypersophisticated in sin. "Children's sources of knowledge are manifold, and astoundingly explicit," she wrote in *The Atlantic.* Repellier may have been the first to propose a movie-rating system, asking "the authorities" to bar children from all shows dealing with prostitution.[10]

The media-abetted breakdown of morality was news again in 1934. "Think of the adolescent's world of electric lights, lurid movies, automobiles, speed, jazz and night clubs, literature tinged with pornography, and the theater presenting problems of perversion, the many cheap magazines with fabricated tales of true love, the growing cults of nudism and open confessions, the prevalence of economic uncertainty," Dr. Ira S. Wile wrote, discoursing on "The Sexual Problems of Adolescence" in the journal of the American Social Hygiene Association.[11]

Sound familiar?

Against such invective has always stood a kind of *faute de mieux* realism, which articulates the same sad tale, but sees the outcome as inevitable. In 1997, a Disney executive explained how media and changes in the family created the sophisticated child, who created the media, which changed the family, who created the child . . . and the beast chased its tail faster and faster until it turned into butter (and went rancid). "Today's eight-year-olds are yesterday's twelve-year-olds. They watch some very edgy programs on television. There isn't this innocence of childhood among many children, what with broken homes and violence. We can't treat children as if they're all living in tract homes of the 1950s and everyone is happy. That is ridiculous."[12]

On kids' sophistication, the evidence was with him. In a survey of 3,200 urban and suburban elementary school kids in the 1970s (before MTV!), "the most productive responses were elicited with the instructions, 'Why children shouldn't be allowed to see R- and X-rated movies'; or 'What is in R- and X-rated movies that children are too young to know about?' Here, the children proceeded with aplomb to tell all that they knew but were not supposed to know." Samuel Janus and Barbara Bess, the psychologists who conducted the study, concluded: "One learns that what the adult world has established is an adult psychic censor that will not admit of children's growth and experience. Selective perception may becloud and avoid awareness of childhood sexuality, but it does not eliminate [that sexuality]."[13]

Curiosity

In young children, curiosity about bodies and the making of babies is considered normal and nice. In fact, curiosity is a reassuring explanation of what otherwise might look like the quest for bodily pleasure. "In a child's mind, this investigation [of the body] is much the same as, say, tinkering with toys to see how they operate or watching birds build a nest," wrote Toni Cavanaugh Johnson, a self-styled expert on children's "touching problems."[14] But if curiosity is cute in the kitten, we suspect it could kill the cat.

Our crudest and oldest fear about letting out too much sexual information is that it will lead kids to "try this at home" as soon as they are able—a sort of user's manual model of sexual knowledge.

The relationship between seeing and doing is, to say the least, complex. On one hand, it is intuitively clear and affirmed by social science that learning about sex affects what a person does and feels about it. "The body has a history and a social context that shape meanings and lived experience," wrote University of Massachusetts sociologist Janice Irvine.[15] Sex is cultural. In the United States, kissing is step one of sex. In Burma, kissing is considered unsanitary and disgusting.[16] Sex is historical. Awareness of the erotic utility of silk may date back millennia, but a rubber fetish could not possibly predate 1823, when the first process was developed for rolling rubber into sheets. Even the idea that people have "sexual identities" is less than a hundred years old, as gay historian Jonathan Ned Katz has shown. Before that, a man who engaged in genital acts with another man is simply a man engaging in acts; he is not a particular kind of person, a "homosexual." Sex is influenced by books, art, movies, TV, advertising, and what your friends say. How many women in the 1970s figured out how to have orgasms by reading other women's techniques in *The Hite Report on Women's Sexuality*?

Learning about a sex act doesn't toggle the desire switch to "on" or the body switch to "go." Rather, one reacts to an image or idea out of his or her own experiences and all the scripts he's learned. For a child, those experiences might include an incident of incest, a thrilling experience of mutual masturbation with another child, a course in good touch and bad touch, or a joke heard on the playground. The relationship between learning about sex and doing sex is "more like the world weather system than a chemical reaction," commented University of Hawaii early childhood educator Joseph Tobin. "It's a chaos model we need: One cause can have various effects or different effects than we expected."

Still, the dark suspicion of a direct link between knowing and doing created from the start a conundrum for sex educators, which has endured: how to inform youth about the facts of sex without inflaming their lust? Educators, like parents, worry that if the right adults ("us") do not tell kids the right things about sex (disease and reproduction) in the right way (clinically), the wrong ones will tell them the wrong things. Put another way, sex education, like obscenity law, was founded on the notion that you can separate clean sex from dirty sex.

For the purposes of edification, clean sex is the sex that occurs in committed, preferably legally sanctioned, age-of-majority, heterosexual reproductive relationships; and it includes responsible pre-coital conversation, safer-sex devices, and post-coital cuddling. Clean sex is "scientific," explicated in anatomically correct language and rendered in two-dimensional drawings of fallopian tubes and vas deferens. Dirty sex is all the rest: the sex of the servants' quarters, the street, the schoolyard, of *Penthouse Letters, Baywatch,* 1-900-923-SUCK, and Hotbutts.com. It comes in willy-nilly, festooned with advertising.

But the enterprise of sanitizing sex is always quixotic. For one, clean sex doesn't capture the attention of the young. "When schools teach you about sex, it's just a big blah," one high-school girl told a CBS reporter. "This is a penis, this is a vagina," a male classmate elaborated.

At the same time, even Shakespeare or ancient Indian miniatures can be as filthy as a barnyard. The anthropologist Mary Douglas tells us that dirt is "matter out of place," but to the child who is forbidden it, all sexual knowledge is knowledge out of place, and therefore dirty. Ask the child who has thrilled at uncovering a little cache of penis-related words, right there in the dictionary between *peninsulate* and *penitence,* and she will agree with Douglas: "Dirt is in the eyes of the beholder." A resigned father summed it up in answering a *New York Times* survey about media and children: "Kids are always going to want to watch what we don't want them to."[17]

In part, it's because we don't want them to. Confessing the schoolboy misdemeanor of stealing forbidden fruit, St. Augustine, one of the fathers of Western sexual anxiety, put it this way: "My pleasure was not in those pears. It was in the offense itself."

Harm

The idea that young minds (and female minds and feeble minds) are vulnerable to bad thoughts, which might lead to bad acts, may be considered the founding principle of obscenity law. In 1868, an English anti-clerical pamphlet called "The Confessional Unmasked" was deemed punishably obscene because its text might "suggest to the minds of the young of either sex, and even to persons of more advanced years, thoughts of a most impure and libidinous character."[18]

However, from the seventeenth century to the twenty-first, evidence of the harm of exposure to sexually explicit images or words in childhood is inconclusive, even nonexistent. The 1970 U.S. Commission on Obscenity and Pornography, the "Lockhart Commission," uncovered no link between adult exposure to pornography and bad behavior and called for dismantling legal restrictions on erotica. Not only did the panelists fail to find harm to children in viewing erotica, moreover, they went so far as to suggest it could "facilitate much needed communication between parent and child over sexual matters."[19] Interviews of sex criminals including child molesters reveal that the children who eventually became rapists were usually exposed to pornography less than other kids;[20] if they'd seen the same amount, they didn't see it earlier in life.[21] According to Johns Hopkins University's John Money, one of the world's foremost authorities on sexual abnormalities, "the majority of patients with paraphilias"—or deviant sexual fantasies and behaviors—"described a strict anti-sexual upbringing in which sex was either never mentioned or was actively repressed or defiled."[22]

But such data are, in a sense, politically irrelevant. Marjorie Heins, former head of the ACLU's Arts Censorship Project, found that laws prohibiting minors' access to sexual materials are routinely passed and upheld without recourse to any evidence whatsoever.[23] The moral wisdom of shielding minors from sexy materials was seen as self-evident.

Since Attorney General Edwin Meese's 1985 Commission on Pornography, this presumed harm has become even more "evident." When the commission sat, the Right was in ascendancy and a rump caucus of feminists had singled out pornography not only as the cause of sexual violence to women but as a species of sexual violence in itself. So while the lion's share of the testimony it heard concerned adult materials and consumers, the commission pitched its pro-restriction recommendations to popular fears about children: "For children to be taught by these materials that sex is public, that sex is commercial, and that sex can be divorced from any degree of affection, love, commitment, or marriage," the report read, "is for us the wrong message at the wrong time."[24]

The commission lent new legitimacy to the idea that pornography causes harm, especially to children, and since its hearings that notion has mushroomed, morphing into the suspicion that exposing children to *any* explicit sexual information can hurt them. In recent years, whether the target was nude photos in museum exhibitions, contraceptive information videotapes, or the satanic Barney the Purple Dinosaur, censorship proponents have advertised nearly every assault on speech as a defense of children.

The story of one sex-ed curriculum demonstrates this change in attitude over a third of a century. Around the time of the Lockhart commission, the national Unitarian Universalist Church devised a sex-education program called "About Your Sexuality" for preteen and teenage church members. In some AYS sessions, educators screened filmstrips featuring naturalistic, explicit drawings of people engaged in sexual activities from masturbation to two men kissing. For decades, the program received praise and gratitude from parents, and graduates of the program were glad to enroll their own children in it.

Then, in 1997, two parents in Concord, Massachusetts, protested. Someone informed CBS's right-wing libertarian commentator Bryant Gumble, who rushed in to expose the shocking truth. "Guess who's showing sexually explicit films to children? The church!" blared the segment's teaser. One of the aggrieved mothers was filmed in tears, and a child-abuse "expert" intoned, "It could be disturbing to some kids—and even harmful." The hour wound up with an instant poll of viewers: 74 percent said it is "never okay to show graphic sexual visuals to teenagers in the context of sex education."[25]

Shortly thereafter, the church introduced a new sex-ed curriculum, "Our Whole Lives." According to the church's curriculum director, Judith Frediani, OWL was "far more inclusive and pro-active" than AYS in its "positive message about sexuality." For instance, the discussion of transsexuality is extensive and "sympathetic," and while the curriculum explores abstinence, "we don't tell [youngsters] what decision to make." Nevertheless, the explicit visuals were removed and repackaged as an optional supplement available only to UU-affiliated congregations; parents must now preview the visuals and give written permission for their children to see them.

Did the pictures suddenly become harmful to minors? Current conventional wisdom says yes, and, said Frediani, "Like everyone else, our folks are more cautious, more conservative." Still, anecdotes adds up. Although thirty years of preteens and teens have cycled through About

Your Sexuality—a sufficient subject pool in any social scientist's estimation—the psychological literature contains no reference to a disproportionate number of Unitarians among sexual deviants.

What Is Premature?

It is hard to say what "children" are "taught" by porn or any other sexual imagery or words they encounter in the media. Many sexologists suspect that sexual information gleaned before a person can understand it either bores or escapes or possibly disgusts him or her, but doesn't hurt.[26] Given the gradual and idiosyncratic nature of children's maturation and learning, the timing mechanism of sex education probably resembles a sundial more than the IBM Olympic stopwatch. Still, "timing" or "age-appropriateness" is widely portrayed as a determination of high sensitivity, with miscalculations carrying grave, possibly irreversible, consequences. "Although secrecy makes for dangerous ignorance, too much openness can turn on what is meant to stay turned off until later," childraising adviser Penelope Leach warned the readers of *Redbook*.[27]

In the 1990s, concerns about "timing" inspired two strategies of restriction. Movie producers, and later their colleagues in TV, sliced the young viewing public into precise age categories: this film was "appropriate" for thirteen-year-olds but not twelve-year-olds, that one for seventeen-year-olds accompanied by an adult (who could be eighteen), but not without one. A series of Internet "decency" bills took the opposite tack, instituting a category of "minors" that covers territory as wide as Siberia. For these laws' purposes, the class of people vulnerable to the trauma of seeing a picture of a penis entering a vagina included both the seventeen-year-old sexually active high-school senior and the three-year-old preschooler who pronounces the word "bagina."

All this classification reveals deep anxieties about what childhood is—and about the waning ability to separate the boys and girls from the men and women. The liberal educator Neil Postman dated the "disappearance of childhood" to the invention of the telegraph in the mid-1800s, which eventually spurred a mass media that availed all people at all ages of all sexual secrets. And "without secrets," he wrote, "there is no such thing as childhood."[28]

Perhaps there are no longer any secrets, and media are not the only culprit. Global capitalism and modern warfare dictate that the world's children partake in every activity considered exclusively adult—commerce, crime, soldiering, sex. Indeed, twenty-first-century children may be more like adults than they have been since the seventeenth century, when historians tell us "childhood" was invented.

It is unlikely the air will get less dense with information, or with sex. No law, no Internet filter, no vigilant parent will be able to keep tabs on every page and pixel that passes before a child's eyes beyond about the age of two. But censorship is not protection. Rather, to give the young a fighting chance in navigating the sexual world, adults need to saturate it with accurate information and abundant images and narratives of love and sex, then help kids sort them out.

Notes

1. Jenny Kitzinger, "Children, Power, and the Struggle Against Sexual Abuse," in *Constructing and Reconstructing Childhood,* ed. Allison James and Alan Prout (London: Falmer Press, 1990): 161.
2. Marc Silver, with Katherine T. Beddingfield and Kenan Pollack, "Sex, Violence and the Tube," *U.S. News & World Report* (September 1993): 76–79.
3. Susan N. Wilson, "Who's Afraid of the Big Bad Word?" *Censorship News* (New York: National Coalition Against Censorship: winter 1996): 5.
4. I borrow this term from Agnes Repellier, at note 10.
5. This term was coined by Henry Jenkins, of the Massachusetts Institute of Technology.
6. "A Child's Eye View," *New York Times* (December 31, 1997).
7. Sherry Turkle, *Life on the Screen: Identity in the Age of the Internet* (New York: Simon & Schuster, 1995): 26.
8. Roy Porter, "Forbidden Pleasures: Enlightenment Literature of Sexual Advice," in *Solitary Pleasures: The Historical, Literary, and Artistic Discourses of Autoeroticism,* eds. Paula Bennett and Vernon A. Rosario II (New York: Routledge, 1995): 81.
9. *Fifteenth Annual Report,* Case 39,591 (New York: New York Society for the Prevention of Cruelty to Children, 1890): 15–16.
10. Agnes Repellier, "The Repeal of Reticence," *The Atlantic* (March 1914): 207–304.
11. Ira S. Wile, "The Sexual Problems of Adolescents," *Journal of Social Hygiene* 20, No. 9 (December 1934): 439–440.
12. Bernard Weintraub, "Fun for the Whole Family," *New York Times* (July 22, 1997).
13. Samuel S. Janus and Barbara E. Bess, "Latency: Fact or Fiction?" *The American Journal of Psychoanalysis* 36, no. 4 (1976): 339–346.
14. John Rosemond, "Talking to Kids About Sex," *Better Homes and Gardens* (September 1993): 166.

15. Janice Irvine, "Cultural Differences and Adolescent Sexualities," in *Sexual Cultures and the Construction of Adolescent Identities,* ed. Janice Irvine (Philadelphia: Temple University Press, 1994): 21.
16. Author interview with Leonore Tiefer, May 1996.
17. Elizabeth Kolbert, "Americans Despair of Popular Culture," *New York Times* (August 20, 1995): 23.
18. Marjorie Heins, "INDECENCY: The Great American Debate Over Sex, Children, Free Speech, and Dirty Words," Andy Warhol Foundation for the Visual Arts/Paper #7 (1997): 4.
19. *Report of the Commission on Obscenity and Pornography* (Washington: Lockhart Commission, 1970): 23–27.
20. Mary R. Murrin and D.R. Laws, "The Influence of Pornography on Sexual Crimes," in W.L. Marshall, D.R. Laws, and H.E. Barbaree eds., *Handbook of Sexual Assault* (New York: Plenum Press, 1990): 83–84.
21. David E. Nutter and Mary E. Kearns, "Patterns of Exposure to Sexually Explicit Material Among Sex Offenders, Child Molesters, and Controls," *Journal of Sex and Marital Therapy* 19 (Spring 1993): 73–85.
22. See John Money, *Love Maps: Clinical Concepts of Sexual/Erotic Health and Pathology, Paraphilia and Gender Transposition, Childhood, Adolescence and Maturity* (New York: Irving Publishers, 1986); Irene Diamond, "Pornography and Repression: A Reconsideration," *Signs* (summer 1989), 689; David Futrelle, "Shameful Pleasures," *In These Times* (March 7, 1994): 17.
23. Marjorie Heins, *Sex, Sin, and Blasphemy: A Guide to America's Censorship Wars* (New York: New Press, 1993).
24. *Report of the Surgeon General's Workshop on Pornography and Public Health* (Washington: U.S. Dept. of Justice, 1986): 344.
25. "Public Eye," CBS-TV (Oct. 8, 1997).
26. *Report of the Surgeon General's Workshop,* 36–8.
27. Penelope Leach, "Kids and Sex Talk," *Redbook* (October 1993): 178.
28. Neil Postman, *The Disappearance of Childhood* (New York: Vintage Books, 1994): 80.

21
"NOT A PRETTY PICTURE": FOUR PHOTOGRAPHERS TELL THEIR PERSONAL STORIES ABOUT CHILD "PORNOGRAPHY" AND CENSORSHIP

Marian Rubin, Jacqueline Livingston, Marilyn Zimmerman, and Betsy Schneider

Marian Rubin

On the morning of February 3, 2000, on my way to work, I dropped off a roll of film at MotoPhoto in Upper Montclair, New Jersey, with a note stating that I would pick up my pictures some time around 3:30 the same day.

When I went to pick up my film, the police was waiting for me. They proceeded to question me about my photographs. The images were of my granddaughters, ages three and eight, naked, frolicking around the bedroom prior to taking a bath. They were having fun showing me their Britney Spears and Christina Aguilera "moves." We were all laughing and giggling; just unselfconscious "girl" stuff.

I could understand the police questioning me and felt certain that when they learned that the children were my grandchildren, that would be the end of it. Shockingly, it was far from the end of "it."

I was *booked,* fingerprinted, "mugged" and finally released on $50,000 bail (usually reserved for murderers). I was charged with six counts of child endangerment (felonies) and was not allowed to go home until the police had obtained a warrant to search my house. Police seized photographs, my computers, my printer, scanner, every CD-Rom, and every floppy disk. My eight-year-old granddaughter was awakened and questioned by the Division of Youth and Family Services (DYFS). My son's family was threatened: if they did not cooperate, the children could be removed from their home. For several weeks I was denied any contact with my granddaughters, while my family was "investigated." A social worker in the public school system for thirty-two years, I was immediately suspended from my job.

Initially, I really couldn't believe the police were serious. When the reality of the situation finally landed, I cried buckets. I couldn't believe that a trained prosecutor, head of the Sex Crimes Unit, would not be able to tell the difference between a criminal and a loving, adoring grandmother with a passion for photography. I was humiliated and yet very angry. The seizure of my work and my computer was a major violation and I felt like I imagine a victim of a rape might feel. I was distraught, degraded, and very depressed; I considered suicide. I was extremely upset for my children and my precious little girls. I was furious about the suggestions DYFS put into my granddaughters' head by asking her disgusting questions about things totally outside the realm of her experience.

I completed a Pre-Trial Intervention Program (this is a program designed to keep "first-time offenders" out of the criminal justice system) and was given one year of probation. The case was finally dismissed in February 2001.

After the case was dismissed (without any admission or adjudication of guilt), I was told that my original photographs of the children had been "shredded and burned" and that the prosecutor was refusing to return other photographs, journals, etc. on the grounds that they were "contraband." I hired another attorney to sue for the return of my property. In June 2001, the federal court judge stated that "these were innocent, harmless photos, family photos, and should be returned." Just before this hearing, among some stuff returned to me by the Montclair Police, I discovered all of the "shredded and burned" photos, intact.

Today, I am far less naive and trusting. It is frightening to realize the fragility of our civil rights and how easily they may be violated, on someone's whim.

I am appalled at the lack of integrity in the whole justice system from the police to the prosecutors, to the lawyers and judges. They are all willing to go along with a charade no matter what the cost to the innocent, in order to save face or serve their own agendas. They are even willing to lie, alter, delete, and, if necessary, plant "evidence." At best, they are inept.

It is amazing that determination of my innocence or guilt is left to the perception of the beholder, that someone with a contaminated imagination holds my fate in her hands. I resent being told what to think by people with dirty minds and twisted perceptions.

It is a bitter irony that in a society where much of the advertising and entertainment industries focus on sexuality, an innocent nude photograph of a child is automatically pornography.

I guess you can tell that when I talk about this, I still get very angry. Maybe I need an anger management program.

Since the "event," I have had another little granddaughter. She will soon be two. She is the most precious and beautiful child and I feel blessed by her existence. I have taken numerous photos of her but almost no nudes. I am now conscious of what "private" parts may be showing and how that might be interpreted, so I am censoring my own images and can no longer be spontaneous.

I see through a camera lens and this is the way I preserve memories, whether they be of my children, my grandchildren, childhood friends, long gone relatives or places I've been. My images are windows into my mind. They represent how I see the world, the people I love, my sense of beauty, my sense of anger or my sense of humor. My deepest resentment about what happened is that it has affected my work: it has altered my vision.

April 11, 2004

Jacqueline Livingston

In 1976, as an Assistant Professor of Photography at Cornell University, I exhibited a few photographs of male nudes, including one of my six-year-old son, Sam, playing with himself. My life quickly changed. I was called into the dean's office and told to remove my photographs from the exhibition because complaints had been filed; some were worried that children might see them. I refused to remove my photographs and argued in their defense, "My photographs were meant to challenge a sexually repressed culture, to open its eyes to the beauty of the male nude and the beauty of a child raised to be comfortable with nudity, owning his own body. Who better to see these photographs than children?"

A month later I was told my contract would not be renewed. In speaking to the art department chair, I was told bluntly, "You cannot be a feminist and stay at Cornell and furthermore, you cannot photograph male genitalia and expect to stay here either."

I had moved across country from San Francisco to Ithaca for this job. My marriage had ended; I had my child to support. Another move at this point seemed out of the question. After months of bargaining with Cornell, I threatened a sex-discrimination suit. Within one week, a one-year, nonrenewable contract arrived. At the end of that year (June 1978), when Cornell still did not provide reasons in writing for denying me further employment, I filed a sex-discrimination suit against the university with the Human Rights Commission of New York State.

In the fall of 1980, four other plaintiffs and I entered court with a class action sex-discrimination suit against Cornell. During the five years of litigation, thirty-six other women, ex-Cornell faculty, joined the suit. Cornell settled out of court for $250,000—$16,000 each for the five original plaintiffs. It was hardly a year's academic salary.

In October of 1979, I refinanced my home and published a series of fourteen posters (each 18 x 24 inches) containing over 200 photographic images of three generations of men—my son Sam, my husband John, and my father-in-law Richard. Each character's story is completed on four separate posters and ends with the final (fourteenth) poster showing the three males together again.

In Poster #1, running down the left of the poster, are four photos of my son. Sam is nude with his back to the camera, a boy of six, wearing a wig, lying on a bed with a rose-covered sheet. As the series progress, Sam looks over his shoulder at me (his photographer-mother) and says with his facial expression, "What are you up to? What's with the wig? You want people to think I'm a girl?" In the last frame, he flips over, spreads his legs, showing full frontal nudity with a grin from ear to ear, as if to say, "Hey! I am a boy! Take a look." The series title is "Sam on a Bed of Roses."

The second poster continues with Sam. Here he is still full of mischief, joking around. The camera moves in for close-ups of him playing with himself, unselfconscious. (This was the series of nine photos first exhibited at Cornell in 1976.)

In the second poster about Sam, he is eight and playing in the bathtub with a phallic-shaped balloon that he clearly recognized as such. He has fun pretending it is a gun and his penis, putting it between his legs, bending it, hugging and squeezing it, bouncing and sucking it—his toy.

In the third poster Sam is ten and nude in the first frame, then frame by frame he adds a piece of clothing and finally, with a bit of wishful thinking, he puts on his father's suit coat. Its oversize arms nearly cover his hands, only the ends of his fingertips show.

In the fourth and final poster about Sam, he is holding a cardboard cut-out of a suit coat nearly the size of his father's coat. It is covered with a collage of stereotypical male-role-icons representing cultural expectations. Sam takes the collaged coat to a cemetery, buries it, and leaves with its reverse shadow, a white cardboard cut-out of a suit coat, symbolic of a clean slate on which he can create his own future.

In the photographic posters about Sam's grandfather and father, each man starts out clothed and gets undressed (symbolically freeing themselves from cultural duress) in the process of transformation. In a series of ten photos, they make strained gestures and attempts at touching.

I sent a set of these 14 posters to a total of 300 museums, galleries, critics, and artists, asking them to hang the posters in whatever venue they could during the month of October 1979. This was a way to confront and bypass art-establishment practices that in essence censor (potentially) controversial work. Some of my peers in academe showed and discussed the posters in their art classes. At one school a professor attempted a public exhibition of the entire set only to be foiled by the school's president. The professor rented a space off-campus at his own expense and advertised. Hundreds lined up to see the show, and all four local TV stations reported the event.

On October 8, 1979, the *Village Voice* printed an interview with me by Howard Smith. They published three of the posters, including the one of Sam playing with himself. I received over 400 letters of congratulation and support from around the country, surprisingly only one was condemning, and sold nearly 100 sets. The negative side soon arrived. Howard Smith called saying, "Hide your posters. The American Society for the Prevention of Cruelty to Children is pounding at our door, threatening legal action against the *Voice.* They are calling your photos 'kiddie porn.' Their lawyers are talking to ours. If they bring charges, they could confiscate your work."

Then someone called the child abuse hotline about me. A letter from New York Child Protective Services informed me that I was under investigation for suspected child abuse; my character and fitness as a parent were questioned. I had to hire a lawyer. He got me a copy of New York State's child pornography law. I felt relieved that it seemed to allow for artistic merit and intent, and didn't automatically label all nudes "obscene." I was under the impression that my art was under the protection of the First Amendment. With this assurance, my son and I met with a social worker who questioned us with our lawyer present. My son was asked how he felt about the photographs of him ("Fine, we're nudist."), and I was asked, "Are you photographing other children nude?" ("No.")

The social worker had seen my fourteen posters in the local gallery in a feminist bookstore and said he supported my work. According to him, I was fortunate to have him assigned to my case; anyone else would have given me a hard time. Four months later, I received a letter declaring the accusations "unfounded." That was one of the happiest days of my life.

[Flashback:] Months before the *Voice* publication, I'd photographed Sam nude in a friend's New York City loft. Sam stood next to a brass birdcage almost as tall as him with a beautiful parrot. As I always did with slide film, I mailed it to be processed at Kodak in Rochester. It seemed to be taking a long time. I finally heard from Kodak. They were holding eight rolls of my film and giving me the choice of allowing them to destroy the film or turn it over to the district attorney.

My lawyer advised me that I let Kodak destroy my film because the district attorney was up for reelection and had already created a name for himself by "successfully" prosecuting seven "porn" cases. He was almost certain to prosecute me, so I felt I had no choice but to succumb; and Kodak destroyed my film.

With no teaching position on the horizon, I realized that the controversial nature of my photography might mean my demise in academe. So I was forced to find a new career. I began investing in real estate. In 1982–83, with the help of my future husband Leo, I opened "Jacqueline Livingston—A One Artist Gallery" in Soho. I planned to exhibit my photography with a different show monthly and to also display the fourteen posters of my family throughout the year I'd be open.

As soon as I opened, the FBI showed up. They sent a powerful looking man nearly weekly to confront and harass me face-to-face; later his visits tapered off to monthly. Each confrontation was the same; he'd ask,

"How are you able to get away with your exhibition of kiddie porn?" I felt protected by the First Amendment and said so. I explained that not every nude picture of a child is pornography and that my photography was art, it had a message. And it was owned by major art museums.

The $100,000 the gallery project cost was much more than I'd anticipated. To maintain it I had to sell and refinance some of my newly acquired real estate. From that point on, I had to work mostly at menial jobs that left me exhausted. There was no extra time or energy to realize my most ambitious photographic ideas or to edit, promote, and exhibit the photographs that I did make.

I continued applying for academic jobs, but it was hopeless. I never stopped photographing, but I simply could not find the time and energy to give voice to my images by writing autobiographical texts to accompany them or to produce a book of my photography. I no longer saw myself as the triumphant veteran of censorship. I began to think it was my fault that I was silent and submerged.

I received some vindication for my work in 1999 when the Herbert F. Johnson Museum of Art at Cornell University presented the exhibition "Children Seen and Not Heard" and included my poster of Sam in the bathtub, playing with the phallic-shaped balloon. The show's catalogue describes how exhibiting the photos of my son at Cornell cost me my teaching position there, explains that I believe in "bringing up children liberally and openly addressing their sexuality," describes the poster and continues by saying, that "Ultimately, it is undeniable that this child is having fun playing and it is the [sic] only the adults who find this problematic."

July, 2004

Marilyn Zimmerman

August 1993. Roxanne's third birthday party! My friends and their children and Roxanne's cousins and grandparents are crowded in my small living area on a hot day. I have sewn an angel outfit for Roxanne as a gift and she opens it and puts on the chiffon dress with angel wings. But she is hot in the dress and she decides to take it off, partying in complete innocence in her "birthday suit" with gossamer wings. "Ariel the Mermaid," hired to entertain the children, arrives in sequined top and tail. Ariel puts a golden crown on Roxanne; initiates each new event with the chorus "Happy Birthday, Roxanne!"; paints the requested rainbow on Roxanne's cheek and fulfills all the other children's orders. While photographing (the lens an extension of the adoring mother's eye), I turn to a friend and comment, "angel wings, a crown, and a rainbow . . . how more empowered can a little girl be?!"

Marilyn Zimmerman, "Roxanne's Birthday Party 8/31/93." Courtesy of the artist.

November 1993. Working in the photography lab at Wayne State University (WSU), I contact-print several rolls of black-and-white film of home portraits of my family and my three-year-old daughter. In one, she is just out of a bath and lounging on her bed before getting dressed. With the camera on continuous frame, there are four frames frozen at 1/60 of a second as she casually touches her genital area. The contact sheet also includes close-ups of her face as she gazes directly into the lens.

December 1993. I am called to the WSU police station, where I am confronted with my contact sheet under a ¼-inch glass, a tape recorder, and a male and female police officer. I claim the contact sheet and, with excruciating naivete, address the police as if in a classroom: I speak of the collapse of the private and public, of the misinterpretation of Mapplethorpe's work and its censorship at the Cincinnati Art Museum, about how I photograph my daughter constantly and exhibit photographs as an artist. They ask which of the images on the contact sheet I would exhibit. I tell them that I shoot a great deal of film, and only a small percentage is exhibited. They ask me if I would blow up the images so that they could look for identifying signs, such as bruises. They point to the close-ups and describe my daughter as "dazed" or "traumatized." Aghast, I tell them they can contact Roxanne's daycare or her grandparents and then ask if I may leave and when I can get my contact sheet back. They tell me that they will contact me the following week. (I learn later that neither the prosecuting attorney nor the university police officials in charge have children.)

In the warrant, which I acquire later through the Freedom of Information Act, the police claim that I admitted that the photographs were controversial—the folly of mentioning Mapplethorpe and thinking I would thereby exonerate myself!—and that I take thousands such images. As a result, a search for "sexually abusive material" is requested. The prosecuting attorney suggests that a male family member shot the images in question or that I was teaching my daughter to masturbate! I think of how entrenched is the idea of the female nude as the passive object of the projected male gaze, and the notion that children are inherently nonsexual in their innocence.

December 7, 1993. Day of Infamy. I am in my office talking to a graduate student. There is a knock at the door and four police officers with a search warrant swarm into my office and rummage through all my negatives and photographs. "Open up your safe or we'll blow it up! There are police officers at your home. You can either let them in, or they'll knock down your door!" The scene is surreal; the police confiscate the 1991 issue of the *Art Journal* depicting the most controversial photographs by Mapplethorpe, as well as negatives of my daughter breastfeeding. I am escorted home where seven police officers spend the next four hours going through twenty years of image-making.

Attorney Arthur Spears arrives at my home and we go back to campus to talk to my department chair. Both the chair and the dean are very supportive. Afterward they both tell me that they went to the university president asking for support, citing the importance of freedom of expression in an academic environment. The WSU president, however, assumes a public stance of neutrality, apparently unwilling to touch the issue of "protecting a child." (I learn later from a sympathetic janitor that the president told his valet to take his own garbage directly to the city dump from then on, since my original contact sheet had been retrieved from the trash by a janitor. Trash is public property!)

December 8, 1993. Prosecuting Attorney Nancy Diehl is willing to consider information provided by artists and academics that will place my photographs in an artistic (rather than abusive or pornographic) context. At that time, the clause in the state penal code for sexually abusive material of children (with a maximum of twenty years, $20,000, or both) excludes depictions of nudity that have a "primary literary, artistic, educational, political, or scientific value."

Carol Jacobsen, from the University of Michigan, organizes the Michigan Anti-Censorship Task Force to mobilize the art and academic communities. A letter-writing campaign is mounted; letters flood Diehl's office. My attorney suggests discretion; if the story hits the media before a decision is made, the publicity may alert religious fanatics who may pressure the prosecutor's office into pressing charges.

December 23, 1993. My attorney calls the art department to tell my chair and me the good news that the charges have been dropped.

January 1994. Roxanne's father begins custody action. He is recently married, and has had Roxanne with him since September in his new home in South Carolina. Initially supportive of me and knowing it was all ludicrous, he became frightened for Roxanne's welfare, saw a hand he could play for full custody, and went for it. My private life will again be subject to public litigation! My heart and stomach literally, physically ache. I miss her so!

February 1994. Michigan House Bill 4177 eliminates the intent clause which grants exceptions for "material that has primary literary, artistic, political, or scientific value" and raises the penalty on sexually abusive material regarding children. When it is brought to a vote, Representative Gubow cites my case, asserting, "without the exceptions we are putting people at risk of having their homes and offices searched by overzealous police and prosecutors and further putting artists, educators, and scientists at risk of arrest and prosecution. One only needs to look at the recent case of a Wayne State University professor where a janitor found a nude picture of her daughter that caused her office and home to be searched and charges [initiated] against her. Child pornography and child abuse are totally unacceptable behavior, but this bill puts totally innocent people in jeopardy." The bill passes 95 to 5.

The first child pornography laws were passed in 1982, a result of right-wing think tanks. If you can control representation of the body, you can control the body politic. Overly broad child pornography laws are a red herring pulling resources and attention from the tougher issues that mean truly protecting children: poverty, real physical abuse, and rooting out the causes of the international child prostitution trade.

2005. Having lectured frequently about my experience has helped me to achieve some perspective and healing. At dinner with artist Carolee Schneemann, she observes that the loss of custody of a child is often the cost of a woman's exploration of alternative lifestyles. But the experience has strengthened my sense of mission in reclaiming what has been exiled into shame and negativity: the sacredness and joy of expression of our bodies. More than ever, I strive for a mediating dialogue, to be an activist, a trickster rebel, a communitarian, to work toward a society of unique and diverse voices living in harmony, to empower and inform women, and to work toward a safe environment for us to be our own creative and sexual agents, to smuggle what was exiled and made taboo back into sacred ground: the big life passages of sex, aging, and death.

Roxanne is fifteen now. I am the noncustodial parent who pays child support and sees her on holidays. Her father and I vowed to keep our egos on the shelf, to be positive and supportive toward one another, and deal directly with each other and not through her. There have been challenging times stretching my sense of safety and love.

When she visits, I mention the infamous photo event. It is uncomfortable for her, I can tell. When she googles my name this censorship issue is on top of the list. What is so private is made so public! With future conversations I hope we can reframe and reclaim the infinity of our tender ties.

September, 2005

Betsy Schneider

Three years ago, while I was living and teaching in London, I had a student who was arrested when she went to pick up her processed film. Apparently her film contained images of unclothed children and someone in the lab had reported this to the police. During the nine hours of interrogation, she mentioned that she had a teacher—myself—who photographed her daughter naked every day. Upon their request, I showed the Child Protection Team at Scotland Yard my daily photos from the first three and a half years of my daughter's life. Both detectives informed me that my work was not "indecent" (The UK term for defining porn). A month later the charges against my student were dropped.

Soon afterwards, however, I was arrested myself when I went to pick up a film from another London lab. It was September 14, 2001, and I quite vividly remember walking down the street on my way to the lab with my three-and-a-half-year-old daughter, Madeleine, trying to answer her question as to why the planes flew into the buildings. Minutes later we were in a police car driving off to a Central London precinct. After a few hours, I met with a couple of detectives who found my explanation of the photos to be adequate. They drove me home where I showed them slides of the work to prove that I was an artist and these photos were part of an ongoing project. That was the end of that.

So, I was not totally surprised when, in the spring of 2004, my photos were again the subject of controversy. "Photo of the Day" is a project in which I have made two photos of my daughter every day since she was born in December of 1997. In one of these two daily photos she is usually unclothed. In March 2004 I showed a selection of this work for the first time as part of an exhibition on the theme of childhood at the Spitz Gallery in London. For the exhibition I chose to display only a small part of the project, three nine-week panels, each consisting of sixty-three images. One panel covered birth to nine weeks, another was from when my daughter was two and a half, and another from when she was five. The images had been digitally scanned, composited, and output as large inkjet prints in which each of the individual images were the size of a standard machine print 4x6 inches.

Although the show was hosted by the gallery, it was not curated by them. A few hours after the midday Sunday opening, the gallery director became uncomfortable with the work. Without consulting me or the organizers of the exhibition, she ordered the gallery closed, the windows covered, called in the police, and took down my work. Frustrated by the lack of discussion and communication, the organizer of the event, the curator, and I contacted the *Guardian.* The next day the story was front-page news. During the next two days, there was a massive media blitz. Some of the coverage was fair and actually explored important issues. Much did not. The show reopened on Tuesday but without my images.

By the end of the day on the Monday the *Guardian* article ran, more than thirty reporters had contacted me. During the course of a few hours I became a public figure and a target for the tabloids. Late in the afternoon I was advised by a friend, who was taking phone calls, to remove the images from "Photo of the Day" from my Web site: *The Sun,* Rupert Murdoch's notorious daily tabloid was going after me and would have no qualms about taking images off the Web site. So I removed all the images from "Photo of the Day" from the Web, but left other work, which also featured my daughter. Someone from *The Sun* took a picture from another body of work, cropped it from the sides, erased the background, manipulated the hair to look more messy and placed black bars across her face and at the bottom of the image where the vulva would have been had the image been fully frontal (it was not). Next to my image they placed another image, one which they claimed to have taken from a "child porn site." The images are similar in that both have white backgrounds, both contain young girls, both are cropped at the very top of the legs and both have black bars over the genital area and the eyes. The headline of this full-page spread read "One of These Pictures Is From a Trendy London Gallery, the other is from a child porn site: Can You Tell The Difference?" For an entire week, *The Sun,* whose readership is in the millions, ran articles attacking me, called me a child pornographer, my work an "evil tide of filth," and suggested that I be "dragged by the hair through the streets kicking and screaming."

Thursday, the day after I returned to the United States, *The Sun* printed a photo of my husband, which had been surreptitiously taken in front of our house in Arizona. I felt extremely unsafe. Yet I wasn't sure of whom I was afraid: the press, stalking pedophiles, or vigilantes who would be out to get someone they could call a pervert. I knew for sure that I did not want Madeleine to know about the intensity of this, I did not want her to be made to feel in any way ashamed about her body or the way we live our life.

I also was quite concerned that if the story broke in Phoenix, not only would my daughter be affected and my job as an untenured professor be in jeopardy, but I might face legal charges and my kids could be taken from me.

Of course I questioned what I had done. How could I not? Before arriving back in the States I ached for my two kids, afraid that I had somehow done something to damage them. I stood strong while I was questioned by the press, but if you are asked anything enough times, you eventually begin to doubt your own answer.

The kids' dad took the daily photos while I was gone and the first day after I was back when I took the daily photo I was really nervous—I really hoped Madelaine would want to wear clothes for the rest of the project. Of course she had very little sense of what had happened and, to my relief, that day was really no different from the two thousand others in which I had taken photos. Madeleine did seem to think I was being a bit overaffectionate and indulgent, but it was very comforting to get back and see that I didn't seem to be the awful mother/monster/pornographer that I was starting to internalize. I knew she was safe and okay; she didn't know that her picture was plastered across UK tabloids next to the picture of another little girl who is not identifed by name.

This incident has drastically changed the way I look at my work—now I comb the pictures for the ones which are slightly more provocative, I see them out of context and through the eyes of someone out there ready to attack me for exploiting my child. I am relieved now on days when my daughter decides to wear clothes for the photo, we cover the windows at night, and I do see more through the lens of other people's eyes.

I realize I probably could take advantage of the publicity and show the work in a place that is willing to capitalize on the attention. Yet, while I think it is important that we have a conversation about these issues, I wonder what I will sacrifice if I show the work now. Will people ever see my work in all its complexity? Or will they merely see the controversy and the nakedness? Perhaps I should be happy that my work has generated a discussion. I'm still not sure. This work—of which only a small fraction has been shown for only a few hours—now has a set meaning for millions who have never seen it. I guess that's what censorship is about and why it is so dangerous.

On some days what has happened makes my resolve stronger. I want people to consider the confusion and double standards we have in regard to children and sexuality and nudity. On other days I feel defeated and powerless. My work has been reproduced in the millions in a form I find demeaning and frightening to both me as an artist and to my child (And who is that other little girl? Am I somehow responsible for her image being published too?). I believe that it is essential that we resist the threat to open expression. But the stakes are high. I don't know exactly what I am going to do with this work. I may have to sit on it for a while and wait until the time is right. I don't know. What I do know is that I can't let this stop me from doing what I think is important and right, I will keep making the pictures as long as my kids are willing. Showing the work is another matter entirely.

June 2004

22

CHILD PORNOGRAPHY LAW AND THE PROLIFERATION OF THE SEXUALIZED CHILD

Amy Adler[1]

> Most of us carry in our heart the Jocasta who begs
> Oedipus for God's sake not to inquire further.
>
> —letter of Schopenhauer to Goethe

Child pornography law is a remarkably recent invention. Not until 1982 did the Supreme Court consider the distinct problem of child pornography, create it as a special category of constitutional inquiry, and expel it from the protection of the First Amendment. Since its conception, legal scholars have largely ignored it as an area of study. Unlike the burgeoning academic discourse that has grown up around obscenity law and adult pornography, the law of child pornography has been left alone to occupy its own peculiar and unpleasant realm. Yet left to its own devices, child pornography has spawned an extraordinary and troubling body of case law. As legal scholars occupy themselves with more tasteful topics—and ones that may appear to present more serious challenges to free speech jurisprudence—the law of child pornography has undergone a significant expansion, largely unchecked by critical inquiry. From its relatively recent birth, the law of child pornography has come into adulthood, and an ungainly creature it is.

The dramatic expansion of child pornography law has not occurred in a vacuum. Rather, it has been caught up in a cultural maelstrom. Since the late 1970s, the problem of child sexual abuse has been "discovered" as a malignant cultural secret, wrenched out of its silent hiding place and elevated to the level of a "national emergency."[2] At the center of this dark secret lurks child pornography, constituting both a hideous product—and some would say cause—of child molestation.

Child pornography law presents the opportunity for a case study of how censorship law responds to and shapes a cultural crisis. We have two corresponding events. On the one hand, we have the "discovery" in the late 1970s of the twin problems of child sexual abuse and child pornography, and the continuation of the problems to the point where they have reached the level of an ongoing, "ever-widening" crisis.[3] On the other hand, we have child pornography law. Born in the same period, created to solve the problem of child sexual abuse, child pornography law too has grown dramatically in the past twenty-five years, expanding and proliferating along with the underlying problem that it targets. Yet, curiously, the law's expansion has not solved the problem, but only presided over its escalation. As child pornography law has expanded since the late 1970s so has a "culture of child abuse," a growing "panic" about the threat to children.[4]

What, if any, is the relationship between these two concurrent phenomena—the expansion of child pornography law and the growing problem of child sexual abuse, including child pornography? Does their correlative temporal connection allow us to draw any conclusions about a possible causal relationship? There is a standard, conventional explanation for this correlation. This account casts law in a reactive stance: as the sexual exploitation of children, or at least our awareness of the problem, has risen, legislatures and courts have responded by passing and upholding tougher child pornography laws. As the crisis has surged, so has the law. In this view, law is always a step behind the problem, racing to keep pace with a burgeoning social crisis. I am sure that is at least part of what is going on.

Here I propose an alternate reading, not to exclude the conventional account described above, but to supplement it. In this reading, I view law and the culture it regulates not as dialectical opposites, but as intermingled. Child pornography law may represent only another symptom of and not a solution to the problem of child abuse or the cultural fascination with sexual children. The cross purposes of law and culture that we normally assume (law as prohibition, which both halts and incites desire) may mask a deeper harmony between them: The legal discourse on prohibiting child pornography may represent yet another way in which our culture drenches itself in sexualized children.

Child pornography law explicitly requires us to take on the gaze of the pedophile in order to root out pictures of children that harbor secret pedophilic appeal. The growth of child pornography law has opened up a whole arena for the elaborate exploration of children as sexual creatures. Cases require courts to engage in long, detailed analyses of the "sexual coyness" or playfulness of children, of their potential to arouse.[5] Courts have undertaken Talmudic discussions of the meaning of "pubic area" and "discernibility" of a child's genitals in a picture at issue.[6] But even when a child is pictured as a sexual victim rather than a sexual siren, the child is still pictured as sexual. Child pornography law becomes, in this view, a vast realm of discourse in which the image of the child as sexual is preserved and multiplied.

The point of this essay is that laws regulating child pornography may produce perverse, unintended consequences and that the legal battle we are waging may have unrecognized costs. Of course, I do not doubt that child pornography law has substantial social benefits. In fact, I strongly suspect that these benefits outweigh the costs detailed. I nonetheless focus on these costs as a means to unsettle the confident assumption of most courts, legislators, and academics that the current approach to child pornography law is unequivocally sound. I question their conviction that the more regulation we impose the more harm we avert. Ultimately, I raise questions about the nature of censorship itself.

The Law of Child Pornography

In *New York v. Ferber*[7] a unanimous Supreme Court created a previously unknown exception to the First Amendment, proclaiming that "child pornography" was a new category of speech without constitutional protection. Since *Ferber*, federal courts, so disquieted by the dangers of child sexual abuse, have tolerated statutes that define child pornography in increasingly broad and subjective terms.[8]

The law upheld in Ferber prohibited photographic depictions of children engaged in sexual conduct. Sexual conduct was in turn defined to mean: "intercourse, sexual bestiality, masturbation, sado-masochistic abuse, or lewd [or lascivious] exhibition of the genitals."[9] This latter term, "lascivious exhibition of the genitals" launched the most problematic aspect of defining child pornography. Determining whether a photo depicts a child engaged in intercourse, for example, would appear to be a relatively straightforward task. But what exactly is "lascivious exhibition of the genitals"? How does it differ from an innocuous photograph of a naked child—a family photograph of a child taking a bath, or an artistic masterpiece portraying a naked child model? It is at this margin of child pornography law, where its prohibitions bump up against "innocent" speech, that, ironically, the definition of child pornography has grown.

Since Ferber, the Supreme Court and lower courts have expanded the definition of lascivious exhibition.[10] In the 1994 case of *United States v Knox,*[11] for example, the Third Circuit held that a depiction could constitute a "lascivious exhibition of the genitals" even if a child is fully clothed. The defendant, Knox, possessed videotapes that zoomed in on the genital areas of clothed girls. The Third Circuit approved Knox's conviction under federal law, deciding that the definition of "child pornography" did not require child nudity. The Circuit held its ground, even after the Supreme Court remanded the case to the Circuit for reconsideration in light of a brief by the Solicitor General of the United States in which he argued that the Circuit had gone too far, and that the statute required at least "discernibility" of the genitals if not outright nudity. Meanwhile, other district and circuit courts have been busily amplifying the meaning of "lascivious exhibition."

Surveillance and the Pedophilic Gaze

> All seems infected that th' infected spy
> As all looks yellow to the jaundiced eye.
>
> —Alexander Pope, "Essay on Criticism" (1711)

Yet as child pornography law has expanded, so has child pornography. Indeed, we now live in a culture in which we are continually bombarded by images of sexualized children. Here I explore the relationship between this growing crisis and the growth of child pornography law.

Call the theory I present the disease model of child pornography law. Like everything else, law has been infected by our cultural sexualization of children; it is symptomatic of the illness it fights. And once infected, the doctor spreads the disease to his other patients. In this view, law does not merely invite its own transgression; it reenacts and disseminates the very cultural problem it attacks. Child pornography law socially constructs the child as sexual. One result of this construction may be that more people feel sexual desire for children. But that is not the only possible result. Others may feel increased horror or repulsion. Others may be driven to activism. What I mean to show is that child pornography law has deepened the link between children and sex. The reaction to their union will vary with each observer.

Child pornography law has changed the way we look at children. I mean this literally. The law requires us to "study"[12] pictures of children to uncover their potential sexual meanings, and in doing so, it explicitly exhorts us to take on the perspective of the pedophile. Congress feared in its 1996 virtual child pornography legislation (since ruled unconstitutional) that one danger of child pornography is that it "encourag[es] a societal perception of children as sexual objects."[13] But child pornography law unwittingly encourages the same perception. It, too, sexualizes children, and thereby promotes one of the very dangers it purports to solve. I begin with a cultural example that illustrates the changed way we look at children and then turn to case law to explain it.

In February of 1999, Calvin Klein launched an advertising campaign introducing his first line of children's underwear. The centerpiece of the campaign was a black-and-white photograph of two boys—about age 4 or 5—jumping on a sofa in their underwear. The company said the ad showed "children, smiling, laughing and just being themselves."[14] Klein unveiled the new ad in a huge billboard in Times Square. He also ran full-page ads in the *New York Times Magazine* and other newspapers.

The reaction was swift and furious: critics saw the ads as "child pornography." The accusations were the front-page story the next day in newspapers and tabloids. *The New York Post*'s cover story called the pictures "provocative ads, featuring semi-nude kids." Boycotts were threatened. Talk show host Rosie O'Donnell vowed on national TV never again to buy anything by Calvin Klein. Klein had the billboard removed a day after it was unveiled and never ran the ads again. (It was too late to remove them from some newspapers, where they appeared once.)[15]

How did this happen? Why did so many people come to see child pornography in this picture of children "smiling, laughing and just being themselves"? Even Klein's critics acknowledged, "You can envision this photo taken by accident—an innocent photo taken by a mom." A curator at the International Center for Photography described the picture as a "very ordinary image."[16] It was similar to a family snapshot but with "a sense of nostalgia and classicism."[17] What made this "ordinary image" become "provocative"[18] and "pornographic"? The same critic who recognized that a "mom" could have taken the photo by accident pointed to the following evidence to show that this picture was not an accident at all, that it was child pornography: "If an outline of the little boy's genitals can be seen in a photograph taken by a professional photographer, that's not an accident," he said.[19]

After I read this criticism, I went back and looked at the picture in the *New York Times Magazine.* One of the little boy's underpants seem baggy as he jumps in midair. Is that an outline of his genitals I wondered? It was then, as I scrutinized the picture of the five-year-old's underwear, that I realized I was participating in a new order, a world created and compelled by child pornography.

I do not believe that thirty years ago people would have seen the photograph the way we do now. Our vision has changed. I think that child pornography law is part of the reason we have come to think about the picture this way, searching for signs of sex in a "very ordinary image" of children.

It is essential to the legal definition of child pornography for us to understand that pedophiles see differently. Once we understand this, however, we have to take another step: We must look at pictures as a pedophile would. Consider the argument made to the Supreme Court in the Knox case:

> Because lasciviousness should be examined in the context of pedophile voyeurs, this Court should view visual images of young girls in playgrounds, schools and swimming pools as would a pedophile. Pedophiles associate these settings with children, who to pedophiles, are highly sexualized objects. It therefore follows as a matter of course that viewing videocassettes of young girls in these settings permits the pedophiles to fantasize about sexual encounters with them.[20]

This argument exhorts the Court to see children as "highly sexualized objects." The Third Circuit seems to have accepted this argument when the case was remanded to it from the Supreme Court. In examining the videotapes of clothed girls, the court found significant that "[n]early all of these scenes were shot in an outdoor playground or park setting where children are normally found." This aspect of the videotapes—that they were filmed in a setting where "children are normally found"—became one of the details that the court specifically, though not exclusively, relied on in concluding that the material in question was child pornography that "would appeal to the lascivious interest of an audience of pedophiles."[21] According to this logic, a place "where children are normally found" is now suspiciously erotic. If the picture "permits . . . pedophiles to fantasize," then it requires us to do so, too.

Why did the law develop like this? The problem for legal regulation is that pedophiles often find stimulation from the very same pictures that nonpedophiles consider innocuous, that we extol and value: Consider the Pedophilic magazine *Paidika,* a self-described online "journal of paedophilia." Its Web site depicts not grotesque sex acts with children, but pictures of kids that I could only call "cute." *Paidika* also provides links for the interested pedophile to *Vogue Bambini,* an Italian fashion magazine for children's clothes. *Paidika* features on its Web site a *Vogue* cover, depicting a young child actor and a blonde girl. The children, wearing heavy winter coats and hats, smile angelically at the camera.

In fact, certain pedophiles may *prefer* "innocent pictures."[22] According to some theorists, the stimulation of a picture may be inversely proportional to its overtly sexualized nature: It may be the very innocence of the child subject that is sexually stimulating.[23] Thus the peculiar nature of pedophilic desire itself may make the governance of child pornography an impossible task. One writer reports that members of the "North American Man Boy Love Association" or "NAMBLA" find erotic stimulation by watching children on network television, the Disney channel, and mainstream films. As the writer puts it: "I have found NAMBLA's porn and it is Hollywood."[24]

With this in mind, it becomes easier to understand why this territory of "lewd exhibition of the genitals" has proved fertile ground for legislative action and judicial approval. Take the facts of *United States v. Knox*[25] the controversial Third Circuit decision discussed above. According to the facts, here was a pedophile whose apparently preferred form of child pornography existed on this very margin: Although the court found that the material was bought by *Knox* for sexual stimulation, the videotapes seized from the defendant did not portray explicit sexual acts such as intercourse. Indeed, they did not even depict nudity; rather, they contained "vignettes of teenage and preteen females" engaging in baton twirling and gymnastics routines and sometimes "striking provocative poses for the camera." The girls, aged eleven to seventeen, were all wearing "bikini bathing suits, leotards, underwear, and other abbreviated attire."[26]

By criminalizing this type of material, it becomes harder and harder to draft a definition of prohibited speech that evades overbreadth. How do we at once prohibit the material at issue in *Knox* and yet avoid sending a parent to jail for taking a picture of her eleven-year-old daughter wearing a bikini on the beach? Or for that matter, how do we distinguish between the material Knox possessed and mainstream fashion magazines and advertisements, often featuring fifteen- or sixteen-year-old models "striking provocative poses" and wearing "abbreviated attire"—sometimes even nude?

In 1986 the Attorney General's Commission on pornography noted these problems in a footnote to its report: "There is also evidence that commercially produced pictures of children in erotic settings, or in nonerotic settings that are perceived by some adults as erotic, are collected and used by pedophiles. . . . [F]or example, advertisements for underwear might be used for vastly different purposes than those intended by the photographer or publisher."[27] Yet the Attorney General's Report also indicated that although it was "important to identify" this kind of material, "[t]here is little that can be done about" it.[28] Legislatures and prosecutors did not agree. The push to criminalize this sector of "child pornography" was already underway. Thus the law presses inexorably in the direction of prohibiting more and more speech that is susceptible of at least two different interpretations.

As a result of this pressure, the pedophilic gaze has become central, not peripheral, to child pornography law. It is relevant in the law's premise as well as in its application. First, the obligation to see the world through the eyes of a pedophile arises from the basic assumption in the definition of child pornography described above. Once we accept that prohibited depictions of "sexual conduct" by children can include not only explicit sex acts, but also the more subjective notion of "lascivious exhibitions," this process begins. The law presumes that pictures harbor secrets, that judicial tests must guide us in our seeing, and that we need factors and guidelines to see the "truth" of a picture. That even a clothed child can be engaging in lascivious exhibition of his genitals only makes the process more urgent and more difficult. Once the law acknowledges that pedophiles like many pictures of children, and that clothed children can be sexy children, then we have to redouble our efforts and to doubt our instinctive ways of seeing.

Second, the mechanisms of applying the law usher us step-by-step into a pedophilic world. The leading case on the meaning of "lascivious exhibition" is *United States v. Dost*.[29] The "Dost test" identifies six factors that are relevant to the determination of whether a picture constitutes a "lascivious exhibition," asking whether:

1) the focal point of the visual depiction is on the child's genitalia or pubic area;
2) the setting of the visual depiction is sexually suggestive, i.e., in a place or pose generally associated with sexual activity;
3) the child is depicted in an unnatural pose or in inappropriate attire, considering the age of the child;
4) the child is fully or partially clothed, or nude;
5) the visual depiction suggests coyness or willingness to engage in sexual activity;
6) the visual depiction is intended or designed to elicit a sexual response in the viewer.[30]

The application of the test requires an inquiry into the intended effect of the material on an audience of pedophiles. The sixth and most important Dost factor asks if the picture is "designed to elicit a sexual response in the viewer," which targets not just any viewer, but a pedophile viewer. As the Ninth Circuit explained, "lasciviousness is not a characteristic of the child photographed but of the exhibition which the photographer sets up for *an audience that consists of himself or like-minded pedophiles.*"[31] To answer this question obligates us to get inside the head of the pedophile and to see the world from his eyes.

However, it is not only this factor of the Dost test that requires us to take on the perspective of the pedophile. The application of each Dost factor demands a heightened awareness of the erotic appeal of children. We must search out whether the child's genitals are the focal point of the picture, whether the pubic area is prominent, if the child is in a setting normally associated with sex, if the child conveys an erotic acquiescence in his gaze, or if there is some suggestion of his "coyness or willingness to engage in sexual activity." If a videotape depicts a clothed child dancing, we must look closer; the Court insists that we ask: is the child innocently dancing or is she engaging in "gyrat[ions] indicative of adult sexual relations"?[32]

Consider, for example, the scrutiny necessary to determine whether a picture suggests "sexual coyness or a willingness to engage in sexual activity." In the Dost case, the court described a photograph of a ten-year-old girl sitting naked on the beach:

> Her pelvic area appears to be slightly raised or hyperextended and her legs are spread apart. . . . Her pubic area is completely exposed, not obscured by any shadow or body part.[33]

The court then analyzes whether such a photograph is lascivious—in particular, whether the girl expresses a sexual "willingness"—and concludes that the young girl does seem sexually inviting. Why? Although "nothing else" about the child's attitude conveys this, the court nonetheless concludes that the girl's "open legs do imply such a willingness [to engage in sexual activity]."[34]

What does it do to children to protect them by looking at them as a pedophile would, to linger over depictions of their genitals? And what does it do to us as adults to ask these questions when we look at pictures of children? As we expand our gaze and bend it to the will of child pornography law, we transform the world into a pornographic place. Our vision changes the object that we see. Child pornography law constitutes children as a category that is inextricable from sex.[35] The process by which we root out child pornography is part of the reason that we can never fully eliminate it; the circularity of the solution exacerbates the circularity of the problem. Child pornography law has a self-generating quality. As everything becomes child pornography in the eyes of the law—clothed children, coy children, children in settings where children are found—perhaps everything really does become pornographic.

Congress passed the 1996 Child Pornography Prevention Act in part because it feared that child pornography was changing our view of children. Congress found:

> The sexualization and eroticization of minors through any form of child pornographic images has a deleterious effect on all children by encouraging a societal perception of children as sexual objects . . .[36]

Although I contest the constitutionality of banning speech based on this finding—indeed, the Supreme Court later struck down the legislation[37]—the fundamental insight of Congress was fair: Child pornography changes the way we perceive children. What Congress failed to see is that child pornography law itself has also done that. Even more directly than child pornography, child pornography law explicitly requires us to take on a "perception of children as sexual objects," to see, for a moment, as a pedophile does.

Conclusion

In a sense, even to ask the questions I raise in this essay is to open a Pandora's box. Ultimately, they challenge deeply held assumptions about the nature of censorship, and about the relationship between law and the culture it regulates. Not only do these questions suggest the possibility that some kinds of rules are inevitably counterproductive; the questions also place law in a different light, as an institution that actively creates sexual culture rather than an institution that merely responds to it.

Notes

1. This piece is adapted from Amy Adler, "The Perverse Law of Child Pornography," 101 *Columbia Law Review* 209 (2001).
2. Ian Hacking, "The Making and Molding of Child Abuse," 17 *Critical Inquiry* 253 (1991).
3. *Philip Jenkins, Moral Panic: Changing Concepts of the Child Molester in Modern America* 147 (1998) (Quoting Ernest Volkman and Howard L. Rosenberg, *The Shame of the Nation,* Fam. Wkly., Jun. 2, 1985, at 4).
4. Hacking, *supra* note 2.
5. *See, e.g., United States v. Dost,* 636 F. Supp. 828, 833 (S.D. Cal. 1986) (observing that 14-year-old girl in photograph has a "sexually coy attitude").
6. *See Knox v. United States,* 32 F.3d 733, 746 (3d Cir. 1994) (discussing the discernibility of young girl's genitals through "thin but opaque clothing"); *Knox v. United States,* 977 F. 2d 815, 819 (3d Cir. 1992) (evaluating medical treatises to determine whether the inner thigh is part of the "pubic area").
7. 458 U.S. 747 (1982).
8. For an in depth account of the law of child pornography, see my article, Amy Adler, "Inverting the First Amendment," 149 *University of Pennsylvania Law Review* 921 (2001).
9. *Ferber,* 458 U.S. at 751 (emphasis added). The federal 1984 Child Protection Act

adopted most of this definition from *Ferber* but changed the word "lewd" to "lascivious."

10. *See Massachusetts v. Oakes* 491 U.S. 576 (1989); *Osborne v. Ohio,* 495 U.S. 103 (1990).
11. *Knox,* 32 F.3d at 733 (3d Cir. 1994).
12. *United States v. Villard,* 700 F. Supp. 803, 811 (D.N.J. 1988).
13. Child Pornography Prevention Act of 1996, Pub. L. 104–208 §21(11)(A).
14. Lenore Skenazy, "Calvin's Not-So-Model Behavior," *N.Y. Daily News,* Mar. 1, 1999, at 29 (editorial) (quoting Calvin Klein).
15. "Calvin Klein Axes Ads for New Kids Underwear," *Advertising Age,* Feb. 22, 1999, at 64.
16. "Calvin Klein Pulls Children's Underwear Ad." *Associated Press,* Feb. 18, 1999 (quoting Bernard Yenelouis of the International Center for Photography in New York.)
17. *Id.*
18. Kirsten Davis and Ed Robinson, "Brief Stay for Calvin Kiddie Ads," *New York Post,* Feb. 18, 1999, at 5.
19. Annie Groer, Ann Gerhart, "The Reliable Source," the *Washington Post* Feb. 18, 1999, p C3 (quoting Robert Peters, President, Morality in Media).
20. 1992 U.S. Briefs, 1183, *Knox v. United States,* No. 92-1183, *Brief of National Law Center for Children and Families,* amici curiae in support of respondent, Sept. 7, 1993.
21. *Knox,* 32 F.3d at 747.
22. For example, the catalogue from which Knox ordered his videotapes described one videotape, featuring girls in panties, as "so revealing it's almost like seeing them naked (*some say even better*)." *Knox,* 32 F.3d at (emphasis added). *See also* Hearings on S1237 before the Senate Judiciary Comm., 104 Cong. Act at 878 (1996) (Testimony of Chief Postal Inspector Jeffrey Dupika) ("Often, we conduct searches in our investigations and we find photographs of children *who are not* involved in sexual activity, photographs taken by pedophiles for their own gratification.") (emphasis added); John Crewdson, *By Silence Betrayed: Sexual Abuse of Children in America* 247 (1988) (a pedophile could "look at the children's underwear section of a Sears catalogue and become aroused . . .") (quoting Rob Freeman-Longo, a researcher at Oregon State Hospital). For other cases in which defendants were arrested for material that seems to fall into this category, *see e.g., Arizona v. Gates,* 182 Ariz. 459, 461 (1994) (material depicted children in "normal situations and poses," in a "ballet costume and in dance class" and in "department store underwear advertisements, National Geographic-type articles and medical textbooks").
23. *See* James R. Kincaid, *Erotic Innocence: The Culture of Child Molesting,* Durham: Duke University Press, 1998, 54–55.
24. Matthew Stadler, "Stranger," March 20, 1997 at 15. (cited in *Kincaid, supra* note 23, at 115).
25. 32 F.3d 733 (3d Cir. 1994).
26. *Id.* at 737.
27. Attorney General's Commission on Pornography Final Report, at 407 n.71 (1986).
28. *Id.*
29. 636 F. Supp. 828 (D. 1986) *aff'd sub nom U.S. v. Wiegand.* 812 F.2d 1239 (9th Cir. 1987).

30. *Dost,* 636 F. Supp. at 831.
31. *United States v. Wiegand,* 812 F.2d 1239, 1244 (9th Cir. 1987) (emphasis added).
32. *Knox,* 32 F.3d at 747.
33. *Dost,* 636 F. Supp at 833.
34. *Id.*
35. Cf. Charles Taylor, "Foucault on Freedom and Truth," 12 *Political Theory* 152 (May 1984) (discourses "bring about a new kind of subject and new kinds of desire and behavior"); Wendy Brown, "Freedom's Silences" in *Censorship and Silencing: Practices of Cultural Regulation* at 322 (Robert C. Post ed., 1998) ("To speak repeatedly of trauma risks encoding it as identity."); Vikki Bell, *Interrogating Incest: Feminism, Foucault and the Law,* London: Routledge, 1993, at 86 (noting social construction of children as "simultaneously sexual and not sexual, as innocent and as provocative").

    Once again, I do not argue that child pornography law makes us all into pedophiles. Rather, I argue that child pornography law makes us share the gaze if not the desire of the pedophile; it thereby shapes the category of "child." For the classic work establishing that the "child" as a category is socially constructed, *see* Philippe Aries, *Centuries of Childhood* (1962).
36. Child Pornography Prevention Act of 1996, Pub. L. 104-208 §21(11)(A).
37. *See* Amy Adler, "Inverting the First Amendment," 149 *University of Pennsylvania Law Review* 921 (2001).

23

INVASION OF THE KIDDYFIDDLERS

Mick Wilson

It is arguably one of the hard-won achievements of the women's movement to have placed child sexual abuse, especially incestuous rape, on the political, legal, and media agenda.[1] However, not unlike other achievements of the women's movement, it has been an ambiguous success. The making over of child sexual abuse into a question of paedophilia is an uneasy translation at best. Guy Hocquenhem has argued: "These new arguments are essentially about childhood, that is to say, about the exploitation of popular sentiment and its spontaneous horror of anything that links sex with the child."[2]

Recently, the question of systematic and collusively obscured sexual abuse of minors has become a central media theme in both Europe and North America. Importantly, the emergence of this media-spectacle has been related to the coming to maturity and thus coming to voice of the victims of such abuse. (Just as significant, however, is the fact that the media have not always been willing to address such themes.) In tandem with the spectre of organisationally protected "paedophile priests," another media-enabled spectre of social-sexual panic has emerged: the "paedophile-at-large" or the "paedophile-in-the-community." Zygmunt Bauman, the social theorist, in his book *In Search of Politics* introduces a discussion of the loss of the possibility of a meaningful politics by citing a spontaneous public protest in response to precisely this spectre of the paedophile-at-large. Bauman retells the story of Sidney Cooke, a paedophile who had been released from prison and returned home. Home, in this case, was Yeovil, in England's West Country. The ensuing protests were described as highly charged emotional outpourings from ordinary people: ordinary people who took to the streets and gathered outside the local police station where it was believed that Cooke was in hiding. Bauman argues that the protests are the only space

left where spontaneous public action and collective political involvement is available to the citizenry. According to Bauman, the powerlessness felt by these people is overcome for a short period when a sense of community, shared belonging, and shared outrage can be expressed powerfully and publicly.[3]

Bauman invokes the theme of *moral panic* as a way of explaining what is at stake in the protests. Moral panic is a sociological construct developed by British academics in the 1960s to address a media-facilated fear of such perceived societal threats as the emergence of youth subcultures. Stanley Cohen in his *Folk Devils & Moral Panics* provides a broad outline:

> Societies appear to be subject, every now and then, to periods of moral panic. A condition, episode, person or group of persons emerges to become defined as a threat to societal values and interests; its nature is presented in a stylised and stereotypical fashion by the mass media; the moral barricades are manned by editors, bishops, politicians and other right-thinking people; socially accredited experts pronounce their diagnoses and solutions; ways of coping are evolved or (more often) resorted to; the condition then disappears, submerges or deteriorates . . . Sometimes the object of the panic is quite novel and at other times it is something which has been in existence long enough, but suddenly appears in the limelight. Sometimes the panic passes over and is forgotten, except in folklore and collective memory; at other times it has more serious and long-lasting repercussions and might produce such changes as those in legal and social policy or even in the way the society conceives itself.[4]

This construct has been criticised, not least as a consequence of it passing into greater and nonspecialised currency. Pointing to the weaknesses of the concept Simon Watney has argued that:

> To begin with, [moral panic] may be employed to characterise all conflicts in the public domain where scape-goating takes place. It cannot, however, discriminate between either different orders or degrees of moral panic. Nor can it explain why certain types of events are especially privileged in this way. Above all, it lacks any capacity to explain the endless 'overhead' narrative of such phenomena, as one 'panic' gives way to another, or one anxiety is displaced across different 'panics.' Thus one moral panic may have a relatively limited frame of reference, whilst an-

> other is heavily over-determined, just as a whole range of panics may share a single core meaning whilst others operate in tandem to construct a larger overall meaning [. . .] the theory of moral panics makes it extremely difficult to compare press hysteria and government inaction, which may well turn out to be closely related.[5]

Accepting the limited power of analyses of moral panic, it is nonetheless interesting to note that the paedophile scare is arguably a classic example of moral panic, and one that is subject to several renewals over the last three decades. Recognizing the paedophile narrative as part of a panic response strongly suggests then that it is serving a function of displacement. Thus Bauman and others will argue that the core meanings at play here do not reside in the ostensible content of the stories told and retold. Rather, it is a question of serving some other need. Essentially this proposes a functional reading of the panic as a mechanism for disavowing a broader set of intractable social and political problems by allowing for the symbolic acting out of a proxy anxiety in a way that is amenable to some potential resolution. Such resolution is usually dependent on attaching blame to a localisable, if not proximate, cause. Thus Bauman sees the clutch of panicked people of Yeovil, protesting the presence of an alien in their midst, as a reflex of the felt loss of a public sphere and of a participative politics. However, it may be that these situations are more complex than is allowed by positing a simple opposition between surface content (paedophile as threat of imminent harm to children) and actual function (reclaim a space of politics/disavow its loss). The need for a more nuanced reading of these panic responses is particularly suggested by the recent upsurge in narratives of child-sex offenses which involve celebrities.

These recent narratives provide a further twist on this narrative of perversity and violence. Such cases as the Gary Glitter conviction, the Tim Allen conviction [husband of a famous Irish TV chef], the Jonathan King prosecution, the Pete Townshend story, and the more recent false accusation of Matthew Kelly are indicative of an emergent trend in the media which forges a relationship between celebrity and child-sex perversity. (It may be that there is a genealogy of these recent narratives to be found in the earlier history of Hollywood and the notorious crimes of stars such as Fatty Arbuckle.)

However, it is not just conventional celebrity that is at issue here: it's not simply about stars; it's primarily a question of media visibility. When the two Soham children were abducted and murdered in the late summer of 2002, the unfolding media coverage culminated in the revelation that the police spokesperson (who had anchored much of the TV coverage) had been named in an FBI report on UK-based, Internet child pornography viewers. As has happened many times before, a public image of civic and moral probity and a private "truth" of perversity collided. This collision took place in the, arguably already *pornographic,* context of a daily news narrative of trauma. (A trauma that was made over into soap opera by a news industry apparently starved of other hot content during the August holiday period.) The extra charge of sensation generated by this case was the proximity of the compromised police officer to a massively exploited story of child-murder.

Media exposure becomes, in these cases, an integral aspect of the narrative of paedophilia: the paedophile is in a sense already famous and becomes infamous, is already exposed in the media and is then subsequently further exposed, *outed* as a pervert.

Central to this renewed currency of paedophile stories is the trope of "child pornography on the Internet" and the organised networks of child abuse. Certain cases in the U.S. and in Belgium were given international media prominence in the 1990s and thus established a very strong relationship between the Internet, consumption of child pornographic imagery, and organised networks of child abduction, trade, and sexual abuse. In 1996, the FBI established its Innocent Images programme which addresses child porn on the internet. This programme has garnered international media coverage because of the exchange of information about consumers of child pornography with other governments and police forces. Thus child porn has become the object of international police collaboration, similar to earlier initiatives to collaborate internationally around drugs trafficking and terrorism. This is indicative of the perceived scale of the threat.

In one famous exposé of the threat of the internet as a medium of paedophile activity, a group of North American police chiefs were presented in a seminar with an FBI agent posing as a twelve-year-old girl in an online chat room. The "girl's" cover story was that she was away from school with the flu. Very quickly, she became the target of enquiries from ostensibly older men who made enquiries about her sex activities and requested pictures of her. One interlocutor sent a digital image of his genitals. In other versions of this story the interlocutor arranges a meeting with the child under the pretence of being a same-age-group peer only to emerge as a middle-aged predator. A key trope in the discussion of organised networked paedophiles is the description of their ability to engage with the child in the child's domestic sphere, since the Internet-enabled computer is in the bedroom or sitting room, and is thus a gateway into the home, a gateway that can often be unpoliced and unprotected. It is important to note that these scenarios of adults recruiting younger children and teenagers online are cited as examples of child pornography. The argument thus made is that there is a smooth and uninterrupted continuum between the consumption of imagery and the actualising of predatory sexual assaults on children. The smooth continuity of this spectrum is guaranteed by the figure of the paedophile: Only a paedophile would look at such images, and a paedophile by definition is one who actively sexually assaults children. (There are interesting parallels with earlier concerns for the deleterious effects of the cinema on children, especially as these pertained to perceived sexual threats to the child in the darkened space of the cinema, and the presumed inherent promiscuity of the cinematic image itself.)[6]

It is noteworthy also that these recent narratives of paedophilia have become, not just part of "news" and "documentary" programmes, but also the stuff of explicitly "entertainment" TV production (accepting that these distinctions are slight anyway). Thus the U.S. TV series *Law & Order Special Victims Unit* in its 2002 season featured a preponderance of storylines centred on child-sex offenders. (This series signals its role as a considered commentary on the moral and legal dilemmas of contemporary U.S. society by referencing specific topical social issues in the storyline and providing context-setting dialogue. Thus it echoes and reinforces the broader currency of the paedophile narrative in the media.) Interestingly these storylines generally entail murder scenarios as the logical extension of the child-sex offence. The abuse stories are generally situated in the context of nonbiological family relations or of state care and welfare initiatives. In one instance the victims are non-U.S. citizens imported as part of an organised trade in children-for-sex, in another instance the victims are children from dysfunctional families where the primary carer is a drug addict or otherwise incapacitated. There is in one storyline a specific address to the North American Boy Love Association, an advocacy group for paedophiles. This organisation is cited in the course of a standard context-setting aside by one character. The effect of this device is to reinforce the topicality of the theme and underline the broad social urgency of the issue.

These narratives of child sexual abuse, whether in the news or in detective shows, refer ultimately, and however heavily mediated, to actual events in the world. What they describe does in some critical sense take place. On the other hand these are not the only stories that might be told about child sexuality or child sex assaults. These narratives clearly service a moral panic reflex by forging a series of linkages between child sexual assault and several key themes: the individualised, pathological type "the paedophile"; the extra-familial networks of these otherwise remote, isolated types (enclaves of clerics or networks of tech-savvy online predators); the pervasive threat, yet extraordinary nature of the pervert; the danger of new technologies (digital imaging, digital networks) as vehicles bringing these, otherwise externalised, threats into the home (the putatively safe place of childhood); the vulnerability of nontraditional family constructs. These stories tell us that child sexual assault is a pathology of *the contemporary, of modernity.* It should be remembered that when feminist authors began to produce narratives of sexual assault on children, among the key themes were the family, male authority, incest, the construction of femininity as childlike, and the collusive societal repression of these stories of abuse. For earlier feminist accounts child sexual abuse was thus a *pathology of patriarchy, of authority.*

Returning then to the moral panic interpretation, it appears that the paedophile scare is overdetermined. It is symbolically operating many and various anxieties but also displacing and obscuring other dilemmas. It obscures the simple fact that children are primarily vulnerable to sexual exploitation in their family homes at the hands of their parents, their carers, their siblings, their relatives, and other figures of trust. It obscures the simple fact that children, internationally, are subject to all manner of chronic and fatal abuses, under systems that are collusively maintained by a whole host of international players. It displaces our profound ambivalence for this historically recent construct, the child, and does not allow us to ask why the child can be so sexually charged, for so many "ordinary people." It obscures that which is arguably the primary locus of most violence, of most sexual pain and dysfunction, the family. It services the recurrent anxieties that have traditionally emerged in the face of technological change. And indeed, as Bauman notes, it does seem to

enable a fleeting sense of community, identity, and belonging in the face of horror.

The paedophile scare appears to brook no dissenting positions, no hesitant critique or even anything that obliquely suggests that the whole spectrum (from Internet imagery to child-murder) is not an absolute, integral, and uniform evil. Indeed if the child-sex question was properly a question, a topic on which publicly reasoned exchange and dialogue could proceed, the moral panic would be punctured. It requires the quenching of all and any ambiguity, all and any scruple, so that an absolute and binding consensus may hold. It may be that this is the one point at which moral panic responses and some feminist accounts of child sex offences converge: there must be no confusion; the juxtaposition of sex and the child is always and everywhere monstrous. But of course historically children have not been listened to, or believed in respect of these matters, while adults have often been protected by family collusions and the support of other social structures, and so the fear of slippage is understandable. Ambiguity in these matters, it is believed, will accrue benefit only to offenders and predators.

Notes

1. Bell, Vikki, *Interrogating Incest: Feminism, Foucault and the Law,* London: Routledge, 1993, 154.
2. Foucault, Michel, *Politics, Philosophy, Culture: Interviews and Other Writings* 1977–1984, L. Kritzman [ed.]. New York: Routledge, 1988, 273.
3. Bauman, Zygmunt, *In Search of Politics.* London: Routledge, 1999.
4. Cohen, Stanley, *Folk Devils & Moral Panics.* McGibbon & Kee, 1972, 9.
5. Watney, Simon, *Policing Desire: Pornography, AIDS and the Media.* London: Cassell, 1987, 41.
6. Hansen, Miriam (1990) "Early Cinema: Whose Public Sphere?" in Thomas Elsaesser (ed.) *Early Cinema: Space, Frame, Narrative.* London: BFI.

PART IV

Cultural Diversity & Hate Speech

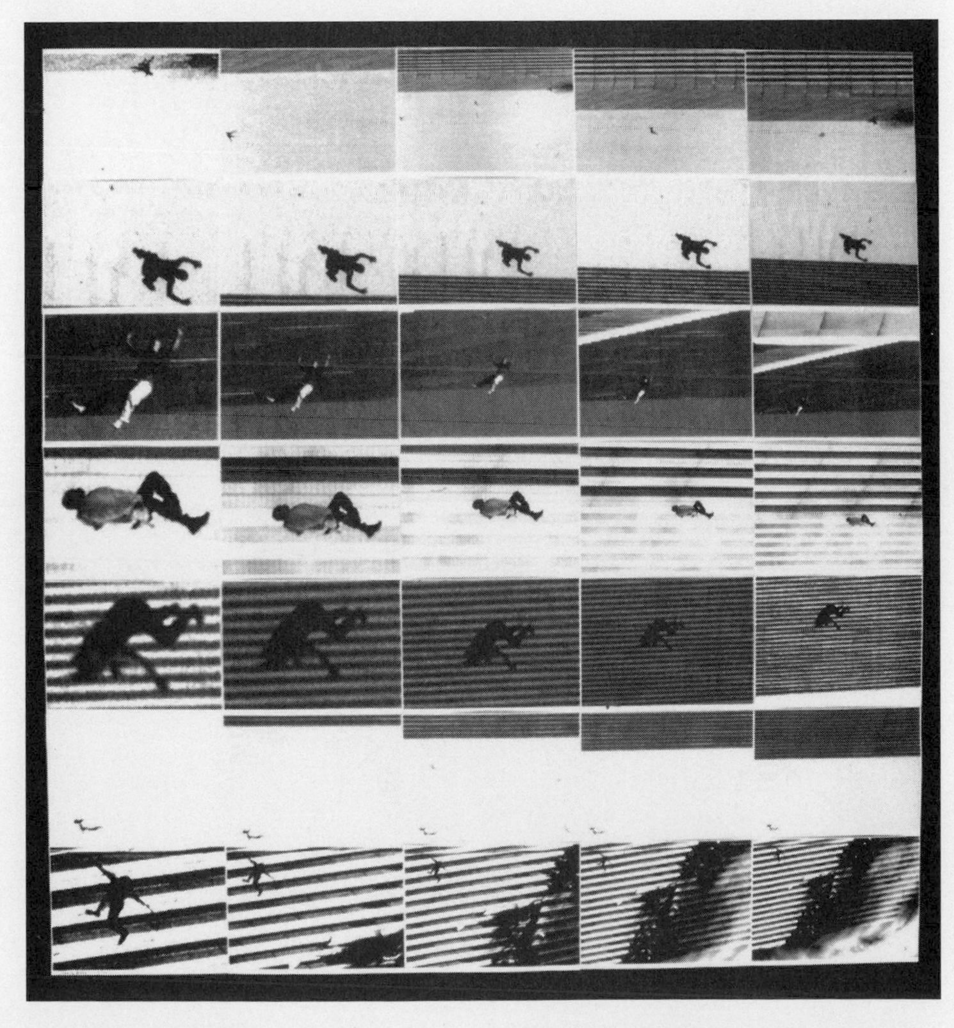

Carolee Schneemann, "Terminal Velocity," 2001. Black and white computer scans of falling bodies from 9/11—inkjet on paper. Enlarged sequences: 7 columns x 5 rows—35 units, each 12" x 16"; total 84" x 80". Courtesy of the artist.

24

WHEN WORDS AND IMAGES CAUSE PAIN: THE PRICE OF FREE SPEECH

Svetlana Mintcheva

In 2004, Dutch filmmaker Theo van Gogh was stabbed and shot dead in Amsterdam by a Muslim extremist in retaliation for making a controversial film about Islamic culture. The murder offered tragic testimony to the power of words and images to offend cherished values, to outrage, and even to incite violence. It spurred a passionate debate about the regulation of speech that "incites religious and ethnic hatred." Should government control, even ban, such hateful expression? Governments in Europe have answered in the affirmative: They have not only criminalized hate speech, they are actively prosecuting—and occasionally convicting—artists, curators, and writers accused of stirring anti-Muslim or anti-Christian hatred.

In the U.S., things are different. The drafters of the U.S. constitution, haunted by fresh memories of religious intolerance in the Old World, were uncomfortable with the idea of government control of expression, whether political or religious. Thus, the First Amendment protects, among other types of expression, speech that might offend particular social groups.

The only exception to that protection occurs when hateful speech constitutes a direct threat. Unfortunately, in practice, it is notoriously difficult to distinguish a threat from purely expressive activity. The creators of an antiabortion Web site, for instance, claimed that their site, which featured a list of names and addresses of physicians (the names of those who were killed by antiabortion zealots had a line struck through them), was entitled to free speech protections. Nevertheless, in 2002, the Ninth Circuit Court of Appeals ruled that the Web site's contents constituted illegal "threats," not free speech. Resolving how to treat cross burning—as symbolic expression or intimidation—posed another serious challenge to the Court. The nuanced 2003 decision presented no clear cut solution and left further such controversies to be resolved on a case-by-case basis.

Most initiatives to repress "hateful" or "offensive" material in the United States, however, do not call for the wholesale withdrawal of First Amendment protections. Instead, they are camouflaged as demands for respect, sensitivity, appropriateness, or decency. The "say what you like, but not with my tax dollars" catchphrase, familiar from the culture-war controversies of the late eighties and nineties, is accompanied today by a number of variations ranging from "not in my community" to "not in my children's school system." And offended sensibilities are not solely the province of Jesse Helms and his ilk. Previously disenfranchised groups—racial, ethnic, and sexual minorities—make their own demands for sensitivity and respect for their feelings or for their histories of victimization.

The unprecedented cultural presence of ethnic or sexual minorities is raising questions that, until not that long ago, seemed outside the public discourse. Is insight into history attained only through personal experience or suffering? Do citizens and, more to the point, taxpayers have a right to not be disturbed by museum programming or school curricula? Are cultural stereotypes to be overcome by banning them from sight? Does victimhood convey special privileges? *Who is* allowed to speak about the painful history of an ethnic or racial group? Indeed, who *owns* identity and history?

When film director Spike Lee criticized Quentin Tarrantino's use of the word "nigger," he also claimed his own right to use it as an African American. Randall Kennedy, who recounts the incident in "Pitfalls in Fighting 'Nigger'," notes, "For many people, *nigger* and its cognates take on completely different complexions depending on the speaker's race." Kennedy recounts the history of the cultural stigmatization of *nigger* and how this otherwise positive process morphed into a prime instance of the excesses of political correctness unchecked by common sense. One of the most egregious examples of a good-thing-gone-bad he cites is the attack on David Howard, a white civil servant in Washington, D.C., for Howard's use of the word "niggardly." Even though niggardly bears no relation to *nigger,* its use was interpreted, against all logic or common sense, as racist. Kennedy narrates the unfolding of this and other sometimes similarly ridiculous political and media events. They provide an eye-opening view of how easy it is for some to exploit the new sensitivities of cultural diversity.

Racial and ethnic sensitivity becomes an even more complicated problem when the drama unfolds *within* a community. In 1997, African American artist Bettye Saar publicly attacked a younger African American artist, Kara Walker, for her racially charged depictions of African Americans in sexual and violent contexts. In 2003, Holocaust survivors vociferously denigrated *Mirroring Evil,* an exhibition at the Jewish Museum in New York, which included, among other controversial material, the work of Alan Schechner, an Anglo-Israeli artist who served as a peace agitator in the Israeli military. Schechner digitally manipulates archival photographs so as to raise awareness about the ideological exploitation of the Holocaust.

The controversy surrounding Kara Walker's work engendered passionate debate about African American artists' use of black stereotypes. It coincided with an expanded an already raging dispute over whether African Americans should collect black memorabilia. The ensuing discussion focused on the role of positive images of African Americans and the psychological realities of internalized self-hatred and resentment, which Walker's art investigates. Psychological reality, being honest about one's own fears and insecurities, are also subjects explored in "The Past Is a Prologue," an exchange between Michael Harris and Lowery Sims, which focuses on derogatory stereotypes in art and in black memorabilia and the pain and outrage they sometimes cause to African Americans.

In the case of *Mirroring Evil,* the controversy, which preceded the show, seemed to determine its very presentation: The exhibition was framed by an extraordinary quantity of explications and justifications; an effort, no doubt, to make sure that viewers interpreted it "correctly." The conversation between the show's curator and assistant curator and the editors of this volume, included in this section, is a behind-the-scenes glimpse into the long and exhausting process of negotiation that goes into making possible an exhibition on a controversial topic. Sadly, the media firestorm around *Mirroring Evil,* which focused almost exclusively on the question of whether a Jewish museum should host such a show, almost completely submerged the art and the questions it raised.

The attacks of 9/11 immediately led to a new piety: Anything that would bring back the reality of the trauma—be it a disaster movie, John

Adams' opera *The Death of Klinghoffer,* or Eric Fischl's sculpture of a fallen body shown in Rockefeller Center—was deemed off-limits. At the same time, the "proper" discourse around 9/11, a discourse of mourning for the "innocent" and righteously opposing the forces of "evil," was quickly established and nurtured by a docile, uncritical press and compliant entertainment media. Finally, in the summer of 2005, New York Governor George Pataki offered an ultimatum to the cultural institutions chosen to occupy space in the new Snohetta Cultural Center: "guarantee" that they would have no programming that "denigrates America and could be offensive to the memory of the victims" (read: "art that criticizes U.S. policies"). Eventually the Governor decided that the space should become part of the 9/11 Memorial as any cultural institution presents the risk of controversy.

Not surprisingly, the production of "proper discourse" went into high gear for the wars in Afghanistan and Iraq. When Chicano artist/art instructor John Leanos made a poster critical of the political and media exploitation of the image of Pat Tillman, an Army Ranger killed by friendly fire in Afganistan, he encountered a wave of anger and hatred and no support from the University of Arizona, his home institution, which, instead, launched a review of his teaching practices. Woe to him who questions the image of a war hero and, by extension, of a heroic war!

Whereas taboos on words, topics, and images are everywhere in twenty-first-century U.S. culture, they are most fully codified within the educational system. Calls to remove books from curricula and school libraries because of offensive words are almost daily occurrences somewhere in the country. Bias and sensitivity reviews are routine in the production of textbooks as well as in standardized testing. In the 2003 New York English Language Arts Regents Exam, a passage about racial identity by Annie Dillard was stripped of references to race, rendering it incomprehensible, and references to Jews and Poles were deleted from Isaac Bashevis Singer's works about Jews in Poland. In *The Meaning of Bias,* Diane Ravitch details the bias and sensitivity guidelines of Riverside Publishing, the testing company contracted to produce President Clinton's "voluntary national test" of reading for fourth graders. As Ravitch reports, such guidelines are the norm for major American publishers of educational materials. The goal is to remove any content that might possibly be offensive to anyone, whether it be the "stereotype" of depicting women as homemakers, or the presence of an owl (apparently taboo in Navajo culture).

Censoring disturbing or even offensive speech, especially in art and literature, often violates not only the intentions or spirit of the speaker or writer, but suggests a perhaps willful lack of understanding of language itself: the inherent ambiguity of words and images, as well as the role of context in determining meaning. What some see as an assault on religious symbols or historical sacred cows, others regard as a criticism of the commercial uses of faith, a multicultural expansion of religious iconology, or an inquiry into how consumer society deals with the traumas of the past. Some words and images may hurt—no matter how they are used—because they are deeply rooted in the scars and unhealed wounds of history and social discord. Banning them, unfortunately, is not likely to erase the pain of historical reality.

25

PITFALLS IN FIGHTING "NIGGER": PERILS OF DECEPTION, CENSORIOUSNESS, AND EXCESSIVE ANGER

Randall Kennedy

In 1939, when David O. Selznick was in the throes of producing *Gone With the Wind,* he received hundreds of letters from blacks warning him to remove all "nigger" references from his upcoming film. The letter writers were concerned because the novel on which the film was based was full of such references. So, too, were early drafts of the film script. Initially Selznick sought to solve the problem by promising that the N-word would not be spoken by any white characters, but once he had been made aware of the intensity of blacks' feelings, he resolved to prohibit its use entirely and took pains to publicize his decision. A form letter declared that his studio had been "in frequent communication with Mr. [Walter] White of the Society for the Advancement of Colored People, and has accepted his suggestions concerning the elimination of the word 'nigger' from our picture."[1]

In the years that followed, blacks began to win other, similar battles. By the 1940s, "sensitivities were sufficiently aroused for Joseph Conrad's *The Nigger of the Narcissus* (1897) to be removed from open shelves in school libraries; for Marjorie Kinnan Rawlings's *The Yearling* (1938) to be released in a 'school edition' that omitted two passages containing the word [*nigger*]; and for Agatha Christie's play *Ten Little Niggers* (1939) to be retitled for American consumption as *Ten Little Indians* (and then retitled again as *And Then There Were None*)."[2]

In the 1960s and the decades thereafter, campaigns against racial indecency gained unprecedented support in mounting countless challenges to racist cultural artifacts. Scores of landmarks on official maps, for example, once bore such names as Nigger Lake, Niggerhead Hill, and Old Nigger Creek. *Nigger,* as we have seen, can have many meanings. But in the context of naming landmarks—an endeavor monopolized until recently by white men—it is clear that the *nigger* memorialized on maps was not the *nigger* of irony or affection but the *nigger* of insult and contempt. Widespread anger at cartographic slurs prompted Secretary of the Interior Stewart Udall to insist in 1963 that the Board on Geographic Names replace all references to *Nigger* with *Negro.*[3]

In Mississippi in 1964, during a *successful* gubernatorial campaign, Paul Johnson repeatedly joked that the acronym NAACP stood for "Niggers, Apes, Alligators, Coons, and Possums."[4] Such an electoral outcome would be inconceivable today in any state. No serious politician, not even a David Duke, could casually and unapologetically refer to "niggers" and hope to win an election. *Nigger* has been belatedly but effectively stigmatized—an important, positive development in American culture.

Progress, however, begets new problems, and our subject is no exception. The very conditions that have helped to stigmatize *nigger* have also been conducive to the emergence of certain troubling tendencies. Among these latter are unjustified deception, overeagerness to detect insult, the repression of *good* uses of *nigger,* and the overly harsh punishment of those who use the N-word imprudently or even wrongly.

The stigmatization of *nigger* has unavoidably created an atmosphere in which people may be tempted to make false charges in order to exploit feelings of sympathy, guilt, and anger. The most notorious instance of such deception involved an allegation made by a black teenager named Tawana Brawley, who claimed that several white men had abducted her, raped her, and scrawled *nigger* on her body with feces. Her charges have now been fully discredited, though some still profess to believe her story.[5] Brawley, however, was not alone in seeking to exploit goodwill through a hoax. In 1995 Tisha Anderson, a black woman, and William Lee, her white boyfriend, insisted that they had received hateful messages ("Niggers don't belong here") and been victimized by vandals who had scrawled racist slurs on the walls and steps of their apartment building ("Niggers live here"). It was all a lie: *They* were the ones who had defaced the building, in an attempt to escape their lease.[6]

In yet another case, Sabrina Collins, a black freshman at Emory University, claimed that someone had targeted her with death threats and racist graffiti. Her alleged ordeal became national news. At one point it was reported that she had been so traumatized by racist mistreatment that she had curled up into a fetal position and ceased speaking. Subsequently, however, it became clear that Collins herself had committed the acts in question. That a college student would perpetrate such a hoax was bad enough, but worse still was the reaction voiced by Otis Smith, the president of the Atlanta branch of the NAACP, who dismissed as largely irrelevant the finding that Collins had lied. Echoing Tawana Brawley's apologists, he maintained that to him, it did not matter "whether [Collins] did it or not."[7] Rather, what concerned Smith was "all the pressure these black students are under at these predominantly white schools."[8] If the hoax served to highlight that issue, he suggested, then he had no problem with Collins's means of publicity. It is difficult to imagine anything that could be more discrediting to a civic leader than the remarks attributed to Smith. Not only do they exhibit an egregious indifference to truthfulness in public discussion; they also indicate an inability to distinguish between a coherent political strategy and a pathetic escapade that was probably nothing more than a desperate plea for help.

Of all the things that have hurt the campaign against *nigger*-as-insult, unjustifiable lying and silly defenses have inflicted the most damage. But worrisome, too, are the badly mistaken attacks undertaken against people who never should have been seen as enemies.

One infamous round of wrongheaded protest was directed against David Howard, the white director of a municipal agency in Washington, D.C. Howard unwittingly entered the fray when he told members of his staff that in light of budgetary constraints, he would have to be "niggardly" with the money at his disposal. Apparently believing that *niggardly* (which means miserly or stingy) was related to *nigger,* a couple of Howard's black subordinates began a whispering campaign that blossomed into a public outcry. Howard resigned. The mayor of Washington, Anthony Williams, immediately accepted his resignation, declaring that Howard had shown poor judgment.

For several days afterward this incident became a focus of discussion in forums high and low. Eventually Mayor Williams, who has been criticized as insufficiently "black" by many Washingtonians, offered Howard another position in the D.C. government and admitted that he had been wrong to accept his resignation without first educating himself fully about what had transpired. By then, though, the damage had been done. By fearfully deferring to excessive and uninformed outrage, the mayor had lowered his own standing in public opinion.

A misplaced protest notable for the distinguished character of its antagonists erupted in the pages of *Boston Magazine* in May 1998, following the publication of a long, largely complimentary article by Cheryl Bentsen about Henry Louis Gates Jr., the chair of the Department of Afro-American Studies at Harvard University. Gates is a controversial figure about whom it is virtually impossible to write without getting involved in the disputes that surround his celebrity. In this instance, however, disputation arose not from Bentsen's profile itself but from the title given to it by the editors of the magazine. The cover of the April issue featured the phrase "Head Negro in Charge," a softened version of a term well known in black circles: "Head Nigger in Charge," or HNIC. Scores of readers objected.

In truth, the anger directed at *Boston Magazine* had to do not so much with the content of the disparaged title as with its provenance—that is, the fact that the phrase had been co-opted by the magazine's white editors. For many people, *nigger* and its cognates take on completely different complexions depending on the speaker's race. Had the "HNIC" profile and title appeared in *Essence, Emerge, Ebony,* or some other black-owned publication, there would have been no controversy. But *Boston Magazine* is white-owned and marketed mainly to whites, situating "HNIC" in a context that, for some observers, raised several difficulties: the embarrassment of discussing certain racial topics before a predominantly white audience; fear of, and anger about, a white entrepreneur intruding into black cultural territory; and the suspicion that whatever the setting, whites derive racist pleasure out of hearing, saying, or even alluding to "nigger." For these reasons, even blacks who use *nigger* themselves adamantly insist that it is wrong for whites to do so.[9] On the album containing his "I hate niggers" skit, for example, Chris Rock also presents a sketch in which a white man approaches him after a performance and appreciatively repeats some of what Rock has just said onstage. The next sound heard is that of the white man being punched.[10] Rock's message is clear: White people cannot rightly say about blacks some of the things that blacks themselves say about blacks. Just as a son is privileged to address his mother in ways that outsiders cannot (at least not in the son's presence), so, too, is a member of a race privileged to address his racial kin in ways prescribed to others.

Although many whites follow this convention, some rebel. Two noteworthy examples are Carl Van Vechten and Quentin Tarantino. In *True Romance,* Tarantino orchestrates a confrontation between a white man and a Sicilian mobster. The man knows that the mobster is about to kill him, and in a final gesture of defiance, he laughingly tells him that since North African moors—"niggers"—conquered Sicily and had sex with Sicilian women, his ancestors must have been niggers. Further, the condemned man speculates that the Sicilian's grandmother "fucked a nigger" and that therefore the mobster himself is "part eggplant." And in Tarantino's *Pulp Fiction,* a scene featuring a black hit man, his white partner, and a white friend of the black hit man has the professional assassins showing up unexpectedly at the home of the friend to dispose of a bloody car with a corpse inside. Exasperated, the white friend complains to his black hit-man buddy that "storing dead niggers ain't my fucking business." It isn't so much the fact that he will be breaking the law by helping to conceal a murder that worries him; rather, it's the fear that his wife will divorce him if she comes home while the hit men are still in the house. This white man who talks of "dead-nigger storage" loves his wife and is absolutely terrified by the prospect of losing her. It is important to note that she is black.

Spike Lee, among others, has taken exception to Tarantino's playfulness with *nigger.* When it was noted in response that some of his own films also make extensive use of *nigger,* the director replied that as an African American, he had "more of a right to use [the N-word]."[11] Lee himself has not articulated the basis for that asserted "right," but at least three theories are plausible. One is that the long and ugly history of white racist subordination of African Americans should in and of itself disqualify whites from using *nigger.* A second holds that equity earned through oppression grants cultural ownership rights: having been made to suffer by being called "nigger" all these years, this theory goes, blacks should now be able to monopolize the slur's peculiar cultural capital.[12] A third theory is that whites lack a sufficiently intimate knowledge of black culture to use the word *nigger* properly.

All three of these theories are dramatized in Lee's film *Bamboozled,* a farce about a black scriptwriter who, in order to keep his job, creates a television-network variety show featuring all of the stereotypical characteristics through which blacks have been comically defamed: blackface, bugging eyes, extravagant buffoonery, the omnipresent grin. Lee takes care to make the worst of *Bamboozled*'s many villains an obnoxious, presumptuous, ignorant white man—Dunwitty—who deems himself sufficiently "black" to boast to his African American subordinates that he knows more about "niggers" than they do.[13]

The great failing of these theories is that, taken seriously, they would cast a protectionist pall over popular culture that would likely benefit certain minority entrepreneurs only at the net expense of society overall. Excellence in culture thrives, like excellence elsewhere, in a setting open to competition—and that includes competition concerning how best to dramatize the N-word. Thus, instead of cordoning off racially defined areas of the culture and allowing them to be tilled only by persons of the "right" race, we should work toward enlarging the common ground of American culture, a field that is open to all comers regardless of their origin. Despite Spike Lee's protests to the contrary, Quentin Tarantino is talented and has the goods to prove it. That is not to say that he should be exempt from criticism, but Lee's racial critique of his fellow director is off the mark. It is almost wholly ad hominem. It focuses on the character of Tarantino's race rather than the character of his work—brilliant work that allows the word *nigger* to be heard in a rich panoply of contexts and intonations.

Advocates of broader prohibitions against "hate speech" maintain that the current legal regime is all too tolerant of *nigger*-as-insult and other forms of racial abuse. Several of the most prominent of these advocates—notably Charles Lawrence, Mari Matsuda, and Richard Delgado—have, in their positions as professors in law schools, provided intellectual underpinnings for campaigns aimed at banishing hate speech.[14] They and their allies have succeeded in persuading authorities at some colleges and universities to enact new speech codes. They have succeeded, too, in shaking up and enlivening civil libertarians, a group that had become intellectually complacent in the absence of a strong challenge. They have been unable, however, to sway the judiciary and have thus been forced to witness the invalidation of speech codes tested in litigation.[15] They have also largely failed to capture opinion. In the American culture wars of the 1980s and 1990s, the left-liberal multiculturalists who sought increased regulation of hate speech were soundly trounced by a coalition of opponents who effectively derided them as censorious ideologues—otherwise known as the P.C. (Political Correctness) Police.

The point, however, is not simply that the champions of speech codes lost on a variety of important fronts; it is that they *rightly* lost. For one thing, proponents of enhanced hate-speech regulation have typically failed to establish persuasively the asserted predicate for their campaign—that is, that verbal abuse on college campuses and elsewhere is a "rising," "burgeoning," "growing," "resurgent" development demanding countermeasures.[16] Regulationists do cite racist incidents on campus—the African student at Smith College who found a message slipped under her door reading, "African Nigger do you want some bananas?";[17] the counselor at Purdue University who was greeted by the words "Death Nigger" etched onto her door;[18] the taunt written on a blackboard at the University of Michigan: "A mind is a terrible thing to waste—especially on a nigger"[19]—but too often the dramatic retelling of an anecdote is permitted to substitute for a more systematic, quantitative analysis. Indeed, some commentators do not even seriously attempt to document their assertions but instead simply note a number of apparently outrageous events and then charge, without substantiation, that these episodes are, for example, representative of "a rise in the incidence of verbal and symbolic assault and harassment to which black and other traditionally subjugated groups are subjected."[20] A list of twenty, fifty, one hundred, or even three hundred racist incidents may appear to offer a terrible indictment of race relations on American campuses—until one recalls that there are hundreds of institutions of higher education across the country. Bearing in mind the numbers of young collegians who are constantly interacting with one another, often in close quarters, is a useful aid for keeping in perspective the catalogue of racist episodes that regulationists point to as the predicate for what they see as urgently needed reform.

A persuasive assertion that racially assaultive speech is on the rise ought logically to entail positing that there was a greater incidence of such speech in year *Y* than in year *X*. Demonstrating such a trajectory, however, is a daunting enterprise. After all, even when one is able to say that the number of reported incidents in a certain year was greater than the number of reported incidents in another year, there remains the problem of determining whether the reporting itself was a mirror of reality or a result of efforts to elicit from subjects their dissatisfaction with conduct they perceived to be offensive. Acknowledging such complications opens the way to considering alternative interpretations to those put forth by the regulationists. One alternative is that the growing number of reported episodes involving hate speech is a function of both an increased willingness to report perceived insults and an increased willingness to record them, which would mean that the perception of a rising tide of racial vilification is an illusion that paradoxically signals progress rather than regress. Or it may be that the regulationists are correct—that increased reporting does in fact reflect a greater incidence of verbal abuse. Even if that is so, however, there remains a question of interpretation. Here again, it is possible that episodes of verbal abuse are actually indicative of racial progress. On some campuses, for example, racist verbal abuse may not previously have been a problem simply because there were too few blacks around to generate racial friction. More recently, with the advent of a critical mass of black students, the possibilities for racial conflict may have escalated. At institutions where this is the case, increasing numbers of racial insults could be merely a function of more frequent interracial interaction and all that comes with it—for good and for ill.

Proponents of enhanced speech codes portray blacks on predominantly white campuses as being socially isolated and politically weak. Yet the regulationists clearly believe that the authorities to whom they are appealing are likely to side with these students and not with their antagonists. This, as Henry Louis Gates Jr. observes, is the "hidden foundation for the [anti–] hate speech movement. . . . You don't go to the teacher to complain about the school bully unless you know the teacher is on your side."[21]

Resorting to school authorities, however, has had its own costs. In stressing the "terror" of verbal abuse, proponents of hate-speech regulation have, ironically, empowered abusers while simultaneously weakening black students by counseling that they should feel grievously wounded by remarks that their predecessors would have shaken off or ignored altogether.

An examination of the substance of the regulationists' proposals turns up suggested reforms that are puzzlingly narrow, frighteningly broad, or disturbingly susceptible to discriminatory manipulation. In 1990, after much debate, Stanford University prohibited "harassment by personal vilification."

The Stanford code covered a single, specific type of speech: vulgar racial insults directed from one person to another in a face-to-face encounter. Such exchanges do happen; at the University of Wisconsin, for instance, a group of white, male students reportedly followed some black female students, all the while shouting, "I've never tried a nigger before."[22] But conduct of this sort is sanctionable via traditional legal machinery (or if not through reputation-besmirching publicity) without resort to newfangled modes of repression. It is likely, moreover, that especially on a college campus, antiblack polemics that are polite, skillful, and conventionally garbed—think of *The Bell Curve*—will be far more hurtful to African Americans than the odd *nigger, coon, jigaboo,* or other racial insult, which in any case will almost certainly be more discrediting to the speaker than to the target. Yet under the Stanford code, the damaging but polite polemic is protected, while the rude but impotent epithet is not. This problem of underinclusiveness is a major embarrassment for the regulationist camp because, as Gates notes, "the real power commanded by the racist is likely to vary inversely with the vulgarity with which it is expressed. Black professionals soon learn that it is the socially disenfranchised—the lower class, the homeless—who are more likely to hail them as 'niggers.' The circles of power have long since switched to a vocabulary of indirection." By focusing on vulgar words that wound, regulationists "invite us to spend more time worr[ying] about speech codes than [about] coded speech."[23]

Because speech codes of the Stanford variety fail to address what some regulationists see as intolerable forms of speech, broader prohibitions have been proposed. Professor Charles Lawrence, for example, has urged that the ban on racial epithets be extended beyond the context of face-to-face encounters, while Professor Mari Matsuda has advocated punishing "racist speech" in general. Such proposals, however, encroach upon legal doctrines that have helped to make American culture among the most open and vibrant in the world.[24]

The cumulative effect of these speech-protective doctrines is a conspicuous toleration of speech and other representations that many people—in some instances the vast majority of people—find deeply, perhaps even viscerally, obnoxious, including flag burning, pornography, Nazis' taunting of Holocaust survivors, a jacket emblazoned with the phrase "Fuck the Draft" worn in a courthouse, *The Satanic Verses, The Birth of a Nation,* or *The Last Temptation of Christ.* Just as acute wariness of public or private censorship has long furthered struggles for freedom of expression in all its many guises, so has resistance against censorship always been an important and positive feature of the great struggles against racist tyranny in the United States, from the fight against slavery to the fight against Jim Crow.[25] For this reason, we may count ourselves fortunate that the anti–hate-speech campaign of the regulationists fizzled and has largely subsided. This particular effort to do away with *nigger*-as-insult and its kindred symbols was simply not worth the various costs that success would have exacted.

Finally, I turn to the eradicationists—those who maintain that *all* uses of *nigger* are wrongful and hurtful and ought to be condemned by dint of public opinion. Their absolutist position simply fails to acknowledge adequately either the malleability of language or the complexity of African American communities. Even the proponents of enhanced speech codes—the "regulationists" whom I have just criticized—make a distinction between racist and nonracist, impermissible and permissible usages of the N-word. Professor Delgado has proposed, for example, that whites who insultingly call blacks niggers should be subject to suit for money damages. He goes on to explain, however, that the salutation " 'Hey, nigger,' spoken affectionately between black persons and used as a greeting, would not be actionable" under his scheme.[26] Similarly, though without expressly mentioning *nigger,* Professor Matsuda has indicated that her approach would allow words generally seen as racial insults, and thus otherwise prohibitable, to be protected in the context of a "particular subordinated community" that tolerated the use of such terms as a form of "word-play."[27] She elaborates, "Where this is the case, community members tend to have a clear sense of what is racially degrading and what is not. The appropriate standard in determining whether language is persecutorial, hateful, and degrading is the recipient's community standard. We should avoid further victimization of subordinated groups by misunderstanding their linguistic and cultural norms."[28]

Matsuda, however, minimizes the reality of cultural conflict within groups. As we have seen, for example, blacks differ sharply over the use of *nigger.* Some condemn it absolutely, unequivocally, across the board, no matter who is voicing the hated N-word and no matter what the setting.

Addressing African American comedians, Bill Cosby has argued that when *nigger* pops out of their mouths as entertainment, all blacks are hurt. He fears that white onlookers will have negative impressions of African Americans reinforced when blacks laughingly bandy about the N-word. He fears that many whites largely ignorant of black America will be all too literal-minded and will fail to understand the joke. Notwithstanding Cosby's criticisms and pleas, many black comedians have continued to give *nigger* a prominent place in their acts. Several of them were mainstays of *Def Comedy Jam,* a popular show that appeared on the Home Box Office cable-television network in the 1990s. Taking aim at *Def Comedy Jam,* Cosby likened it to an updated *Amos 'n' Andy:* "When you watch [*Def Comedy Jam*], you hear a statement or a joke and it says 'niggers.' And sometimes they say 'we niggers.' And we are laughing [at it], just as we laughed at *Amos 'n' Andy* in the fifties. But we don't realize that there are people watching who know nothing about us. This is the only picture they have of us other than our mothers going to work in their homes and pushing their children in the carriages and dusting their houses. . . . And they say, 'Yeah, that's them. Just like we thought.' "[29]

Today's conflicts over *nigger* replicate yesterday's conflicts over *Amos 'n' Andy.* Among the supporters of that show were black entertainers who stood to make money and gain visibility by participating in its production. Among the supporters of *Def Comedy Jam* and other, similar programs of our own day are black performers hungry for a break; to them, Bill Cosby's militant aversion to the N-word as entertainment is an indulgence that they themselves are hardly in a position to afford. Black critics of the campaign against *Amos 'n' Andy* charged that the show's detractors were excessively concerned about white people's perceptions. Today a similar charge is leveled. Some entertainers who openly use *nigger* reject Cosby's politics of respectability, which counsels African Americans to mind their manners and mouths in the presence of whites. This group of performers doubts the efficacy of seeking to burnish the image of African Americans in the eyes of white folk. Some think that the racial perceptions of most whites are beyond changing; others believe that whatever marginal benefits a politics of respectability may yield are not worth the psychic cost of giving up or diluting cultural rituals that blacks enjoy. This latter attitude is effectively expressed by the remark "I don't give a fuck." These entertainers don't care whether whites find *nigger* upsetting. They don't care whether whites are confused by blacks' use of the term. And they don't care whether whites who hear blacks using the N-word think that African Americans lack self-respect. The black comedians and rappers who use and enjoy *nigger* care principally, perhaps exclusively, about what they *themselves* think, desire, and enjoy—which is part of their allure. Many people (including me) are drawn to these performers despite their many faults because, among other things, they exhibit a bracing independence. They eschew boring conventions, including the one that maintains, despite massive evidence to the contrary, that *nigger* can mean only one thing.

Notes

1. See Aljean Harmetz, *On the Road to Tara* (1996), 144; Leonard J. Leff, *"Gone With the Wind* and Hollywood's Racial Politics," *Atlantic Monthly,* December 1995.
2. Hugh Rawson, *Wicked Words* (1989), 270.
3. At the same time, Secretary Udall changed all "Jap" references to "Japanese." See Mark Monmonier, *Drawing the Line: Tales of Maps and Cartocontroversy* (1995), 52. See also Lois Thomas, "What's in a Name," *In These Times,* October 20, 1997; Richard Willing, "Cripple Creek, Squaw Tits, and Other Mapmaking No-Nos," *Washington Magazine,* June 1996.
4. William Bradford Huie, *Three Lives for Mississippi* (1965), 35.
5. See Robert McFadden et al. *Outrage: The Story Behind the Tawana Brawley Hoax* (1990); Grand Jury of the Supreme Court, State of New York, County of Dutchess, Report of the Grand Jury and Related Documents Concerning the Tawana Brawley Investigation (1988).
6. See Kathryn K. Russell, *The Color of Crime: Racial Hoaxes, White Fear, Black Protectionism, Police Harassment, and Other Microaggressions* (1998), 157; James Merolla, "Newport Woman Reports Getting More Racist Messages: Tisha Anderson Says She Is Afraid to Leave Her Apartment after Receiving Telephone Threats and a Note," *Providence Journal-Bulletin,* November 16, 1995; "Anonymous Donor Offers Reward in Racist Threat; Police Report No New Leads on Slurs Scrawled on Walls and Steps of the Newport Green Apartment Complex," *Providence Journal-Bulletin,* November 14, 1995. For a glimpse of the wasted effort, damaging confusion, and hurtful recrimination generated by this episode, see Celeste Katz, "Newport NAACP Branch Meets over Racist Attacks; They Question the Newport Police's Efforts and Demand Further Action in the Case of Tisha Anderson," *Providence Journal-Bulletin,* November 18, 1995. For a

murky case that seems to have involved another racial hoax in Providence, see Marion Davis, "Charges against Clemente Dismissed; Garrick Clemente Was Accused of Hiring Someone to Paint a Racial Slur on His Front Door," *Providence Journal-Bulletin,* August 5, 1996.

7. Peter Applebombe, "Woman's Claim of Racial Crime Is Called a Hoax," *New York Times,* June 1, 1990; see also Russell, *The Color of Crime,* 160.
8. Applebombe, "Woman's Claim of Racial Crime Is Called a Hoax."
9. See, e.g., Stan Simpson, "In Defining the N-word, Let Meaning Be Very Clear," *Hartford Courant,* November 3, 1997: "What would happen if a white friend were to come up to me and say [as does my black brother], 'Hey, Nigger! How are you doing?' Well, excuse my ebonics, but we be fightin'."
10. Listen to Chris Rock, "Niggers vs. Black People," on *Roll with the New* (1997). For the video performance, see Chris Rock, *Bring the Pain* (1996).
11. See Kevin Merida, "Spike Lee, Holding Court: The Director Talks Movies, Hollywood, Basketball and, Oh Yes, Controversy," *Washington Post,* May 1, 1998.
12. See Lynne K. Varner and Hugo Kugiya, "What's in a Name?—A Hated Racial Slur Finds New Currency—and Controversy—in Popular Culture," *Seattle Times,* July 6, 1998.
13. See Richard Corliss, "The Scheme of a Notion," *Time,* October 9, 2000; "Spike's Minstrel Show," *Newsweek,* October 2, 2000.
14. See Richard Delgado, "Words That Wound: A Tort Action for Racial Insults, Epithets and Name-Calling," *Harvard Civil Rights–Civil Liberties Law Review* 17 (1982): 133; idem, "Campus Antiracism Rules: Constitutional Narratives in Collision," *Northwestern University Law Review* 85 (1991): 343; Charles Lawrence III, "If He Hollers Let Him Go: Regulating Racist Speech on Campus," *Duke Law Journal,* 1990, 431; Mari J. Matsuda, "Public Response to Racist Speech: Considering the Victim's Story," *Michigan Law Review* 187 (1989): 2320.
15. See, e.g., *UWM Post, Inc., v. Bd. of Regents,* 774 F. Supp. 1163 (E.D. Wis. 1991); *Doe v. Univ. of Michigan,* 721 F. Supp. 852 (E.D. Mich. 1989).
16. For examples of this rhetoric, see Lawrence, "If He Hollers Let Him Go," 434, 449; Matsuda, "Public Response to Racist Speech," 2370 ("Marked rise of racial harassment, hate speech, and racially motivated violence marks our entry into the 1990s"). Even fervent opponents of speech codes accede without sufficient questioning to their antagonists' portrayal of rising waves of campus racism; see, e.g., Nadine Strossen, "Regulating Racist Speech on Campus: A Modest Proposal?," *Duke Law Journal,* 1990, 484, 488. For useful commentary on this point, see James B. Jacobs and Kimberly Potter, *Hate Crimes: Criminal Law and Identity Politics* (1998), 45–64; Richard Bernstein, *The Dictatorship of Virtue* (1994), 183–215.
17. Lawrence, "If He Hollers Let Him Go," 433.
18. Ibid., 432.
19. Ibid., 433.
20. Ibid., 434.

21. Henry Louis Gates Jr., "War of Words: Critical Race Theory and the First Amendment," in *Speaking of Race, Speaking of Sex: Hate Speech, Civil Rights, and Civil Liberties* (1994), 42.
22. Lawrence, "If He Hollers Let Him Go," 448.
23. Gates, "War of Words," 47.
24. See Strossen, "Regulating Racist Speech on Campus," 484.
25. See William Lee Miller, *Arguing about Slavery: The Great Battle in the United States Congress* (1996); Harry Kalven Jr., *The Negro and the First Amendment* (1965); Michael Kent Curtis, "The Curious History of Attempts to Suppress Antislavery Speech, Press, and Petitions in 1835–37," *Northwestern University Law Review* 89 (1995): 785.
26. Delgado, "Words That Wound," 180. Note, though, that Delgado adds yet another complication: if *nigger* "was intended and understood as demeaning, minority plaintiffs could sue other members of the same or another minority group" (ibid.). He does not broach the question of whether it would be permissible under any circumstances—e.g., if done with affection—for a white person to call a black person "nigger."
27. Matsuda, "Public Response to Racist Speech," 2364.
28. Ibid.
29. Quoted in Laura A. Randolph, "Life after the *Cosby Show,*" *Ebony,* May 1994.

26

THE PAST IS PROLOGUE, BUT IS PARODY AND PASTICHE PROGRESS?

Michael Harris and Lowery Stokes Sims in conversation
with Karen C.C. Dalton

Karen Dalton: Let's begin this conversation with the reason that we are having the conversation, which is an article that you did called "Memories and Memorabilia, Arts and Identity: Is Aunt Jemima Really a Black Woman?" In this article you open early on with the sentence, "It is time for an extended discussion about a recent confusing cultural phenomenon, black memorabilia and the fact that blacks collect it. Are vicious, hurtful caricatures worthy of remembrance by their targets?" So I thought that we could springboard from that point if you'd talk to us a bit about your article and some of the points you're trying to make therein.

Michael Harris: There was an article in a popular black magazine based in Atlanta several years ago that talked about people collecting black memorabilia and one collector was gushing about how profitable it was. Something seemed strangely out of kilter for me in hearing that. As I explored the area more and more, I began to see psychological implications that perhaps related to Duboisian double consciousness in a certain way and to some of the black psychology that I had been exposed to through N'aim Akbar, Bobby Wright, Joe Baldwin, and people like that from the Association of Black Psychologists. It [collecting black memorabilia] seemed to either smack of a sense of self-hatred or at least a terribly uncritical understanding about how images have been used intentionally to affect people, identity, and consciousness.

KD: Could we talk a little bit specifically about some of those images so we all know we are talking about the same things?

MH: You know, well, the basic ones. Sambo and Aunt Jemima come out of a long literature that categorized Africans in certain essentialist ways and by extension, any person of African descent in the New World. So you have the asexual mammy who is the perennial servant and is nonthreatening. With the black male you have either the buffoon who is childlike and inept, or you have the threatening, bloodthirsty savage. The motivation for the production of this imagery was to control black people within white society as well as to justify taking over their African territories. These images codified notions of who black people were and I believe that they really affected nineteenth-century African American artists in profound ways. Twentieth-century African American artists have been reacting to or against these images for the whole century.

KD: What do you think about that, Lowery? We know that this image reversal or the actual images themselves really come from the late nineteenth century. They show up in the late 1870s after Reconstruction, and they move, according to Kenneth Goings, right up into the 1960s.

Lowery Sims: Well, I guess I come at this issue as someone who's been collecting black dolls and figurines since the early 1970s. I've also been involved in supporting the work of Bob Colescott since 1970, so this has been a twenty-year odyssey for me. I think that certainly Michael is absolutely correct. These images were always specters that haunted one's childhood.

Last night I was thinking about all the social interdictions of our parents: Don't wear loud clothing, don't talk loud, don't laugh loud, don't eat watermelon in public. All of these restrictions were laid down so that you wouldn't seem to conform to stereotypes. I remember growing up as a young black girl and dealing with people being so preoccupied with the size of one's lips. There were few role models. Thank God for Annette Funicello who, though Italian, as a kid did have curly hair, and Sophia Loren. At one point when I started wearing lipstick, I remember my mother very sternly told me I should control the line on the bottom of my lips. I said well look at Sophia Loren. She has full lips. So I had the example of two Italian women who gave me some kind of leeway.

I first got involved in black memorabilia—I guess it was in the mid-1970s—because my friends, Leslie King Hammond and her husband,

Home Craft Magazine cover, January 1936. Collection of Kevin W. Thomas.

O'Neil Hammond were collecting posters, dolls, and that sort of thing. I wanted to buy them a present. This was just at the time when I first saw Bob Colescott's work. I remember walking into the Razor Art Gallery and I just couldn't believe this stuff. I was horrified and extraordinarily relieved at the same time because having come through the 1960s with another kind of stereotype—the black nationalist, big breasted, big buttocks, big Afro stereotype of black womanhood—the Pam Grier which I certainly couldn't live up to—I was relieved to encounter Colescott. You see, Colescott takes another approach and turns it around. His work liberated me psychologically. I knew we were treading in dangerous waters but I was attracted to the humor, after twenty years of just holding everything in—it was like wearing girdles.

When I got involved in both buying presents for Leslie and her husband and getting to know Bob, I found myself moving through the whole landscape of black memorabilia in an interesting kind of way, because it was invading a lot of areas of my life. I became aware of the richness of the imagery. It's everywhere in every form. If you start collecting the stuff, you can specialize. You can do the Pinkham labels, Currier & Ives, paperwear, dolls—it just goes on.

I think that at the same time this imagery was difficult and denigrating. I certainly don't want to minimize the political impact. I began to wonder (and I think Carrie Mae Weems has done this in some of her *American Icon* series) what it meant to have this imagery at every point in your house: In an odd sort of way, it kept black people at the center of American consciousness. We didn't disappear into a reservation, we didn't disappear into the fringes, we were everywhere. I think this is one aspect of this whole thing that I find fascinating.

MH: Well, I have to raise some questions and I have to locate myself as being a member of AfriCobra. I became a member in the late 1970s. It had changed somewhat but it was one of the groups producing those big, big, big women you were talking about. The group did evolve aesthetically and consciously.

I do have a sort of Pan Africanist perspective. And since my studies have been in primarily African art and culture, I tend to use Yoruba culture as a touchstone, as a comparison. That being said, I'd like to raise a question for people who collect so-called "black memorabilia": If it is the equivalent of Confederate flags and Klan memorabilia—because they are all sourced in a white racial consciousness (the very identity of whiteness being racial, being a counter-identity of black, but an identity not based in the reality of those people labeled "black")—should you be so fond of "black memorabilia"?

If we take that approach, then Aunt Jemima is not a black woman. She would be a white male in drag in a minstrel posture, in blackface. Perhaps there's a limited understanding of black women that was drawn upon, but I don't think there is a black woman underneath this character. I certainly wouldn't find any women in my family that I could extract from the Aunt Jemima mythology.

LS: What about, let's say, images from real life? You know, images in film, images from Africa, depictions of sports figures—a Tiger Woods, a Michael Jordan, a Dennis Rodman—how they appear in commercials, how they appear on talk shows, how they are being commodified. I mean let's face it, we are in a society that commodifies everything, we're not going to get away from that.

MH: Isn't the Tiger Woods phenomenon an example of the hunger people have had for a successful African American who's dignified, who's accomplishing?

LS: But who's creating that? Is it African Americans or the white world? That's my question.

MH: I think that's an important issue. I've read where both Kara Walker and Michael Ray Charles have struggled with the fact that so many African Americans disliked their images. So I would ask if we were creating images, would these memorabilia have been the images that we created of ourselves in 1890 or 1910? Would we have made *Birth of a Nation* to discuss the South? Would we make Steppin Fetchit the character, even if he was the trickster, is he the trickster that we would have created, and my answer is of course, no.

LS: For all the artists that we have mentioned and others that we haven't mentioned, I would bet that each one has a motivation that is completely different from the others. Some may be extremely personal and some more opportunistic. I would say for somebody like Bob Colescott, it is confronting his own demons at this point. I can't say that I agree with everything that he does. We used to have real arguments about his treatment of women in general, black and white.

With regard to the work of the younger artists, I think it is clear that the controversy about them comes from the fact that the black body is still certainly a very powerful visual icon. If you looked at Lorna Simpson's photographs, there is something very powerful about the seemingly straightforward representation of the body in conjunction with words that really clarify the sexual politics of the black body in an extremely powerful way.

The *New York Times* just had an article on black erotica and how controversial that is, because in trying to escape certain stereotypes about black sensuality, blacks have also put themselves in a position where they can't fully explore their natural sensuality. When do we get to be fully sexual beings like everybody else in this society?

KD: One cannot ignore the fact that a number of these young artists really seem to believe that they are doing positive things, that they are creating acts of liberation. Wendell Brown, talking about his watermelon quilts, is uninterested in turning negative images as have been portrayed in the past, into positive images. He believes that images like watermelons, chicken, sports—these are things that you like or do well and should be celebrated.

MH: I read that and I've read statements by Kara Walker—her father sent me a package of material—and I read the interview with Michael Ray Charles, and I hope that they develop more political and historical and critical acumen as they develop as artists. I know that they have a great deal of talent. Kara is to be congratulated on her McArthur Award, but I do think that they need to really look at why their own community has such trouble with their work, and why they are enthusiastically received by the white art apparatus.

They might want to look at parallels between their experience and the primitivist notions and patronage of a few whites that sparked what we do call the "Harlem Renaissance": the Harmon Foundation, Van Vechten, "the Godmother," and all of that. It seems as if there is something very similar going on now.

LS: The media also co-opts certain kinds of statements that may even stem from one kind of political motivation and diffuses the effect of it by commercializing it right away. Bruce Springsteen's *Born in the U.S.A.* all of a sudden became the all-American album when he was critiquing what was happening to the working class. It's very hard to be truly revolutionary in a society where everything can be a commodity.

I certainly would not dismiss the possibility that the white art world may gravitate towards the images of Kara, Michael, and other artists like that precisely because of that edge their work treads. They may not want to examine the problematic aspect of their support of this kind of imagery, particularly since it is so obvious that they're going toward one thing. But we also must be careful not to isolate and ostracize these young artists who feel that they may be doing something very genuine—genuine and serious.

MH: I think that these artists, first of all, deserve to face the critique of their own community. If their community reacts and critiques them, I think they deserve to deal with that but I also feel that the art community at large was tending to become more comfortable with work that either flowed with the mainstream or if it was critical, talked about white people. So we have some of Carrie May Weems' work, we have Adrian Piper, some of Lorna's work, also feminist critique—things that were of interest to whites.

I have a friend who is doing a program teaching history through poetry and creative writing in Pittsburgh. She told me some of the white students had difficulty sitting there for 30 to 40 minutes if there was no talk about whites. That would be my indictment of the art world in general, because I've seen some artists who I think are doing outstanding work but they're drawing from a tradition coming out of Alain Locke: looking to Africa, looking to their own cultural communities, issues in those communities, and it's rare that we get someone who breaks through who's not talking about, or to, whites.

LS: I think that's absolutely true. I think that the art world is narcissistic and tends to be self-referential. But the power structure in this country is like that. It doesn't necessarily tolerate difference. It tends to deal with things that deal with its concerns, interests, anxieties, and fears. I imagine that Latino, Native American, or Asian artists are now probably facing the same kinds of dilemmas as African Americans. The images that the mainstream art world tolerates from communities of color do not necessarily have anything to do with issues within them.

MH: To go back to what you said about people trying to be revolutionary, I think we learned in the 1960s you can co-opt through incorporation. So people who shout "racist, racist" can be brought in to quiet them down.

LS: I suspect what we are asking from these young artists has much to do with how we expect artists to position themselves in the art world. Most individuals coming out of art schools now are going to gravitate towards the market, let's face it. If there's a general call for artists to return to the community, that's a whole other matter. The whole system now is so big artists feel they can do one thing or another, whereas in the 1960s and 1970s, somebody like a Benny Andrews could be both an artist in the market and in the community. It's very hard to do that now. Art schools really encourage young artists to basically position themselves to make the money. There is a question you have to ask. How is the black community going to react and support artists? Are we going to make a place for them? Are we going to be able to tolerate it when they don't do things that are exactly what we think they should? For every criticism we may have of these artists' work, there is the opposite point of view. In that case, they have to do the best they can to get over. When Michael (Harris) was starting out, he could look to AfriCobra which was extremely community based and very conscious of a responsibilities to a larger entity.

KD: And you could depend on a unified community.

MH: And I'm just a dreamer and idealist anyway. Of all the options, of all the possibilities in the universe and all the creativity that's there, couldn't we find some other way to make a critique than to make six foot Sambos? Isn't there something else? That's all I ask. I'm dazzled by the creativity and the new ideas that many young people bring to their work. And artists deserve room to do what they want and need to do. But at the same time, art is not individual. People have that illusion, but art is sanctioned by society and when it goes too far out society will crush it. They did that to Mapplethorpe and Serrano. The society will come up and smack you if they don't like what you are doing. So art is more communal than people may acknowledge.

LS: But that's not what these kids are being taught in art school. Every time I go to be a visiting critic at an art school, all they want to know is how to make it in the art world. They're not talking about how to relate to the community. I think there's a way in which the whole notion of artistic freedom, what exactly censorship is—self-censorship or censorship from the outside—this has gotten totally misconstrued. Particularly over the last ten years since Jesse Helms took on the NEA. I think that individual responsibility means that you have to accept the consequences for your actions. That's something that is still not discussed widely in art schools. We need to talk about taking responsibility and thinking about where you are positioning yourself in the world.

27
BEYOND GOOD AND EVIL

Norman Kleeblatt and Joanna Lindenbaum in conversation with Robert Atkins and Svetlana Mintcheva, regarding the exhibition *Mirroring Evil: Nazi Imagery/Recent Art*

In March, 2002, The Jewish Museum opened the exhibition Mirroring Evil: Nazi Imagery/Recent Art. *Due in large part to the publication and release of the exhibition catalog in January of that year, controversy erupted before the show had even been installed. The show opened to protests from Holocaust survivors' groups, center- and right-wing pundits, and only tepid support from Mayor Michael Bloomberg, a patron of the museum. Norman Kleeblatt is The Jewish Museum's Susan and Elihu Rose Curator of Fine Arts and the guiding force behind the exhibition, and Joanna Lindenbaum was the show's assistant curator.*

The following conversation was conducted by e-mail between November 2004 and March 2005.

Robert Atkins and **Svetlana Mintcheva:** We're very interested in how the show's potential for controversy affected its development and realization. When did you first realize it was likely to be controversial? How did the museum's board of directors react to the potential controversy?

Norman Kleeblatt and **Joanna Lindenbaum:** We always knew there was the potential for the show to be controversial. We also knew that some audiences who would come to engage in the ideas of the show might not be familiar with the language of conceptual art, which is after all the lingua franca of the artists in the exhibition.

The exhibition was originally scheduled to open in March of 2001. During the previous summer, we began to seek feedback from members of communities who were interested in the ideas of the exhibition. Feedback from these meetings were evaluated and taken into careful consideration during the planning stages of the project. Early in 2001, we realized we had the responsibility to develop the interpretation for the show and decided to postpone the opening a year, until March 2002.

RA: What went into the process of developing the interpretive materials?

JL & NK: One of our biggest objectives was to ensure that we didn't close down the subject matter, but rather open it up for discussion. To do this, we knew we would need to shape a dialogue. In order to create a framework for the dialogue, we tried to look critically at the art to determine the major questions it asked. These questions are tough ones that confront viewers in their everyday lives: Who can speak for the Holocaust? How has Nazi imagery come to represent evil? When does the mundane become dangerous? What are the limits of irreverence? How has art broken the silence?

We arrived at these questions by discussing reproductions of works in the show with a wide range of community members, museum professionals, artists, and scholars. We reached out to many different individuals from many different communities, both in the U.S. and abroad. In group or one-on-one meetings, we spoke with Holocaust survivors, children and grandchildren of survivors, grandchildren of perpetrators, victims of other genocides, artists, art historians, museum and Jewish educators, lay leaders from the Jewish community, and those involved in the study and teaching of the Holocaust, and human rights.

Your first question pointed to our board of trustees and their importance to this institution and that's an apt observation. Many of our board members serve as barometers for public response; they're connected to and represent various communities. We met with the majority of them, either individually or in small groups. We used their comments, concerns, and ideas, along with those of others we consulted, in shaping the interpretation. Our board members were remarkably supportive. Some even became spokespersons for the show.

SM: Some observers criticized the abundance of interpretive material framing the show—presumably the end-result of this process—as excessive. How do you decide when an interpretive frame begins to work against the art by reducing its ambiguities and complexities?

NK & JL: To us, the criticism of interpretation within a contemporary art exhibition sounds like a mandate to return to formalism. That is a view in which art is worshipfully regarded as totally isolated, insulated from social concerns and accessible only to a chosen few.

SM: But surely varying amounts of interpretation are always possible within varying institutional contexts and surely not every charge of over-interpretation is a covert call for formalism. Is there a point where there *is* too much interpretation?

JL & NK: Most of the criticism of the quality and quantity of interpretation came from the art press. This show and its subject matter reached—and affected—more than just those who are contemporary-art savvy. We felt it was our obligation to make the individual works and the exhibition as a whole accessible to a large and diverse public. There was, in fact, no more text in *Mirroring Evil* than in [Norman Kleeblatt's] *Too Jewish* exhibition of 1996, in which the interpretation also focused on the ways popular culture could represent both the images and ideas behind the art.

RA: Let's return to this issue of community and who speaks for whom. We know you reached out to "the community." Who exactly constituted that community(s)? Did you conceptualize it first as a community of Holocaust survivors? And then a larger circle of Jews?

NK & JL: One of the cornerstone questions of the exhibition was "Who can speak for the Holocaust?" We felt it was important to ask this question and just as important not to answer it. Instead we tried to let audiences find their own answers. *Mirroring Evil* was not about the Holocaust per se, but about how certain concepts and propaganda techniques employed by the Nazis continue to be used (and consumed) today. So the exhibition was targeted not just at Holocaust survivors, but at anyone, Jewish or not, who could be asked tough moral questions about the decisions we all make in everyday life.

SM: Part of the "frame" for the show was the museum itself. Given the political and cultural climate of 2002, is there any other institution but this one that could have presented *Mirroring Evil?*

JL & NK: First of all, *Mirroring Evil* began to be planned as early as 1999. Granted, the climate for showing challenging contemporary art changed considerably in the wake of September 11th. But we were continuing a long museum tradition of showing such work and the subject matter itself certainly resonates with the programmatic mission of The Jewish Museum. So, despite some resistance, perhaps at that particular time we were the logical place for this exhibition, although at an earlier moment a similarly focused exhibition might have appeared at another institution. And this was, by no means, meant to be an exhibition just for The Jewish Museum audience. We strove to listen to the voices of people outside Jewish communities to make sure they were also part of the dialogue during the run of the exhibition.

RA: How did you do that?

NK & JL: We organized daily dialogues which became remarkable sites for intimate emotional and intellectual discourse. Audiences from all sorts of backgrounds participated in these dialogues.

RA: What did the museum learn from its experiences producing and presenting *Mirroring Evil*? And what did each of you, personally, learn?

JL & NK: As an institution, the museum learned how difficult it is to manage an exhibition with such complex and challenging subject matter. The intensity of the project's mission and the sensitivity of the project's issues required both individuals and departments to find new ways of collaborating and working together in order to actualize the exhibition and surrounding programs. Throughout the planning stages of *Mirroring Evil,* the curatorial team worked much more closely with the education, public programming, and public relations departments than previously.

We also learned that the public was willing, if they took the trouble to come to the exhibit, to engage in a dialogue with the works, with each other, and with docents, scholars, and educators. Similarly, we found an eagerness to read and understand, and to form opinions and communicate them among these people. Of course this was a self-selected sample that came in spite—or because—of the press coverage. The bottom line is that they were willing to come through the door. This is stimulating knowledge and provides inspiration for future exhibitions that will keep this dialogue going.

NK: Given the complexities of mounting such an exhibition, it might have been easier to give up on it midway. I didn't give up and nor would I, if I had to make the choice again. But at times, I do think we all wondered if it was worth the energy we had to expend. The possibility of debating [fundamental issues of identity] that had been off-limits for nearly a decade made it worthwhile.

In a more personal sense, I also learned that in order to do a project that means so much intellectually and morally, I had to give up some of my control. That meant empowering others, both inside and outside the institution, to exercise major roles and have major voices in the project.

RA: That's fascinating. What about you Joanna?

JL: I can say that I learned a countless number of things from working on this project. In particular the importance of educating the entire staff—including those not usually involved in educational outreach such as administrators, guards, and volunteers—about a sensitive and potentially controversial project. We presented the exhibition's art and ideas to each staff member well in advance of the opening in order to understand and respond to their feedback, enthusiasms, discomforts, and concerns about the show. This dialogue helped create community within the institution by both acknowledging staff apprehension and providing concrete suggestions for interacting with museum visitors.

Unfortunately I also learned, that much of the press would rather create a firestorm of controversy than do something constructive. Why no in-depth discussions of touchy subject matter? Or assessments of the nuances of the exhibition and the art? Shouldn't they want to stimulate thought and reflection among their readers and viewers? Wouldn't you?

28
MY MEMORIAL TO PATRICK TILLMAN

John Leanos

As a Chicano artist, part of my job is to comment on society and to critically engage issues that some consider taboo, unpopular, or culturally sensitive. As an assistant professor at Arizona State University, I quickly realized that performing such work can lead to trouble.

In October of 2004, I created a Day of the Dead artwork and memorial to fallen U.S. Army Ranger and ex-professional football player, Patrick Tillman. Its spirit was critical: Tillman's death in Afghanistan in April, 2004, was utilized by the U.S. military, the federal government, and the media to construct an image of a glorified war hero who had died while bravely fighting the evil Al'Qaeda. The truth, however, was quite different. It was reported that Tillman had died by so-called "friendly fire" and not until December of 2004 did the military disclose that he died at the hands of his own platoon because of "botched communications, mistaken decisions . . . and negligent shooting."[1]

The canonization of Patrick Tillman as a war hero and martyr created an atmosphere that restricted critical analysis of Tillman's heroic image. At the same time, many were capitalizing and profiting from Tillman's story. There were two unauthorized books published about Tillman, a Hollywood screenplay reportedly in the works, hats, jerseys, helmets, pins, and photos. Arizona State University, Tillman's alma mater, produced several military-sport themed memorial pamphlets. The Arizona Cardinals, a professional football team, sold tickets that offered free rubber bracelets with Tillman's name and ID number on them to the first 10,000 fans at the game. (The bracelets were quickly sold on eBay for up to seventy dollars apiece).

This branding, profiteering, and propagandistic use of Tillman's image and name were acceptable to the powers that be so long as it fit within a patriotic and heroic ideological framework. When my more

John Jota Leanos, "Friendly Fire," 2004. Courtesy of the artist.

critical memorials were placed around the Arizona State University campus and in Phoenix, local ABC, and *CBS Nightly News* ran sensationalized stories about them. CNN then picked up the story and broadcast it nationally over the weekend that preceded the second Bush–Kerry presidential debate, which took place at Arizona State University. I received hundreds of phone calls and email messages filled with hate, bigotry, racism, homophobia, and threats of death and violence. My home address was posted online. The president of Arizona State University sent out letters that publicly decried the work and the Board of Regents launched a fruitless investigation into my classroom activities.

On the one hand, I am not surprised by the violent reaction of politically conservative males to this artwork (over 90 percent of the hate mail I received was from men). It is business as usual on the extreme right to launch hate campaigns, ad hominem attacks, character assassination, and witch hunts to destroy the professional lives of those who breach certain ideological *fronteras.* On the other hand, the artwork was not slanderous, obscene, pornographic, or racist. That it could incite such vicious reactions is all-too-revealing of the times in which we live.

For a full account of this art controversy, please go to http://www.leanos.net

Notes

1. Steve Coll, "Barrage of Bullets Drowned Out Cries of Comrades," *Washington Post,* Dec. 5, 2004:A01.

29

THE NEW MEANING OF BIAS

Diane Ravitch

> Do you know that Newspeak is the only language in the world whose vocabulary gets smaller every year?
>
> —George Orwell, *1984*

FOR MONTHS after I participated in the appraisal of President Clinton's proposed voluntary national test, I continued to reflect on the experience. The bias and sensitivity reviewers saw insult in words and ideas that most people would find unexceptional. They employed a set of assumptions that were outside the realm of what seemed to be common sense.

As I tried to understand the reasoning of the reviewers, I remembered that in 1998 the president of Riverside Publishing had met with our committee to explain how reading passages for the voluntary national test would be selected. We expressed our hope that the test would be of high quality, that it would be more than just a basic skills test. We wanted the publisher to include passages based on good literature. We thought that children should read something worthwhile when they took the test, not just banal selections. We asked whether his company would choose some readings drawn from myths and fables and other classic literature. He said that they would try, but we had to bear in mind that "everything written before 1970 was either gender biased or racially biased." He said this very casually, as though he was uttering a truth too well known to need explanation or defense. This belief provided the backdrop for the document that he gave us that day, titled "Bias and Sensitivity Concerns in Testing."

When I first read this document, I was astonished by the list of topics that the test publisher considered out-of-bounds, and I filed it away. Two years later, in 2000, when I saw the results of the bias and sensitivity review, I retrieved this document and found that it held the key to the reviewers' assumptions. "Bias and Sensitivity Concerns in Testing" explained how the concept of bias had been redefined. It contained rules for self-censorship that most Americans, I believe, would find deeply disturbing.

The Riverside guidelines are a mixture of sensible general reminders about the unacceptability of bias, as well as detailed lists of words and topics that must be avoided on tests. "Bias," it declares, is anything in a test item that might cause any student to be distracted or upset. Bias is the presence of something in a test item that would result in different performance "for two individuals of the same ability but from different subgroups." So, for example, a test question that is upsetting to a member of group A (for instance, a girl) would prevent her from doing as well as someone who was from a different group (for instance, a boy). Bias, says the publisher, can cause inaccurate scores and measurement errors. It seems to be a settled principle that tests should not contain anything that is so upsetting to certain students that they cannot demonstrate what they know and can do. Presumably a very graphic description of violence, for example, would be so disturbing to some students that they would not be able to answer test questions. Presumably students would be upset by a test question that contained language that demeaned their race, gender, or religion. Riverside says that its tests "are designed to avoid language, symbols, gestures, words, phrases, or examples that are generally regarded as sexist, racist, otherwise offensive, inappropriate, or negative towards any group." In addition, tests should not contain any subject matter that anyone might consider "controversial or emotionally charged." Such things would distract test takers and prevent them from showing their true ability. It would be unfair, certainly, and the goal of a bias and sensitivity review is supposed to be fairness.

But then look at where the logic of fairness leads. There are three ways, the guidelines assert, to ensure fairness in testing. One is by "representational fairness," another is by reviewing "language usage," and a third is by removing "stereotypes." In addition, certain inflammatory topics must be avoided. Each of these versions of "fairness" leads the publisher to specify precisely what language and which ideas will be allowed and which will be banned. As I read through the guidelines, I began to understand why the publisher advised us that everything written before 1970 was biased. Few writings before that date could possibly meet the specifications laid out in the guidelines.

The bias guidelines list certain topics that are so controversial or "emotionally charged" that they must be avoided on a test unless they are directly relevant to the curriculum (in a test of reading, no particular subject matter is directly relevant, so all of these topics must be avoided). Such topics are:

Abortion
Creatures that are thought to be scary or dirty, like scorpions, rats, and roaches
Death and disease
Disrespectful or criminal behavior
Evolution
Expensive consumer goods
Magic, witchcraft, the supernatural
Personal appearance (such as height and weight)
Politics
Religion
Social problems (such as child abuse, animal abuse, and addiction)
Unemployment
Unsafe situations
Weapons and violence

The guidelines advise that accuracy should be the goal when dealing with historical information, but on a reading test historical accuracy may be sacrificed when it involves stereotypes.

In addition to the list of banned controversial topics, there is an exhaustive description of "negative" and "sensitive" material that cannot appear on a test. Negative material includes (but is not limited to) parents quarreling, children mistreating each other, children acting disobediently toward their parents, and children showing disrespect for authority. Sensitive material includes paganism, satanism, parapsychology, magic, ghosts, extraterrestrials, Halloween, witches, or anything that might conjure up such subjects, even in the context of fantasy. Anything related to Halloween, such as pumpkins and masks, must be avoided. Gambling must be avoided, as must references to nudity, pregnancy, or giving birth, whether to animals or people. "Controversial" styles of music like rap and rock and roll are out.

But that is not all. Religious and political issues must be avoided. Reading passages must not contain even an "incidental reference" to anyone's religion. There must not be any mention of birthdays or religious holidays (including Thanksgiving), because some children do not have birthday parties and do not share the same religion. In any material about Native Americans, care must be exercised to steer clear of religious traditions.

There must be no reference in any test passage to evolution or the origins of the universe. Writers must avoid any mention of fossils or dinosaurs. Their very existence suggests the banned topic of evolution. However, it is acceptable to refer to "animals of long ago" if there is no mention of how old they are and no suggestion that the existence of these animals implies evolution.

Still more topics are banned as upsetting to sensitive children. There is some overlap with the first set of banned topics, but this list adds some additional caveats. These include:

Someone being fired or losing their job
Rats, mice, roaches, snakes, lice
Cancer or other serious illnesses
Death
Catastrophes such as earthquakes and fires (natural events like tornados or hurricanes may be okay if the context is not too frightening)
Unnecessary violence (reference to guns or knives is forbidden except in a historical context)
Gratuitous gore, like animals eating other animals
Serious social problems, like poverty, alcoholism, divorce, or addiction of any kind
Slavery and racial prejudice

The bias guidelines require that test questions "model healthful personal habits." Any references to smoking, drinking, or junk food must be eliminated. Writers must be cautious when depicting someone drinking coffee or tea and must take care not to mention even aspirin. Children must never be shown doing dangerous things, "no matter how good the moral of the story is."

The test passages must avoid beliefs, attitudes, or values that are not embraced by just about everybody. Fables are a particular concern, because they often conclude on a cynical note or have "a pragmatic moral" that someone may find offensive. Particularly taboo, the guidelines warn, is anything that suggests secular humanism, situation ethics, or New Age religion.

The people who select reading passages for tests are directed to seek out "uplifting topics." Anything depressing, disgusting, or scary should be eliminated.

Many topics are prohibited because testing experts agree that any less than ideal context will be so upsetting to some children that they will not be able to do their best on a test. But would children really be distracted if they read a story in which someone was fired or unemployed? Would they be disoriented if they read a story in which someone was seriously ill or parents were divorced? No educational research literature supports these prohibitions. There are no studies that show that children were unable to finish a test or do their best because they were asked to read a story in which the characters were rich or poor. Farewell then to *Great Expectations, Little Lord Fauntleroy,* and "The Little Match Girl," with their unacceptable images of wealth and poverty.

The prohibitions are there not because of research findings, but because the *topics upset some adults,* who assume that they will upset children in the same way. Some adults sincerely believe that children will project themselves into everything they read and that they will be deeply disturbed to read that someone else is taller than they, or that other children had a birthday party or live in a big house when perhaps they are not similarly privileged. It is hard to imagine that a fourth-grade student would be paralyzed by dread by reading a story that included descriptions of mice. Clearly forbidden by such a prohibition is any excerpt from books like E.B. White's *Stuart Little* or Robert Lawson's *Ben and Me,* not to mention stories of Mickey Mouse, Mighty Mouse, and other fictional mice beloved by generations of children.

Most of the prohibitions are a direct response to longstanding complaints from the religious right. Many of the banned topics are intended to avert the controversy that might erupt if the test referred to evolution or witchcraft or religion. Spokesmen for the religious right consider any description of behavior they do not like as an endorsement of that behavior. They reject depictions of magic, witchcraft, and the supernatural; they don't want education materials to show people engaging in bad behavior, like children disobeying their parents. They have gone to court in several jurisdictions to protest against "secular humanism," "situation ethics," and "New Age" religion, because such ideas conflict with the moral code that is fixed in the Bible.

Test publishers have found that the best way to avoid controversy is to eliminate anything that might cause controversy. As the bias guidelines of Riverside Publishing show, quite a large number of topics are avoided (i.e., censored) because of fear of complaints by the religious right. But the bias guidelines try to mollify not only conservatives, but also feminists and advocates for multiculturalism, the handicapped, and the aged. The publishers want everyone to be happy, or at least not to be unhappy. Whereas the right gets topic control, the left gets control of language and images. To see how this works, we must consider what the test publisher describes as the three types of fairness: representational fairness, language usage, and stereotyping.

The Riverside guidelines define "representational fairness" to mean that no group will be overrepresented or underrepresented. Thus, with few exceptions, reading passages are supposed to include equal numbers of males and females, and proportionate representation of all groups in terms of ethnicity, age, socioeconomic background, gender, community setting, and physical disabilities. Another way that Riverside defines "representational fairness" is that the materials on tests should be "relevant" to the life experiences of those taking the test. For example, southern students should not be expected to understand the "concepts" of snow and freezing winters, which are outside their own personal life experience. To expect them to know about such weather conditions when they have not experienced them is considered regional bias.

Language usage refers to the specific words in a test passage or test question, and here the bias guidelines become strongly proscriptive. Gender bias is implied by any use of the term *man,* as in "mankind" or "man in the street" or "salesman." All of these are now forbidden terms that must be replaced by "the human race," the "average citizen," or a "sales representative." Bias against people with a disability occurs whenever a disabled person is identified by that disability. For example, it is biased to refer to "the blind"; one must say instead, "a person who is blind." It is biased to say that someone is "wheelchair bound"; one must refer instead to "a person who uses a wheelchair." It is biased to say that someone was "a victim of polio"; one must refer instead to "a person who had polio." Then there is elitist bias, which is also unacceptable. An example of this bias is the sentence "Even though she was a poor, Hispanic woman, Maria was able to start a successful company." The sentence must be reworded as "Through hard work and determination, Maria Sanchez started a successful company."

It is easy to see how publishers might well conclude that everything written before 1970 is racially biased or gender biased. Certainly John Steinbeck's *Of Mice and Men* makes racial references that are inappropriate under the guidelines (even its title, referring to both mice and men, is unacceptable); so does Mark Twain's *Adventures of Huckleberry Finn;* so do the novels of Richard Wright, Zora Neale Hurston, and James Baldwin. The novels of Jane Austen, Edith Wharton, and Charles Dickens contain what the bias reviewers consider gender stereotypes. The publisher of Riverside was right: Most classic literature is unacceptable when judged by the new rules governing references to gender, ethnicity, age, and disability.

In addition to representational fairness and language usage, the bias guidelines warn against stereotyping. In the early years of the feminist movement, activists complained that women were shown only as housewives and mothers, rather than as scientists, professionals, and business leaders. African Americans complained that they were portrayed only in subservient roles, rather than as scientists, professionals, and business leaders. The effort to eliminate stereotypes was intended to banish any notion that certain high-status careers and activities were closed to women, blacks, and other minorities.

The definition of stereotyping, like the definition of bias, has become far more elaborate and refined as time has gone by. Educational publishers know that they must avoid showing people of a certain gender, race, ethnicity, age, or disability group in roles that might contribute to a stereotype. What was once a fairly sensible notion of fairness—don't always show women as homemakers—has turned into a presumption that they should never be shown in that role. The bias guidelines suggest that it is stereotypical to depict women as wives and mothers, even though most women are, at some time in their lives, wives and mothers. Since men cannot be portrayed as wives and mothers, no one may fairly be presented in those roles. Although the guidelines note that "all group members should be portrayed as exhibiting a full range of emotions, occupations, activities, and roles," writers are forewarned that certain representations are not acceptable because of their past history as stereotypes.

A person with the job of writing test questions has the thankless task of portraying American society in all its diversity, without at the same time giving any stereotypical attributes to any person who is portrayed. Thus, while the rest of us might imagine that the purpose of a test is to find out whether students have learned what they studied in class, test developers spend as much time balancing social imperatives as they do on the academic and cognitive content of test questions.

The definition of bias and sensitivity is so broad and so proscriptive that it guarantees the exclusion from national and state tests of many valued works of literature. Whether classic or contemporary, most recognized authors will almost certainly violate the rules about topic or language usage or stereotyping because such authors did not tailor their writing to meet the guidelines. One looks to literature for expressions of imagination, reality, paradox, and complexity rather than carefully crafted orthodoxies. There are stories that are not appropriate for fourth-grade children because of their language or imagery, but none of those censored by the bias reviewers came anywhere near that threshold.

There is no valid educational reason to exclude such a broad list of topics other than to placate the religious right; children should be able to read a test passage about dinosaurs or literary flights of fancy. Similarly, there is no valid educational reason to regulate language usage so tightly other than to placate the feminist and multicultural left; children should be able to read a passage in which a mother prepares dinner or an African American family lives in a city neighborhood without setting off a furor about stereotyping. Furthermore, banning words like "mankind" is just plain silly. By now, our society has evolved to the point where some people will say "humankind" or "the human race" and others will say "mankind." We should be mature enough to live with diversity of language usage. We have never had a language police or a thought police in this country, and we should not have one now.

What kinds of educational materials can survive this heavily proscriptive review? What's left after the language police and the thought police from the left and the right have done their work? Stories that have no geographical location. Stories that have no regional distinctiveness. Stories in which all conflicts are insignificant. Stories in which men are fearful, and women are brave. Stories in which older people are never ill. Stories in which children are obedient, never disrespectful, never get into dangerous situations, never confront problems that cannot be easily solved. Stories in which blind people and people with physical disabilities need no assistance from anyone because their handicaps are not handicaps. Stories in which fantasy and magic are banned. Stories about the past in which historical accuracy is ignored. Stories about science that leave out any reference to evolution or prehistoric times. Stories in which everyone is happy almost all the time. The result of all this relentless purging is dishonesty, a purposeful shielding of children from anything challenging, controversial, or just plain interesting. It is a process that drains literature of its life and blood, converts it into dreary reading materials, and grinds reading materials into pabulum.

The Riverside bias and sensitivity guidelines are not unique. Indeed, Riverside cites guidelines issued by other test publishers and by the American Psychological Association to show that its recommendations are right in the center of the educational publishing mainstream. Once I understood what the guidelines meant and how they were implemented, I could not shake the feeling that something important and dangerous was happening in American education that few people knew about. The more I thought about the ubiquitous application of censorship at the source, the more it seemed to me to be a major intellectual scandal, the more it looked like political correctness run amok, far from public view.

PART V

Self-Censorship

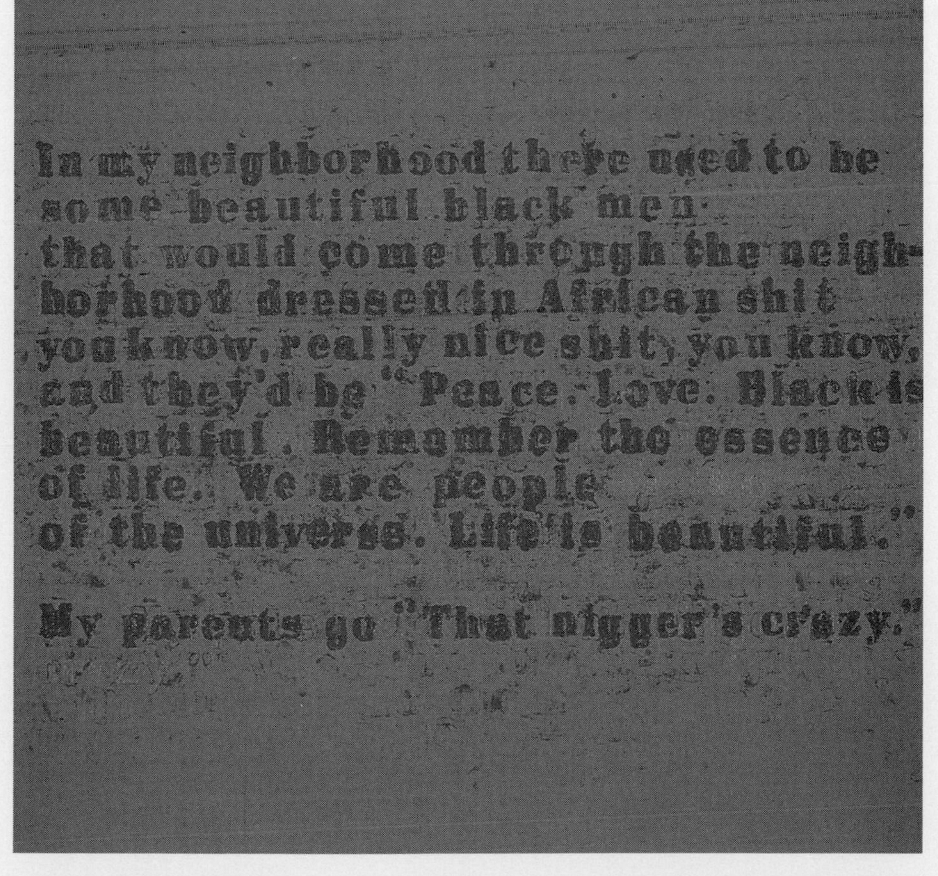

Glenn Ligon, *Beautiful Black Men,* 1995. Oilstick and acrylic on canvas, 32" x 32". Collection of Peter Norton. Courtesy of the artist.

30

THE CENSOR WITHIN

Svetlana Mintcheva

The ultimate dream of censorship is to do away with the censor. Writers and artists in totalitarian regimes are forced to learn what subject matter is off-limits and which aesthetic forms are taboo. Self-censorship is rewarded with membership in exclusive groups, which grant sought-after privileges; failure to conform is swiftly punished—in the worst cases by jail or even a death sentence. In the United States, however, political repression is not the primary concern of the majority of artists and writers. What they usually fear is not imprisonment but the more mundane, albeit powerful, pressures derived from the difficulties of publishing or exhibiting their work.

Both ubiquitous and invisible, self-censorship in modern democracies is frequently invoked but little explored. Just as censorship is often disguised under the rubric of "protecting children" or sensitivity to religious values, self-censorship masquerades as a search for political balance, respect for one's audience, consideration for the feelings of others, or adherence to the standards of the art world. But can every modification of content made in response to such concerns be deemed self-censorship? When an artist opts to rework a performance or hesitates about working with cultural taboos, who is to say this is self-censorship and not a legitimate creative decision? When a museum alters an exhibition so as not to anger and alienate its audience, it may just be fulfilling its central mission: to serve the community and demonstrate respect for its diverse values.

Self-censorship occurs both in the creative process and in everyday life; it can affect an individual or an institution: "Whoever believes that they are immune, is the first victim," insists Hans Magnus Enzensberger, the German poet, essayist, and publisher. Before condemning the censor within, however, we need to be aware of its multiple motivations and subtle methods.

To understand institutional self-censorship, it is necessary to unravel the decision-making process that museums embark upon when they plan what to include and what to exclude from an exhibition. Exhibitions are highly collaborative enterprises involving personnel of many kinds—curators, museum directors, administrators—who are responsible for dealing with artists and trustees while also taking into account the needs of the audience. Pressures come from inside, but also from outside: from politicians, the media, as well as from funding agencies and sponsors. Museum professionals are expected to organize popular shows and to take into account the diverse beliefs and sensitivities of their increasingly heterogeneous audiences. They are also called upon to increase the cultural capital of their institutions through socially relevant and cutting edge programming, yet tread lightly when assessing the social role of the exhibition's sponsor. These multiple requirements are rarely in complete harmony. When they clash, some degree of self-censorship is often the result. As the roundtable discussion with museum directors Tom Finkelpearl and Thomas Sokolowski, included in this section, suggests, balancing the desires of artists and the mission and needs of an institution requires extensive dialogue, education, and compromise.

At its best, the dialogue begins well in advance of an exhibition. Thomas Sokolowski recounts the sometimes tense discussion with the NAACP and other religious and social service groups in the planning process of a potentially troublesome show of lynching photographs at the Warhol Museum in Pittsburg, Pennsylvania. As most concerns had been voiced before it even opened, the exhibition itself ran smoothly. Occasionally, however, in response to controversy flaring up after a show has been installed, a work is modified. This happened with a controversial piece by Palestinian artist Emily Jacir, which was part of a show at the Queens Museum of Art. Tom Finkelpearl relates the complex interplay of pressures and interests that led to the compromise.

The strident patriotism, flag displays, and the polarized "you are with us or against us" mentality nurtured by the White House after September 11th, together with the political polarization of the country around the war in Iraq, has put new pressures on exhibition spaces. A ubiquitous search for political "balance" today often results in the suppression of even relatively mild critique—most visibly in the media, but also in academia and virtually elsewhere else. The planning for a 2004 exhibition of politically themed art at the galleries of Arizona State University in Phoenix, for instance, prompted anxious inquiries by local legislators, which, in turn, motivated the University administration to insist on political "balance"—that is, any work critical of George W. Bush or his policies had to be "balanced" either by work celebrating him or work attacking his rival, Senator John Kerry (the exhibition coincided with one of the preelection presidential debates). The curators acceded to pressure and eventually the show was trimmed of some of the work categorized as "anti-Bush." Only inquiries by a local reporter who obtained the internal e-mail correspondence related to the planning of the exhibition brought the university administration's censorious actions to light.

Institutional self-censorship may be invisible to the larger world but, because there are many witnesses, it is much easier to identify than personal self-censorship. When it comes to individuals the first reflex is to deny the internal censor—until one begins considering the numerous choices and considerations that arise during the creative process. The personal narratives in "The Ubiquitous Censor: Artists and Writers on Self-Censorship" provide a rare, and thought provoking, glimpse into this process.

Sometimes, when economic considerations are at play, the call to censor oneself is straightforward: a publisher, for instance, might press an author to make slight changes to a manuscript so that school libraries would buy the book and book clubs would adopt it. Taken by surprise, an author sometimes agrees, as we learn from Judy Blume, a writer whose novels, immensely popular with young women, top the American Library's Association list of frequently banned books for reasons ranging from profane language and sexual content to promoting "the stranglehold of humanism on life in America," and showing children cruelly teasing a classmate.

Other examples are more subtle—and insidious. The very institution of contemporary art, with its rigid, unwritten rules as to what comprises art, what constitutes "cool," and what, therefore, deserves the spotlight, is a powerful force in shaping what artists allow themselves to do and often prompts self-censorship. Afghan-born New York curator Leeza Ahmadi writes of the necessity non-Western artists feel to produce work conforming to a Western definition of art if they want to be exhibited. Barbara Pollock, artist, critic, and mother, writes of the fear that her motherhood-themed work will never have the requisite hipness for the contemporary art world.

Self-censorship works best when it is imperceptible—not only to outsiders, but to its very perpetrator. Indeed, as Carolee Schneemann points out, it is doubtful that an artist today, living in a "profoundly, pervasively self-censoring" culture, "inundated with increasingly suppressive government control; our psyches . . . sucked into Mc-Malled soullessness," would even recognize self-censorship.

But is self-censorship always bad? Can a more nuanced understanding of the censor within redeem some of its manifestations? Or, put another way, is it a trade-off worth making? As we learn, self-censorship sometimes originates in the legitimate need to protect family members or in respect for the internal taboos of one's community, as performance artist Guillermo Gómez-Peña relates from experience. Or, it might be a calculated compromise allowing an alternative voice to be heard, even if filtered. Such is the deal playwright Betty Shamieh made with herself when she offered a less politically pointed monologue to the Brave New World festival in New York, hoping to ensure the presence of an Arab-American playwright in the festival. Or it could be that some material is simply too culturally loaded, too explosive, or "too close to home, too black, and too strong," as Glenn Ligon writes of his struggle to incorporate the comic material of Richard Pryor within his visual artwork.

One of the first things we learn as children is that there are things you can say and do at home, but cannot say or do on the bus, or at school. Most of the artists we invited to share thoughts on self-censorship are keenly aware of this. Ligon recalls an incident where a visitor to the Whitney, who otherwise confessed he loved Richard Pryor's routines, was upset to see a reference to them on museum walls. Gómez-Peña speaks of the difficulty of presenting sexually explicit content in Chicano art spaces and, conversely, the difficulty of presenting radical political content in Anglo "spaces"—whether art centers or public radio stations. Nobody who creates work for an audience can deny that s/he takes out the editor's red pen to excise a phrase or idea that might be "alienating" or "offensive" to an imagined viewer or listener.

Questions of what to express and what to repress are issues we grapple with every day. Self-repression often derives from fear: fear of ostracism, fear of not being understood, published, exhibited. This fear threatens creative activity: J.M. Coetzee insists that the interiorization of the censor into the writer's psychic life "bring[s] with it humiliation, self-disgust, and shame." But self-censorship can also arise from a sense of consideration for others. Psychoanalyst Janice Lieberman notes that some of the most groundbreaking modern artists—Pablo Picasso and Jackson Pollock—were unusually narcissistic and oblivious to others' needs. She hypothesizes that this trait served their art well.

Are artistic genius and social connectedness at odds? Is creativity beyond conventional morals and is the acceptance of social norms already a form of self-censorship? Our concern for ethical principles necessarily constrains us, limits what we say and do. And although such principles may be overzealously applied, or less altruistic than we think, sensitivity to the feelings of others is obviously not altogether a bad thing. But carried too far, sensitivity and caution begin to stifle.

Ultimately, we do censor ourselves out of fear: whether that is the fear of political repression or the fear that our not quite politically correct inner thoughts would emerge and condemn us in the eyes of our peers. In contrast to those working under openly repressive regimes, we are unwilling to admit that we are not really free to say what we like: we all want to deny the censor within. Perhaps it is impossible to really speak about how we censor ourselves—for to speak about one's internal censor is to expose what we most want to hide.

31

TO DISCERN, TO DISCRIMINATE, AND TO DECIDE: CENSORSHIP AND INSTITUTIONS

Tom Finkelpearl (director of the Queens Museum of Art) and Thomas Sokolowski (director of the Andy Warhol Museum in Pittsburgh) in conversation with Svetlana Mintcheva and Robert Atkins

Robert Atkins: Let's talk first about how you conceive of your audiences. Is there such a thing as community or is it a construction of politicians and foundation heads? Given that Queens is one of the most racially diverse places in the U.S., why don't we start with you, Tom Finkelpearl.

Tom Finkelpearl: We aspire to be the people's museum. And we are located in the second-most-used park in the city. The folks using the park are our greatest potential audience: lots of Latinos, South Asians, and East Asians living in Flushing and Corona. And we are making a very concerted effort to not have our audience be upper middle class, to not have the "normal museum audience." We've made staff changes, and we have initiated multi-year programs aimed specifically at audience development. We have a trolley running from Jackson Heights through Corona to the museum and back to get people from those communities into the museum. We have just hired a head of public programming who is completely conversant with the second-generation, multicultural Queens crowd. Next weekend, for example, we are producing "Fatal Love," which is a joint Indian-Pakistani celebration. Both Indian and Pakistani independence days are this week. In Manhattan they are celebrated as independent nationalistic holidays. In Queens we are doing them together. The event is called "Fatal Love," because these are two peoples who hate and love each other.

RA: So you don't have a traditionally elite, moneyed audience to "offend"?

TF: No we do, we do. And you know what it is? There is a kind of upper middle class, quite traditional audience that is largely Italian and Jewish, which is diminishing as a percentage, yet remains in control of the politics. But this is also a very open minded, liberal group of people. We have many trustees from this group and they are all for becoming part of the cultural mix of Queens.

Tom Sokolowski: And do they show up at the "Fatal Love" celebrations and such and such? I think too often when cultural institutions do this, with the most admirable of intentions, it is ultimately bringing the "them" in, to use old-fashioned words, without bringing the "us" in, and it becomes just as elitist in a different kind of way.

TF: They don't have to come, they just have to embrace it. And, of course, there are trustees and trustees. First of all, the old Jewish grandmother members are open-minded and will come to anything. They are a great and loyal audience. Last year, the highlight of "Fatal Love" was a classically trained Indian drag queen. And when s/he performed, it was Ecuadorian day in the park and a Hong Kong riverboat festival was also happening. There were our members sitting around and there was a huge South Asian contingent. And they all loved it. And half the audience didn't notice it was a man. We were laughing at some of the jokes but we didn't get it because we don't know enough Bollywood film, but we appreciated his or her artistry. That was a great moment. Now not every moment is like that, but the older Jewish and Italian crowd does come to the whole range of events.

TS: That is great. But having such a diverse constituency you cannot but be aware that there are serious conflicts there, too.

TF: One of the things about Queens that is very different than Brooklyn or the Bronx, is that it's very middle class. There aren't many poor people and there aren't many rich people. There are a lot of homeowners and they have a lot in common. Sixty percent of households in Queens are headed by people born outside the United States. Ninety percent of the people in our community are minorities; the majority is a minority. So there are many underlying similarities as well as, of course, underlying differences. One thing in common among all these groups is the second-generation experience. Because, whether you are from India or from Azerbaijan or Guatemala, your parents often cling to a traditional culture and consider themselves to be from their native land, but *you* are American, making for these huge generation gaps.

I have to tell you about something that's made me miserable. We had a show called *Queens International.* It was a show of international artists who all live in Queens. And so one of the artists was a Palestinian artist, Emily Jacir. One of the quirks of our museum is that the U.N. General Assembly met in our building from 1946 to 1950. So the partition of Palestine was decided upon in this building.

Emily's mother worked in the World's Fair in 1964 in the Jordanian Pavilion, which was all manned or, rather, womaned, by Palestinian women. So Emily did a piece about the celebratory moment of Israel being admitted into the U.N. and Palestine being partitioned in November, 1947. She found in our archives a brochure from the Worlds Fair in 1964, a very pro-Palestinian, anti-Israeli propaganda piece, which was given out by the Jordanians. She had it reprinted and, without any indication that it was a work of art, left it in a bin where people were picking it up. They freaked out.

So I am trying to figure out what to do. I thought that the most important thing we could do at this point is to create a moment of dialogue, not to strictly adhere to the idea that the work couldn't be changed. And so we got into a discussion with the artist about the fact that people didn't recognize her handout as a work of art and were simply freaking out because they thought that the museum was distributing Palestinian propaganda. We got into lengthy discussions with conservative and orthodox Jewish communities; we were attacked in the press by the right.

Then we invited Marcia Kannry, founder of the "Dialogue Project," to the museum. The project gives Jewish Israelis and Arab Palestinians and Jews and Arabs the opportunity to sit down and talk to one another. I would say my best moment at the museum came during a panel discussion with three Israelis and three Palestinians organized by Emily Jacir. We had a Christian Palestinian, an Iraqi Jew, an Ashkenazi Jew, and so on. It was a whole mix of those two communities. And that came about because Emily did change the piece. She stopped giving out the brochure, though you could still see the brochure, you could read the brochure, and you could even get the brochure if you requested it. However, it wasn't something you just pulled out of an unmarked box. And this, at some level, was censorship. And she felt that even though she agreed to it. I said to a friend of mine, "Well she agreed to it, it wasn't censorship," and he said, "It is not necessarily not censorship because she agreed to it." So we didn't take the hard First Amendment line, "We are never going to change a piece because of controversy," but we did create an opportunity for genuine dialogue.

TS: You were right, that was the smart thing to do. Sometimes you want to sit down with the artist and say, "What the hell were you trying to get out of that?" and they say, "We were trying to bring about such and such," and I say, "Well, you did it badly." If you can go about and say, "I won't hang that abstract painting because it's lousy," why should you not be able to say, "You are not being responsible"? You are not being censorious in the traditional way of saying, "We don't want any trouble," but rather saying, "You are playing with fire and you are going to hurt yourself and others." And someone playing with fire should be slapped for arrogance. I think what you did was a very responsible thing for a cultural institution to do. Because not only did you save your neck, but you brought about a dialogue and that is indeed what that artist's original intention was: to make us look more clearly at the Palestinian-Israeli conflict. So you were the one who effectuated that work of art, not her.

TF: Well no, her agenda was to show the injustice of what happened on November 29, 1947; in the other part of the piece, there was a tent into which were sown the names of the 413 Palestinian villages people were basically kicked out from. Her agenda wasn't, strictly speaking, dialogue; her agenda was to make a point of the fact that her folks had been displaced.

TS: Was that made clear to you when you agreed to do the pictures?

TF: Completely. I knew her work, I invited her. I still think she is a fantastic artist. And we are friends. I think she was agreeable because we are friends. And she didn't attack this museum. Also we treated her well. We paid to get the brochure printed. We had a very interesting dialogue among the different generations of Jewish board members. The board did not say, despite some of the content of the piece, that we should take it down, just that we should differentiate our voice from the artist's. Since then we have done Arab family day and we are planning a show about the Arab Renaissance. What other museum in New York City has done a major project with a Palestinian artist?

Svetlana Mintcheva: A good example of institutional self-censorship.

TS: Definitely. Fifteen years ago or so Mona Hatoum did a video show at the old Artist's Space and that was covered. Has anyone done that since then? So, in other words, forget 9/11, just doing a Palestine-focused show in New York City is close to impossible.

SM: What would you have done if Emily Jacir had not agreed to change the work?

TF: We had an idea of what was the proper thing to do. Which was to have the brochure there, and have it visible, readable, but not takeable. And I brought this to the board. My instructions from the board, with which I concurred, were to see if she would agree. And she agreed, although she said that she thought she was being censored. Then, while on vacation, I spoke with the *Jewish Press,* a right-wing newspaper, and I explained what we had decided to do. And they wrote that we had pulled the brochure from the show. Which was not true. So the right was placated at this point—inaccurately. Then Walter Robinson picked up this story from the *Jewish Press,* and, without calling me, published the same report in *Artnet*. Nobody who wrote saw the exhibit. Emily at that point could have become the darling of a revolt against the Queens Museum and could have garnered all this publicity. But she told her friends, "Look, these guys are not the enemy." She knows every Palestinian artist in New York City, and she is completely tied into the activist community. So the dogs of the right and left were called off, and it didn't end up becoming a big controversy.

SM: Clearly there are some battles you don't want to fight because there are others that are more important.

TF: You see, that is the thing. I wanted to choose dialogue over a battle. And that is what I am interested in—how can you not have a battle? How can you have a dialogue instead?

SM: But you made her choose her battle?

TF: No, no, no. We did lots of public programming around the piece. We also told her, you could hand the thing out at the gallery, that isn't a problem if you want to be there . . .

SM: Yet the framing, the particular way the brochures were distributed appears crucial to her piece . . .

TS: Along with that, I think the thing that is often missed is that is for many years there is this notion that the space that takes on a project—no matter how mundane or how fractious—has to engage in all of the incunabula that this particular individual artist brings. And I don't think that is something that an institution should have to take on. Especially when it is taken by surprise. (Not that that was necessarily your case.) Obviously, to appear at the Queens Museum, as opposed to some nonprofit space in the middle of nowhere says something: that is, you are giving your credibility as an institution. It is totally fraudulent to say, "I want that credibility, but if someone in that institution doesn't agree with me, then you are censoring me." I think in many instances artists who play that game are guilty of the worst kinds of reverse censorship, as in "I am going to raise some really touchy issues here and get all the Palestinians who are mad as hell for all sorts of good reasons to support me and you are not going to have a goddamned chance." As opposed to saying that by presenting me, you are giving me credibility. So I have to take with that credibility some of your logic and order and the architecture of your institution.

RA: But don't you think that most artists show in good faith . . .

TS: No. No. No. I have done this for many years and I think no. There are some who do and are fabulous, and there are some who like to sucker you.

TF: I don't necessarily agree with that and it may sound corny, but when you are working with an artist, it is a partnership. And it shouldn't be antagonistic.

TS: No, it shouldn't be.

TF: And that goes both ways. And that is what I think you are saying, "We are going to work with you and you are going to work with us." Emily is a wonderful artist.

SM: From what you are saying, it seems that in the relationship between the museum and the artist, the museum has control.

TS: No, no, no. The museum has a responsibility to the artist, but also a responsibility to the institution.

SM: So what are the museum's responsibilities to the artist?

TS: To present something that is appropriate to what that artist's intentions are but also understanding how these intentions relate to the institution's mission and the institution's history and its community. You need to know you are taking that on and that you want to take that on as an institution and you bring the battery of your board, your education department, and your funders to do that.

TF: I think the responsibility of the museum is first and foremost to the audience. And that the point of having a museum is that it is an educational institution and it brings people spiritually and intellectually to a different place. My ideal is to really stimulate the audience with fabulous programs and great imaginative leaps. And I think Emily is a really good artist, so we did a big project with her. We fulfilled our responsibility for her to communicate with our audience. Our first responsibility remains to the audience.

RA: Collaboration is certainly at the heart of the presenting process. Similarly, in the writing world, it's just assumed that there are certain roles, that is, that a writer does not produce or design the book. That an editor is there in a book or a magazine to say to the writer, "This works, and this doesn't."

SM: At what point, however, does selection become self-censorship?

TS: I live in Pittsburgh, Pennsylvania. It is a very different place from New York, a very cautious community. And my institution has set its goals, or more appropriately, I have set its goal of being a gadfly of this community. We changed the mission statement from a more traditional one—artist/monograph/museum—to being a center for social and cultural change. And that is what we do. Two and a half years ago, one of my staff members proposed that we do the show of lynching photographs that you might have seen in New York, first in a commercial gallery and then in the New-York Historical Society. Pittsburgh, by the way, has a really bad racial situation. It's twenty-five years behind every other major city in America. We first debated the issue internally and we asked ourselves, "Why should we do this." And we based it upon the fact that Andy Warhol collected archival photographs. He actually had some lynching photographs together with the car crashes and suicides. And along with this came the notion that journalistic images could be powerful sources for art.

So we decided to do it, but we could not do it in a vacuum. We can't do a show like this and thrust it in people's faces. People would freak out one way or another. So we decided, six months before the show, that we would bring the community in. So we brought in tons of people from religious groups and social service groups and the NAACP, and we first were going to say, if you think we should not do this show after some discussions we won't. People on my staff said—and they were absolutely right—"We aren't going to allow other people to tell us what we are going to do. What we should say is that we are going to do this show, because we think it is the right thing and we have our mandate. But how can you help us do it, because we think you could help others understand the context and the importance of it."

And so this group met. After the second time they met, they started challenging us quite vociferously about certain things. They said, "Well, if you really want to do this, why don't you bring so-and-so in." And we did, and we talked to other people. But at one point many people said you just can't show these very strong images to really young kids who may go out distraught, or they may start fights and burn things down. You must show some more positive images. And we did, we created this sort of African-American timeline of history and culture, which has since been used throughout the entire state of Pennsylvania. Then we started to have people come in and talk to the staff and the board. I went to the board and said we are going to do the show. "But what happens if . . . ? And this is going to cause problems because . . ." And I gave them all the really sort of nasty possibilities and they all sat there saying, "UHHHHHHH." But then we took a vote and everyone said we should do it. So we moved forward. And at one point we had people coming from the African American community, some academics who were dealing with the notion of prejudice in this country. But as they told us about their personal lives, we began hearing homophobia, misogyny, and anti-Semitism. So I said, "Whoa! This doesn't go." And I got into a heated argument with one woman who said, "You know you shouldn't have images of nonblack people being lynched." And I said, "Well that is history; you know it happened." "You're taking away our thing, we want it," was her reply. And I said we are not going to cut those images out. And there were a few tense weeks about that. But they backed down.

Later on when the show was up, I had a very intense meeting with one of our guards who said, "Oh, these black people are going to come in and they are going to kill people and we are going to have guns in the galleries and I don't trust these kids, you know what they are like." We didn't have one violent experience. We never heard complaints from any member of our board or from any black organization in the city. Nobody ever mentioned censoring anything, because we made it clear we weren't going to allow for that. But we said we weren't going to allow for censorship, after we promised to hear first what everyone has to say. We will hear what you want, but you are also going to know from where we are coming. And I think that is the important message from the institution—it has a role to play beyond collecting images. Because, no matter who the artist is, or what the subject matter is, the institution is the one that remains in your community.

SM: Would you say that controversy is good publicity?

TF: Unfortunately controversy sometimes is news.

TS: One place where that didn't work was the Jewish Museum and its *Mirroring Evil* show. Even with the controversy, there was dreadful attendance. To their credit, they decided to do this very intense show. They knew it was an intense show, which is why they put off doing it for five years. And then when the controversy came, they weren't willing to say, "Well we knew this was going to be difficult, and we are going to do it to be difficult." They kept backtracking. And as they backtracked, the people who were against it got even more vocal. They had so many disclaimers: You just walked in the door and it was all explanatory videos and texts on the walls. It really took away all the bite from a show that was supposed to have bite.

RA: Do you really think controversy is good for institutions? Please name names.

TS: Controversy can be good for an institution if the institution, just as Tom [Finkelpearl] said, and I was describing, can weave it in and make the institution answer to the community and act in concert with the community.

RA: You *created* a provocative exhibition, I think that is fundamentally different.

TS: Well, there was potential for some members of the African American community to say we were doing this to be sensationalistic. The only criticism we got was from a national group that is behind reparations. And their issue was why are we talking about this other stuff? The only thing that mattered to them was reparations. But we invited them to panels, and they came and they were pretty obnoxious. Many other black participants just shouted them down, which was great. But who knows what is going to be provocative? You never know.

SM: Isn't it interesting how you talk differently when you are regulating some element of a show: It's always a matter of dialogue, it is never about self-censorship. On the other side, as the one being regulated, you usually feel censored. Is there any point where we can talk about and employ the concept of self-censorship? For instance, we noted that no museum in New York really dares approach Palestinian issues. Is this self-censorship? Can we talk about this concept? When you talk to people directly no one admits to doing it.

TF: Before you even get to something politically engaged like the Palestinian work, most people don't even do daring shows about art, never mind politics, sex, whatever. It is usually Winslow Homer and Cézanne who are being shown in big art institutions throughout the country. This is because there is a paucity of imagination and intellectual courage. Forget political and social courage. And because everyone now is so freaked out about raising the big bucks needed to keep their institutions afloat that the only show that they are going to do isn't selected out of fear of censorship but out of fear of low attendance and low ticket prices.

SM: Wouldn't these anxieties about money also apply to funders? You are worried about your audience but you are also worried about whether your funder will like or dislike what you do.

TS: Oh sure. The question is, will they even have a meeting with us to discuss funding. It doesn't even have to be Palestinians or lynchings or AIDS. If it is considered too recondite it's a problem too. Ozenfant still lifes, for instance, who in the hell is going to pay for that?

SM: How is the Warhol Museum funded?

TS: We get money from private individuals, corporations, and private foundations just like almost any other museum. We also receive state money from the Pennsylvania Council for the Arts, but no city or county money.

SM: Did you have problems funding the lynching photographs exhibit?

Tom S: No, in fact we went to the most conservative foundation in Pittsburgh and we got the largest grant they have ever given—$100,000.

SM: The Queens Museum is city-funded?

TF: Yes, about 35 percent.

SM: Do issues of funding arise in connection with programming and content?

TF: There are different kinds of pressure that come with different kinds of funding. A lot of this pressure is a positive force, as in the pressure by city-funding sources to be inclusive. We had gay and lesbian day at the museum a couple of days ago and that was no problem at all. We are having an event with a guy who spent three years in jail for his art. We do all sorts of things that might stir up controversy in one way or another.

RA: Is there a pressure to be too popular? To cater to the community perhaps a little too much, as with singles nights, for instance.

TF: Well I want our shows to be popular so there isn't any pressure compelling me to make them popular. But we are doing things that are not going to be crowd pleasers—such as performance-art pieces—while we are also doing shows that aren't explicitly art world, but are based instead on the cultural history of Queens.

TS: Without sounding Pollyannaish about it, museums—maybe more than ballet, theater, and opera—now hold the public's imagination. Many people see museums as safe places where difficult issues can be taken up. So we almost have a kind of sacred duty, meaning that if an institution like yours or mine isn't going to do it, then no one will do it. The Met won't do it. Our museums are a kind of forum that very few places, certainly not universities, represent these days. We are able to do projects that really delve into social dilemmas. And I think, if we lose the confidence of communities, they are just not going to come. You can forget about your dollars or whatever then; the point of your very existence is lost.

TF: A museum shouldn't be an island outside of the community. So we are going to be partnering with religious groups. This is not the right-wing, faith-based George Bush agenda, it's simply recognizing that in the minority communities in Queens, religious organizations are very important. Now, I was at this Ford Foundation meeting a couple of weeks ago and we had just had Gay and Lesbian Day at the museum and there was a bunch of people at the meeting from religious groups. I asked a priest what I should do about the relationship between the faith-based groups and the queer groups meeting at the museum, and he said nothing. And I realized that I could say, "Listen guys, we are just going to do Gay and Lesbian Day every year so get used to it," or say, "What do we have in common with you? What social goals are we all interested in?" and leave the rest for later.

TS: If they choose not to come on Gay and Lesbian Day that doesn't mean that you don't have a partnership. And you can't force people to come, but maybe some will. When we do focus groups with kids from poorer backgrounds, the first thing they say—other than "It was cool and we had fun"—is that it is clean and it is safe. This is heartbreaking. Like there is nothing else in their lives that is clean and safe? So if we can act on that, play with it even, and then navigate through these other waters . . .

SM: This is a good note to end on. Usually when we have censorship discussions they are somewhat darker. At NCAC we advocate dialogue as a primary way to resolve controversies. When there is an attempt to respond to the community without taking the work down, usually all goes well. But if there is no dialogue, there are offended people on both sides and nobody wins.

32
TAKING OFFENSE

J.M. Coetzee

At an individual level, the contest with the censor is all too likely to assume an importance in the inner life of the writer that at the very least diverts him from his proper occupation and at its worst fascinates and even perverts the imagination. In the personal records of writers who have operated under censorship we find eloquent and despairing descriptions of how the censor-figure is involuntarily incorporated into the interior, psychic life, bringing with it humiliation, self-disgust, and shame. In unwilling fantasies of this kind, the censor is typically experienced as a parasite, a pathogenic invader of the body-self, repudiated with visceral intensity but never wholly expelled.[1]

The most law-abiding countries are not those with the highest prison populations but those with the lowest offender rates. The law, including the law of censorship, has a dream. In this dream, the daily round of identifying and punishing malefactors will wither away; the law and its constraints will be so deeply engraved on the citizenry that individuals will police themselves. Censorship looks forward to the day when writers will censor themselves and the censor himself can retire. It is for this reason that the physical expulsion of the censor, vomited forth as a demon is, has a certain symbolic value for the writer of Romantic genealogy: it stands for a rejection of the dream of reason, the dream of a society of laws founded on reason and obeyed because reasonable.

Writing does not flourish under censorship. This does not mean that the censor's edict, or the internalized figure of the censor, is the sole or even the principal pressure on the writer: there are forms of repression, inherited, acquired, or self-imposed, that can be more grievously felt. There may even be cases where external censorship challenges the writer in interesting ways or spurs creativity.[2] But the Aesopian ruses that censorship provokes are usually no more than ingenious; while the obstacles that writers are capable of visiting upon themselves are surely sufficient in number and variety for them not to invite more.

Notes

1. Danilo Kis, "Censorship/Self-Censorship," *Index on Censorship* 15/1 (January 1986), 44.
2. This perverse case is made in respect of certain Russian writers by Lev Loseff, *On the Beneficence of Censorship* (Munich: Otto Sagner, 1984). Eugene Goodheart argues that in the case of D. H. Lawrence censorship may have been an enemy but was nevertheless "a necessary and empowering enemy." "Censorship and self-censorship in the fiction of D. H. Lawrence," in George Bornstein, ed., *Representing Modernist Texts* (Ann Arbor: University of Michigan Press, 1991), p. 230.

33

THE UBIQUITOUS CENSOR: ARTIST AND WRITERS ON SELF-CENSORSHIP

Leeza Ahmadi, Judy Blume, Guillermo Gómez-Peña, Glenn Ligon, Barbara Pollack, Betty Shaumeh, and Carolee Schneemann

Leeza Ahmadi

When I immigrated to the U.S., I was thirteen years old. I found myself having to adapt to a whole new "social program," a whole new set of ideological, political, economical, and psychological rules. I felt safer telling people that I was Persian than Afghan. It seemed more acceptable. Possibly because people didn't know too much about Persia, even though it is a requirement in history classes. Afghanistan was pretty popular in the eighties, because it was at war with the Soviet Union. But at thirteen it didn't seem like a very fashionable place to say you are from. Persia was interesting, because it baffled a little and sounded more mysterious and abstract. Besides, Iranians and Persians are much more established in the U.S.: They are doctors, lawyers, big business people, especially in Queens and on Long Island. They have huge houses. It helped my self-image, even though I was not consciously aware of all this.

In college, I was exposed to the idea of identity and cultural pride and how that was valuable. I found it safe to say I was from Afghanistan. It also shocked people who'd say, "Oh, you look so South American." I remember getting a kick out of breaking down people's notions about what Afghans look like. I also engaged in a "Third World victim" role, telling people how the superpowers played their game of soccer, using Afghanistan as their bloody playing field. That was my rebellious stage.

After September 11th, I decided I was going to take a positive stance. But when people asked where I was from, I was once again reluctant to tell them. This time it was not out of an adolescent need to be accepted, but because I was afraid of people's reactions. I would laugh and say, "I am from someplace that is really popular right now," and then wait for their reaction and say, "Afghanistan." I was teaching a combination of Afghan and Indian dances and found myself replacing the word Afghan dance with Persian dance in my email blasts. It took a few months before I could stop doing this.

As an independent curator, I often wonder about the undefined boundaries of formal and conceptual contemporary art, as well as about who decides what is art in the first place. As a curator I am authorized to select works, which means that in the case of my own exhibitions, it is I who decide what art is. Yet a more poignant question would be to ask what activates my choices?

Working with artists from diverse backgrounds helps me to find a common denominator that connects contemporary artists. One common denominator is that today all artists have been trained to speak the language of art: a language that has been developed by the museum and gallery world or by the MFA programs here in the West. Artists from around the world are compelled to express themselves in a Western language in order to be accepted by the establishment. They may express their own cultural sensitivity and political views as long as they fit within the Western definition of art, which reigns in the institutions.

In the past two decades, for instance, artists from around the world seem compelled to make installation and video art. My personal feeling is that this is because that makes them feel accepted. Installation art is highly valued by the art world. Take a work by Roya Ghiasy, an artist from Afghanistan, now living in New York and Holland: The installation is a carpet made out of rice, carrots, and raisins and is related to the idea of the nomad; the nomad moves from place to place just as this piece can be removed and recreated elsewhere. It is beautiful, both visually and conceptually; the rice, the raisins, the carpet, the idea of the nomad, all point to Ghiasy's own cultural background. But if this artist had created her work in a village in Afghanistan and not in her studio in Brooklyn, what would it look like? What medium would qualify as acceptable if she had no reference to Western contemporary art or access to 300 galleries in Chelsea?

Judy Blume

I began to write when I was in my mid-twenties. By then I was married with two small children and desperately in need of creative work. I wrote *Are You There God? It's Me, Margaret* right out of my own experiences and feelings when I was in sixth grade. Controversy wasn't on my mind. I wanted only to write what I knew to be true. I wanted to write the best, the most honest books I could, the kinds of books I would have liked to read when I was younger. If someone had told me then I would become one of the most banned writers in America, I'd have laughed.

When *Margaret* was published in 1970, I gave three copies to my children's elementary school but the books never reached the shelves. The male principal decided on his own that they were inappropriate for elementary school readers because of the discussion of menstruation (never mind how many fifth- and sixth-grade girls already had their periods). Then one night the phone rang and a woman asked if I was the one who had written *that* book. When I replied that I was, she called me a communist and hung up. I never did figure out if she equated communism with menstruation or religion.

In that decade I wrote thirteen other books: eleven for young readers, one for teenagers, and one for adults. My publishers were protective of me during those years and didn't necessarily share negative comments about my work. They believed if I didn't know some individuals were upset by my books, I wouldn't be intimidated.

Of course, they couldn't keep the occasional anecdote from reaching me: the mother who admitted she'd cut two pages out of *Then Again, Maybe I Won't* rather than allow her almost thirteen-year-old son to read about wet dreams. Or the young librarian who'd been instructed by her male principal to keep *Deenie* off the shelf because in the book, Deenie masturbates. "It would be different if it were about a boy," he'd told her. "That would be normal."

The stories go on and on but really, I wasn't that concerned. There was no organized effort to ban my books or any other books, none that I knew of, anyway. The seventies were a good decade for writers and readers. Many of us came of age during those years, writing from our hearts and guts, finding editors and publishers who believed in us, who willingly took risks to help us find our audience. We were free to write about real kids in the real world. Kids with feelings and emotions, kids with real families, kids like we once were. And young readers gobbled up our books, hungry for characters with whom they could identify, including my own daughter and son, who had become avid readers. No mother could have been more proud to see the tradition of family reading passed on to the next generation.

Then, almost overnight, following the presidential election of 1980, the censors crawled out of the woodwork, organized and determined. Not only would they decide what *their* children could read but what *all* children could read. It was the beginning of the decade that wouldn't go away, that still won't go away almost twenty years later. Suddenly books were seen as dangerous to young minds. Thinking was seen as dangerous, unless those thoughts were approved by groups like the Moral Majority, who believed with certainty they knew what was best for everyone.

So now we had individual parents running into schools, waving books, demanding their removal—books they hadn't read except for certain passages. Most often their objections had to do with language, sexuality, and something called "lack of moral tone."

Those who were most active in trying to ban books came from the "religious right" but the impulse to censor spread like a contagious disease. Other parents, confused and uncertain, were happy to jump on the bandwagon. Book banning satisfied their need to feel in control of their children's lives. Those who censored were easily frightened. They were afraid of exposing their children to ideas different from their own. Afraid to answer children's questions or talk with them about sensitive subjects. And they were suspicious. They believed if kids liked a book, it must be dangerous.

Too few schools had policies in place enabling them to deal with challenged materials. So what happened? The domino effect. School administrators sent down the word: Anything that could be seen as controversial had to go. Often books were quietly removed from school libraries and classrooms or, if seen as potential troublemakers, were never purchased in the first place. These decisions were based not on what was best for the students, but what would *not* offend the censors.

I found myself at the center of the storm. My books were being challenged daily, often placed on *restricted* shelves (shades of Elizabeth, New Jersey, in 1955) and sometimes removed. A friend was handed a pamphlet outside a supermarket urging parents to rid their schools and libraries of Judy Blume books. Never once did the pamphlet suggest the books actually be read. Of course I wasn't the only target. Across the country, the Sex Police and the Language Police were thumbing through books at record speed, looking for illustrations, words or phrases that, taken out of context, could be used as evidence against them.

Puberty became a dirty word, as if children who didn't read about it wouldn't know about it, and if they didn't know about it, it would never happen.

The Moral Tone Brigade attacked *Blubber* (a story of victimization in the classroom) with a vengeance because, as they saw it, in this book evil goes unpunished. As if kids need to be hit over the head, as if they don't get *it* without having the message spelled out for them.

I had letters from angry parents accusing me of ruining Christmas because of a chapter in *Superfudge* called "Santa Who?" Some sent lists showing me how easily I could have substituted one word for another: *meanie* for *bitch: darn* for *damn: nasty* for *ass.* More words taken out of context. A teacher wrote to say she blacked out offending words and passages with a felt-tip marker. Perhaps most shocking of all was a letter from a nine-year-old addressed to *Jew*dy Blume telling me I had no right to write about Jewish angels in *Starring Sally J. Freedman as Herself.*

My worst moment came when I was working with my editor on the manuscript of *Tiger Eyes* (the story of a fifteen-year-old girl, Davey, whose beloved father dies suddenly and violently). When we came to the scene in which Davey allows herself to *feel* again after months of numbness following her father's death, I saw that a few lines alluding to masturbation had been circled. My editor put down his pencil and faced me. "We want this book to reach as many readers as possible, don't we?" he asked.

I felt my face grow hot, my stomach clench. This was the same editor who had worked with me on *Are You There God? It's Me, Margaret; Then Again, Maybe I Won't; Deenie; Blubber; Forever*—always encouraging, always supportive. The scene was psychologically sound, he assured me, and delicately handled. But it also spelled trouble. I got the message. If you leave in those lines, the censors will come after this book. Librarians and teachers won't buy it. Book clubs won't take it. Everyone is too scared. The political climate has changed.

I tried to make a case for why that brief moment in Davey's life was important. He asked me *how* important? Important enough to keep the book from reaching its audience? I willed myself not to give in to the tears of frustration and disappointment I felt coming. I thought about the ways a writer brings a character to life on the page, the same way an artist brings a face to life on canvas—through a series of brush strokes, each detail adding to the others, until we see the essence of the person. I floundered, uncertain. Ultimately, not strong enough or brave enough to defy the editor I trusted and respected, I caved in and took out those lines. I still remember how alone I felt at that moment.

What effect does this climate have on a writer? *Chilling.* It's easy to become discouraged, to second-guess everything you write. There seemed to be no one to stand up to the censors. No group as organized as they were; none I knew of, anyway. I've never forgiven myself for caving in to editorial pressure based on fear, for playing into the hands of the censors. I knew then it was all over for me unless I took a stand. So I began to speak out about my experience.

What I worry about most is the loss to young people. If no one speaks out for them, if they don't speak out for themselves, all they'll get for required reading will be the most bland books available. And instead of finding the information they need at the library, instead of finding the novels that illuminate life, they will find only those materials to which nobody could possibly object.

Some people would like to rate books in schools and libraries the way they rate movies: G, PG, R, X, or even more explicitly. But according to whose standards would the books be rated? I don't know about you but I don't want anyone rating my books or the books my children or grandchildren choose to read. We can make our own decisions, thank you. Be wary of the censors' code words—*family friendly; family values; excellence in education.* As if the rest of us don't want excellence in education, as if we don't have our own family values, as if libraries haven't always been family-friendly places!

And the demands are not all coming from the religious right. No . . . the urge to decide not only what's right for their kids but for all kids has caught on with others across the political spectrum. Each year *Huckleberry Finn* is challenged and sometimes removed from the classroom because, to some, its language, which includes racial epithets, is offensive. Better to acknowledge the language, bring it out in the open, and discuss why the book remains important than to ban it. Teachers and parents can talk with their students and children about any book considered controversial.

I gave a friend's child one of my favorite picture books, James Marshall's *The Stupids Step Out,* and was amazed when she said, "I'm sorry, but we can't accept that book. My children are not permitted to use that word. Ever. It should be changed to 'The Sillies Step Out,' " I may not agree, but I have to respect this woman's right to keep that book from her child as long as she isn't trying to keep it from other people's children. Still, I can't help lamenting the lack of humor in her decision. *The Stupids Step Out* is a very funny book. Instead of banning it from her home, I wish she could have used it as an opportunity to talk with her child about why she felt the way she did, about why she never wanted to hear her child call anyone *stupid*. Even very young children can understand. So many adults are exhausting themselves worrying about other people corrupting their children with books, they're turning kids off to reading instead of turning them on.

In this age of censorship I mourn the loss of books that will never be written, I mourn the voices that will be silenced—writers' voices, teachers' voices, students' voices—and all because of fear. How many have resorted to self-censorship? How many are saying to themselves, "Nope . . . can't write about that. Can't teach that book. Can't have that book in our collection. Can't let my student write that editorial in the school paper."

Guillermo Gómez-Peña

I'm one of those artists who occupy an interstitial space, a border zone; I work in multiple mediums and cultural contexts. For this reason my tribulations with censorship and self-censorship take many forms.

Often when working in Chicano art spaces, I feel the pressure to not engage in what producers perceive as "extreme sexual behavior" 'cause, "our organization is a family-friendly space." And I must confess that a few times I've complied with their wishes. Why? Perhaps because of my desire to be accepted by the larger Chicano/Latino community or, perhaps, because I don't wish to be perceived as irrational or immature. My consolation has been, "Well, after all, there are more important issues to fight for."

For a Mexican artist, family matters and *pudor* inevitably come into play. Once when performing in Mexico City, the morning before opening night, I found out that my beloved mother was coming to the show along with several aunts, uncles, cousins, and nephews. I flipped out. I truly did. I decided to sacrifice some of my nude sections. In retrospect, I think I did it because I stupidly felt I didn't want to embarrass my family. They had already endured enough during my wild life as a performance artist—potential deportations, run-ins with the police, media scandals, and the ongoing circulation of extreme images. When I told the members of my troupe about my decision, they were very tough on me. One of them called me a coward. And perhaps she was right.

In Anglo and European art spaces, while I am allowed to be as experimental and sexually explicit, my radical politics often cause discomfort. I almost can read producers' minds: "If only Gómez-Peña were more elliptical and indirect, he would be a great artist." And my attitude has been polite but firm: "Sorry, take it or leave it. That's the Gómez-Peña package. It's a bit thorny."

In the first months after 9/11, when touring U.S. art spaces, I was told by some producers, "Please [don't] express all your radical opinions about the Bush administration and the war on terror because . . . we may lose our funding . . . or the Christian right might attack us." (I heard the latter in some conservative states.) Whether their fears were mythical or real, I sometimes complied. Why? Because I didn't want to hurt producers who had been committed to my work throughout the years. Later, I was furious with myself for complying, because I feel that it was precisely this sensitivity that has helped the right gain so much ground. They perceive our sensitivity as either hesitation or weakness.

For more than fifteen years I did commentaries for National Public Radio. I agreed to do that not as an artist impersonating a journalist, but as an artist who sees himself as a social commentator and public intellectual and who speaks as such. However, editors often forgot the reason why they originally invited me and tried to domesticate me. Once, I remember an editor told me, after reviewing the script of a commentary about a Clinton visit to Mexico, that I was "too hard on him and he was one of the few friends of public radio left in the White House." I agreed to lighten up the piece a bit because I had worked too long on it and didn't want to lose it. I felt like shit afterwards.

I witnessed from within the move of public radio towards the right; as this happened I became more incensed and protective of my voice. I wrote a tough commentary on Bush's "other war on terror," the war against people of color and immigrants within the U.S. Before recording it I was told: "Gomez-Peña, we already have other commentators dealing with this issue. Stick to what you know. What we want from you is border pop culture and art." That was hard to stomach, and so I resigned. A week later they managed to persuade me to return. After 9/11 they began to censor me openly. My relationship with *All Things Considered* became an ongoing dance macabre: them wanting to water down my material and turn me into an intellectual lite and me fighting for more control and salsa. I finally told them: I'll see you guys when Bush leaves office and you recapture your fangs. I don't regret it.

When I venture into university contexts to teach performance workshops, I tend to overstate the ethical rules of our performance games and rituals and always start with a disclaimer: "If you think you can solve personal issues through performance, this is not your workshop; if you have issues with physical contact, this is not your workshop." Why do I do this? Perhaps out of fear that if I open the door for students to express themselves on political and sexual issues within the puritanical university context, my colleagues and I will be blamed if a student goes overboard or even complains. Is this my Catholic guilt working or my cultural sensitivity? I truly don't know. The truth is that, in the performance workshop, crossing social, psychological, and gender boundaries is always a necessary risk. This can be dangerous when a student is immature, inexperienced, or feels extremely entitled. How far are we willing to go in a university setting? I don't have an answer but I'm struck how infrequently these fears arise when teaching abroad, in Europe or Latin America. And I do know that our answer matters—both for a future generation of students and, no less, for ourselves.

Glenn Ligon

My cousin Derby had a collection of Richard Pryor records. He was a bit older than my brother and me so the fact that he had money to buy albums, comedy albums with dirty words in them at that, was a source of envy. He would play the albums for us on a little plastic record player he had up in his room, the volume turned down so the adults in the house wouldn't hear. It was the mid-seventies, I was fifteen and Pryor was at the peak of his fame.

My mother never let me listen to any Pryor records at home. "Too grown," she said. She was more into Moms Mabley and Redd Foxx, though it was the domesticated PG versions of their acts that she enjoyed on TV. Pryor's own short-lived network show, cancelled in its first season, was barely tolerated. "He's no Flip Wilson," my mother said. Still, between the illicit sessions in my cousin's bedroom and the cancelled TV show, Pryor was an important part of my childhood.

What I liked most about Pryor was that he used the word "nigger" in practically every joke. Blackness in any form was a difficult subject for me. I remember being embarrassed when singing the call and response chorus to James Brown's "Say It Loud." I could sing the "say it loud" part okay, but when I got to "I'm black and I'm proud" all I could manage was a whisper.

I have been thinking a lot about Richard Pryor lately because I am making text paintings using his routines. I made a couple of Pryor paintings back in the early 1990s but never developed them into a body of work. At the time I thought it was because they were too close to the work of Richard Prince, who had been making silkscreen paintings of borscht-belt comedians' jokes for many years. Actually Pryor's explorations of race and raw sexuality were miles away from the jokes in Richard Prince's paintings, but I took no comfort in that. The few pieces I did make were a hit: They were included in an exhibition at the Whitney Museum and sold to prominent collectors. Still, the project stalled after four paintings. I returned to it again only a couple of weeks ago.

I have been sitting at my desk for several days listening to Richard Pryor jokes on my iPod. There is one routine where Pryor talks about going to Africa at the advice of his therapist. Possibly responding to some snickering in the audience, Pryor says:

> Black people are frightened to death of therapists. For some reason, of all the people on the planet, in America we some motherfuckers that need some therapy. You believe me, 'cause we are fucked up. We fucked up 'cause we got to be insane 'cause we ain't killed you motherfuckers.

When I heard that joke, I realized why it had taken me ten years to continue the series: too scared. The deep critique of whiteness and racism in his work, his anger and his carnivalesque sense of sexuality frightened me. Although it was all expressed through jokes, in the end the jokes simply weren't funny. They were too close to the nasty unconscious of American society. Too close to home, too black and too strong. And if they scared me, then what of my audience?

I recalled a story a friend told me about leading tours at the Whitney when some of my paintings were exhibited. Someone on the tour objected to the presence of Pryor jokes in the show. When asked if he liked Richard Pryor's routines, he responded, "I love Richard Pryor, just not on the walls of the Whitney Museum." That people make hierarchies of spaces, that there are spaces where some things are considered appropriate and others where they are not, is not surprising. What surprised me was the realization that I adhered to those hierarchies too and that the spaces where Pryor was not appropriate included the space of my studio and my own head.

So why have I returned to Pryor after all these years? Perhaps it is that Pryor is funny again. Not that he wasn't funny back in the seventies, it's just that all his militancy, his rage at social and economic injustice, his breaking down of sexual taboos seems amusing now, almost quaint. The jokes don't scare me anymore because the world they promised to bring seems even farther away than it did then. As Pryor says, "Remember the Revolution brother? It's over. Lasted six months." When I listen to Pryor records now, I laugh and I am a little sad—nostalgic for my fear, I guess.

Barbara Pollack

Way back in 1974, when Lucy Lippard took stock of the state of feminist art in her essay "The Pains and Pleasures of Rebirth: Women's Body Art," she concluded her survey of recent work with a question:

> One curious aspect of all this women's work . . . is the fact that no woman dealing with their own bodies or biographies have introduced pregnancy or childbirth as a major image . . . Is it because many of these artists are young and have yet to have children? Or because women artists have traditionally either refused to have children or have hidden them

away in order to be taken seriously in a world that accuses wives and mothers of being part-time artists?

Thirty years later, the question is just as valid, as I survey recent work by younger women artists, who now in these supposedly post-feminist times continue to bare their breasts but rarely reveal a midriff with a Caesarian scar.

I have consciously chosen "motherhood" as a topic in my work, front and center, because of the voices—inside and outside my head—that have warned me that to reveal myself as a mother, a Jewish mother no less, means revealing an identity that is antithetical to the hip, cool irony of contemporary art. I make these works, always collaborating with my son, Max, in order to combat these voices, but also to bring a new voice to the dialogue about contemporary art.

When I began making this work, a decision that coincided with my pregnancy in 1987, "the family" was first beginning to be used by the Religious Right as a reason to censor contemporary art. In reaction to the dialogue surrounding the Culture Wars, I decided to make work revealing that artists too have "families." We reproduce as well as produce, procreate as well as create; that not all families want censorship or share the Right's definition of "family values."

But from the moment my project was shown publicly—ten years of these photographs were installed in the exhibition, *The Family of Men,* at Thread Waxing Space in 1999—it became clear that censorship was not solely the prerogative of the Jesse Helms contingency. While many curators were supportive, many others found it difficult to digest "motherhood" within their rubric of identity politics. Apparently, some identities are more aesthetic than others. Motherhood, as I know from my daily experience, is confusing and messy and chaotic, running contrary to postmodernism's slick production values and the prepackaged transgression of commercialized bohemia. Yet, I thought I could address at least my own predicament with humor and irony and all the other prerequisites of contemporary art.

The question that my more recent projects, video works in which Max appears as the ostensible subject and performer, continue to raise these issues. On the one hand, now that Max is sixteen there is a way that the work has become more in keeping with the youth culture of contemporary art. On the other hand, revealing that I have a child who is sixteen means that I am identifying myself as a full-fledged adult, definitely getting older, a not-often mentioned taboo for a contemporary artist. Since many of these works show Max engaged with popular culture—violent video games, sexy music videos, chat rooms—the question always comes up about why I, as his mother, let him engage in these activities. Apparently, both art world types and general audiences believe that I, as mother, should be Max's censor.

Inside my process, I have to say that the greatest issue of self-censorship does not come from my role as mother or my relationship with Max. Though this could be a problem for other artists working in this terrain, I have spent a lot of time working with Max and discussing at length this ongoing project with him. He is not treated as "my subject" but as a full-fledged participant. So, even though the work may look like I am intruding on his privacy or violating his boundaries, we have actually investigated his comfort level. It is very important to me that he comes through this experience of art-making feeling proud of his contribution and with his integrity intact. But, of course, wanting to retain integrity—mine and his—may be an insidious form of self-censorship.

Yet, the greatest, loudest, most nagging voice in my head goes something like: YOU'RE NOT COOL. YOU WILL NEVER BE HIP. WHO ARE YOU KIDDING?

That's it in a nutshell. I would love to say that I have gotten past this issue. I would love to say that my work is clearly about deeper, more complex issues—and it is. But, though I have gained recognition and respect for my projects, I continually worry that the mere mention of motherhood takes me out of the running for the kind of short-lived, but very bright, spotlight that leads to art-world fame. It is difficult, even painful, to know that that kind of attention is reserved solely for women artists who make work about sexuality, preferably getting naked themselves. It is truly painful to know that I am making work that, as Max and I get older, has less and less of a chance of being recognized in the current contemporary art world. The more long-term experience of being a woman—motherhood is one example, but also love, aging, breast cancer, menopause—will certainly never find a spot, even among the wide range of issues often on view, in Chelsea galleries on a Saturday afternoon. And, by being eliminated from the networks of marketing and promoting contemporary art, these issues will never wedge their way into the pantheon of art history.

Yes, by openly trying to insert motherhood into the canons of art—move over Virgin Mary!—I know I am making a fool of myself. And it is that feeling, of falling on my face without the safety net of *cool,* is the greatest fear of all.

Betty Shamieh

I am a Palestinian-American Playwright—and I'm Christian. Significant numbers of Arabs are Christian, which is something many Americans do not know; Arab society is not by any means homogeneous.

I was born in San Francisco, so I'm a citizen of this country. I went to Harvard and Yale and what attending institutions like that provides is access to people in positions of power.

Yet, part of me is terrified to be writing these words singling myself out as an Arab American at this stage in American history, because I don't know what the ramifications of that are or will be. Part of me wants to heed President Bush when he lets it be known on national television that he thinks citizens better "watch what they say," but part of me is extremely cognizant of the fact that over a thousand Arab and Muslim Americans were picked up and held for months without trials and without our government releasing their names following the attacks of September 11; that it was eighteen months after Pearl Harbor that Japanese Americans were sent to internment camps; and that this country does not have a history of showing tolerance toward any racial minority whose members are easy to pick out of a crowd.

There are certainly acts of intolerance short of internment of which governments are capable. I have been censored in many ways. But I think the most overt example of censorship I have yet faced is my experience with a project called the Brave New World Festival.

The Brave New World Festival at New York City's Town Hall was—as its Web site declared—designed for artists to explore "the alternate roots of terrorism." For the most part, only very well-established playwrights were asked to participate, but I—who had just finished Yale School of Drama a year before—was invited partly because of my work at the "Imagine: Iraq" reading, which drew 900 people to Cooper

Union in New York City in November 2001, to hear plays about the Middle East. I am an actress as well as a playwright, and, at the "Imagine: Iraq" reading, I performed a monologue I wrote about the sister of a suicide bomber who mourns not knowing what her brother planned to do and not being able to stop him. The piece is very clearly a plea for nonviolence.

When the organizers of the Brave New World Festival asked me to perform the same monologue for them, my first thought was that I did not want to be in Town Hall on the first anniversary of Sept. 11 presenting a play that deals with such potent subject matter. Then I realized that it was especially important at that time and in that place to present precisely such work. So, despite all my fears and concerns, I agreed to their request—but asked the organizers to get Marisa Tomei (who was already involved in the project) or an actress of that caliber to play the role. I felt that if there was going to be a backlash, I didn't want to be dealing with it alone.

I got a call from an organizer a few weeks later. She told me she loved the piece and that—at my request—she had given it to Marisa Tomei. But she also said that some of her colleagues had objected to the content of my piece. She informed me that I was welcome to write something different but that they were rescinding their offer to present my monologue.

At this time, I did not know that they were also censoring people like Eduardo Machado, who is the head of the playwriting MFA program at Columbia and one of the best-known playwrights of his generation.

So, in an Uncle Tom–like manner, instead of holding my ground, I wrote another piece. I did so because I was the only Arab American playwright in the lineup. Arab American artists are largely faceless in this country and I felt that, by dropping out, I would be helping those who are trying to keep it that way.

The new piece I wrote for them was a very mild and humorous short play. The narrator, an Arab American girl, tells the audience of a fantasy she has about ending up on a hijacked plane and talking the hijackers out of their plans. The people on the plane listen to the hijackers' grievances and actually refuse to get off the flight until all people have a right to live in safety and freedom. Then, in her fantasy, the narrator ends up on *Oprah,* and has a movie made about her starring Julia Roberts.

Harmless, right? Especially for a forum designed to present theater that asked real questions.

But when I got into rehearsal on the day of the performance with the director, Billy Hopkins, and actresses including Rosie Perez, I realized someone had censored the text, deleting chunks of my work that deal with the main character talking to the hijackers and making them see the error of their ways.

Of course, I had my own original copy with me. I had just begun to distribute it when the stage manager stepped into the rehearsal. She announced that because the performance schedule had grown overlong, my piece, the token Arab American playwright's play, had been cut, along with a number of others.

What made the experience particularly disturbing was that the organizers had touted this event as a venue for alternative ideas and voices. To censor voices that present exactly those perspectives made it seem as though those voices don't exist.

Many people ask me if I—as a Palestinian American playwright living in New York in a post–September 11 world—have been facing more censorship in the wake of that horrific event that changed all of our lives. The answer—which might surprise many—is no.

The reason is that there was such an astounding level of censorship in American theater when it comes to the Palestinian perspective before September 11, that I really haven't felt a difference in the past two years.

Indeed, the last time there was a serious attempt to bring a play written by a Palestinian to a major New York stage was in 1989. Joe Papp, artistic director of the Joseph Papp Public Theatre, asked a Palestinian theater troupe that had toured throughout Europe to bring its highly acclaimed show, *The Story of Kufur Shamma,* to his theater.

Joe Papp was a theatrical visionary. In other words, he wasn't going to stick a piece of mindless propaganda on his theater's stage. But his board objected to his decision to bring the show to New York.

Papp, arguably the most powerful man in the history of American theater, did not feel he could stand up to his board members. He rescinded his offer because, as the *Philadelphia Inquirer* reported, "[H]e had come under a great deal of pressure and that he could not jeopardize his theater."

I'm telling this story only because I think its relationship with my work is intriguing. For the three years I was a graduate student at the

Yale School of Drama, I, in effect, censored myself. I did not produce a single play about the Palestinian experience, which is an enormous part of who I am as a person and an artist.

I wanted to avoid confronting the kind of censorship anybody faces when portraying the Palestinians as human beings. I wanted to avoid that kind of controversy until I had a bit of a name for myself, a bit of a following.

Unfortunately, what happened as a result of my self-censorship was my work was eviscerated. Now, I write about the Palestinian experience not only just because it deserves—as all stories deserve—to be heard, but also because if I hope to make vital theater I can only write about what I care deeply about. And vital theater is the only kind of theater I'm interested in making.

It came down to a very clear choice for me. I either had to give up writing for the stage or decide to write about what I knew and cared about and, therefore, face what it meant to be a Palestinian American playwright working in New York at this time. I, either wisely or unwisely, have chosen the latter.

When you think of all the ethnic minorities in this country who have had their story told multiple times in the theater, you wonder—would it do such harm to add to that mosaic one story about the Palestinian perspective?

Are the people involved in the incidents I mentioned being rational when they try so hard to keep a Palestinian perspective out of the public eye, which they unfortunately and—in my opinion—unnecessarily see as contrary to their own?

Aren't they overreacting a little bit? I mean, really. Is theater that powerful?

The answer is yes. A good play, a play that makes you feel, allows you to see its characters as fully human, if only for two hours.

If more people actually saw Palestinians as human beings, our foreign policy could not and would not be the same.

Carolee Schneemann conversation with Svetlana Mintcheva

Carolee Schneemann: Among my many censored works, an installation of video and painting-constructions shown at Max Hutchison Gallery in 1985 elicited an especially insidious response. The exhibit referenced the destruction of Palestinian communities in Beirut and refugee camps in Southern Lebanon. I gathered photographs of ancient villages, serene landscapes, and evidence of bombardment connected with the Israeli invasion of Southern Lebanon. I began to combine them with large paintings, juxtaposing images of my everyday life with images of savage and seductive destruction.

Then an unprecedented disaster for my established gallery occurred: Its entire printed mailing list of announcements for the exhibit "disappeared." Then a section of a triptych was stolen while we were installing it. During the exhibit, some viewers tore up the informational brochures I had prepared. Was some low-level, disruptive censorship at play? As if to suggest that exploring the chaotic destabilization of Lebanon was as taboo as my erotic images from the 1960s or my Vietnam atrocity film of 1965?

Svetlana Mintcheva: You knew as you were making this work that you were entering volatile territory—that this was a very explosive topic, didn't you?

CS: I never plan to enter "volatile territory," but I am drawn to demystifying, to clarifying displaced meanings, to questioning contradictions. Media and cultural censorship can provoke my need for visual equivalence, for exposing political deformations, aesthetic distractions, and the loss of empathy. *Fuses,* my self-shot erotic film (1965) was inspired by the censorious morality of the time and the absence of a creative precedent for my lived experience of heterosexual pleasure. *Viet-Flakes* (1965) was inspired by the censorship of Vietnam atrocity images.

SM: How does it feel to have your work attacked?

CS: Threatening. I might feel intimidated but also outraged, alarmed. Censorship's effect is disproportionate, out of scale. My work is a small part of a larger activist conversation, which may at any time provoke censorship. At the same time, censorship points to resistance and creative explication. I am surprised that *Devour,* my recent dual-projection video, which loops fragments of current warfare disasters and domestic intimacy, was rejected by venues I thought would be welcoming.

SM: Do you think this is a result of institutional self-censorship?

CS: Our suppressive media and pacified population bear the psychological trauma of the 1960s, where every leader, every humanist activist, as well as many "counter-culture" artists and entertainers were mysteriously assassinated or died suddenly. The mysterious killers were furtive figures, who seemed to emerge from central casting. In our cultural unconscious these shadow murders imply dangers in asserting a dissenting voice, in fighting for constitutional rights, in protesting and organizing. But artists often exhume these suppressed figurations and the forces behind them.

SM: In the case of a gallery owner today who won't show politically radical expression, you don't really think it's an actual fear for her life stopping her, do you?

CS: No, gallerists do not fear for their *life,* although they may fear for their economic and social position. Radical exhibits can redefine a gallery, marginalize it, separate it from conservative collectors, critics, or acquisition committees. Political controls are often veiled, unconscious, deflected now as increasing academic and bureaucratic constraints manipulate what we can see, how we question the deceptions within our social fabric. The increasing suppression of dissent, of analysis, the terrible costs of this war [in Iraq] have been confabulated in linguistic acronyms, propaganda, slogans—until our feelings go dead in confusion.

SM: How does the present political climate affect the way you think about your work?

CS: It's a politically oppressive atmosphere, more turbid and turbulent even than our wars in Vietnam, Philippines, Nicaragua, etc. In popular culture the "righteous heroic" is our mantra: "We had to destroy this Iraqi city/infrastructure for your own good." We Americans aren't allowed to see the images of the caskets, we can't see the images of our own wounded, we can't see the images of destroyed cities, villages, mutilated civilians. "Embedded Reporters" give us only predigested "information." I'm obsessed by the intensive suppression of real issues.

SM: Let's talk a little bit about your more sexually explicit work, which has been accused of being obscene or pornographic. American culture has so much trouble with erotica, sexually explicit material is always on the point of sliding into pornography. Do you worry about controlling the way your work is interpreted?

CS: Censorship and pornography are blood brothers. The lack of historic context, the inability to grasp the formal properties of my work is always shocking. I may have no control over how my work is interpreted, but it belongs to an historic, aesthetic context. My erotic works extend classical visual traditions, informed by feminisms redefining what can be seen/what is obscene. As a painter, there should be nothing that I may not look at, or consider . . .

SM: Did you ever go home and say, "Oh my god, I just can't do that!"?

CS: Oh yes, Absolutely. What helped me was that, for many years, I had a collaborator and loving partner; he was there when I felt I could succumb to [self] censorship and we also belonged to a wider community of artists and students sharing creative and political concerns.

SM: Was there anything that you didn't do as a result of cultural/political pressures, because you wouldn't be able to show it perhaps?

CS: To the contrary, there are certain energies made active by censorship. I have experienced thirty years of censorship simply by creating visualizations of lived experience and the body. Even *Infinity Kisses,* the cat-kissing photographic sequences have been found objectionable, obscene! I continue to explore *why* certain imagery is objectionable: I pursue research on taboos as various as war rituals, bodily fluids, bestiality, genital sexuality, witchcraft trials—the old Eros and Thanatos.

SM: Do you think there are times when self-censorship *might* be good.

CS: Our present cultural framework is already profoundly, pervasively self-censoring in its distractions and deflections of reality. As we are inundated with increasingly suppressive government control; our psyches are sucked into Mc-Malled soullessness. Yet there remains the fog of history, activism, Wobblies, Feminists, peaceniks, hallucinogens, patchouli, fierce music—a coherent resistance. In this maelstrom, I have to question the artist—Would s/he even recognize self-censorship?

Note

1. This essay was adapted from Part Two of the series of panel discussions, "Censorship in Camouflage," held at the New School University, in New York, in June 2002.

34

A PSYCHOANALYST'S PERSPECTIVE ON ARTISTS AND CENSORSHIP[1]

Janice Lieberman

What are the conscious and (especially) the unconscious mechanisms that result in self-censorship? How does the artist's psyche anticipate other people's reactions and alter and/or omit what might, perhaps, only be expressed in its original form in a different context? Is the self-censoring artist like Woody Allen's *Zelig,* a chameleon-like person who automatically adapts to those around him?

Artists have a different degree of awareness when creating their work. Some may be exquisitely tuned to the body language, to the look in the eye of others; those artists limit themselves to the detriment of their work. Some, on the other hand, may be so narcissistic that they are completely unaware of the other, the other serving merely as a mirror reflecting his/her own grandiosity. Picasso, for example, was in his personal life completely blunt and insensitive, a character trait that served his art by preventing him from censoring himself. Jackson Pollock was similarly uncaring about the public and created something completely new.

So what goes on inside the psyche that creates self-censorship? And I ask, is self-censorship, be it conscious or unconscious, deceptive? Is it lying?

Self-censorship is rooted in the use of defense mechanisms. Our everyday defense mechanisms lead us to distort what we think, say, or do in order to protect ourselves from facing what is too uncomfortable to face. We deceive ourselves all the time. We repress (forget) or suppress (keep under the surface). Unconscious denial or disavowal of what we know or desire to express automatically inhibits thought and actions. As George Orwell noted, "Circus dogs jump when the trainer cracks his whip, but the really well trained dog is the one that turns his somersault when there is no whip." However, rationalization and intellectualization enable us to turn more basic and more primitive thoughts and actions into higher-level behavior that mask their origins.

We also avoid speaking about or facing certain truths with omissions and lies. In my book *The Many Faces of Deceit: Omissions, Lies and Disguise in Psychotherapy,*[2] I wrote about omissions on a conscious, preconscious, and unconscious level—the whole spectrum from leaving out what is threatening to the self or others, to just blatantly lying.

Artists consciously or unconsciously shape their work in all these ways. Yet why are some artists able to rebel and make this rebellion the essence of their art and why do others submit to the social order and censor themselves? I think that this has to do with the unconscious reasons for becoming an artist in the first place. To me—and there are those who will disagree—the artist, by definition, makes something new and changes and challenges the social order. I think that yielding to the judgments of others reflects a conflict about being an artist. The conflict can be so great that the artist may be blocked in doing his/her work. The conflict may have to do with the fear that any expression will be an expression of rage; or fear of success and its various symbolic implications; or, perhaps, fear of others' envy, or, finally, a fear of exhibiting oneself.

Despite popular notions about artistic freedom, I would argue, however, that some self-censorship is necessary: As a writer, I write in order to communicate with others, not just myself. When I write I am acutely aware of my audience. I want my work to be published and reviewed. I want my books to be purchased. I therefore cannot write everything that is in my head. I also must disguise the identity of those patients about whom I write. Shouldn't this creative deception be termed self-censorship?

Sometimes I should censor myself but, due to ignorance about my future audience, I do not. A number of years ago I presented a paper on Arshile Gorky and his proclivity to lie. I spoke in passing of his adolescence, in which members of his Armenian family became victims of the Turkish genocide, something I had read as a fact in many books about Gorky. I was unaware that a group of Turks act as watchdogs over all academic references to these historic events. One such person interrupted me at the start in a way that made it impossible to read the entire paper. In subsequent presentations, I decided to censor myself and did not refer to the Turks in this way. This war between the two countries was incidental to my topic and I wanted to talk about it free of interference.

On the other hand, I quite consciously wrote a negative review of a book by a noted and much revered art critic. I thought it was a nasty and dyspeptic book and said so. I was surprised that the journal editor, a friend of the critic, agreed to publish it. But the art critic then took me on and publicly exposed my lack of advanced degrees in art history, something I did not enjoy, to say the least. So we choose our battles and our wars.

But let me illustrate what I am talking about by not censoring my remarks to come, although I believe that many of you will disagree with some of what I have to say and I will be unpopular.

I sometimes feel that certain artworks should never have been made. For example, the photographs Sally Mann took of her naked children should not have been sold, shown, or published. Schoolchildren should not be taken to see artworks in museums that arouse overwhelming feelings, like the work of artists such as Cindy Sherman and Nan Goldin. I found several works in the current *Mirroring Evil* exhibition at the Jewish Museum to be not only trivial but perpetuators of negative stereotypes about Jews. I loved the *Sensation* show, and I like and have written about Andres Serrano's *Morgue* Series, yet I find his *Sex* Series and "Piss Christ" to be puerile. However, if adult audiences want to look at them, why not?

Imagine that most of you disapproved of my initial four sentences and approved of my last two—Have I risked your wrath? Would I say what I did in another setting? Am I being aggressive and provocative by not censoring myself or, am I being masochistic, if punished for my honesty?

As a psychoanalyst I censor myself with my patients and students everyday. Is self-censorship lying? It would be quite harmful if I did not do so. In fact, if I told the truth, the whole truth, and nothing but the truth, I would not have any patients. In my work, the "art" has to do with the timing, tact, and dosage of the "truth" I prescribe.

Notes

1. This article was adapted from Part Two of the series of panel discussions, "Censorship in Camouflage," held at the New School University, in New York, on June 2002.
2. Janice Lieberman, *The Many Faces of Deceit: Omissions, Lies and Disguise in Psychotherapy.* New York: Jason Aronson, 1966.

About the Editors

Robert Atkins is a UC Berkeley–trained art historian, activist, and writer, who has taught at numerous universities and art schools, most recently the University of Michigan and the Rhode Island School of Design. A former columnist for the *Village Voice,* he has written for more than 100 publications throughout the world and received awards for art criticism from the NEA, Manufacturers Hanover Bank, and (in 2001) the first Penny McCall Award for the Visual Arts. In 1993, Abbeville Press published *ArtSpoke: A Guide to Modern Ideas, Movements and Buzzwords 1848–1944,* a companion to his bestselling *ArtSpeak: A Guide to Contemporary Ideas, Movements and Buzzwords,* which is now available in five languages in its updated 1997 edition. He is also the co-author of *From Media to Metaphor: Art About AIDS,* the exhibition catalog and accompanying book for the show of the same name, the first traveling museum exhibition of its kind.

Atkins's interests in art, technology, and mass media have resulted in his organizing exhibitions at far-flung venues throughout the world and in his groundbreaking coverage of the cyber-artworld for publications such as *Art in America.* He is an associate at the STUDIO for Creative Inquiry at Carnegie Mellon University, former media-arts editor for The Media Channel (http://www.mediachannel.org), and the initiating editor/producer of *Artery: The AIDS-Arts Forum* (http://www.artistswithaids.org/artery). From 1996 to 1998, he held the position of vice president/editor-in-chief of the Arts Technology Entertainment Network, a *New York Times* startup company producing arts programming for the Internet and cable TV. And in 1995, he founded the City University of New York–sponsored *TalkBack! A Forum for Critical Discourse* (http://talkback.lehman.cuny.edu/tb), the first American online journal about online art and cyberculture. He is a co-founder of Visual AIDS, the group of arts professionals that conceived Day Without Art and the Red Ribbon; and 911—The September 11 Project: Cultural Intervention in Civic Society. He is currently at work on an anthology of his own writing entitled *Seismic Shift: The Collision of the Art World and the Real World in the Late Twentieth Century.* His Web site is http://www.robertatkins.net.

Svetlana Mintcheva directs the arts program at the National Coalition Against Censorship, the only national initiative devoted to the arts and free expression. NCAC is an alliance of fifty nonprofit organizations, including artistic, religious, educational, labor, and civil-liberties groups. Since the creation of the Arts Advocacy Project in 2000, Mintcheva has been directly involved in many local arts controversies. Drawing on her singular perspective on the state of creative freedom in the U.S., she writes regularly on emerging trends in censorship, organizes public discussions, and mobilizes support for individual artists. She initiated and supervises the online projects *Art Now: Art After September 11,* which evolved into *The Patriotism of Dissent: Artists Responding to the Political Present,* and *Law, Art and Free Expression,* a database of legal case summaries for the general public (at http://www.ncac.org).

Previously, Mintcheva worked for the Center for Documentary Studies in Durham, North Carolina, organizing arts outreach to public schools. She has also taught at the University of Sofia, Bulgaria, and at Duke University, from which she received her doctorate with a dissertation about provocative American art in the late twentieth century. She has published numerous articles about postmodern art and literature.

About the Contributors

Amy Adler, a law professor at the New York University School of Law, is an expert on the legal regulation of art, speech, and sexuality.

Leeza Ahmadi is an independent curator, born in Afganistan, and now living in New York.

Judy Blume is a best-selling, award-winning, and oft-censored writer specializing in fiction for teens. She is also a passionate anticensorship activist and sits on the board of the National Coalition Against Censorship.

J.M. Coetzee is a South African writer of worldwide renown. He was awarded the 2003 Nobel Prize for literature.

Giselle Fahimian is an intellectual property attorney in San Francisco. She is a recent graduate of Harvard Law School, where her backgrounds in art history, film studies, and radio broadcasting led to her exploration of the growing tensions between the arts and the law.

Tom Finkelpearl recently assumed the directorship of the Queens Museum. He was previously director of New York's Percent for Art Program and has held various positions at P.S. 1 in Queens, New York.

Alexander R. Galloway is an assistant professor at New York University. He is founder of the software development group RSG and author of *Protocol: How Control Exists After Decentralization.*

Guillermo Gómez-Peña is a performance artist and writer, who was born in Mexico and splits his time between Mexico City and San Francisco. His work investigates border culture and transcultural identity.

Stephanie Elizondo Griest is a writer and the founding director of the Youth Free Expression Network, the national coalition of teens and adults committed to defending the free expression rights of young people.

Hans Haacke is a German-born conceptual artist based in New York and a former professor at Cooper Union. He is known for his probing, socially engaged art, which has been collected and exhibited by institutions throughout the world including The Solomon R. Guggenheim Museum, The Museum of Modern Art, Documenta, and the Venice Bienale.

Dee Dee Halleck is a co-founder of Paper Tiger Television and the Deep Dish Satellite Network, the first grass-roots community television network. She is professor emerita in the Department of Communication at the University of California, San Diego.

Michael Harris is associate professor of art history at the University of North Carolina, Chapel Hill. He is the author of *Colored Pictures: Race and Visual Representation.* An artist as well, Harris has been a member of the art collective AfriCobra since 1979.

Marjorie Heins, the founder of the Free Expression Policy Project, is a fellow in the Brennan Center for Justice at NYU School of Law Democracy Program. *Not in Front of the Children: "Indecency," Censorship, and the Innocence of Youth,* her most recent book, received the American Library Association's 2002 Eli M. Oboler Award for the best published work in the area of intellectual freedom.

Randall Kennedy is professor of law at Harvard University. In addition to *Nigger: The Strange Career of a Troublesome Word,* his books include *In-*

terracial Intimacies: Sex, Marriage, Identity and Adoption, and *Race, Crime, and the Law.*

Seth Killian consults on gaming for both commercial and nonprofit groups, including the Electronic Software Association, the Digital Futures Library Initiative, and venture capital firms. He also runs the internationally known eVo fighting game tournaments and works at the University of Illinois Press.

Norman Kleeblatt is the Susan and Elihu Rose Chief Curator of Fine Arts at The Jewish Museum in New York and the organizer of such exhibitions as *The Dreyfus Affair: Art, Truth and Justice; Too Jewish?: Challenging Traditional Identities;* and *An Expressionist in Paris: The Paintings of Chaim Soutine* (with Kenneth E. Silver). He writes for *Art in America, Artforum,* and *Art Journal.*

Wallace Kuralt was an independent bookseller and the owner of the Intimate Bookshop in Chapel Hill, North Carolina.

John Jota Leaños is a Chicano artist, digital cultural worker, and assistant professor of Xicana/o Studies at Arizona State University in Tempe.

Ruby Lerner is the founding executive director and president of the Creative Capital Foundation, an innovative arts foundation modeled on venture capital concepts. It was established in 1999 to support individual artists in all disciplines.

Lawrence Lessig is a law professor and the founder of the Center for Internet and Society at Stanford University in Palo Alto, California. He was named one of *Scientific American*'s Top 50 Visionaries, for arguing "against interpretations of copyright that could stifle innovation and discourse online." Besides *The Future of Ideas,* he is the author of *Code and Other Laws of Cyberspace.*

Judith Levine's work explores the ways in which history, culture, and politics are entwined in personal life. Her latest book is *Not Buying It: A Year Without Shopping* (Free Press, 2006). *Harmful to Minors: The Perils of*

Protecting Children from Sex won the *Los Angeles Times* Book Prize in 2002.

Dr. Janice Lieberman is a faculty member and Training and Supervising Analyst at the Institute for Psychoanalytic Training and Research. She is the author of *Body Talk: Looking and Being Looked at in Psychotherapy* and co-author of *The Many Faces of Deceit: Omission, Lies and Disguise in Psychotherapy.*

Glenn Ligon is an artist working in New York. His work has been shown and collected by major museums throughout the country, including The Walker Art Center in Minneapolis, Minnesota, where he was a recent artist-in-residence.

Joanna Lindenbaum is a Curatorial Assistant at The Jewish Museum in New York.

Jacqueline Livingston is a photographic artist who divides her time between New York, Arizona, and Hawaii.

Antoni Muntadas is a Catalan artist living in New York, whose work addresses the relationship between public and private space and the promulgation and censorship of information and ideas. Muntadas's work has been exhibited at venues throughout the world, including The Museum of Contemporary Art, Barcelona, the Sao Paulo Bienal, Documenta, and the Venice Bienale.

Barbara Pollack is a New York–based artist who frequently collaborates with her son, Max. Her articles on contemporary art have appeared in *Art in America, Artnews,* the *Village Voice,* and the *New York Times.*

Diane Ravitch is research professor of education at New York University and Non-Resident Senior Fellow at the Brookings Institute. An historian of education, she served President George H.W. Bush as assistant secretary of education and President Clinton as a member of the National Assessment Governing Board.

Marian (Seid) Rubin has balanced her lifelong passion for photography with a thirty-five-year career as a school social worker and advocate for children with disabilities. Rubin specializes in portraiture and lives in New Jersey.

André Schiffrin is the founder and director of The New Press in New York. He previously served, for thirty years, as managing director of Pantheon.

Carolee Schneemann is a multidisciplinary artist whose video, film, painting, photography, performance art, and installations have been widely shown in the United States and Europe. In 2002, MIT Press published her book, *Imaging Her Erotics: Essays, Interviews, Projects.*

Betsy Schneider is a photographic artist whose work—which addresses issues of childhood, time, decay, the body, and culture—has been exhibited throughout the world. She is an assistant professor of art at Arizona State University in Tempe.

Betty Shamieh is a Palestinian American playwright living in New York. A graduate of Harvard University and of the Yale School of Drama, Shamieh is currently a screenwriting professor at Marymount Manhattan College.

Lowery Stokes Sims directs the Studio Museum in Harlem in New York. Previously, she was a curator at the Metropolitan Museum of Art.

Thomas Sokolowski has been director of the Andy Warhol Museum in Pittsburgh since 1997. He previously directed the Grey Art Gallery at New York University.

Lawrence Soley is Colnick Professor of Communication and Journalism at Marquette University in Milwaukee, Wisconsin. In addition to *Censorship INC.: The Corporate Threat to Free Speech in the United States,* his books include *Free Radio, Leasing the Ivory Tower, The News Shapers,* and *Clandestine Radio Broadcasting.*

Eugene Thacker is an assistant professor at the Georgia Institute of Technology. He is the author of *Biomedia* and *The Global Genome,* and a member of the Biotech Hobbyist collective.

Douglas Thomas is an associate professor in the Annenberg School for Communication at the University of Southern California, in Los Angeles, where he directs the Thinking Through Technology project, which examines emergent new media and technologies in relation to entertainment, learning, and the nature of its user cultures.

Siva Vaidhyanathan, a cultural historian and media scholar, is an assistant professor of Culture and Communication at New York University. In addition to *Copyrights and Copywrongs: The Rise of Intellectual Property and How It Threatens Creativity,* he is the author of *The Anarchist in the Library.*

Mick Wilson is an artist and writer who lectures on art and digital media at the Institute of Art, Design & Technology and the Department of Computer Science, Trinity College, in Dublin, Ireland. He has exhibited widely in a variety of media and is completing the research project entitled *The Conflict of the Faculties?: Interdisciplinarity, Criticism and the University.*

Marilyn Zimmerman, an artist, critical thinker, and postmodern feminist, is associate professor of photography at Wayne State University in Indiana. Her work ranges from portraits of her family to collaborative, community-oriented installations.

"Teens Talk About Censorship" participants: **Stephen Opong,** seventeen, is a senior at Columbia Prep in New York; **Damali Slowe,** fourteen, is a sophomore at Westminster School in Simsbury, Connecticut; **Ife Collymore,** sixteen, is a senior vocal major at LaGuardia High School in New York; **Christopher Davis,** sixteen, is a senior art major at LaGuardia High School. Stephen, Damali, Ife, and Christopher work for *Harlem Live,* a webzine produced by New York teens. **Kehinde Togun,** nineteen, is a sophomore at Rutgers University, who served, from 2000 to 2002 on the editorial board of *Sex ETC,* a national newsletter written by and for teens. **Tynesha McHarris,** eighteen, is a freshman at Rutgers. Tynesha and Kehinde are co-founders of Breaking the Chains, an after-school mentoring program in Westside Newark, New Jersey.